LANGUAGE ACQUISITION

LANGUAGE ACQUISITION

THE GROWTH OF GRAMMAR

Maria Teresa Guasti

A Bradford Book
The MIT Press
Cambridge, Massachusetts
London, England

First MIT Press paperback edition, 2004
© 2002 Massachusetts Institute of Technology

This book was set in Times New Roman in 3B2 by Asco Typesetters, Hong Kong, and was printed and bound in the United States of America.

Library of Congress Cataloging-in-Publication Data

Guasti, Maria Teresa.
  Language acquisition : a linguistic perspective / Maria Teresa Guasti.
    p.   cm.
  "A Bradford book."
  Includes bibliographical references and index.
  ISBN-13: 978-0-262-07222-9 (hc.: alk. paper)—978-0-262-57220-0 (pbk.: alk. paper)
  ISBN-10: 0-262-07222-X (hc.: alk. paper)—0-262-57220-6 (pbk.: alk. paper)
  1. Language acquisition. I. Title.
P118 .G83   2002
401'.93—dc21   2001044322

10 9 8 7 6

To Aditi, Alessandro, and Natale

Contents

Preface

My goal in writing this introduction to language acquisition has been to present a wide range of evidence and theoretical advances to upper undergraduate and graduate students as well as to researchers interested in new developments in language acquisition.

In presenting acquisition data and theories, I have adopted concepts developed in linguistic research, thereby assuming that the reader is somewhat familiar with them—say, from having taken an introductory linguistics course or having read an introductory textbook (Akmajian et al. 2001; Haegeman 1994; Radford 1997; Roberts 1998). However, at the beginning of each chapter I summarize the basic assumptions to ensure a common background. Beyond the introductory chapter, this textbook includes nine chapters that cover acquisition of specific aspects of language from birth until about 5–6 years: the abilities of newborns and acquisition of phonological properties of languages (chapter 2); acquisition of the lexicon (chapter 3); acquisition of various aspects of syntax such as clause structure, subject omission, and movement transformations (chapters 4–7); acquisition of the interpretation of pronouns (chapter 8); acquisition of the interpretation of universally quantified sentences (chapter 9); and children's interpretation of subordinate infinitive structures (control structures) (chapter 10). Chapter 11 is dedicated to specific language impairment and to dissociations between language and other cognitive capacities.

Several pedagogical features have been adopted. Each chapter begins with an outline. Intermediate summaries, summaries of hypotheses and predictions, and methodological information about critical experiments are included to help the reader follow the arguments and focus on how a scientific argument is constructed. Chapters 2–10 end with a summary of linguistic milestones; suggestions for further reading (to enable the reader to find specific works on topics not discussed in the text); a list of key words (key words are printed in boldface the first time they appear in the text); and study questions and exercises (to help the reader grasp the major concepts by trying to design experiments or explain certain facts). A glossary of terms appears at the end of the book.

Where necessary, I have introduced linguistic hypotheses that are useful to explain certain accounts of children's production. For simplicity, however, these hypotheses may not figure in later chapters. For example, in chapter 4 I introduce the hypothesis that subjects are generated in the VP. However, for simplicity I later draw trees that disregard this hypothesis (unless it is required by a particular argument being presented), placing subjects directly in Spec IP. Similarly, I use the symbols NP and DP interchangeably for projections of nouns. Unless a more articulated clausal representation is required for explanatory purposes, I adopt the view that a clause includes only one functional projection, IP.

Throughout the text I give examples of children's utterances. To avoid repetition, I acknowledge all the sources of the data here rather than in the text. Data from the two French children Daniel and Nathalie are from Lightbown 1977; data from the German child Simone are from Miller 1976; and data from the Danish children Jens and Anne are from Hamann and Plunkett 1998. Unless otherwise acknowledged in the text, the other data come from the CHILDES database (MacWhinney and Snow 1985). Sources include Miquel Serra and Rosa Sole (for Guillem); Wijnen 1992 (for Hein, Thomas); Wijnen 1988 (for Niek); Brown 1973 (for Adam, Eve, Sarah); Suppes 1974 (for Nina); Schaerlaekens and Gillis 1987 (for Maarten); Suppes, Smith, and Leveillé 1973 (for Philippe); Christian Champaud (for Grégoire); Wagner 1985 (for Andreas); and Cipriani et al. 1989 (for Diana, Guglielmo, Martina, Raffaello, Rosa).

Acknowledgments

This is the time to express my gratitude to the individuals who helped in the preparation of this book. First, I would like to thank Gennaro Chierchia and Marina Nespor for their initial support, their advice, and their continual availability while I was writing. Across the Atlantic, I wish to acknowledge the support of Stephen Crain and Rozz Thornton. I profited greatly from their expertise and from discussing various linguistic issues with them. Rozz deserves special gratitude for reading and commenting carefully on the entire manuscript.

Special credit should be given to the people who read and commented on chapters of the manuscript: Adriana Belletti, Carlo Cecchetto, Gennaro Chierchia, Anne Christophe, Giuseppe Cossu, Stephen Crain, Bob Frank, Alessandra Giorgi, Andrea Gualmini, Michael Kenstowicz, Claudio Luzzatti, Marina Nespor, Jacques Mehler, and Orin Percus. Their expertise has helped me to present the material better and to fill in some gaps. Thanks also to an anonymous reviewer for useful comments on the entire manuscript.

I have benefited greatly from personal or e-mail discussion with Luca Bonatti, Marica DeVincenzi, LouAnn Gerken, Jim Huang, Nina Hyams, Gary Marcus, Franck Ramus, Mabel Rice, Luigi Rizzi, and Ken Wexler.

For sending me their work, I am indebted to Piero Bottari, LouAnn Gerken, Myrna Gopnik, Cornelia Hamann, Heather van der Lely, Reiko Mazuka, Dana McDaniel, Laura Petitto, Mabel Rice, Lyn Santelmann, and Ken Wexler.

For the drawings included in this book that aren't explicitly acknowledged, and for always being available to discuss issues about language, my thanks to Natale Stucchi.

I am grateful to Anne Mark for the masterful editing.

I wish to express profound gratitude to my husband Natale and to my son Alessandro Omero for the patience and understanding they showed during the whole enterprise, whose end was cheered up by the birth of my daughter, Aditi Chiara.

Abbreviations

A-	Argumental
Ā-	A-bar or nonargumental
A	Adjective
AP	Adjectival Phrase
Agr	Agreement
AgrP	Agreement Phrase
Asp	Aspect
AspP	Aspectual Phrase
C	Complementizer
CP	Complementizer Phrase
D	Determiner
DP	Determiner Phrase
I	Inflection
IP	Inflectional Phrase
LF	Logical Form
Neg	Negative head
NegP	Negative Phrase
N	Noun
NP	Noun Phrase
OI	Optional infinitive
QR	Quantifier Raising
RI	Root infinitive
T	Tense
TP	Tense Phrase
UG	Universal Grammar

Chapter 1

Basic Concepts

INTRODUCTION

The study of language acquisition raises questions such as these: How do children break into language? How does knowledge of language emerge in early infancy, and how does it grow? What are the milestones of the language acquisition process? What kinds of linguistic knowledge do children display at given points of development?

The framework adopted here to answer these questions is the generative theory of Universal Grammar (Chomsky 1975, 1981, 1986). According to this theory, human beings are innately endowed with a system of richly structured linguistic knowledge, which guides infants in analyzing incoming linguistic stimuli. Such a theory makes possible clear and falsifiable predictions about children's linguistic competence and offers the tools needed to precisely characterize this competence at given points of development. As a first step in this enterprise, this chapter characterizes what it means to know a language and discusses how knowledge of language becomes available. In so doing, it introduces basic concepts underlying the approach taken in the book and presents the general framework of the research to be discussed.

1.1 REFLECTIONS ON THE COURSE OF LANGUAGE ACQUISITION

Mother: Do you want to get dressed to go see piglet?
Nina: I wanna take the play dough to piglet. (2;10)

Diana: Li faccio vedele a Luca la bambola. (2;6)
(I) to + him make see to Luca the doll
'I make Luca see the doll.'

Eve: I ride a funny clown.   (1;9)

Diana: C'ha   capelli lossi.   (2;6)
           (she) has hair   red
           'She has red hair.'

Adult: I don't think you write with pencil on that, Adam.
Adam: What you write with?   (3;3)
Adult: You write with some crayons.
Adam: Why d(o) you carry it by de handle?

Rosa: Dov'è   un' atta   seggiola?   (2;10)
          where is a   other chair
          'Where is another chair?'
Rosa: Una seggiola dov'è?
          a   chair   where is
          'Where is a chair?'
Mother: È   qui?
            is (it) here

Human language acquisition is an astonishing process. Let us consider what these children have accomplished in about 3 years. Although their language may still not be perfect, they put words in the correct order. Nina produces quite a complex sentence, putting the complements in the right order (first the direct object and then the prepositional complement) and applying *wanna*-contraction. Scrambling complements is possible in Italian, and Diana shows that she can take advantage of this option, by putting the prepositional complement (*a Luca* 'to Luca') before the direct object (*la bambola* 'the doll'). Eve places the adjective *funny* before the noun *clown*, as required in English, while Diana places the adjective *lossi* (*rossi*) 'red' after the noun *capelli* 'hair', since she speaks Italian. One of Adam's questions features preposition stranding, although it lacks the auxiliary *do* (though Adam does include it on other occasions, as his second question shows). Forming nonadult questions (by failing to use the auxiliary) seems to be specific to English learners; note that Rosa, an Italian-speaking child, forms adultlike questions, putting the subject at the right (*un'atta seggiola* 'another chair') or left (*una seggiola* 'a chair') periphery of the sentence.

For children, acquiring a language is an effortless achievement that occurs

- without explicit teaching,
- on the basis of positive evidence (i.e., what they hear),[1]
- under varying circumstances, and in a limited amount of time,
- in identical ways across different languages.

Let us look at each of these accomplishments in more detail.

1.1.1 Acquiring Language without Explicit Teaching

Unlike learning a second language in adulthood, acquiring a first or native language does not require systematic instruction. Parents usually do not teach children the rules of language or tell them what kinds of sentences they can and cannot say. Language develops spontaneously by exposure to linguistic input, that is, on the basis of what children hear. Children are rarely corrected, and even when they are, they resist the correction. For example, for a while English-speaking children say *goed* rather than *went* even though parents may occasionally correct them. For about three years my Italian-speaking child said *facete* rather than *fate* 'make + 2PL', although I often corrected him. McNeill (1966, 69) reports the following conversation between a child and his mother:

(1) *Child:*   Nobody don't like me.
    Mother: No, say "nobody like*s* me."
    Child: Nobody don't like me.
    (eight repetitions of this dialogue)
    Mother: No, now listen carefully; say "*nobody likes me.*"
    Child: Oh! Nobody don't like*s* me.

The child in this exchange uses double negation (*nobody don't*), an option that is not allowed in standard English. As the exchange shows, correction does not seem to have helped the child very much: he eventually notices the use of *likes* (though he uses it incorrectly), but he fails to take advantage of the whole content of the correction.

1.1.2 Acquiring Language on the Basis of Positive Evidence

Parents' corrections should inform children of what is *not* possible in the language they are exposed to; such information coming from correction is called **negative evidence**. As noted, however, corrections are rare, and they do not seem to improve children's linguistic behavior. Much research has been conducted to establish whether negative evidence is available to children in the form of parents' disapproval or failure to understand, parents' expansion of what children say, and frequency of parents' reactions to children's utterances (see Bohannon and Stanowicz 1988; Demetras, Post, and Snow 1986; Hirsh-Pasek, Treiman, and Schneiderman 1984). Although the question is still much debated, the general conclusion is that negative evidence is not provided to all children on all occasions, is generally noisy, and is not sufficient (see Brown and Hanlon 1970; Bowerman 1988; Morgan and Travis 1989; Marcus 1993). Thus, negative evidence is not a reliable source of information. Children have the best chance to succeed in acquiring language by relying on **positive evidence**, the utterances they hear around them—a resource that is abundantly available.

1.1.3   Acquiring Language under Varying Circumstances and in a Limited Amount of Time

Children acquire language under different circumstances, and the linguistic input they are exposed to may vary greatly from child to child (see section 1.5.3 regarding acquisition of American Sign Language and creoles). Nevertheless, they all attain the same competence and do so in a limited amount of time.[2] By about 5 years of age they have mastered most of the constructions of their language, although their vocabulary is still growing.

1.1.4   Acquiring Language in Identical Ways across Different Languages

Children achieve linguistic milestones in parallel fashion, regardless of the specific language they are exposed to. For example, at about 6–8 months all children start to babble (see chapter 2), that is, to produce repetitive syllables like *bababa*. At about 10–12 months they speak their first words, and between 20 and 24 months they begin to put words together. It has been shown that children between 2 and 3 years speaking a wide variety of languages use infinitive verbs in main clauses (see chapter 4) or omit sentential subjects (chapter 5), although the language they are exposed to may not have this option. Across languages young children also over-regularize the past tense or other tenses of irregular verbs. Interestingly, similarities in language acquisition are observed not only across spoken languages, but also between spoken and signed languages. For example, at the age when hearing babies start to babble orally, deaf babies start to do the same manually (see Petitto 1995). It is striking that the timing and milestones of language acquisition are so similar and that the content of early languages is virtually identical, despite great variations in input and in conditions of acquisition.

1.2 THE LOGICAL PROBLEM OF LANGUAGE ACQUISITION

Looking at the facts described in the last section, researchers have characterized the problem of language acquisition as follows (see Baker and McCarthy 1981):

- Children come to have very rich linguistic knowledge that encompasses a potentially infinite number of sentences, although they hear a finite number of sentences.
- The data that children draw upon consist of positive evidence (sentences that are acceptable in the language they are exposed to).
- Children are not told which sentences are ill formed or which interpretations sentences cannot have in their language, but eventually they attain this knowledge; all mature speakers can judge whether a sentence is acceptable or not (under a given interpretation).
- Although children make "errors," they do not make certain errors that would be expected if they generalized from the linguistic input. For example, although children hear sentences like *Who do you wanna invite?* and *Who do you wanna see?*, they do not generalize from these to impossible English sentences like *Who do you wanna come?* (see section 1.4); although this generalization would seem reasonable, children never say such sentences.

These points are part of an argument about the mechanisms underlying language acquisition—the so-called **argument from the poverty of the stimulus**. Essentially, this argument starts with the premises that all speakers of a language know a given fairly abstract property and that this property cannot be induced from the evidence available to children (positive evidence).[3] What conclusion can we draw from these premises? That is, where does linguistic knowledge come from? After a brief excursion into background assumptions, this is the question we will explore.

1.3 THE NOTION OF GRAMMAR

To know a language means to possess a system of knowledge called grammar. A **grammar** is a finite system since it is somehow represented in the mind/brain. As Chomsky showed in the 1950s, it is a **mental generative procedure** that uses finite means to generate an indefinite number of sentences. The term *grammar*, as used here, refers to a psychological entity, not to an inventory of sounds, morphemes, inflectional paradigms, and syntactic constructions (e.g., passives, relative clauses). Although we will be using terms such as *passive*, *relative clause*, and *interrogative* and will be discussing the acquisition of the corresponding constructions, it should be clear that we are using such terms only for convenience. They do not have an independent status in the framework adopted here. For example, interrogatives are the result of movement operations that displace constituents in certain ways. These movement operations are not specific to interrogatives, but are shared by other constructions.

Our linguistic knowledge allows us to produce and understand sentences we have never heard before. It also gives us the tools to establish whether a sentence is acceptable in our language or not. For example, although (2) is comprehensible, it is not an acceptable sentence in English. It does not comply with what we know to be licit in English.

(2) Dog a old a bone ate.

It is again our grammar that permits us to say that the sentence in (3) is perfectly sound, but only on the interpretation that Mary washed another female individual. It cannot mean that Mary washed herself.

(3) Mary washed her.

In other words, the pronoun *her* in (3) must refer to or pick out an individual distinct from the individual picked out by *Mary*. As (4) shows, however, pronouns need not always be interpreted in this way.

(4) Mary washes her socks.

The sentence in (4) is ambiguous: it can mean either that Mary washes some other female individual's socks or that Mary washes her own socks. Unlike the pronoun in (3), the pronoun here can be interpreted in two ways: either it refers to the same individual picked out by *Mary* or it refers to another salient individual in the extralinguistic context.

Linguistic ambiguity is pervasive. Sentence (5) is also ambiguous, having the two readings in (6a) and (6b) (example from Lightfoot 1982, 19).

(5) John kept the car in the garage.

(6) a. The car that John kept was the one in the garage.
    b. The garage was where John kept the car.

Human beings have the resources to cope with linguistic ambiguity. We know whether a sentence is ambiguous or not, whether we can interpret it in certain ways or not, because our grammar assigns sentences structural representations constrained in specific ways. The string in (5) can be associated with two structural representations, (7a,b), each corresponding to one of the two legitimate interpretations of this string, (6a,b).

(7) a.

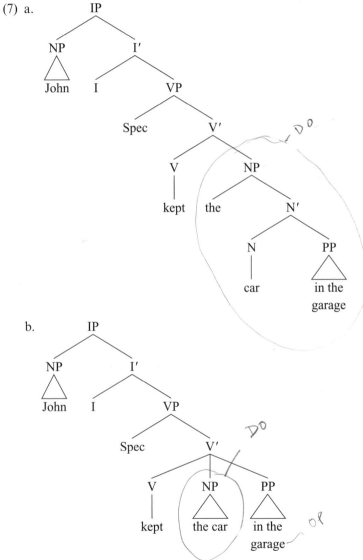

b.

On the interpretation in (6a), whose structural representation is given in (7a), the sequence *the car in the garage* forms a constituent. On this interpretation (5) means that, among the things available, John chose the car that was in the garage. On the interpretation in (6b), whose structural representation is given in (7b), the same sequence is split into two constituents, *the car* and *in the garage*. On this interpretation it means that the garage is the place where John kept the car. The different interpretations that we assign to (5) are based on the different structural representations that our mental grammar associates with it.

In summary, we can do certain things with language because we have a grammar, a psychological entity realized somehow in our mind/brain. This grammar assigns certain structural representations to sentences, and it sanctions certain interpretations while banning others. It does this by means of constraints that establish what is possible and what is not possible in language. In the next section we will look more closely at the notion of constraints.

1.4   CONSTRAINTS

Constraints are linguistic principles that prohibit certain arrangements of words, certain operations, and certain associations of sounds and meanings. They encode properties that hold universally (i.e., in language after language) and are all inviolable (i.e., no violation of any sort is tolerated). In the framework adopted here, constraints are not ranked with respect to one another. (In this sense, this conception of constraints differs from the one advocated in Optimality Theory, where constraints are violable and ranked, and where different constraint rankings are held to underlie differences between languages; see Archangeli and Langendoen 1997; Barbosa et al. 1998.) Sentences must conform to linguistic constraints if they are to be considered well formed or acceptable. For example, the question in (8b), obtained from the declarative sentence in (8a), is judged ill formed by English speakers, as conventionally indicated by the "star" (*), because it violates a constraint of English grammar.

(8) a.   John regrets that Paul behaved badly.
     b.   *How does John regret that John behaved?

In this book the term *constraints* will be used as defined above, although in the literature about language it is also used otherwise.

Constraints are of two kinds: **constraints on form** and **constraints on meaning**. Constraints on form encode the linguistic information that certain sentences are ill formed. An example of a constraint on form is the one operative in (8b). Notice that a minimal variant of (8b)—namely, (9b), obtained from (9a)—is well formed.

(9) a. John thinks that Paul behaved badly.
    b. How does John think that Paul behaved?

The question of interest here is this: how does the child who has heard (8a) and (9a,b) refrain from abstracting a rule that would yield (8b)? In fact, English speakers all share the knowledge that questions like (8b) are ill formed. Linguists propose that a constraint on grammar is responsible for this knowledge. Moreover, speakers of all other languages investigated thus far also know that the counterpart of (8b) is ill formed in their languages, and that the counterpart of (9b) is well formed. Thus, the kind of knowledge that allows us to say that (8b) or its counterpart in another language is not acceptable cannot be language specific, but must be universal.

Another constraint on form is that governing the optional contraction between *want* and *to* in English.

(10) a.   Who do you wanna invite?
     b.   Who do you want to invite?

(11) a.   When do you wanna go out?
     b.   When do you want to go out?

(12) a. *Who do you wanna come?
     b.   Who do you want to come?

It is possible to contract *want* and *to* in (10a) and (11a). However, in (12a) the result of *wanna*-contraction is ill formed, something that speakers of English implicitly know, although they may not be able to formally express this prohibition. Essentially, *wanna*-contraction is not possible when the questioned element is the subject of the infinitival clause, for example, *John* in *I want John to come*. Although linguists speak of "a constraint governing *wanna*-contraction," remember that terms naming specific syntactic constructions are used only for convenience. In its general formulation this is a universal constraint that blocks a certain process from occurring in certain structural configurations.

In summary, a constraint on form underlies our ability to say that certain sentences are ill formed. It is a piece of linguistic knowledge that restrains us from making wrong generalizations—for example, from inducing (12a) from (10) and (11).

Beyond constraints on form, grammars include constraints on the meaning that speakers assign to acceptable sentences. Consider the sentences in (13). Both sentences are perfectly well formed, but while in (13a) the two italicized expressions *he* and *John* cannot pick out the same individual, in (13b) they can (here, "*" indicates that the sentence in (13a) is ruled out when the two italicized expressions pick out the same individual).

(13) a. **He* danced, while *John* was singing.
     b. While *he* was singing, *John* was dancing.

In other words, (13b) is ambiguous: the pronoun *he* can refer either to the same individual that *John* refers to (anaphoric interpretation of the pronoun) or to another salient character in the extrasentential context (exophoric/deictic interpretation of the pronoun). By contrast, in (13a) the pronoun *he* can only be interpreted as referring to some individual other than John. Interestingly, in all languages investigated so far, the counterparts of (13a,b) work the same way; that is, the constraint governing the interpretation of (13) holds universally. Constraints on meaning can be represented as pairs prohibiting the association of certain sentences (S) with certain meanings (M).

(14) *⟨S1, M1⟩

The association between sentence and meaning in (13) is governed by a constraint prohibiting an anaphoric interpretation of the pronoun in certain structural configurations. This constraint, to be discussed in chapter 8, is Principle C of the binding theory. Principle C, or whatever subsumes its effects, bans an anaphoric interpretation of the pronoun in (13a), but not in (13b).

In summary, linguistic knowledge about the possible form of sentences and about the possible association of form and meaning is couched in terms of constraints that hold universally (as linguistic research since the 1960s has shown) and that are not violable. Our linguistic behavior is guided by these constraints, witness the fact that we can judge whether or not it is licit to contract *want* and *to* in certain sentences, and that we know how to interpret pronouns depending on the linguistic context.

1.5   WHERE DOES KNOWLEDGE OF LANGUAGE COME FROM?

How do we know that a sentence is ill formed, that it cannot have a given meaning, or that it is ambiguous? Four hypotheses have been advanced, involving imitation (section 1.5.1), reinforcement (section 1.5.2), association procedures (section 1.5.3), and Universal Grammar (section 1.5.4).

1.5.1   Language Learning through Imitation

One hypothesis holds that children learn language by imitating what adults say, by trying to repeat what they hear. However, several facts, showing that there is no necessary similarity between linguistic input and linguistic output, militate against this hypothesis.

First, studies of parents' speech suggest that children are usually not influenced by caregivers' speech style. Newport, Gleitman, and Gleitman (1977) have shown that a high proportion of parents' utterances are questions (*What do you want?*) and commands (*Get the toy car!*) and only 25% are simple declaratives. By contrast, simple declaratives are the first kind of sentence that children mostly produce.

Second, children continually produce novel utterances, in two senses. For one thing, they hear a finite number of sentences, but they come to be able to produce and understand indefinitely many sentences, including vast numbers they have never heard and therefore cannot be imitating. For another thing (and this is the most compelling evidence against the acquisition-through-imitation hypothesis), children produce utterances that they *cannot* have heard before, because the adult speakers in their environment do not produce them.

It is well known that English learners overregularize irregular past tense verbs and say for example *goed* instead of *went* and *singed* instead of *sang*, although they have never heard these forms, because adults do not use them. In the same vein Guasti, Thornton, and Wexler (1995) have found that English-speaking children aged 4–5 years produce negative questions with the form in (15). No adult utters such sentences; thus, children cannot have learned them by imitation. (Although (15a,b) are not acceptable in the adult language, they are part of children's grammar and therefore are not marked with "*". This practice is followed throughout the book.)

(15) a. What does he doesn't eat?
　　 b. Why could he couldn't wash his hands?

Similarly, Thornton (1990) has shown that English learners produce long-distance extraction questions in which an interrogative pronoun occurs twice, in both sentence-initial and intermediate positions.

(16) What do you think what the puppet has eaten?

All these examples demonstrate that children go beyond their linguistic input and try to say things they cannot have heard. Children do this because they are attempting to discover the "rules" operating in their language, rules that may vary from one language to another. These facts point toward the conclusion that imitation does not play a crucial role in language acquisition.

1.5.2   Language Learning through Reinforcement

Behaviorist psychologists have claimed that language is learned through the mechanism of reinforcing the contingent association between stimulus and response—the same general-purpose mechanism that is invoked to explain other learning processes in animals and in humans (see Skinner 1957). According to this view, children learn language because they are positively reinforced when they produce correct verbal expressions, negatively reinforced when they make errors.

Although the learning-through-reinforcement hypothesis is simple, it cannot explain how humans acquire language and cannot characterize human linguistic competence, as Chomsky (1959) details in his review of Skinner 1957. First, like the acquisition-through-imitation hypothesis, it cannot explain the fact that children acquire competence over an indefinite number of sentences: they understand and produce sentences they have never heard and produced before, that is, for which no reinforcement was provided. Second, parents generally pay attention to what children say and not how they say it. If a child asks a question, the adult will hardly check for its grammatical correctness, but will simply answer, as the following exchanges illustrate:

(17) *Adam:*   Where penny go?   (Adam, 2;5)
    Mother: I don't know.

(18) *Adam:*   Where penny go?   (Adam, 2;5)
    Mother: Didn't you drop your pennies on the floor?

These exchanges show that the notion of reinforcement is vague. In a sense, by responding, the mother is reinforcing the child: she has understood the question. But if the child were to take this reinforcement as a sign that his question was grammatically correct, he would never converge on the correct grammar. Eventually, children attain adult competence and form adultlike questions, but this does not seem to happen through reinforcement. In fact, as we saw in section 1.1.1, even when parents correct children's ungrammatical sentences, these corrections go unnoticed. In sum, positive and negative reinforcement do not explain human linguistic attainment.

1.5.3 Language Learning through Association

Another hypothesis about how language acquisition occurs is expressed by an approach called **connectionism**, neural networks, or parallel distributed processing. (See, e.g., Elman 1993; Elman et al. 1996; Rohde and Plaut 1999. See Pinker and Prince 1988 and Marcus 1998 for criticism; and see Pinker 1999 for an introductory discussion.) At the outset it is worth noting, as does Marcus (2001), that the term *connectionism* is ambiguous. Generally it is associated with the idea that brain circuits do not support the representation of symbols and rules; connectionist models are thus usually opposed to models in which symbols are manipulated. However, in addition to symbol- and rule-free models, there exist connectionist models whose goal is to explain how symbolic manipulations can be implemented in a neural substrate (see, e.g., Shastri and Ajjanagadde 1993; see Marcus 2001 for an extensive discussion of these issues). The remarks that follow apply to models that aim at eliminating symbols and rules.

Connectionist models or artificial neural networks are inspired by a coarse metaphor of the brain, in that they consist of several interconnected neuronlike processing units modified by learning associations between input (stimulus) and output (response) patterns. Interactions among these units give rise to behavior that simulates, sometimes very accurately and precisely, actual human behavior. A network consists at least of input and output units connected by modifiable weighted links. During the learning phase the network is presented with examples of both input and output. Given an input, the network modifies the weights of its connections so as to produce the correct output. After learning, the network can generalize to new stimuli provided they belong to the same class of stimuli used in the training phase. Notice that in these models neither nodes nor links correspond to linguistic categories or rules. These are represented in the network by various patterns of activation among links.

Here we will briefly look at some linguistic phenomena connectionists have sought to account for, noting simply that many intricate aspects of language acquisition and of human linguistic competence still await explanation within a connectionist approach (for more detail on debates surrounding connectionism, see the works just mentioned).

Some connectionist models assume that the mental mechanism employed for acquiring language operates on the basis of analogy or similarity. To gain some insight into how these models operate, let us examine an aspect of acquisition they are most frequently used to simulate: the acquisition of the English past tense. We will then consider whether such models can indeed explain how children learn language.

Regular verbs in English form the past tense by adding the morpheme spelled *-ed* to the stem, regardless of the phonetic features of the stem, while irregular verbs are grouped in family resemblance patterns that form the past in various idiosyncratic ways (e.g., *drink/drank*, *sing/sang*, in which a vowel is changed).

Connectionists claim that acquisition of the past tense of regular and irregular verbs consists in learning associations between the phonetic properties of verb stems and the phonetic properties of their past forms and in generalizing these associations to similar-sounding words (Rumelhart and McClelland 1986). In the connectionist view, children learn that verbs ending in *alk* [ɔ:k] (e.g., *talk* and *walk*) are associated with the past tense form *alked* [ɔ:kt]; similarly, verbs having the pattern *consonant-consonant-i-nk* (e.g., *drink*) are associated with a past tense form having the pattern *consonant-consonant-a-nk* (e.g., *drank*). Children are said to exploit these associations to form the past tense of verbs: whenever they hear a new verb with a specific phonetic pattern (input), they will produce the past tense form associated with that pattern. (See Rumelhart and McClelland 1986; Plunkett and Marchman 1993. For criticism, see Pinker and Prince 1988; Kim et al. 1994.)

Connectionist models mimic some aspects of the process of morphological acquisition; for example, they make the overregularization errors that children make in learning the past tense. However, on closer inspection the actual process of language acquisition and these connectionist simulations are not greatly similar, as far as regular verbs are concerned. Marcus (1995) points out that some connectionist models overregularize vowel-change verbs (*sing* becomes *singed*, rather than *sang*) less frequently than no-vowel-change verbs, while children overregularize the former more frequently than the latter; in addition, these models cease to overregularize verbs only after an abrupt change in the training input, while children do the same although there is no change in the input.

Connectionist models regularize irregular verbs on the basis of resemblance to similar-sounding regular verbs—for example, producing *holded* by analogy with *molded*, *folded*. However, Pinker (1994b) shows that more than similarity of sounds is at work in overregularization: children treat the same phonetic string differently depending on its grammatical status. Stromswold (1990) found that children overregularize main verb *have*, *do*, and *be* just as they overregularize other main verbs, but they do not overregularize the same verbs when they are used as auxiliaries. For example, children say *I doed it* rather than *I did it* or *I haved it* rather than *I had it*, but they do not say *Doed you come?* rather than *Did you come?* or *I haved eaten* rather than *I had eaten*. Evidence also shows that in some groups of people with language impairments the production of regular and irregular verbs is differently affected (see chapter 11; also see Pinker 1999 for a discussion of these issues). These facts cast doubt on the view that a single learning mechanism based on association is responsible for the acquisition of the past tense and of language more generally.

Many connectionist models have attempted to simulate aspects of morphological acquisition; some have also attempted to simulate limited aspects of syntax—for example, sequencing of Noun-Verb, or Noun-Verb-Noun, where the noun can be modified by a relative clause (see Rohde and Plaut 1999; see also Elman 1993).

Although connectionist models can learn some sequencing of words, to date it is unknown whether they can learn the knowledge expressed by linguistic constraints of the kind mentioned in section 1.4 and thus refrain from generating the incorrect sentences discussed there, which children do not produce (see also Marcus 1999). It is also unclear how such models can come to know whether a sentence is ambiguous—indeed, to know all the intricate and abstract aspects of linguistic knowledge discussed in Chomsky's review of Skinner 1957. This criticism is not intended to deny that association and some form of stochastic information are involved in language acquisition. Indeed, some stochastic information may help infants in segmenting speech into word units (see chapter 3). Moreover, an associative mechanism may be appropriate to handle certain linguistic phenomena. Pinker (1997) discusses a theory, called the *word-and-rule theory*, that includes both rule-based and associative components. The rule-based component manipulates symbols and is responsible for the inflection of regular words. It operates on members of syntactic categories (e.g., Verb, Noun) and generates inflected words. For example, it generates the past tense of a regular verb by adding the morpheme spelled *-ed* to the stem; it forms the plural of a regular noun by adding the morpheme spelled *-s* to the stem. The associative mechanism is responsible for the inflection of irregular words and operates on the basis of (sound) similarity. For example, a novel verb such as *spling* is held to have the past tense form *splang* by virtue of similarity to pairs of forms already stored in memory such as *sing-sang* and *ring-rang* (see Prasada and Pinker 1993). Sound similarity plays no role in the inflection of regular words. Thus, according to the word-and-rule theory, two mechanisms—one rule-based, the other associative—are involved in the acquisition of inflection, each subserving different aspects of acquisition (see sections 11.2.1.4, 11.3.2). Association may account for the acquisition of some aspects of linguistic knowledge, but it can hardly answer the entire question of how children acquire language.

Another area where we can compare connectionist models and human learners is the ability to acquire language from radically degenerate input. Human beings clearly demonstrate this ability, as proven by data from creole languages and sign languages (see Bickerton 1988; Goldin-Meadow and Mylander 1984; Kegl 1994). In the nineteenth century people on plantations and in slave colonies often developed a rudimentary form of language to communicate—a lingua franca or pidgin. Once a pidgin has native speakers—the children of the individuals who originate it—it develops into a full language, called a creole. Unlike pidgins, creole languages have function morphemes and a more elaborated structure. Creoles are thus expanded and refined by children on the basis of rudimentary, degenerate input, the pidgin. A similar situation occurs with sign languages. Deaf children born to late learners of American Sign Language (ASL) receive very rudimentary linguistic input, because their parents avoid complex structures and often omit function morphemes. In spite of this degenerate input, these children achieve a more refined competence than their parents, acquiring a sign language that includes complex structures and function morphemes (see Newport 1988).

As Bickerton (1996) points out, connectionist models cannot simulate this ability of human learners. Since a connectionist system learns exclusively on the basis of its input, it will learn a degenerate language if the input is degenerate. If it is to expand and refine the input, it must be endowed with a program that does just that; but such an adjustment does nothing else than supply the model with an innate component, which amounts to recognizing that language acquisition requires innate (possibly language-specific) structures.

In summary, the connectionist models discussed in this section are based on the assumption that language can be acquired through association. However, much linguistic knowledge seems to resist an explanation in such a paradigm, calling instead for a theory that incorporates innate structure, rule-based mechanisms, and constraints.

1.5.4 The Innateness Hypothesis

Recall the premises of the argument from the poverty of the stimulus: that all speakers of a language know a fairly abstract property and that this property cannot be induced from the evidence available to children (positive evidence). The conclusion that these premises invited us to draw is the answer to the question we started with: where does linguistic knowledge come from? Imitation, reinforcement, and association having failed to answer this question, we must look further. In fact, the answer that Chomsky (1959) gave in arguing against behaviorist views and that conclude the argument from the poverty of the stimulus is that *this knowledge is inborn*.

There is a debate as to how rich the genetic makeup supporting human linguistic abilities is. Researchers in the Chomskyan tradition assume that inborn human knowledge is richly structured and must consist of the kinds of constraints (or of something equivalent in its effects) discussed above. It is very unlikely that these constraints are learned since they hold universally. It would be very curious that all languages conform to these constraints if this crosslinguistic similarity were not somehow dictated by our mind/brain: languages "are all basically set up in the way that human biology expects them to be" (Gleitman and Lieberman 1995, xxi). Thus, children are born expecting that, whichever language they are going to hear, it will have the properties that their genetic equipment is prepared to cope with.

The hypothesis that the language capacity is innate and richly structured explains why language acquisition is possible, despite all limitations and variations in the learning conditions. It also explains the similarities in the time course and content of language acquisition. How could the process of language acquisition proceed in virtually the same ways across modalities and across languages, if it were not under the control of an innate capacity? Of course, not *all* linguistic knowledge is innate, for children reared in different linguistic environments learn different languages. That languages vary is obvious. For example, in Italian the sentential subject can be phonologically silent, while in English it cannot. However, this variation is not unlimited. **Universal Grammar** (UG) is the name given to the set of constraints with which all human beings are endowed at birth and that are responsible for the course of language acquisition. UG defines the range of possible variation, and in so doing it characterizes the notion of possible human language. A characterization of UG is a characterization of the initial linguistic state of human beings, the genetic equipment necessary for acquiring a language.

According to this nativist view, acquisition results from the interaction between inborn factors and the environment. Language is not learned, but, under normal conditions, it is deemed to emerge at the appropriate time, provided the child is exposed to spoken or signed language. Obviously, children have to learn the words of their language, its lexicon. They also have to figure out what the regularities of their language are, and how innate constructs are instantiated in their linguistic environment (Fodor 1966).

1.5.5   The Principles-and-Parameters Model

Our genetic endowment makes it possible to learn any human language. Children raised in an English-speaking environment speak English, those raised in an Italian-speaking environment speak Italian, and those raised in a Tibetan-speaking environment speak Tibetan. Although all languages have the same basic underlying structure, there are variations. For example, in some languages (e.g., English and Italian) the verb comes before complements; in others (e.g., Turkish and Bengali) it comes after. So, while an English speaker would say *John bought books*, a Turkish speaker would say something equivalent to *John books bought*. Some languages (e.g., Italian and Spanish) allow the sentential subject to remain phonologically unexpressed; others (e.g., English) do not. So, while *Bought a book* is ungrammatical in English, its counterpart is acceptable in Italian or Spanish.

The model of language adopted here makes sense of these variations by holding that UG consists of two types of constraints: **principles** and **parameters**. Hence, it is called the *principles-and-parameters model* (Chomsky 1981). Principles encode the invariant properties of languages, that is, the universal properties that make languages similar. For example, the constraint discussed in section 1.4 governing the interpretation of pronouns is a principle; in any human language this principle regulates the interpretation of pronouns. Parameters encode the properties that vary from one language to another; they can be thought of as switches that must be turned on or off. An example is the pro-drop or null subject parameter governing the phonological expression of the sentential subject.

As a first approximation, we can formulate the pro-drop parameter as in (19).

(19) Can the sentential subject be phonologically null?

Depending on the particular language, the answer to the question in (19) will vary. If a child is exposed to Italian, the parameter in (19) will be set to the positive value; if the child is exposed to English, it will be set to the negative value.

Under the principles-and-parameters model, children are innately endowed with principles and parameters, because both are given by UG. The children's task is to set the parameters to the value expressed by the language of their environment. In this model, then, language acquisition consists (among other things) in selecting the appropriate values of the parameters specified by UG.

The theory of language acquisition endorsed here is a selective theory, rather than an instructive one. "Under an instructive theory, an outside signal imparts its character to the system that receives it, instructing what is essentially a plastic and modifiable nervous system; under a selective theory, a stimulus may change a system that is already structured by identifying and amplifying some component of already available circuitry" (Lightfoot 1991, 2). In other words, under an instructive theory genuine learning takes place; under a selective theory no learning takes place because the stimulus works on what is already inborn.

Selection, rather than instruction, operates in other biological systems besides language. Niels Kaj Jerne has defended a selective theory of antibody formation, whereby antigens select antibodies that already exist in an individual's immune system (for discussion of these issues, see Jerne 1967, 1985; Piattelli-Palmarini 1986). He has also conjectured that certain central nervous system processes might work selectively and has pointed out that in the history of biology selective theories have often replaced instructive theories.

In summary, UG is the human genetic endowment that is responsible for the course of language acquisition. It includes principles and parameters that encode the invariant and variant properties of languages, respectively. Parameters define the range of variation that is possible in language; and together, principles and parameters define the notion "possible human language." Language acquisition is a selective process whereby the child sets the values of parameters on the basis of the linguistic environment.

1.6 THE CRITICAL PERIOD

Innate behaviors are often distinguished by the existence of **critical periods** during which the ability to acquire the competence reaches its peak; thereafter, the ability to acquire that competence declines. For example, visual abilities in animals develop naturally only if animals receive appropriate visual stimulation early in life. Cats seeing only vertical stripes become blind to horizontal stripes and vice versa (Blackmore and Cooper 1970). The same critical period effects are observed in the development of imprinting in ducks and of attachment in young of various species (Hess 1972) and in song learning in birds (Marler 1970). For example, ducklings become emotionally attached to the first moving thing they see, be it the mother duck, a human being, or an object.

Since language is also innate, we may wonder whether its acquisition is subject to critical period effects. Lenneberg (1967) suggested that language can develop fully only if it is acquired before puberty. Since then, evidence has accumulated that a native competence is acquired only if language is acquired before puberty.

One such piece of evidence is provided by children deprived of linguistic and social interaction during their childhood. The girl known as Genie was reared in such conditions until she was discovered at the age of 13 (Curtiss 1977). Even after several years of linguistic rehabilitation, Genie's language abilities were very limited, especially in syntax.

Evidence in favor of the critical period hypothesis also comes from congenitally deaf people who are exposed to a first language, American Sign Language (ASL), at different ages. Singleton and Newport (1994) tested production and comprehension of ASL verb morphology by congenitally deaf individuals exposed to sign language from birth, from 4 to 6 years of age, or after age 12. They found that performance linearly declined with age of first exposure. Individuals exposed to ASL from birth performed better than those exposed from 4 to 6 years of age, and the latter in turn performed better than individuals exposed after age 12.

That early exposure is critical in attaining native competence is also supported by studies showing that a foreign accent can already be detected in individuals first exposed to a foreign language at age 3 and that accents get stronger as age of first exposure increases (Flege, Yeni-Komshian, and Liu 1999). Similarly, Johnson and Newport (1989) have shown that only speakers who have been exposed to American English, as a second language, before age 7 achieve native performance on an examination testing mastery of morphology and syntax. Speakers who are exposed after age 7 do not acquire native competence.

In summary, the evidence to date shows that there are critical period effects for acquiring the phonology, morphology, and syntax of one's native language. While all human beings are endowed with a richly structured system of linguistic knowledge, this system can develop naturally and fully only if the individual is exposed to appropriate stimuli early in life. This explains the fact that acquiring a language (native or foreign) is a natural achievement for children and becomes more difficult as one gets older.

Key Words

Argument from the poverty of the stimulus
Association procedure
Connectionism
Constraints on form
Constraints on meaning
Critical period
Grammar as a mental generative procedure
Imitation
Negative evidence
Parameters
Positive evidence
Principles
Universal Grammar

Chapter 2

First Steps into Language

INTRODUCTION

Already at birth infants start processing the speech stimuli of their linguistic environment. Infants display a surprising sensitivity to the acoustic cues that express constructs of natural language (syllables, phonemes, words). This suggests that they are biased to pay attention to speech stimuli—to perceive speech in certain ways and then to map the acoustic stimuli onto the phonological system of their native language. Initially, infants are sensitive not merely to acoustic stimuli that have a phonological value in the language they are exposed to, but to any acoustic stimulus that has a phonological value in some human language. This is because infants are potential native speakers of any human language and are thus endowed with a mechanism that adjusts itself to any language. Infants start as universal learners and become speakers of one or more specific languages, depending on their linguistic environment. This can be conceived of as a **selective process**, in which experience narrows perceptual sensitivity and thus enables learners to choose the phonological system instantiated in the input from among those that characterize human languages as a whole and that are encoded in Universal Grammar.

In this chapter we will investigate infants' abilities to perceive the properties of the speech input. Section 2.1 shows that by using aspects of the suprasegmental structure of the language they are exposed to (i.e., its stress patterns and intonation), infants are able to discriminate between languages. It then examines how infants represent languages. Section 2.2 investigates infants' ability to cope with individual speech sounds or segments, an ability critical for acquiring words. Section 2.3 examines infants' early speech production.

2.1   THE QUEST FOR THE NATIVE LANGUAGE

Infants start to produce their first meaningful linguistic expressions (single words) around 10–12 months. Does this mean that they start to be interested in language only around that age? Not at all. Infants are sensitive to language immediately after birth, if not already in the womb. At 4 days they display amazing capacities; for example, they can discriminate their native language from a foreign language. They can do so even if they are not familiar with the speaker's voice, showing that they are indeed discriminating between languages and not between voices. This result hints that newborns can disregard irrelevant variations such as voice quality, speech rate, and accent. It also suggests that they are somehow able to encode linguistic stimuli and form some sort of representation of what they hear; that is, they are able to discover some regularities in the speech input.

It is well known that babies born into a multilingual environment can easily pick up more than one language. This shows that infants can distinguish not only between utterances in the language of their environment and utterances in other languages, but also between utterances in two or more languages spoken around them. Learning a language requires discovering the rules of that language—for example, how words are ordered in clauses, and how questions are formed. If infants could not distinguish between utterances from different languages, they might make bizarre conjectures concerning the properties of what they hear. Without this ability, how could a child hearing sentences from, say, French and Spanish ever figure out the properties of French?

To explore this issue in more detail, let us look at the results of several experiments showing that babies discriminate between different languages.

2.1.1   Language Discrimination: Native versus Foreign Languages

If infants are endowed with the capacity to learn any language, they should show this ability in some way. As we will see, infants can cope with the extraordinary variation manifested in the world's languages.

The fact that infants discriminate their native language from a foreign language is a robust finding confirmed in numerous experiments with different pairs of languages, conducted with infants in the first few days and months of life. These studies are summarized in table 2.1, beginning with the pioneering study by Mehler et al. (1988). (One exception has been documented: 2-month-old babies exposed to British English do not discriminate English from Dutch, a fact we will come back to.)

Table 2.1
Pairs of languages used in studies of discrimination between the native language and a foreign language. Unless noted otherwise, the pairs of languages were discriminated.

Languages discriminated	Infants' native language	Age at testing	Source
French-Russian	French	4 days	Mehler et al. 1988
English-Spanish	Spanish, English	2 days	Moon, Cooper, and Fifer 1993
English-Italian	English	2 months	Mehler et al. 1988
English-Japanese	English	2 months	Christophe and Morton 1998
English-French	English	2 months	Dehaene-Lambertz and Houston 1998
English-Spanish	Spanish	4 months	Bosch and Sebastián-Gallés 1997
English-Catalan	Catalan	4 months	Bosch and Sebastián-Gallés 1997
Spanish-Catalan	Spanish	4 months	Bosch and Sebastián-Gallés 1997
Spanish-Catalan	Catalan	4 months	Bosch and Sebastián-Gallés 1997
English-Dutch (no discrimination)	English	2 months	Christophe and Morton 1998
English-Dutch	English	5 months	Nazzi, Jusczyk, and Johnson 2000

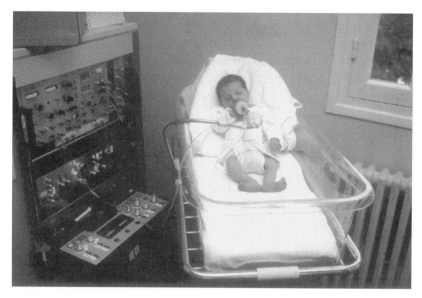

Figure 2.1
A typical experimental setting for the high-amplitude sucking procedure (HAS).
Newborns are placed in a crib in a semireclining position and suck a pacifier linked
to a pressure transducer connected to a computer that controls the delivery of
stimuli from a loudspeaker. (Picture kindly made available by Jacques Mehler.)

But how can researchers establish that young babies discriminate languages? The standard technique is a habituation-recovery procedure that
exploits infants' sucking behavior: the **high-amplitude sucking procedure** (HAS) (see also Jusczyk 1997 for a description of this technique). In
a typical experiment using the HAS, infants suck on a pacifier, which is
linked to a pressure transducer connected to a computer, enabling their
sucking rate to be measured. Stimuli are presented through a loudspeaker.
Infants hear stimuli contingent on their high-amplitude sucks. A typical
setting is presented in figure 2.1.

An experiment using the HAS procedure starts by measuring infants'
sucking rate in the absence of any stimulation, to determine each infant's
baseline. Then the habituation phase starts. During this phase linguistic
stimuli are presented, in general contingent on infants' sucking rate. This
aspect of the experiment exploits the fact that infants are very good at
learning the connection between sucking and sounds, and then using
sucking to trigger stimulation. When infants have heard the same stimulus
for a while, they become habituated to it and suck less. When the infant's

sucking rate has reached a predetermined habituation criterion (a one-third decrement in sucking rate), the experimental phase starts. Infants are assigned to one of two conditions. In the experimental condition infants are presented with new stimuli, while in the control condition infants continue to receive the same stimuli they have heard in the habituation phase. To demonstrate that infants discriminate between two sets of stimuli, one must compare the sucking responses of the experimental group with the sucking responses of the control group before and after the change. If infants in the experimental group are sufficiently interested by the new stimuli, they should suck more than infants in the control group. Since the only difference between the two groups before and after the change is the occurrence or nonoccurrence of new stimuli, a different response (increased sucking or lack thereof) by the two groups is interpreted as discrimination between the two sets of stimuli. This technique can be used with infants up to 3 months of age.[1]

For concreteness, let us consider the experiment carried out by Mehler et al. (1988). In the habituation phase infant French learners from both the experimental and the control groups heard Russian utterances. When they were habituated—that is, when their sucking rate declined to a predetermined criterion—the experimental phase started. During this phase the control group continued to hear Russian utterances and the experimental group started to hear French utterances. While the habituation phase was identical for the two groups of babies, the experimental phase differed. Therefore, a difference in the sucking responses of the experimental and control groups must be attributed to the single change that occurred during the experimental phase, that is, the delivery of new stimuli to the experimental group. Figure 2.2 displays the sucking responses of infant French learners to Russian and French. As the figure indicates, during the habituation phase sucking rate increased and then decreased for both the control group and the experimental group. During the experimental phase infants in the experimental group sucked more than infants in the control group. From this difference, we infer that the experimental group detected the change.

2.1.2 Discrimination between Two Foreign Languages

From the previous discussion it is apparent that babies can discriminate their native language from a foreign language soon after birth. It is possible that language-specific influences have already left a trace after a few days of exposure or even that infants have already become familiar with

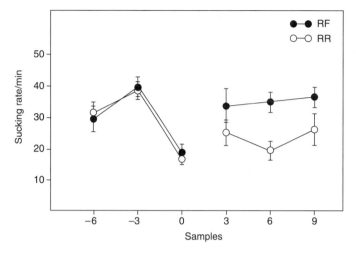

Figure 2.2
Sucking rate averaged over three consecutive samples during the habituation phase and the experimental phase of a study in which infant French learners heard utterances from Russian and French. The graph displays the sucking rates of infants who heard Russian during the habituation phase. Group RF heard French during the experimental phase and group RR continued to hear Russian. The bars above and below each point indicate the standard error of the mean. (Reprinted from *Cognition*, volume 29, Mehler, Jusczyk, Lambertz, Halsted, Bertoncini, and Amiel-Tison, "A Precursor of Language Acquisition in Young Infants," pp. 144–178. Copyright 1988, with permission from Elsevier Science.)

certain properties of their linguistic environment before birth.[2] However, neither possibility explains newborns' ability to distinguish between foreign languages, that is, languages they have not been exposed to. Four-day-old infants born into a French-speaking environment distinguish between English and Italian utterances (see Mehler et al. 1988, reanalyzed in Mehler and Christophe 1995) and between English and Japanese utterances (see Nazzi, Bertoncini, and Mehler 1998; and see Cristophe and Morton 1998 for evidence that this also occurs at 2 months). Table 2.2 summarizes the major results from studies of foreign language discrimination by babies, some of which we will examine later.

The early capacity to distinguish the native language from a foreign one and even one foreign language from another is very intriguing. Since infants can discriminate between two foreign languages they have never heard before participating in the experiment, it must be the case that during the experiment they can rapidly build some sort of representation

Table 2.2
Pairs of languages used in studies of infants' discrimination between foreign languages. Unless noted otherwise, the pairs of languages were discriminated.

Languages discriminated	Infants' native language	Age at testing	Source
English-Japanese	French	5 days	Nazzi, Bertoncini, and Mehler 1998
English-Italian	French	4 days	Mehler et al. 1988 (reanalyzed in Mehler and Christophe 1995)
Dutch-Japanese	English	2 months	Christophe and Morton 1998
French-Russian (no discrimination)	English	2 months	Mehler et al. 1988
French-Japanese (no discrimination)	English	2 months	Christophe and Morton 1998
English-Dutch (no discrimination)	French	4 days	Nazzi, Bertoncini, and Mehler 1998

of what they hear. All these facts suggest that there exist certain salient acoustic properties that capture infants' interest and that can be extracted from utterances in very little time and with limited exposure.

Beyond showing that babies can discriminate between foreign languages, table 2.2 shows that in some cases they fail to do so. For example, 2-month-old American English learners are unable to discriminate French from Russian, something that 4-day-olds born into a French-speaking environment can do (see table 2.1). Similarly, 2-month-old British English learners cannot discriminate French from Japanese (see Christophe and Morton 1998) (we will look later at other findings reported in table 2.2). One reason for this failure to discriminate may be that some developmental change occurs within the first months of life. As the table shows, newborns can discriminate between any two foreign languages (babies born into a French-speaking environment can discriminate English from Japanese and English from Italian), while at 2 months their ability is more constrained (babies born into an English-speaking environment can discriminate Dutch from Japanese, but not French from Russian or French from Japanese). It is not clear why there are such differences in discriminating between pairs of languages (see section 2.1.4.2). Moreover, there is one pair of languages that even newborns cannot discriminate: 4-day-olds born into a French-speaking environment cannot discriminate English from Dutch (see Nazzi, Bertoncini, and Mehler 1998). We will return to this fact in section 2.1.4.1.

A word of caution is needed, however. One might object to a developmental explanation, since the pairs of languages used and the native languages of the babies tested vary across studies. Although we know that at 2 months infant English learners cannot discriminate French from Russian and French from Japanese, we do not know what they would have done at 4 days with the same pairs of languages. Moreover, we know that at 4 and 5 days infants born into a French-speaking environment can discriminate English from Italian and English from Japanese, respectively, but we do not know what they would do at 2 months. To be certain that the change in performance between younger and older babies is due to developmental factors, additional experimentation is needed.

2.1.3   The Source of Discrimination

We have seen that very young infants can discriminate between pairs of languages, even though they are not familiar with them; they do so on the basis of very little information. Dehaene-Lambertz and Houston (1998) showed that infants can recognize their native language after hearing 1200 ms of an utterance, or roughly half a dozen syllables (see also Bosch and Sebastián-Gallés 1997). But how did the infants in these studies manage to discriminate between pairs of languages? It is very implausible that they could have recognized some words of the languages, because at 4 days, the age at which infants were tested, they are unlikely to have any lexical knowledge. One possibility is that the babies responded to some coarse acoustic characteristics of the samples, such as the mean energy of the utterances or the pitch. To test this hypothesis, Mehler et al. (1988) presented the same French and Russian stimuli used in the experiment discussed in section 2.1.1, but played backward. In this way the prosody of the utterance is modified, but the energy of the signal is the same. If babies exploit some gross acoustic property of speech, they should discriminate between languages even when the stimuli are played backward. This prediction did not stand up: under these conditions 4-day-old babies born into a French-speaking environment were unable to discriminate French from Russian.

Another possibility is that infants accomplish the discrimination task by recognizing segmental properties of the languages. Indeed, in some of the experiments mentioned in sections 2.1.1 and 2.1.2 real-language samples were used. To figure out whether infants draw upon segmental information to accomplish the language discrimination task, Mehler et al. (1988) and other researchers have tested infants with low-pass-filtered speech, that is, speech in which only frequencies below 400 Hz were retained. This transformation reduces segmental content (single sounds can no longer be identified) and preserves prosodic or suprasegmental information (intonation, rhythm).[3] If infants were relying on segmental information, they should not have been able to discriminate between low-pass-filtered samples from different languages, because in these samples the segmental information was gone. The finding that infants nonetheless succeeded under these conditions indicates that infants do not rely on segmental information to discriminate between languages, but on some prosodic properties of speech.

Prosodic information is thus sufficient for telling languages apart. Is it also necessary? In low-pass-filtered speech some rudimentary segmental information is indeed retained, and this may be enough for infants to discriminate between languages. To discard this explanation, Dehaene-Lambertz and Houston (1998) presented infants with multisyllabic words extracted from sentences and reassembled in a scrambled order. The aim

of this manipulation was to destroy the suprasegmental coherence of the
utterance and to preserve phonemic information and information about
the prosody of single words. If phonemic information or word-level
prosody is enough to discriminate between two languages, babies listening
to words reassembled in scrambled order should have no trouble discriminating between languages. By contrast, if phonemic information or
word-level prosody is not sufficient, babies listening to scrambled words
should not be able to discriminate between languages. Indeed, 2-month-
old American English learners failed to discriminate between English and
French in the scrambled-order condition, but they succeeded when the
prosodic information of the utterances was preserved as with low-pass-
filtered stimuli. Thus, the prosodic information contained in brief (1200
ms) utterances is both sufficient and necessary for telling languages apart.
(Note that what matters is prosodic information at the level of the *utterance* and not at the level of single words. In fact, in the scrambled-order
condition the prosodic structure of words was available, but did not elicit
a discrimination response.)

Table 2.3 summarizes hypotheses, predictions, and results regarding
language discrimination by babies.

In sum, newborns can discriminate between their native language and a
foreign language and between two foreign languages by relying on prosodic information. Since infants do not know anything *specific* about their
native language (i.e., about phonological constructs, stress, syllables, etc.),
the prosody of languages must include some very robust and reliable
acoustic cue that infants can easily pick up in a very short time and use
for classifying languages.

2.1.4   The Rhythm-Based Language Discrimination Hypothesis

We have seen that infants rely on some prosodic information to discriminate between languages. Can we be more precise about the nature of the
information they rely upon? Discrimination requires infants to build a
representation of the first set of stimuli (utterances from one language),
then compare it with a second set of stimuli (utterances from a new
language), and determine whether these new stimuli match the earlier
representation. This leads to a new question: what is the nature of the
representation that infants rely on during a language discrimination task?
Mehler et al. (1996) propose that infants extract and build a representation of languages based on rhythmic properties, which are known to vary
across languages. Dutch and English sound very different from Spanish
and Italian, a difference that Lloyd James (1940) described by saying that

Table 2.3
Summary of hypotheses, predictions, and results regarding language discrimination by babies

Hypothesis	Prediction	Result
Babies discriminate languages on the basis of the mean energy of the signal or pitch.	Babies should discriminate languages even when the stimuli are played backward.	Babies do not discriminate languages when the stimuli are played backward.
Babies discriminate languages on the basis of segmental properties.	Babies should not discriminate languages when the stimuli are low-pass filtered.	Babies discriminate languages even when stimuli are low-pass filtered.
Babies discriminate languages on the basis of word-level prosody or of some residual phonemic information available when the stimuli are low-pass filtered.	Babies should discriminate languages when words are artificially reassembled so as to maintain the prosody of the words, but not the prosodic coherence of the utterance (scrambled-order condition).	Babies do not discriminate languages in the scrambled-order condition.

Conclusion: Babies must discriminate languages on the basis of prosodic information at the utterance level.

the first two languages have a "Morse code rhythm" and the second two a "machine gun rhythm." Building on this intuition, linguists have coarsely classified languages into stress-timed, syllable-timed, and mora-timed languages (see Pike 1945; Abercrombie 1967; Ladefoged 1975).

(1) a. Stress-timed languages: Dutch, English, Russian, Swedish
    b. Syllable-timed languages: Italian, French, Greek, Spanish
    c. Mora-timed languages: Japanese, Tamil

What distinguishes these classes of languages is the subjective perception of their temporal organization. In stress-timed languages listeners perceive a regular recurrence of stress, in syllable-timed languages a regular recurrence of syllables, and in mora-timed languages a regular recurrence of morae. It is now believed that this distinction in classes of languages is not a primitive property, but the result of interactions between phonological properties of languages—for example, syllable structure and vowel reduction. Stress-timed languages have a greater variety of syllable types than syllable-timed languages; in these languages heavy syllables tend to be stressed and light ones to be stressless. Moreover, unstressed syllables tend to be reduced or absent (see Lehiste 1977; Dasher and Bolinger 1982; Dauer 1983; Bertinetto 1989; Nespor 1990 for discussion of this issue). On the basis of investigating eight languages (Catalan, Dutch, English, French, Italian, Japanese, Polish, Spanish), Ramus, Nespor, and Mehler (1999) and Ramus and Mehler (1999) have shown that the distinction among the three rhythmic classes in (1) reflects phonetic properties of the speech signal, thus supporting the validity of the notion of rhythmic class.

As noted, Mehler et al. (1996) propose that infants discriminate between languages on the basis of a rhythmic representation (the **rhythm-based language discrimination hypothesis**) (see also Nazzi, Bertoncini, and Mehler 1998). The rhythmic representation is a coarse representation in terms of "a succession of vowels of variable duration and intensities, alternating with periods of unanalyzed noise" (standing for consonants) (Ramus, Nespor, and Mehler 1999, 270). This hypothesis grants a central role to vowels. In fact, vowels are acoustically very salient: they carry most of the energy of the speech signal, are louder than consonants, and attract infants' attention more than consonants do (see Bertoncini et al. 1988). For example, newborns are able to count the number of syllables and thus of vowels in a word; in addition, infants perceive accent (see Bijeljac-Babic, Bertoncini, and Mehler 1993; Bertoncini et al. 1995; Sansavini, Bertoncini, and Giovanelli 1997; van Ooyen et al. 1997).

Infants' representation of utterances as a sequence of vowels varies depending on the rhythmic properties of the language, that is, whether it is stress-timed, syllable-timed, or mora-timed. (2) is an approximate depiction of infants' rhythmic representations, where V stands for a heavy vowel and v for a light one.[4]

(2) a. V   V v   V V v V   stress-timed (e.g., English)
    b. V   V V   V   V V   V   syllable-timed (e.g., Spanish)
    c. V V V V V V V V V   mora-timed (e.g., Japanese)

In stress-timed languages, (2a), the interval between vowels is long and irregular, because of these languages' greater variability of syllable structure. In stress-timed languages there is great variability in the number of consonants per syllable; for example, English and Dutch have 16 and 19 syllable types and a maximum of seven segments per syllable (see Nespor 1990). Finally, in these languages there is great variability in the duration of syllables.

In syllable-timed languages, (2b), the distance between vowels is shorter and more regular since there are few types of syllables. For example, Spanish has 9 syllable types that contain at most five segments (see Nespor 1990); Italian and Greek have 8 syllable types.

In mora-timed languages, (2c), the distance between vowels is even shorter than in syllable-timed languages and even more regular, for these languages have long vowels, which correspond to two regular vowels.

2.1.4.1 Evidence for the Rhythm-Based Language Discrimination Hypothesis According to the hypothesis that infants build a representation of languages in terms of rhythm and that they use rhythmic information to discriminate between pairs of languages, infants classify languages on the basis of their global rhythmic properties and disregard the specific identity of a language; that is, they classify languages within rhythmic classes. This hypothesis predicts that infants can discriminate between languages with different metrical patterns, but not between languages with the same metrical pattern—for example, two stress-timed languages such as Dutch and English. The predictions (P) are summarized in (3).

(3) *P1:* Infants discriminate stress-timed from syllable-timed languages.
    P2: Infants discriminate stress-timed from mora-timed languages.
    P3: Infants discriminate syllable-timed from mora-timed languages.
    P4: Infants do not discriminate (at least initially) two syllable-/stress-/mora-timed languages from each other.

As shown in section 2.1.1, newborns can discriminate their native language from a wide variety of languages. Looking back at table 2.1 through the lens of the rhythm-based language discrimination hypothesis, we realize that three of the predictions in (3) are fulfilled.

(4) *P1:* Infants discriminate stress-timed from syllable-timed languages: *English-Catalan, English-Italian, English-French, English-Spanish, French-Russian.*
P2: Infants discriminate stress-timed from mora-timed languages: *English-Japanese.*
P4: Infants do not discriminate (at least initially) two syllable-/stress-/mora-timed languages from each other: *English-Dutch* (stress-timed languages).

So far no experiment has tested infants' ability to discriminate a syllable-timed from a mora-timed language with babies exposed to either a syllable-timed or a mora-timed language. Therefore, we have no evidence bearing on prediction P3.

The findings summarized in (4) provide ample evidence that infants discriminate languages from different rhythmic classes. Interestingly, newborns living in a French-speaking environment cannot discriminate between two foreign languages from the same rhythmic class: Dutch and English (see Nazzi, Bertoncini, and Mehler 1998; see table 2.2). The same finding is replicated with 2-month-old British English learners (see Christophe and Morton 1998; see table 2.1). These results support the hypothesis that the rhythmic information infants rely upon is *class-specific* and *not language-specific*. Eventually, at 5 months, babies learning English are able to discriminate Dutch from English, likely because they have become more familiar with their native tongue or have access to a more detailed representation of their language (see Nazzi, Jusczyk, and Johnson 2000; see table 2.1). The same explanation can be extended to account for why 4-month-old Catalan and Spanish learners can discriminate between Spanish and Catalan, two syllable-timed languages. It would be interesting to know how these babies would have responded at 4 days.

The most convincing confirmation of the rhythm-based language discrimination hypothesis comes from an experiment carried out by Nazzi, Bertoncini, and Mehler (1998). In this experiment filtered utterances were drawn from four languages: two syllable-timed languages (Italian and Spanish) and two stress-timed languages (Dutch and English). No language was familiar to the babies tested, who were from a French-speaking

Table 2.4
Summary of Nazzi, Bertoncini, and Mehler's (1998) experimental design

	Habituation phase	Experimental phase
Rhythmic group	Italian/Spanish	Dutch/English
	Dutch/English	Italian/Spanish
Nonrhythmic group	English/Italian	Dutch/Spanish
	Dutch/Spanish	English/Italian

environment. Four-day-old infants were assigned to one of two groups. The rhythmic group was habituated to a combination of filtered sentences from two languages of the same rhythmic class (Italian/Spanish or Dutch/English); the nonrhythmic group was habituated to a combination of filtered sentences from two languages belonging to different rhythmic classes (English/Italian or Dutch/Spanish). During the experimental phase the infants in the rhythmic group experienced a class change: they listened to filtered sentences from two languages belonging to the other rhythmic class (if they first heard Italian/Spanish, they then heard Dutch/English, and vice versa). The infants in the nonrhythmic group also listened to new stimuli, but these were drawn from the same two rhythmic classes used in the habituation phase (if these infants first heard English/Italian, they then heard Dutch/Spanish, and vice versa). The design is summarized in table 2.4. The main finding of the experiment is that after the change the rhythmic group started to suck significantly more than the nonrhythmic group. Therefore, it must be inferred that only the rhythmic group detected a change in stimuli, that is, a change from one rhythmic class to the other. As the stimuli presented to the nonrhythmic group also changed—the individual languages were not the same in the habituation and experimental phases—it must be deduced that this change did not result in a discrimination response. The conclusion must be that infants discriminate between classes of languages and not individual languages.

2.1.4.2 Language Discrimination and Development We have seen that although 4- or 5-day-old infants can discriminate between some pairs of foreign languages, at 2 months they cannot. For example, 2-month-old American English and British English learners cannot discriminate French from Russian or French from Japanese, respectively (Mehler et al. 1988; Christophe and Morton 1998; see table 2.2). Interestingly, however, 2-

month-old babies learning English can discriminate Dutch from Japanese. How can this be? Why are some pairs of foreign languages still discriminated at 2 months, while others are not?

As noted earlier, we do not know how these babies would have responded if they had been tested at 4 days. But suppose that they had discriminated between all pairs of foreign languages from different rhythmic classes and that the ability to discriminate between foreign languages becomes more constrained at 2 months, that is, that some development takes place. Then, one possible explanation for the findings just presented is offered by the rhythm-based language discrimination hypothesis. At 2 months infants have some sort of representation of their native language that, we now know, is based on rhythm. Since Dutch has a rhythm that is very close to that of English in various ways (vowel reduction, complex syllabic structure, same sort of word stress), it is possible that Dutch and English both fit the 2-month-old infant's representation. Thus, Christophe and Morton suggest that 2-month-old English learners are still able to discriminate Dutch from Japanese, because one of the languages (Dutch) is regarded as native. In other words, they accomplish this discrimination as if they were discriminating the native language from a foreign language. By contrast, French, Japanese, and Russian do not fit the rhythmic representation of 2-month-old English learners; they are thus all considered foreign languages and cannot be discriminated, under the hypothesis that the ability to discriminate between foreign languages becomes more constrained after some months of life. According to this explanation, Dutch and English are equivalent for 2-month-olds. We know that these two languages are not equivalent for 5-month-olds since they discriminate between them. We thus expect that at 5 months infant learners of English will not be able to discriminate between Dutch and Japanese, since Dutch can no longer be regarded as native. So far no experiment has addressed this expectation.

Intuitively, this explanation seems plausible in that it correctly predicts the failure to discriminate French, a syllable-timed language, from Japanese, a mora-timed language. Both languages certainly do not fit the stress-timed representation of 2-month-old British English learners. It is less intuitive to understand why 2-month-old American English learners cannot discriminate French from Russian, because Russian, like Dutch, is a stress-timed language. One conjecture is that the Dutch rhythm is close enough to the English rhythm, but not to the Russian one. This hypothesis lends support to the view that the classification among stress-timed, syllable-timed, and mora-timed languages results from the interactions of different phonological properties (vowel reduction, syllable structure). It is possible that within classes of languages, some pairs of languages are more similar than others.

2.1.5   The Syllabic or Vocalic Nucleus as a Universal Unit of Representation of Speech

The rhythm-based language discrimination hypothesis holds that infants perceive and represent speech in terms of syllable-like units, or more likely some covariant unit, the vowel. In other words, the syllable or a covariant unit, the vowel, is the universal unit that infants use at first to organize speech. Is there any evidence to support this view?

Three studies suggest that there is. First, 4-day-olds born into a French-speaking environment have been shown to detect a change from bisyllabic to trisyllabic items (see Bijeljac-Babic, Bertoncini, and Mehler 1993), but they do not detect a change in the number of phonemes when the items involved have the same number of syllables. Second, 4-day-olds born into a French-speaking environment have been found to discriminate between bi- and trisyllabic Japanese items (e.g., *to-mi* and *to-mi-ta*), but not between pairs of bisyllabic items varying in number of morae (e.g., *se-ki* and *se-Q-ki*—where *Q* represents a geminate—are both bisyllabic, but *se-Q-ki* is trimoraic; see Bertoncini et al. 1995). In a third set of experiments Bertoncini et al. (1988) habituated one group of newborns to a set of four syllables sharing the same vowel ([bi], [si], [li], [mi]) and another group to a set of four syllables sharing the same consonant ([bi], [ba], [bo], [bə]). Simplifying somewhat, in the experimental phase these infants heard the same sequence of syllables they had been habituated to, plus a new syllable sharing either the vowel or the consonant with the syllables used in the habituation phase. (In fact, more conditions were tested in the experimental phase; but these are irrelevant for the point in question.) Newborns detected the presence of the new syllable when the vowel of the new syllable differed from the vowel of the habituation syllables, but not when the change concerned the consonant. (This set of experiments is summarized in table 2.5.)

These results confirm the hypothesis that infants build a representation in terms of vowels, the highly salient nuclei of syllables that carry acoustic information of length, intensity, and height. It is thus very likely that the syllable or the vocalic nucleus is the universal unit of representation in the initial stages of language development, as suggested by Bertoncini and

Table 2.5
Summary of Bertoncini et al.'s (1988) experiments

Habituation phase	Experimental phase	Results
Same vowel [bi], [si], [li], [mi]	New consonant [bi], [si], [li], [mi], [di]	No detection of the new syllable
Same consonant [bo], [ba], [bi], [bə]	New vowel [bo], [ba], [bi], [bə], [bu]	Detection of the new syllable

Mehler (1981), Bertoncini et al. (1995), and Mehler et al. (1996) (see also Dehaene-Lambertz 1998 concerning syllable discrimination by premature babies).

2.1.6 Intermediate Summary

Infants display a very specialized ability to deal with speech input. At 4 days they can discriminate their native language from a foreign one; they can also discriminate between two foreign languages. Discrimination is based on rhythmic properties of speech. Initially newborns build an underspecified rhythmic representation of speech in terms of syllables or vowels—a highly salient unit to which babies pay great attention. This representation is sufficient for a first classification of languages into rhythmic classes and serves as the basis for building a more fine-grained representation, one that more closely reflects the phonological properties of the native language.

2.2 LEARNING THE PHONEMIC CONTRASTS OF THE NATIVE LANGUAGE

So far we have seen that infants discriminate between languages on the basis of rhythmic properties. Another dimension along which languages vary is the repertoire of sounds used to form words in a given language. While the set of human linguistic sounds is finite, languages differ in the subset of sounds or of phonemic categories they choose from this universal set. A language can have from 20 to 60 phonemes (see Bergeijk, van Pierce, and David 1960); for example, English has about 40 phonemes, and Italian 33. The two sounds /l/ and /r/ are not distinctive in Japanese, where they are mapped into /R/, but they are in Italian and English; that is, in these languages there are pairs of words differing only in that one has /l/ and one has /r/, yet differing in meaning (e.g., English *lace* and *race*). Adult speakers *know* this very well, for discriminating between /l/ and /r/ is almost impossible for Japanese listeners (see Goto 1977; Strange and Jenkins 1978), while it is very easy for Italian and English speakers. Adults are very proficient in dealing with phonemic contrasts valid in their native language, and quite inefficient in dealing with phonemic contrasts valid in foreign languages. But how do children attain adult competence with the sound system of their language? There are two possibilities: either the newborn's mind is a blank slate and infants must learn to make the discriminations that are valid in their target language, or infants are endowed with the capacity to discriminate all contrasts and they "learn" to forget the ones that are not instantiated in their linguistic environment. To see which answer is correct, let us investigate infants' perception of consonants.

2.2.1   Sensitivity to Consonant Contrasts

From the 1970s on, research on speech perception has shown that infants discriminate between native contrasts very early. In a pioneering experiment using the HAS, Eimas et al. (1971) were able to show that from around 1 month of age, infants living in an English-speaking environment can discriminate the contrast between the first phoneme of the syllable [ba], which is voiced, and the first phoneme of the syllable [pa], which is voiceless, as in the words *bad* and *pad*.

Perception of consonantal contrasts is **categorical**. That is, adults presented with synthetic speech stimuli can easily discriminate between sounds belonging to two distinct linguistic categories, such as [pa] and [ba], which differ in the voicing feature. However, they have a hard time discriminating between different sounds belonging to the same category, for example, two different instances of [ba] (Eimas et al. 1971).[5] Is infants' perception of consonantal contrasts also categorical? The answer is yes. Eimas et al. (1971) also found that 1-month-old infants, like adults, discriminate between consonantal contrasts in a categorical manner; that is, acoustic differences that adults map into distinctive linguistic categories are perceived as different by infants, and acoustic differences that are not linguistically relevant for adults are not perceived as distinct by infants.

Since Eimas et al.'s (1971) seminal work, further research has shown that infants can discriminate other consonant contrasts, such as place of articulation (e.g., [ba] vs. [ga]—Morse 1972; Eimas 1974) and manner of articulation (oral/nasal) (e.g., [ba] vs. [ma]—Eimas and Miller 1980; see Jusczyk 1997 for reviews).

One might conjecture that infants' discrimination of native contrasts derives from experience with the ambient language—that infants become acquainted with those contrasts that they hear. A serious challenge for this conjecture comes from work by Werker and Tees (1984), who have shown that infants are able to discriminate nonnative consonantal contrasts. Using the conditioned head turn procedure, Werker and colleagues (see Werker 1995 and references cited there) showed that 6- to 8-month-old infants can discriminate between contrasts both from their native language and from foreign languages. For example, infant English learners can discriminate between Hindi contrasts, like that between retroflex (i.e., apico-postalveolar) and dental place of articulation /ṭa/–/ta/ or between breathy voiced and voiceless aspirated dental stops /dʰa/–/tʰa/ (Werker et al. 1981). They can also discriminate contrasts in Thompson (an Interior Salish language spoken in south central British Columbia), such as the contrast between glottalized velar and uvular voiceless stops /k̓i/–/q̓i/. Experience cannot be responsible for this surprising ability, for infants do not hear nonnative contrasts. At the same time it is clear that adults have (partially) lost this skill, since they find it difficult to discern foreign contrasts. When do infants converge on adult competence?

2.2.2 Developmental Changes in the Perception of Nonnative Contrasts

The extraordinary ability of newborns to discriminate unfamiliar phonemic contrasts rapidly declines. While at 6–8 months infants can still discriminate nonnative contrasts, at 8–10 months they are less successful, and at 10–12 months they are no longer able to do so. Thus, by the age of 12 months English-learning infants behave like English-speaking adults. Figure 2.3 reports data from a cross-sectional study in which three groups of English learners (6–8, 8–10, and 10–12 months of age) were given a task requiring discrimination between foreign contrasts, one from Hindi and one from Salish. These responses were compared with those of native learners (Hindi and Salish learners aged 11–12 months). As the figure shows, most English learners discriminate between foreign contrasts when they are 6 to 8 months old. Between 8 and 10 months, the proportion of English learners able to perform the discrimination task decreases, and between 10 and 12 months of age, only about 20% of English learners can discriminate between Hindi contrasts and only about 10% between Salish contrasts. This effect is clearly due to experience with their native language, since all 11- to 12-month-old Hindi and Salish learners discriminate Hindi and Salish contrasts, respectively.

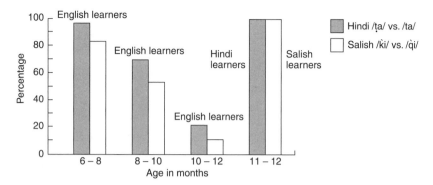

Figure 2.3
Proportion of American English learners from three age groups (6–8, 8–10, 10–12 months) and of Hindi and Salish learners (11–12 months) able to discriminate Hindi and Salish consonantal contrasts. (Reprinted from *Infant Behavior and Development*, volume 7, Werker and Tees, "Cross-Language Speech Perception: Evidence for Perceptual Reorganization during the First Year of Life," pp. 49–63. Copyright 1984, with permission from Elsevier Science.)

These results have been replicated with different infant populations. For example, Tsushima et al. (1994) have found that 6- to 8-month-old Japanese learners can discriminate between the English pairs [ra] and [la]. At 12 months, however, Japanese learners are like Japanese adults: they fail to discriminate between [ra] and [la] (see also Werker and Lalonde 1988 and Best 1995 for additional evidence about the developmental change occurring between 6 and 12 months).[6]

At birth infants can discriminate between native and nonnative contrasts equally well. At 12 months they have become like adults and can handle only native contrasts.[7] These findings favor the hypothesis that infants are born with the ability to discriminate all contrasts, even those not present in the language of their environment. With experience, only the sensitivity to contrasts valid in the native language is naturally maintained. Therefore, the role of experience consists in guiding the child to select, from the universal repertoire of sounds, those that are relevant in the ambient language.

2.2.3   Forgetting as a Way of Developing a Phonological System

We have seen that at the end of their first year infants become attuned to the phonemic contrasts of their native language. How can this developmental change be characterized? Werker and Pegg (1992) and Werker

(1995) propose that the developmental change taking place around 12 months for consonants consists in a **functional reorganization of the sound space**. According to this hypothesis, loss of sensitivity to foreign contrasts does not reflect a change in the auditory system. Instead, it is the expression of a postperceptual process that enables children to attend only to those sounds that have a phonemic value in their language, that is, that permit them to distinguish meanings. Thus, it assists children in the task of mapping sounds into meaning, that is, of learning words (chapter 3). As a consequence of this reorganization, infants are predisposed to attend only to contrasts that have a phonemic value in their language (i.e., contrasts that distinguish meanings, such as the contrast that distinguishes *lag* from *rag*). Contrasts that do not have a phonemic value are disregarded, because they are of no help in building up a lexicon. Thus, the functional reorganization is part of the program that progressively enables children to learn words. It is likely that this program is somehow responsible for infants' sensitivity to various types of segmental information (section 3.1.2.5) and for the incorporation of language-specific segments into infants' linguistic productions, something that occurs around 8–10 months (see Oller 1980; Boysson-Bardies and Vihman 1991). These and other findings are highly suggestive: a schedule coordinates infants' capacities and guides them to pick up exactly the information needed for acquiring words and later other linguistic objects. Although the decline in sensitivity to certain features may at first glance appear to be a loss, it is a gain for the learner (see Newport 1990; Elman 1993). It restricts the search space and minimizes the chances of making errors. In this way, it prepares learners for new achievements.

2.2.4   Early Second Language Acquisition

According to the functional reorganization hypothesis, the loss of sensitivity to foreign contrasts is not permanent. Among other things, this view accounts for the fact that early learners of a second language resemble native speakers, while adults learning a foreign language keep a foreign accent. The later a language is learned, the more a foreign accent is discernible (see Flege, Munro, and MacKay 1995 for review). It has been shown that a foreign accent is already detected in children who are exposed to a second language before age 4 (see Flege, Munro, and MacKay 1995). The effect of age is evident not only in production, but also in perception, although in the former case it is more pronounced (see Flege

1993). Late learners are less proficient in discriminating the phonemic contrasts of the second language than early learners. These data support the functional reorganization hypothesis; the system for detecting foreign contrasts seems to be reactivated in young learners, at least up to a certain age.

Recently it has been established that the reactivation may not occur for some kinds of contrasts, however. Pallier, Bosch, and Sebastián-Gallés (1997) have shown that as a group, Spanish-Catalan bilingual adults with Spanish parents (i.e., Spanish-dominant bilinguals) do not discriminate a particular Catalan vowel contrast, although they have been intensively exposed to Catalan since 6 years of age or earlier (age range 1–6; mean age 4.35). Specifically, they do not distinguish between the two Catalan vowels [e] (as in [te] 'take') and [ɛ] (as in [tɛ] 'tea'), mapping them instead onto the Spanish vowel [e], which is more open than the Catalan [e]. In other words, these adults are assimilating Catalan phonemes to Spanish ones (see also Sebastián-Gallés and Soto-Faraco 1999).[8] These data suggest that once individuals whose native language is Spanish have formed the Spanish category /e/, they are unable to build two new phonemic categories /e/–/ɛ/ partially overlapping with it. Six-year-old children are already too old to acquire a new phonological system with native competence. This finding suggests that there is indeed a permanent loss of sensitivity to some foreign contrasts, a result that challenges the functional reorganization hypothesis. According to this hypothesis, the ability to discriminate foreign contrasts can, in principle, be reactivated, at least in young learners. Further research needs to establish whether the permanent loss concerns only some sounds and under what conditions such a loss is evident. Answers to these questions are crucial for abandoning or refining the functional reorganization hypothesis.

2.2.5   The Nature of Infants' Perception Ability

Infants bring to the process of language acquisition a very specialized ability for discriminating all possible phonetic contrasts in a categorical manner. With experience, they become attuned to those contrasts that have a phonemic value in their native language. It is a matter of debate whether categorical perception is a language-specific ability (see Eimas and Miller 1991) or reflects a general acoustic process (see, e.g., Aslin and Pisoni 1980; Jusczyk 1997). For one thing, other sounds besides linguistic stimuli are perceived categorically (see Jusczyk et al. 1980). It is thus possible that "languages can take advantage of the auditory perception system by placing phoneme boundaries at auditory sensitivity peaks" (Gerken 1994a, 786), that is, in regions to which the human auditory system is particularly sensitive. In fact, not all speech sounds are equally salient; some are more prominent than others and more easily categorized by the auditory system. The auditory system is most sensitive between about 2000 and 5000 Hz (Sivian and White 1933), yet the human vocal apparatus produces speech sounds between 100 and 6400 Hz (Fletcher 1952, cited in Shiffman 1990). Obviously, certain speech sounds are produced in less sensitive regions and are therefore more difficult for infants to discriminate; one example is fricatives (see Jusczyk 1997 for review). Yet the observation that in general phonemic distinctions are placed in a highly sensitive region indicates that language has best exploited human perceptual capacities (which are available independently of language).

Categorical perception might not be an ability specific to humans. Animals (chinchillas, macaques) can perceive speech sounds categorically (see Kuhl and Miller 1975; Pastore et al. 1977; Kuhl and Padden 1982; Pisoni, Carrell, and Gans 1983; Kluender, Diehl, and Killeen 1987). This fact hints that categorical perception may reflect some general acoustic ability; it may very well be that other surprising abilities that infants display are not specific to language.

Preliminary evidence also exists that cotton-top tamarin monkeys can discriminate some pairs of languages, specifically Dutch and Japanese, as babies do (see Ramus et al. 2000). This finding suggests that "some aspect of human speech perception may have built upon preexisting sensitivities of the primate auditory system" (Ramus et al. 2000, 351). Therefore, these skills may not be language specific. However, it is only in humans that they are exploited to acquire language and to map linguistic structures.

2.2.6   Intermediate Summary

At birth infants discriminate a wide variety of sound contrasts. This speech perception ability is very important since it puts children in a position to cope with the phonological properties of any language and thus makes them able to learn any language they are exposed to. This ability changes through exposure to the linguistic environment, and at 12 months infants behave like adults in no longer being able to perform these discriminations, a change that is a prerequisite for acquiring words.

2.3 INFANTS' SPEECH PRODUCTION

Having examined infants' ability to perceive speech, let us turn to their ability to produce it.

While speech perception is evident from birth, speech production abilities are not apparent before 6 months. Infants' first vocalizations consist of cries, vegetative sounds, and isolated vowel-like sounds, occasionally accompanied by consonantal sounds. An important milestone in linguistic development is the onset of **babbling** at around 6–8 months of age, a precursor to language consisting of syllable sequences like *bababa*.

The delay in speech production may be due to the immaturity of infants' speech apparatus, which is not suitable for producing speechlike sounds at birth. But this might not be the only or the primitive reason. Deaf infants engage in **manual babbling** when hearing infants start **vocal babbling**. Since manual babbling does not depend on the maturation of the vocal apparatus, the identical timing in the emergence of vocal and manual babbling has led Petitto and Marentette (1991) to suggest that it is the maturation of the neural substrate supporting language that is responsible for babbling. The close similarity between vocal and manual babbling has implications for our conception of the language capacity. Humans are born with special sensitivity not to sounds, per se, but to the particular units, structures, and regularities found in natural languages, regardless of the modality of expression.

2.3.1 The Maturation of the Vocal Apparatus

From birth to 4 months, the infant's oral tract resembles that of apes. As figures 2.4a and 2.4b indicate, newborns have a higher larynx, a smaller throat, a shorter vocal tract, and a different tongue shape than adults do (see Lieberman, Crelin, and Klatt 1972). This difference in vocal tract shape is responsible for the differences between infants' and adults' resonance cavity, and it limits infants' production of speech sounds. At around 4 months the infant's vocal apparatus undergoes tremendous changes and starts to approximate the adult shape. As is apparent from figure 2.4, one major change is the descent of the larynx. As in chimps, in infants the larynx is high, while in adults it is lower. The descent of the infant's larynx starts at 4–6 months and is not completed until 3 years of age (see Lieberman 1984 for a discussion of modifications in the vocal tract during evolution). Other anatomical changes occur in the vocal tract, as well as in other parts of the body that participate in phonation—

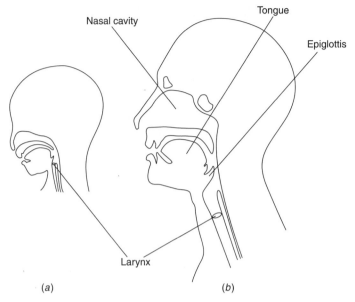

Figure 2.4
Configuration of the vocal tract of an infant (*a*) and an adult (*b*), sectioned along
the midsagittal plane

for example, in the rib cage. While at birth the ribs are almost perpen-
dicular to the spine, at 3 months they start to take the adult shape, that is,
angled downward and outward from the spine. As a result, infants, like
adults, can control air pressure and produce long episodes of phonation.

It is not until the configuration of the oral cavity is ready that babbling, the first form of speechlike production, can start. This does not
imply that the onset of babbling is determined exclusively and mainly by
the anatomical development of the vocal apparatus (but see, e.g., Locke
1983; Studdert-Kennedy 1991), but that this development is a prerequisite
for it.

2.3.2 Vocal Babbling

Babbling is a form of linguistic production characterized by

- a syllabic organization (see Oller and Eilers 1988),
- the use of a subset of the possible sounds found in natural languages
  (Locke 1983),
- the absence of an associated meaning (Elbers 1982).

There are two forms of babbling: **canonical** and **variegated**. Canonical babbling consists of a sequence of the same CV (C = consonant, V = vowel) syllable, the most typical syllable in adult languages (e.g., *bababa*, *dadada*). In variegated babbling the types of syllables and the prosody are more varied and the vocal patterns resemble words. For example, infants can alternate *ba* and *da*, or other syllables. These two forms of babbling do not correspond to two different stages, for infants may produce both at the same time (see Oller 1980; Vihman 1993).

When infants start to babble, their phonetic repertoire displays universal features and is not language specific. For example, in babbling stop consonants and nasals are much more frequent than other sounds; [a] and [æ] are more frequent than [i] and [u]; and CV sequences are more frequent than VCV sequences (for explanations about these universal features of babbling, see Oller 1980; MacNeilage 1980; Elbers 1982; Studdert-Kennedy 1991).

At least by 8–10 months, linguistic experience starts to modulate infants' babbling to some degree. How do we know this? Boysson-Bardies et al. (1989) have shown that the quality of vowels produced by infants reared in different linguistic communities (French, British English, Cantonese, Arabic, Swedish, and Yoruba) varies. Interestingly, these differences reflect those found in the ambient languages. In the same vein Boysson-Bardies and Vihman (1991) have shown that around 10 months infants' production of consonants is also influenced to some degree by the surrounding environment. Infants belonging to different speech communities display a preference for those segments that are more frequent in the words of the target language. For example, labials are more frequent in French words than in English words. Accordingly, infant French learners produce more labials than infant American English learners. Dentals are more frequent in Japanese words than in French words, and infant Japanese learners produce more dentals than infant French learners. Figure 2.5 displays the distribution of labials in babbling and in target words of the adult reference sample for French, English, Japanese, and Swedish. As this figure shows, infants' production of consonantal segments mirrors the statistical tendencies of the target languages. The influence of the environment is also manifest in disyllabic production. The vast majority of disyllabic sequences have the form CVCV in French, English, and Swedish babbling, and the form VCV in Yoruba babbling, mirroring syllable patterns in the target language (Boysson-Bardies 1993).

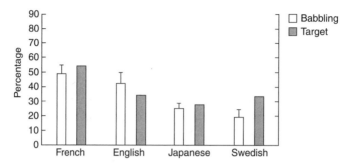

Figure 2.5
Distribution of labials in babbling and target words of the adult reference sample
in four languages. (Adapted from Boysson-Bardies and Vihman 1991. Used with
permission from the Linguistic Society of America.)

Researchers conclude that by 8–10 months the choice of sounds in
babbling is to some degree influenced by linguistic experience. Putting this
together with the fact that by 8 months infants' sensitivity to foreign
contrasts starts to decline, we can see that at this point in development
language specificity is evident both in production (babbling) and in perception (see sections 2.2.2, 2.2.3). Hence, at around 8–10 months infants
are establishing which are the consonantal contrasts of their target language and are progressively converging toward the adult phonological
system (see also section 3.1.2.5 for further evidence that babies are sensitive to segmental information around 9 months).

2.3.3   Manual Babbling

When hearing infants start vocal babbling, deaf infants exposed to sign
language begin to babble manually (see Petitto and Marentette 1991;
Petitto 1995). Manual babbling is distinct from gestures used by all
infants for communicative purposes and from infants' rhythmic manual
motor activity (see Thelen 1991; see also Petitto 1992), and it displays the
same features as vocal babbling. It can be described in terms of linguistically relevant units since, like vocal babbling, it has a syllabic organization. Signs used to babble represent a subset of the inventory of signs used
in signed languages and are employed without meaning. Like vocal babbling, manual babbling is of two types, canonical and variegated. Moreover, from around 10 months the infant's repertoire of signs reflects to
some extent the inventory of signs in the ambient sign language (Petitto
1995).

Thus, the time course, form, and organization of vocal and manual babbling are remarkably similar. What do these findings say about the human language capacity? They suggest that vocal babbling is not driven by the development of the articulatory system underlying speech production, but is controlled by a unitary language capacity, which also governs the onset of manual babbling (see also Meier and Newport 1990 for discussion of the developmental milestones in signed and spoken languages). It is thus possible that the language capacity is not tied to a specific modality, but can express itself in various modalities, provided that these are suitable for conveying the kind of pattern typical of natural languages. The language capacity would then be an **amodal capacity**, sensitive to the kinds of patterns "that correspond to the temporal and hierarchical grouping and rhythmical characteristics in natural language phonology" (Petitto and Marentette 1991, 1495).

Given current knowledge, the relation between manual babbling and the language capacity can be viewed in another way. Speech is the natural mode of expression of the language capacity, and language is a modal capacity tied to the oral modality. However, when this mode of expression is precluded, because of an impairment in the system, the language capacity can reorganize itself and find another means of expression, which can easily be adapted to this task, although it was not originally selected for it.

Remarkably, whether the use of gestures is the result of a rapid adaptation or the expression of an amodal capacity, the use of sign languages is fairly natural in subjects who do not have access to speech. Goldin-Meadow and Mylander (1998) have shown that deaf American and Chinese children who are not exposed to a conventional sign language spontaneously create their own gesture system (see also Feldman, Goldin-Meadow, and Gleitman 1978). Surprisingly, these systems have properties typical of natural languages (order of elements within sentences, case marking of arguments). Moreover, despite the differences between American and Chinese culture, American and Chinese children's gestures resemble each other. These findings would not be expected if the human language capacity did not shape the inventions of gestural systems and was not suitable for different modalities of expression.

2.3.4 Babbling and Word Production

Jakobson (1968) considered babbling as a prelinguistic phenomenon unrelated to the acquisition of language. This view is no longer valid, and babbling is now considered a fundamental step in the development of language: infants try out their articulatory capacities, and they discover and practice the sounds and legal combinations of their language, leading up to the production of words.

At the age of 10–12 months, while they are still babbling, infants start to produce their first identifiable words. So, for a period that may last 4 or 5 months (see Elbers 1982; Vihman and Miller 1988), babbling and first word production overlap. Boysson-Bardies and Vihman (1991) found similarities in the frequency of sounds used in first words and in babbling, suggesting that there is continuity between babbling and word production and that babbling is an important milestone in the process of acquiring a language. Nevertheless, they also found differences between babbling and word production, which reflect the greater demands imposed by the latter. Articulating words requires control and planning of coarticulatory tendencies and of the sequencing of articulatory gestures.

2.4   SUMMARY AND CONCLUDING REMARKS

We have seen that from birth hearing infants display an impressive sensitivity to the properties and structures of natural language phonology. Already at 4 days they can discriminate a wide variety of languages, some of which they have never heard, by relying on rhythm; they can distinguish their native language from a foreign one and even two foreign languages from each other.

Hearing newborns can also discriminate a wide variety of speech sounds drawn from their native language or from a foreign language. Between 6 and 12 months this ability to discriminate foreign sounds declines, since experience urges infants to focus on the sounds they hear in their ambient language, the sounds that form words in their input. At around 6–8 months infants start to babble, vocally or manually. During this activity infants practice the sounds or the signs of their native language and establish a relation between what they perceive and what they produce, something that prepares them for a new accomplishment, building a lexicon.

During the first year of life infants try to orient themselves in the labyrinth of sounds. They hear an input and must work backward to find the underlying structure. Even if we assume that infants are endowed with rich innate equipment, they still must discover how the innate constructs, the units of language, are instantiated in the input. Infants start as potential native speakers of any language, and their language capacity can fit any linguistic input, be it oral or manual. While at birth they are skillful in dealing with global variation, after one year of experience their capacities have been refined. During development, they lose some abilities (e.g., to deal with foreign languages or with foreign consonantal contrasts), but gain access to others that prepare them to learn the units of their ambient language (i.e., words). In their first year of life, then, infants become attuned to global properties (prosodic structure) and the sound system of the language around them.

Summary of Linguistic Development

1. At birth infants
   a. discriminate their native language from a foreign language,
   b. discriminate between two foreign languages,
   c. can count syllables and thus vowels in a word,
   d. perceive accent.
2. At 1 month infants discriminate between consonants.
3. At 6–8 months infants start to babble (vocally or manually).
4. At 8–10 months
   a. infants' vowel quality is influenced by the ambient language;
   b. infants' sensitivity to foreign consonantal contrasts starts to decline.
5. At 10–12 months infants
   a. cannot discriminate consonant contrasts belonging to a foreign language,
   b. use a repertoire of consonants during babbling that is influenced by their native language,
   c. produce their first words.

Further Reading

Boysson-Bardies 1999 is an introductory book that covers language development from birth to 2 years. Petitto 1999 discusses the biological foundation of language by presenting evidence from sign languages. Jusczyk 1997 surveys the development of speech perception and production in great detail. Goodman and Nusbaum 1994 includes articles documenting the changes that infants' speech perception and production undergo during the first 2 years of life. Kuhl 1991 and Kuhl et al. 1992 discuss how infants and adults perceive vowels and how experience shapes humans' perception of the vowel space. How perception of nonnative vowels develops is taken up in Werker and Polka 1993. Gerken 1994a discusses the role of prosody in acquiring a language, interactions between nature and nurture, and individual differences in the acquisition of phonology. Other reviews of various aspects of phonological development are Menn and Stoel-Gammon 1995, Locke 1995, Werker and Tees 1999.

Key Words

Amodal (language) capacity
Babbling
Canonical babbling
Categorical perception
Functional reorganization of the sound space
High-amplitude sucking procedure
Learning as a selective process
Manual babbling
Rhythm-based language discrimination hypothesis
Variegated babbling
Vocal babbling

Study Questions

1. What evidence shows that infants are universal learners?

2. On what basis can we claim that prosody is necessary and sufficient for discriminating pairs of languages?

3. Given the rhythm-based language discrimination hypothesis, would we expect 4-day-old babies to discriminate Italian and Spanish?

4. What linguistic unit do infants choose to represent language? Does this choice depend on the native language or does it reflect a universal tendency?

5. What role does babbling play in language acquisition?

6. How does manual babbling bear on the question of the nature of the language capacity?

7. What is the relation between babbling and word production?

8. Provide evidence for the claim that children learn language by selecting among various possibilities.

Chapter 3

Acquisition of the Lexicon

INTRODUCTION

Children learn the vocabulary of their language at a remarkable pace. At 10–12 months they produce and understand some words (Huttenlocher 1974; Benedict 1979; Oviatt 1980). This is the result of a process that starts at around 6 months, when infants display sensitivity to various phonological properties of native words.

Learning words involves two tasks that can be performed separately by the child: (1) segmenting the speech stream into word-sized units (as a result of which the child has a phonological lexicon of word forms) and (2) associating meanings with word forms. This chapter is built around these two tasks and takes up four main topics: phonological bootstrapping of the lexicon (section 3.1), learning the meaning of nouns (section 3.2), learning the meaning of verbs (section 3.3), and hypotheses about how children bootstrap into syntax (section 3.4). Section 3.4 forms a bridge between the lexicon and the syntax.

Section 3.1 first addresses the problem of finding words in the speech stream and then presents a model for constructing a phonological lexicon. It discusses the idea dubbed phonological bootstrapping of the lexicon, according to which infants can bootstrap lexical acquisition through a phonological analysis of the speech input. The term *bootstrapping* refers to the idea that clues to some abstract symbol or linguistic object (words, categories, syntactic structure) come from (perceptual) properties associated with that symbol or object that are readily available in the input. For example, to find candidate words in the input, various sources of information, including prosody and phonotactic constraints, can be recruited. Once infants have a phonological lexicon, they have to pair word forms with meaning. Performing this mapping is not easy, since a given situation can be described in multiple ways. How can the child establish the meaning of a given word? For nouns, it has been suggested that there are biases that guide children's guesses about their meaning (section 3.2). For verbs, it has been hypothesized that children can infer their meaning from the structural context for their use (section 3.3). This hypothesis raises a new question: how do children have access to syntactic representations? Section 3.4 takes up this question and examines three hypotheses about how children break into syntax.

3.1   WHY FINDING WORDS IS A PROBLEM

Around the end of the first year of life, infants start to produce their first words. But how have they managed to discover words? If you were given a printed text written in a language you do not know, you would be able to identify words by relying on the blank spaces: a word is a chunk that has a blank space to both its left and its right. By contrast, if you heard someone uttering sentences in a language you do not know, you would have a hard time singling out words, that is, figuring out where each word begins and where it ends. Spoken language contains very few consistent physical cues analogous to blank spaces in printed texts for identifying word boundaries. In other words, in fluent speech words are usually not separated by pauses, and they tend to slur into one another. This makes the recovery of word boundaries difficult. Consider the two French sentences in (1), from Christophe and Dupoux 1996. These share the same sequence of phonemes up to the syllable *grin*. While a word boundary must be postulated in (1a) between *chat* /ʃa/ and *grin(cheux)* /grɛ̃(ʃø)/, this boundary does not exist in (1b).

(1) a. C'était *son chat grin*cheux qui le   rendait nerveux.
        it was his cat churlish that him made   nervous
        'It was his churlish cat that made him nervous.'
    b. C'était *son chagrin* fou   qui le   rendait odieux.
        it was his sorrow foolish that him made   hateful
        'It was his foolish sorrow that made him hateful.'

If we look at the acoustic waves of these sentences, given in figure 3.1, we see that there is no break between the syllables *cha(t)* and *grin* in either sentence, even when the two syllables belong to two different words, as in (1a).

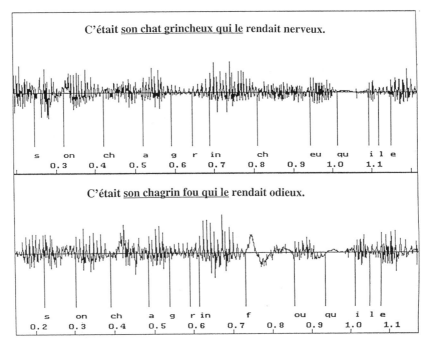

Figure 3.1
Spectrogram of the underlined parts of the French sentences *C'était son chat grincheux qui le rendait nerveux* (top) and *C'était son chagrin fou qui le rendait odieux* (bottom). The vertical lines mark the beginning of each phoneme. (Reprinted from Christophe and Dupoux 1996. Used with permission from Mouton de Gruyter.)

Usually infants hear sentences, where words follow one another without interruptions. Moreover, they are rarely taught isolated words. Aslin et al. (1996) report an experiment in which 12 mothers were specifically instructed to teach new words to their children. Only 3 of them presented words in isolation in more than 50% of their utterances; the other 9 uttered isolated words from 5% to about 30% of the time. Thus, new words are presented to infants in sentences, where word boundaries may be hard to detect.

Even if adults uttered isolated words and infants could form a small lexicon of frequent words, the problem of finding word forms in fluent speech would not be solved, because words can occur embedded in larger words. For example, suppose that an infant knows the word *can*. When she hears *cancer*, *toucan*, and *uncanny*, she may try to match *can* with these words and end up with an incorrect segmentation; for example, she may match *can* with the first syllable of *cancer* and consider the second syllable as belonging to another word. Moreover, certain sequences of sounds can be segmented in different ways. The sequence [aiskrim] corresponds to two different strings of words, *I scream* and *ice cream*.

The upshot of all this is that there are multiple ways to segment a string of sounds. Adults can face this problem and single out words from the speech stream by consulting their lexicon and by appealing to higher-order syntactic, semantic, and pragmatic knowledge. Infants cannot do the same since they have no lexicon. They have to build it!

To sum up, the problem of segmenting the speech stream or of finding word forms arises because

(2) a. speech is continuous (i.e., there are no consistent and reliable breaks between words),
   b. words are not taught in isolation (though even if they were, the problem would remain, because there are words that are part of larger words and there can be multiple ways of segmenting a string),
   c. infants are not born with a lexicon.

And the learnability problem is this: If you have a mental lexicon, you can at least partially solve the problem of recognizing a word in the speech stream by consulting it, that is, by seeing if a given chunk matches an existing word that is stored there. Adults recognize words when they hear something, because they know words in advance. Infants cannot do the same thing, because they do not know words in advance. Then the question is, How do infants break into the lexical system without relying on a mental lexicon, which they do not have?

Despite all the difficulties inherent in extracting word forms from continuous speech, infants do succeed in learning words. We must therefore assume that they are somehow able to segment the speech stream into discrete chunks, that is, to discover word boundaries (something that is hard for a computer to do, witness the fact that no implemented algorithm has yet successfully segmented speech; see Waibel 1986). The next section explores this ability.

3.1.1 Phonological Bootstrapping of Lexical Acquisition

It is possible that children do not look immediately for words in the acoustic input, but that they first try to find larger units such as clauses or phrases. After all, it is easier to recover a word from a clause or a phrase than directly from the acoustic input. This hypothesis is rooted in the observation that when we utter sentences, we tend to group words into prosodically cohesive units, that is, units that are rhythmically and intonationally organized and that roughly correspond to syntactic clauses and phrases (for technical discussion of the prosodic representation of natural language utterances, see, e.g., Nespor and Vogel 1986; Selkirk 1984). (Interchangeably, in this book these units are called *clauses*, *phrases*, *prosodic units*, or *prosodic constituents*.) For example, the string in (3a) (from Thornton and Wexler 1999, 74) has two meanings, conveyed by the two different ways of pronouncing it represented in (3b,c).

(3) a. Bill gave her cat food.
    b. Bill gave her cat FOOD.
    c. Bill gave her/CAT food.

In (3b) the whole string forms a prosodic unit and stress falls on its last element, written in capital letters. When pronounced in this way, the sentence means that the cat was given food, not something else. In (3c) *cat food* is a compound; when English speakers utter this sentence, they tend to group the words *Bill gave her* together and separate them from *cat food* with a short pause. Thus, (3c) consists of two prosodically cohesive units, separated by a prosodic boundary (indicated by "/"). Here stress falls on *cat*—in other words, on the first member of the compound, as is generally the case in English. When pronounced in this way, the sentence means that a female was given cat food. Similarly, the Italian sentence in (4a) is ambiguous.

(4) a. (Al mare) Federico ci   andava solo quando pioveva.
       (to the sea) Federico there went   only when   (it) was raining
    b. (Al mare) Federico ci andava/solo quando pioveva.
       '(To the sea) Federico went there only when it was raining.'
    c. (Al mare) Federico ci andava solo/quando pioveva.
       '(To the sea) Federico went there alone when it was raining.'

On one meaning, (4b), Italian speakers tend to group the words *Federico ci andava* together and separate them from the second group *solo quando pioveva*. When pronounced in this way, the sentence means that Federico went there (to the sea) only when it was raining. On the other meaning, (4c), the prosodic boundary is placed after *solo*, and the sentence means that Federico went there (to the sea) alone, when it was raining.

The prosodic boundaries in (3) and (4) are not just boundaries between two prosodically cohesive units of a certain size, but also boundaries between two words. Thus, if infants can recover boundaries marking prosodically cohesive units, they automatically recover boundaries marking certain words. This procedure therefore allows infants to recover some word boundaries—though, it must be emphasized, not all.

As discussed in section 2.1.3, infants are very sensitive to prosodic properties of speech. Because of this fact and because speech clearly exhibits prosodic organization, Christophe and Dupoux (1996) and Christophe et al. (1997) have proposed that prosody might assist infants in the task of finding word forms. These authors claim that infants may bootstrap lexical acquisition through a phonological analysis of the speech stream segmented into small prosodic units. In other words, infants get a leg up in the acquisition of the lexicon by exploiting phonological information (see Peters 1983; Morgan 1986); that is, they recover words by relying on phonological properties of the speech stream, information that is readily available in the input. This solution is often dubbed the **phonological bootstrapping of lexical acquisition**.[1]

Figure 3.2 shows a possible phonological bootstrapping model for the acquisition of words. According to this model (reading upward), infants hear a sequence of sounds, the acoustic input. From this they build a prelexical representation in terms of phonemes and syllables; that is, they encode the acoustic input in terms of language-specific units. They also mark on this representation various phonological properties such as stress and lengthening. Then, by exploiting a number of acoustic cues, infants extract prosodic boundaries that partition the sequence of phonemes and syllables into small prosodic constituents. Thus, by performing a purely phonological analysis, infants obtain a language-specific prelexical representation of speech segmented into prosodic units of a certain size, each including a limited number of words (e.g., two or three). An example of the kind of information that infants are supposed to extract from acoustic input appears in the middle of figure 3.2. The input (represented as *leiktaho* in the figure) is segmented into prosodic units and is encoded in terms of phonemes, syllables, and so on. It is not clear how detailed this prelexical representation is; it is possible that infants do not represent all phonemic information, but just certain global properties (see Jusczyk 1997 for discussion).

Once infants have built a prelexical representation segmented into prosodic units, they can exploit various sources of information to find word

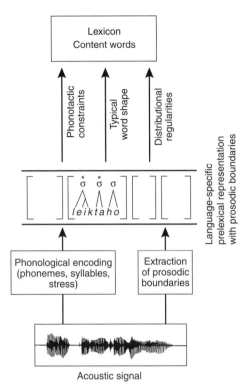

Figure 3.2
A possible model of phonological bootstrapping of lexical acquisition that rests on the prelexical prosodic segmentation hypothesis (see Christophe and Dupoux 1996; Christophe et al. 1997)

forms or to detect word boundaries and thus to build a lexicon of content words. As shown in figure 3.2, these are

(5) a. distributional regularities,
    b. typical word shapes, and
    c. phonotactic constraints.

Distributional regularities refers to statistical information included in sequences of sounds. In a given language the probability (called the **transitional probability**) that one particular sound is followed by another particular sound is higher when the two sounds occur word-internally than when they belong to two distinct words, an observation going back to Harris 1954. The last syllable of any word can be followed by any other syllable. For example, the last syllable of *furniture* can be followed by a high number of other syllables.

(6) the furniture $\begin{cases} \text{is} \dots \\ \text{was} \dots \\ \text{in the room} \dots \\ \text{next to} \dots \\ \text{that John} \dots \end{cases}$

Thus, the probability that *is* follows the last syllable of *furniture* is low (1/5 in (6)), because four other syllables compete with it. By contrast, there is a strong expectation that, given the sequence *ele*, the next syllable will be *phant* or *vator* (example from Saffran et al. 1999). Hence, the probability that *phant* will follow *ele* is 1/2 (just one other syllable competes with it). The point is that sound sequences that occur frequently in speech, that appear in a given order and/or position, are more likely to form a word than sound sequences that occur less frequently. Brent and Cartwright (1996) have implemented a computer algorithm that posits word boundaries by exploiting distributional regularities. They have found that such an algorithm discovers 40% of the words included in a corpus of utterances used by adults in interaction with an infant. This result suggests that using distributional regularities may help the learner, although alone they hardly suffice to solve the segmentation problem.

Regularities in the rhythmic properties of words give rise to **typical word shapes**. For example, in English most content words begin with a strong syllable (see Cutler and Carter 1987). Hence, placing a word boundary before a strong syllable may be an effective strategy for segmenting words in the sound stream.

Phonotactic constraints determine which sequences of phonemes can occur word-internally in a given language. In English, for example, the string of phonemes /dstr/ must be divided by a word boundary between /d/ and /s/, as in *bad string*, since it is not a possible word-internal cluster. There are substantial differences among languages concerning which sequences are legal or illegal. The sequence of phonemes /kt/ is an illegal word-internal cluster in Italian, but a legal one in English—witness the word *phonotactic* itself. Hence, when infants hear a string containing a sequence of phonemes that is illegal in their native language, they may place a word boundary within it.

Distributional regularities, typical word shapes, and phonotactic constraints are all language-specific properties in that they exploit the regularities of a given language. Because the input these strategies apply to must be expressed in the form of categorized units (e.g., phonemes, syllables), learners cannot apply them directly to the acoustic signal; instead, to exploit these properties, learners must have access to some sort of prelexical representation. By contrast, prosodic boundaries can be recovered directly from the acoustic input and thus may be less language specific.

While it is agreed that infants may exploit distributional regularities, typical word shapes, and phonotactic constraints to find word forms, the idea that infants benefit from a prosodically segmented representation in finding words is not common to all approaches.

3.1.2   Plausibility of the Phonological Bootstrapping Model of Lexical Acquisition

Is it plausible to conjecture that infants use phonological cues and regularities to learn word forms? Is there enough information in the input for infants to extract word forms by a purely phonological analysis? To answer these questions, we need to know

(7) a. whether the speech signal contains acoustic cues that mark prosodic boundaries and whether infants perceive them; and
   b. whether infants are sensitive to distributional regularities, typical word shapes, and phonotactic constraints.

3.1.2.1   Acoustic Cues for Prosodic Boundaries

The phonological bootstrapping model of lexical acquisition is viable if the signal includes acoustic cues that mark prosodic boundaries. Phonetic studies have indeed shown that clauses are acoustically marked by three cues:

(8) a. pauses,
   b. syllable lengthening,
   c. F_0 (fundamental frequency) resetting.

In English pauses tend to occur at the end of rather than within clauses (see Scott 1982). The syllable immediately preceding the prosodic boundary of a clause tends to be longer than the other syllables within the clause (see, e.g., Lehiste 1970; Klatt 1975, 1976; Cooper and Paccia-Cooper 1980). Finally, F_0 tends to decline toward the end of a clause; that is, the voice goes down and then rises at the beginning of a new clause (Cooper and Sorensen 1981). In sum, prosodic boundaries of clauses are acoustically signaled by a cluster of cues. Do infants perceive these cues?

3.1.2.2 Sensitivity to Prosodic Boundaries   Various studies have shown that infants gain access to prosodic constituents from about 6 or 7 months of age. Using the head turn preference procedure, Hirsh-Pasek et al. (1987) showed that 7- to 10-month-old infants learning American English (mean age 8 months) prefer to listen to linguistic stimuli with artificial pauses located at syntactic clause boundaries to linguistic stimuli with artificial pauses located within clauses. To demonstrate this, they first tape-recorded samples of infant-directed speech and then manipulated these samples by inserting a 1-second pause at the boundaries between clauses (coincident version) or between words in the same clause (non-coincident version). Two samples of their materials are shown in (9) and (10), where slashes indicate pauses.

(9) *Coincident version*
     Cinderella lived in a great big house/ but it was sort of dark/
     because she had this mean, mean, mean stepmother/ and oh she
     had two stepsisters/ that were so ugly./ They were mean too.

(10) *Noncoincident version*
      Cinderella lived in a great big house but it was/ sort of dark
      because she had/ this mean, mean, mean stepmother and oh she/
      had two stepsisters that were so/ ugly. They were mean/ too.

The effect of the manipulation is that in the coincident version pauses co-occur with the other cues signaling prosodic boundaries (i.e., F_0 or pitch decline and lengthening of the final syllable). By contrast, in the noncoincident version pauses and the other cues signaling the boundaries of prosodic constituents do not form a cluster, which may result in an unnatural speech sample.

  Infants were tested sitting on a parent's lap. They heard sometimes the coincident version and sometimes the noncoincident version, coming from the two loudspeakers placed to their left and to their right. The two measures were the direction and the timing of infants' head turns toward the loudspeakers. It was found that infants listened longer to the coincident version than to the noncoincident one; that is, they turned their head longer toward the loudspeaker uttering the coincident version. This result suggests that when the acoustic cues for prosodic boundaries are put in competition, as in the noncoincident version, infants are likely to perceive the prosody of the sample as aberrant, not typical of natural languages. They hear a pause, but not the pitch decline and lengthening that usually occur with it. By preferring the coincident version, infants react to the disruption of the prosodic coherence. This finding indicates that infants are sensitive to the cluster of cues marking prosodic boundaries—specifically, the boundaries of clauses—and react to the disruption of the prosodic integrity of constituents (see also Jusczyk et al. 1992).

Christophe et al. (1994) extended these results. They showed that 3-day-olds born into a French-speaking environment perceive acoustic cues marking one kind of prosodic boundary. Using the high-amplitude sucking technique, they showed that neonates discriminate bisyllabic stimuli that include a prosodic boundary from stimuli that do not. Bisyllabic stimuli were extracted from two different contexts. For example, *mati* was extracted (1) from within a French word such as *mathématicien* (within-word *mati*), and (2) from a sequence of two adjacent words such as *panorama typique* (between-word *mati*), by taking the last syllable of the first word and the first syllable of the second word. In case (2) the syllables *ma* and *ti* were separated by a boundary that was both a word boundary and a boundary of a larger unit (roughly, a phrase). Infants were then presented with these two sets of *mati* stimuli, one containing a prosodic boundary and one lacking it, and were found to be able to distinguish between them. The authors report two acoustic differences between the sets of stimuli. In the between-word *mati* stimuli, the final vowel *a* of *panorama* was longer than the nonfinal vowels, because French has word-final stress, and the first consonant of the word *typique* was also lengthened. Neither of these acoustic cues was present in the within-word *mati* stimuli. It is likely that in the experiment the infants discriminated the two types of stimuli by drawing on this acoustic difference. This experiment thus shows again that there are acoustic correlates of prosodic boundaries and that infants can perceive them after only a few days of life. This evidence does not prove that infants use prosodic information to recover word boundaries. However, it suggests that they have the perceptual capacity to detect the acoustic correlates of some prosodic boundaries.

In summary, we have seen that there are acoustic correlates of prosodic boundaries, that infants are sensitive to them right after birth, and that from 6 months they are paying attention not merely to boundaries, but to the organization of sounds into coherent units of various sizes. This evidence makes it plausible that babies can extract from the acoustic stream a prelexical representation with prosodic boundaries, as hypothesized by advocates of the phonological bootstrapping model (see figure 3.2).

3.1.2.3   Sensitivity to Distributional Regularities   A source of information that babies could exploit to find words in the acoustic stream is distributional regularities, that is, the frequency of occurrence of a sound (or syllable) given another sound (or syllable). Are infants sensitive to such transitional probabilities between two adjacent sounds (or syllables)? According to an experiment by Saffran, Aslin, and Newport (1996) using the head turn preference procedure (see also Goodsitt, Morgan, and Kuhl 1993), the answer is yes.

For 2 minutes (the habituation phase) these investigators presented 8-month-old American English learners with continuous speech consisting of four three-syllable nonsense words presented in random order. These were generated by a speech synthesizer and uttered in a monotone. The intent was to eliminate pauses and any other prosodic cue to word boundaries, leaving transitional probability between adjacent syllables as the only means to recover words. Infants were divided in two groups, each habituated to a particular sequence of syllables that resulted in two sets of four nonsense words. The two conditions are illustrated in (11).

(11)   *Habituation phase*
       Condition A: pabiku tibudo golatu daropi
       Condition B: tudaro pigola bikuti budopa

A sample of what infants heard would be the orthographic string *pabikutibudogolatudaropi....*

Were infants able to segment these sequences into wordlike units? Segmentation was possible only if infants could notice that certain syllables always occurred in the same order in different contexts, that is, if they could compute the transitional probability between any two syllables and notice that it was higher for certain pairs of syllables than for others. More precisely, in condition A the transitional probability between *pa* and *bi* and between *bi* and *ku* was higher (1.0) than the transitional probability between *ku* and *ti* (0.33), because in the former case the syllables belonged to the same word, while in the latter they belonged to two words—three different words (hence, three different syllables) could follow *ku*.

To assess whether infants can segment sound sequences on the basis of transitional probability, in the experimental phase Saffran, Aslin, and Newport exposed their infant subjects to sequences of stimuli consisting of two words and two part-words. The part-words were obtained by joining the last syllable of one word and the first two syllables of another word: for infants in condition A, *tudaro* (the last syllable of *golatu* and the first two syllables of *daropi*) and *pigola* (the last syllable of *daropi* and the first two syllables of *golatu*). Infants in conditions A and B heard the stimuli listed in (12).

(12) *Testing phase*
pabiku tibudo tudaro pigola

Assume that infants calculate transitional probabilities. Then, for infants in condition A *pabiku* and *tibudo* were words, and *tudaro* and *pigola* were part-words. For infants in condition B *pabiku* and *tibudo* were part-words, and *tudaro* and *pigola* were words. This aspect of the experiment was meant to ensure that infants' responses were not influenced by preference for certain syllable strings. While words and part-words all included syllables that infants had heard during the habituation phase, the syllables' transitional probabilities were different. Since the transitional probability between within-word syllables is 1.0 and that between between-word syllables in the habituation sample is 0.33, if infants do indeed compute the different transitional probabilities, they will respond differently to words and to part-words.

Infants were presented with repetitions of the words and the part-words. It was found that they discriminated between words and part-words and preferred to listen longer to part-words, whichever condition they were assigned to during habituation; that is, they displayed a novelty preference for unfamiliar stimuli. These results suggest that 8-month-olds can extract information about the frequency of occurrence of adjacent syllables from the speech stream.

3.1.2.4 Sensitivity to Typical Word Shapes Another source of information that infants could exploit to find words in the acoustic stream is typical word shapes, that is, rhythmic properties. The rhythmic pattern of words varies from one language to another. For example, in addition to differing in phonetic and phonotactic characteristics, Norwegian and English words differ in prosody; for instance, in Norwegian but not in English pitch often rises on the final syllable of words (see Haugen and Joos 1972). At 6 months American infants prefer to listen to lists of bisyllabic English words than to lists of bisyllabic Norwegian words (see Friederici and Wessels 1993). This preference is evident even when the lists are low-pass filtered at 400 Hz. Since low-pass-filtered speech does not contain much segmental information (see section 2.1.3), this result suggests that 6-month-old infants are capable of recognizing native words in terms of their prosodic structure.

Can babies at 6 months also use other sources of information to recognize words? To answer this question, Jusczyk et al. (1993) tested whether 6-month-old infants can discriminate words by relying on segmental information. They tested infants with lists of words from two languages that have different phonetic and phonotactic properties but similar prosodic properties, Dutch and English (see Reitveld and Koopmans-van Beinum 1987; Crystal and House 1988). They found that 6-month-old American English and Dutch learners were not able to discriminate between English and Dutch lists of words, whether or not the words were low-pass filtered. This result indicates that at 6 months infants are not yet able to use phonemic and phonotactic information to recognize native words, relying on prosody instead.

In section 2.1.4.1 we saw that 5-month-old American English learners can discriminate Dutch from English utterances. This result does not conflict with the result from the experiment just described. The kind of prosodic information that characterizes lists of words is different from the kind of prosodic information that characterizes utterances. Utterances possess a suprasegmental coherence that word lists do not. Recall from section 2.1.3 that newborns cannot discriminate a pair of languages when suprasegmental coherence is destroyed, that is, when stimuli consist of scrambled words extracted from sentences. Lists of words are like scrambled-word stimuli. While 5-month-old infants can discriminate Dutch from English on the basis of natural utterances, 6-month-olds cannot discriminate between lists of words from the same two languages; evidently, the prosodic shape of utterances in these two languages is different enough to elicit a discrimination response from infants but the prosodic shape of words is not.

Prosodic features of words may help infants in segmenting the speech stream. Recall that in English most content words begin with a strong syllable, as in *CANdle*. Adult English speakers seem to exploit this regularity when they parse speech, since they attempt to place a boundary before a strong syllable (see, e.g., Cutler et al. 1986). Are English learners sensitive to this regularity? By 9 months (but not by 6 months), they are. They prefer to listen to bisyllabic words starting with a strong syllable, like *candle* and *cable*, than to bisyllabic words starting with a weak syllable, like *guitar* and *decay* (Jusczyk, Cutler, and Redanz 1993); that is, they prefer to listen to bisyllabic words with a trochaic pattern, a pattern that is very frequent in the language they are exposed to.

3.1.2.5 Sensitivity to Phonetic and Phonotactic Features   Across languages words differ in their phonetic and phonotactic characteristics. The English sound /θ/ as in *thermal* is not found in Dutch, and the Dutch consonant that begins the word *Gouda* is not found in English. In Dutch, but not in English, the phonetic sequences [kn] and [zw] can belong to the same word (e.g., in *knotten, zweten*). In English, but not in Dutch, the sequence [tʃ] can occur word-internally (e.g., in *pitches*). Can infants recognize native words on the basis of phonetic and phonotactic information? We have just seen that 6-month-old American English and Dutch learners could not discriminate English and Dutch lists of words, even though each list contained items with segments and sequences of segments that do not occur in the other language. Hence, at 6 months infants do not yet exploit phonetic and phonotactic information to recognize native words. Interestingly, by 9 months American English and Dutch learners can indeed discriminate lists of English and Dutch words (see Jusczyk et al. 1993). Are they recognizing native words on the basis of phonetic and phonotactic information, or on the basis of prosodic information? When the Dutch and English word lists are low-pass filtered, 9-month-old infants do not display a preference for either language. Since low-pass filtering leaves the prosody of words intact but removes phonetic and phonotactic information, the conclusion appears to be that in the (not low-pass-filtered) word list experiment, the 9-month-old infants were relying not on prosody but on either phonetics or phonotactics.

Can it be shown that infants are specifically sensitive to phonotactic characteristics? Jusczyk et al. (1993) carried out another experiment in which they used lists of Dutch and English words containing phones allowed in both languages, but phonotactic constraints allowed in only one language. Nine-month-old infants were still able to discriminate the two lists of words. Since the phones employed in the lists are present both in Dutch and in English, one must infer that infants have relied on the phonotactic properties of words to perform the discrimination. Thus, at 9 months infants have an idea of which phones are present in their native language and of which strings of phones are allowed. This gives 9-month-olds an advantage over 6-month-olds. It is intriguing that this change occurs during the same period when infants' ability to discriminate foreign contrasts declines in favor of becoming attuned to the phonological system of the target language (see section 2.2.2). Infants around 9–12 months are working on fine-grained properties of the sound system of their native language.

3.1.2.6 How Do Infants Discover the Regularities of Their Native Language? We have seen that infants are sensitive to various properties of language: distributional regularities, typical word shapes, and phonotactic constraints. They could thus use these sources of information to place word boundaries in the speech stream. At this point a natural question arises. If infants are to use (e.g.) phonotactic constraints to place word boundaries, they must know which are the phonotactic constraints in their native language. Consider the sequence [kŋ], which is illicit word-internally in English. When infant English learners hear something like /bæŋknɛkst/ (as part of the phrase *the bank next to the house*), in which the sequence [kŋ] occurs, they are likely to place a word boundary between [k] and [ŋ]. If they do not know words, how did they come to know that [kŋ] cannot be a word-internal sequence in English? Similar questions arise for distributional regularities and typical word shapes. Infants must have a way to know which sound/syllable follows which other sound/syllable most frequently and which are the most common word shapes in their language. How do infants manage to gather this information?

We can conjecture that infants discover distributional regularities through a statistical mechanism that computes the contingency, in the speech stream, between adjacent sounds/syllables. Once they have performed this computation, they can place word boundaries between sequences of sounds that have a low probability of following each other.

Infants can identify the phonotactic constraints—the allowable clusters of sounds—in their language by relying on acoustic cues such as lengthening that signal prosodic boundaries. When a cluster is licit word-internally in a language, the sounds it consists of may sometimes be separated by a prosodic boundary and sometimes not. For example, /kt/ is a licit word-internal cluster in English. Infants learning English might hear words like *phonotactic* or sequences of words like *clock today* (as in the sentence I *would like a clock today*). In the former case the sequence /kt/ is word internal; in the latter it spans two words and likely the two sounds /k/ and /t/ are separated by a prosodic boundary. By contrast, when a sequence of sounds is illicit word-internally in a language, a prosodic boundary will always be present whenever infants hear this sequence. Relying on the frequency with which a prosodic boundary occurs between two given sounds, infants can establish which sound sequences are likely to be allowed or disallowed—that is, likely to occur word-internally or across words. If they always detect a prosodic boundary between two sounds, they will decide that the two sounds do not form a licit word-internal cluster.

Another means whereby infants can find phonotactic constraints is suggested by Brent and Cartwright (1996). According to these authors, infants can find at least some phonotactic constraints in an unsegmented speech stream by assuming that consonant clusters can occur word-initially or word-finally if they can occur utterance-initially or utterance-finally. This proposal is not an alternative to the proposal that capitalizes on the presence of a prosodic boundary between word-internally illicit sequences of sounds; rather, it supplements it. While one strategy relies on the presence of prosodic boundaries, the other does not. Although prosodic boundaries are sometimes present between words, they may not always be. In this respect, the two strategies complement each other.

Finally, infant English learners can exploit the presence of prosodic boundaries before strong syllables, since in this language many words begin with a strong syllable. The presence of a prosodic boundary is a cue for babies to infer that a typical word shape in their language has an initial strong syllable.

To summarize: Initially infants extract a prelexical representation from the acoustic input and recover from this some prosodic boundaries that they superimpose on the prelexical representation. At this point they have not found all the word boundaries, however. Infants also compute the distributional regularities present in the prelexical representation, and, by relying on the location of prosodic boundaries, they identify the licit word-internal sequences of sounds in their language and the most frequent word shapes. Once they have stored this information, they can use it to place other word boundaries.

3.1.3   The Phonological Bootstrapping Model and Universal Grammar

According to the phonological bootstrapping model, infants rely on different strategies to recover word boundaries. It is effective to place a word boundary when the likelihood that one syllable follows another syllable is low; similarly, a word boundary may be placed between phonemes that form an illicit word-internal cluster in a given language or, in English, before a strong syllable. None of these strategies is effective by itself, but together they enable the child to find most word boundaries.

A common feature of these strategies is that they require infants to perform some statistical analysis over the prelexical representation (e.g., compute distributional regularities, find the most frequent word shapes). This means that infants are endowed with a mechanism for computing statistical properties of the language. Is this mechanism specific to language? The answer is no, since infants appear to use it to segment non-linguistic auditory sequences of musical notes (tone) (Saffran et al. 1999). In other words, the same mechanism subserves segmentation of both speech and nonspeech sequences.

The hypothesis that a statistical mechanism exists for locating word boundaries was already hinted by Chomsky (1975, chap. 6, fn. 18). For Chomsky, who built on Harris's (1954) insight, word boundaries ought to be recovered by relying on distributional regularities. We now know that this is not the only kind of strategy available—that other sources of information can also be effective and that infants have the capacity to exploit them all.

Caution must be used in interpreting the data discussed in these sections. While they indicate that babies have a general-purpose (not specific to language) statistical mechanism that is involved in segmenting speech, they do not support the hypothesis that this mechanism is sufficient to acquire any aspects of language. For example, it is hard to see what kind of statistical mechanism can abstract the regularities that underlie the distribution of negative polarity items, that is, expressions such as *any*, *ever*, *give a damn* (see Chierchia and McConnell-Ginet 2000, chap. 9, for an introduction). *Ever*, for instance, is licensed in some contexts (13a), (14a,b), but not in others (13b), (15a,b).

(13) a. Every person who *ever* saw a picture of Picasso will come to this exhibition.
   b. *Every person will *ever* come to this exhibition.

(14) a. No person who *ever* saw a picture of Rembrandt will come to this exhibition.
   b. No person will *ever* come to this exhibition.

(15) a. *Some person who *ever* saw a picture of Picasso will come to this exhibition.
   b. *Some person will *ever* come to this exhibition.

It turns out that a semantic attribute of a class of expressions determines where negative polarity items can and cannot appear, an attribute that a statistical mechanism would be hard pressed to discover.[2]

The approach outlined in chapter 1 holds that language acquisition is made possible by a dedicated and biologically determined mechanism, Universal Grammar (UG), in interaction with the linguistic environment. Language acquisition is viewed not as a process of active learning and of grammar building, but as a process of selecting a specific grammar among those that UG allows. This nativist approach to language is not threatened by the findings discussed in the previous sections or by the conclusion that a statistical mechanism is involved in acquiring some aspects of language. The hypothesis that word segmentation involves a statistical learning skill does not entail that the same skill is necessary and sufficient to acquire all other aspects of language. For example, it is very unlikely that the property responsible for licensing *ever* in (13)–(15) can be learned through some statistical mechanism. Similarly, the phenomena discussed so far do not show that language can be acquired by some general-purpose learning mechanism—indeed, much work in linguistics makes this conjecture highly suspect.

3.1.4   The Two-Step Model of Lexical Acquisition

According to the phonological bootstrapping model, lexical acquisition proceeds in two steps. First, at least some words are identified and stored; then the stored word forms are linked to their meaning. This **two-step model of lexical acquisition** does not entail that in all cases the word form is first identified and a meaning is then attached to it. It merely grants that the process of storing word forms may start before the process of associating words with meanings. How do we know this? Jusczyk and Hohne (1997) exposed 8-month-old infants to recordings of stories for 10 days. After 2 weeks the same infants were presented with either a list of words used in the stories or a list of novel words. It was found that they listened longer to familiar words than to novel words. A control group of infants, who were not familiarized with the relevant words through stories, showed no preference for either list. These results suggest that during the familiarization phase infants were able to extract word forms from stories and to store them, and that later, during the test phase (when they were listening to the lists), they were able to retrieve them. Since stories were told in the absence of referents for the words in the stories and since the meaning of the words was unknown to the infants, it must be the case that word forms were stored without an associated meaning. As far as researchers know, it is not until 10–12 months that infants start to associate meanings with words (see Stager and Werker 1997). Therefore, it is very unlikely that the 8-month-old infants in the study could have comprehended the words used in the story. We can conclude that by 8 months infants start to build a receptive phonological lexicon (see Jusczyk 1997 and Boysson-Bardies 1999 regarding the form of the first stored words). This achievement paves the way for the process of linking word forms with meaning.

3.1.5   Intermediate Summary

According to the phonological bootstrapping model of lexical acquisition, infants can build a prelexical representation of speech based on acoustic cues. This representation is to a large extent language specific and is meant to facilitate the extraction of language-specific regularities. To find word forms, infants do not need to already have a lexicon; they draw on other sources of information such as prosody, distributional regularities, phonotactic constraints, and typical word shapes. Newborns can discriminate stimuli that include a prosodic boundary from stimuli that do not. By 6 months infants are sensitive to the typical word shapes of their native language, by 8 months they have the capacity to notice distributional regularities, and by 9 months they are sensitive to the phonetic and phonotactic properties of native-language words. This sensitivity manifests itself in the same period during which infants' ability to discriminate foreign contrasts is declining; the two phenomena are likely to be a manifestation of a single process that puts infants in a position to acquire native-language words.

3.2   WHY ACQUIRING THE MEANING OF WORDS IS A PROBLEM

The core questions in lexical acquisition are these: How do toddlers know that labels identify objects or describe actions, that is, that words have reference and contribute to the truthfulness of sentences? How do toddlers come to know the meaning of word forms?

Regarding the first question, one conjecture is that toddlers have an initial disposition to refer to things and to recognize the same intention in other humans (Bruner 1978; see also Macnamara 1982). This disposition is likely at the heart of their recognition that words are used to refer to something.

Still, even if children know that words in general are used to refer, they need to figure out what particular words refer to. How does a child understand that a given word labels the object she is holding or the object Mommy is holding? One proposal is that toddlers learn word meanings by a **hypothesis formation and testing procedure**. They make a hypothesis about the meaning of a word by relying on the associative principle of temporal contiguity. That is, they notice the co-occurrence between a word and its referent or between a word and an act of pointing. Once they form a hypothesis about the referent of a word, they test it in new contexts in which the same word is used (see Inhelder and Piaget 1964; Bruner, Olver, and Greenfield 1966). On this view the word-learning task involves associating a word with what is perceived when the word is spoken; in other words, it is a **word-to-world mapping procedure**.

Although this procedure may work to some extent, it does run into problems. For one thing, a particular scene may be compatible with multiple hypotheses. Given a situation that features a cat and an elephant, why should toddlers assume that the word *cat* refers to the cat, rather than to the elephant, the tail of the cat, or the leg of the elephant? Another difficulty arises from abstract nouns, whose meaning is not perceivable.[3] How can the child catch their meaning? The problem becomes even worse when we consider verbs. The meaning of most verbs is not directly observable, and usually the utterance of the verb and the event it describes do not co-occur. When a mother says to her child, "You broke the glass," the event has already taken place and the child is likely to be doing something else. In a similar vein, when a father asks his child, "Bring me the doll," the event has yet to take place. The utterance of a noun is often time-locked to the object that the noun describes, but the utterance of a verb is usually not time-locked to the event it describes; and this makes the word-to-world mapping procedure unsupportive for guessing the meaning of verbs. Another difficulty is that a given scene is open to multiple interpretations, such that it is usually impossible to hypothesize the correct meaning of words only by observing the accompanying extralinguistic context. This is often referred to as the **problem of induction**. For example, the situation described by sentence (16a) can be equally well described by sentence (16b), as pointed out by Gleitman and colleagues, because any event of giving is also an event of receiving.

(16) a. John gives a book to Mary.
     b. Mary receives a book from John.

Figure 3.3
The same scene may be described in different ways: *The cat is under the table,*
The cat is on the mat, The mat is under the cat.

Given one sentence including the word *receive* and a situation in which
a book is transferred from John to Mary, how can the child correctly
conclude that *receive* means what it does, rather than meaning 'give'?[4]
Similarly, figure 3.3 can in principle be described by at least the following
sentences:

(17) a. The cat is under the table.
    b. The cat is on the mat.
    c. The mat is under the cat.

The mappings between an utterance and a scene are many to many: the
same sentence can be used in more than one situation, and the same scene
can be described in more than one way.

3.2.1   Cues to and Biases on Word Meaning

The task of learning words would be facilitated if toddlers had an innate
predisposition to establish joint attention with adults at the moment when
adults speak (see, e.g., Bruner 1978), that is, if they sought to share the
same focus of attention that adults have at the so-called utterance time.

This predisposition would enable infants to recognize that focus of attention and labels converge on the same thing. Word learning would also be facilitated if adults labeled objects or events that infants are focusing on or if they offered nonverbal cues to infants about their focus of attention while they uttered words.

Is there evidence that children can use nonverbal cues to learn word meaning? Baldwin (1991) has shown that at around 18 months toddlers can use the direction of the speaker's gaze to detect the speaker's focus of attention when uttering a word or a sentence. This sensitivity to a nonverbal cue may give children a great advantage in two related ways. At best, it can inform children about what the speaker intends to refer to and thus guide them to establish a correct mapping between a word and its referent; at worst, it can restrain children from establishing an incorrect mapping between a word and its referent (see Bloom 1997 for discussion of the role played in word learning by recognition of the speaker's referential intention).

Although the ability to attend to nonverbal cues gives toddlers a great advantage, these cues may not always be available or may not be sufficient. It is likely that other factors also contribute to the word-learning process. According to some authors, children assume that words are used in certain ways. These assumptions, also called *biases*, facilitate learning word meaning by favoring certain kinds of hypotheses over others.[5] They are part of the learning mechanism and must fade as children grow.

Three **biases on word meaning** have been proposed: the **whole object bias**, the **mutual exclusivity bias**, and the **taxonomic bias** (see Markman 1994 for discussion).

(18) *Whole object bias*
   "A novel label is likely to refer to the whole object and not to its parts, substance, or other properties." (Markman 1994, 155)

The whole object bias leads the child to assume that a novel word refers to a whole object and not to its parts or to the material it is made of (see also Macnamara 1982; Markman and Hutchinson 1984; Markman 1994; Soja, Carey, and Spelke 1991). Therefore, when children hear the word *cat*, possibly in the presence of a cat, they are biased to conjecture that it refers to the whole cat and not to the cat's whiskers, paws, or tail.

Having established that a label refers to a whole object, children must decide how to extend it to other objects. In so doing, they are guided by the taxonomic bias.

(19) *Taxonomic bias*

"[L]abels refer to objects of the same kind rather than to objects that are thematically related." (Markman 1994, 155)

Two objects are *thematically* related if they are linked by some relation— causal, temporal, spatial, or other. For example, cows and milk are thematically related because cows give milk; cribs and babies are thematically related because babies stay in cribs. Two objects are *taxonomically* related if they belong to the same category. For example, cows and pigs belong to the category of animals; cars and bicycles belong to the category of vehicles. How do we know that toddlers extend a label to objects of the same taxonomic category, rather than to objects that are thematically related? In experiments with 4- and 5-year-olds, Markman and Hutchinson (1984) assigned their child subjects to one of two conditions: the no-word condition and the novel-word condition. In both conditions children were first shown a target picture. Then two other pictures were placed next to the target picture, one to the right and the other to the left. One picture depicted an object thematically related to the target, and the other an object belonging to the same superordinate category. So, for example, if the target picture represented a cow, the thematically related picture might depict milk and the taxonomically related picture a pig (see figure 3.4). In the no-word condition the experimenter showed children the first picture and said, "See this?" Then she showed the two other pictures and said, "Can you find another one?" In the novel-word condition the experimenter used a nonsense word to name the target object. While showing the target picture, she said, "See this dax?"; and while showing the other two pictures, she said, "Can you find another dax?"

Figure 3.4
Sample of stimuli used in experiments testing how children extend labels. In the center is the target object, on the left a thematically related object, and on the right a taxonomically related object.

If labels invite children to form categories, one would predict that in the no-word condition children would randomly choose either the thematically or the taxonomically related picture, while in the novel-word condition they would prefer the taxonomically related picture. In fact, children in the no-word condition made a taxonomic choice only 25% of the time; that is, 25% of the time they chose the categorially related object (pig for the target cow). By contrast, children in the novel-word condition made a taxonomic choice 65% of the time. Since the difference between the two conditions was the presence versus the absence of a label for the objects, it must be the presence of the word that influences children's taxonomic choice.

We have seen that children initially take a label to refer to the whole object. However, they eventually learn words for the substance or parts of objects in spite of this whole object bias. This outcome is guaranteed by the mutual exclusivity bias.

(20) *Mutual exclusivity bias*
"Words are mutually exclusive. . . . [E]ach object will have one and only one label." (Markman 1994, 163)

Children assume that there is a one-to-one mapping between words and objects. The rationale for this is that a single object cannot be both a cup and a dish; that is, each object has its own label. Assuming that words are not synonyms may thus be helpful. Hence, when children hear a novel word in the presence of an object, they first conjecture that it refers to the whole object. If this already has a label, then—pressured by the mutual exclusivity bias—they conjecture that the novel word refers to the substance or a part of the object.

Both the mutual exclusivity bias and the whole object bias must be supplanted. For example, a single object may be referred to with its own label or with the label of the categories it belongs to (e.g., a cat is also a pet, an animal, and a mammal). Since children learn words for categories, they must therefore override the mutual exclusivity bias.

Biases encode not absolute prohibitions, but tendencies to favor certain choices. They may help children in solving the induction problem by restricting the space of hypotheses they can entertain. However, their scope is limited since they cannot explain how children learn the meaning of verbs, prepositions, and abstract objects, as pointed out by Bloom (1994b) (for criticism of the bias-based approach, see also Nelson 1988; Bloom and Kelemen 1995). They can also not explain how children decide whether a noun is mass or count. For this, inspection of the syntactic context is necessary. For one thing, whether a noun is classified as mass or count varies across languages (e.g., English *hair* is mass, but its Italian counterpart *capello/capelli* 'hair-SG/hair-PL' is count); moreover, the same object can be referred to with a mass or a count noun (e.g., *footwear* is mass and *shoe* is count; see, e.g., Gordon 1985; Bloom 1994b). For another thing, mass and count nouns have different syntax: in English, for example, unlike a singular count noun, a mass noun cannot be introduced by an indefinite article (*a boy* vs. **a water*); a mass noun, but not a singular count noun, can occur without a determiner (*I want water* vs. **I want orange*). Clearly, then, children must have access to other information besides the above-mentioned biases if they are to advance in the acquisition of word meaning. And indeed, for instance, Gordon (1985) has found that from age 2 American English learners use syntactic information to decide whether a noun is mass or count.

3.2.2   Intermediate Summary

Building up a lexicon requires finding word forms in the speech stream and mapping these onto meanings. One hypothesis is that this mapping can occur through a word-to-world mapping procedure: children fix the meaning of a word by observing the external contingencies for its use. But there are multiple hypotheses that children can entertain when they hear a word in a given context; for example, a word might refer to an object, to its parts, or to the material it is made of. To limit the number of hypotheses, it has been proposed that toddlers are assisted by a set of biases on possible word meanings.

A word-to-world mapping procedure may be of some help in learning the meaning of concrete nouns. However, it can hardly account for how children fix the meaning of other kinds of nouns (abstract, mass) and of verbs.

3.3   ACQUISITION OF VERBS

In this section we will consider how children establish global aspects of verb meaning. Let us begin, however, by looking at a crosslinguistic asymmetry between nouns and verbs observed in early lexicons.

3.3.1   Nouns versus Verbs

An important generalization emerging from studies about lexical acquisition is that children's early productive vocabulary consists almost exclusively of nouns, regardless of the culture in which they are reared (Gentner 1982; see also Bates, Dale, and Thal 1995; Caselli et al. 1995; Gillette et al. 1999). Verbs appear later, and for a while they remain a minority. This advantage of nouns over verbs is likely to arise because the meanings of nouns and verbs, at least to some extent, are learned in different ways. The meaning of at least some nouns (e.g., concrete nouns) can be fixed by relying on a word-to-world mapping procedure, whereby the word is mapped onto the object to which it refers. In this task the child may be aided by the sort of bias discussed in section 3.2.1. Gillette et al. (1999) attempted to model the child's learning situation by presenting adults with silent videos of mothers and their children playing together. The adults were asked to identify a mystery noun uttered by the mother at a given point in the video signaled by a beep. Although this is an idealized situation since adults know nouns and verbs and are told in advance that they have to identify a noun or a verb uttered by the mother, nonetheless the results are instructive. Adults correctly identify the noun uttered by the mother 45% of the time. These findings show that nouns are frequently used in child-directed speech when the referent is present and consequently that the external contingencies may be informative enough for establishing the meaning of at least some nouns. Although extralinguistic information may help the child in figuring out the meaning of some nouns, it is hardly sufficient for figuring out the meaning of verbs. In the same experiment Gillette et al. found that by watching the silent videos adults correctly guessed a mystery verb uttered by mothers less than 15% of the time, much lower than the 45% rate for nouns. The external contingencies do not support fixing the meaning of verbs, because (as noted earlier) there is a temporal gap between the utterance of the verb and the extralinguistic context this utterance is meant to describe.

At about 20–24 months children experience a vocabulary spurt, learning between five and nine new words a day up to the age of 6 years (see Carey 1978). When they are using between 50 and 200 words, most children start putting words together (Bates, Dale, and Thal 1995). When they are using around 400 words, a correlation is also observed between vocabulary size and sentence complexity (Bates, Dale, and Thal 1995). One may conjecture that this correlation is a sign that children have access to some new source of information for learning word meaning, that is, syntactic information, as Gleitman and coauthors propose. But how are syntax and the acquisition of verb meaning related? In the next section we will look at a procedure for determining the meaning of verbs that appeals to the syntactic context for their use.

3.3.2   Syntactic Cueing of Verb Meaning

"A picture is worth a thousand words, but that's the problem: a thousand words describe the varying aspects of any one picture" (Gleitman and Gillette 1995, 417). As noted earlier, the ongoing scene is open to a multitude of linguistic descriptions, and this makes it difficult to figure out what the meaning of a verb is by looking only at the scene. **Syntactic cueing of verb meaning** is a way to get past these difficulties: to determine the meaning of a verb (or of a noun), one needs to look at the syntactic context in which the verb is inserted.[6]

Syntactic cueing of verb meaning refers to the idea that children can use the multiple structural contexts in which a verb is used in combination with the extralinguistic situation to infer verb meaning. It replaces a word-to-world mapping procedure with a **sentence-to-world mapping procedure**, in which syntactic structures narrow the range of interpretations possible in a given situation.

Syntactic cueing of verb meaning is inspired by Brown's (1957) idea that children can use morphosyntactic cues in determining whether a word is a noun or a verb. Brown presented children with pictures that he described by using nonsense words inserted in different syntactic contexts. For example, he asked, "Show me a sib" (noun syntax), or "Show me sibbing" (verb syntax). In the former case children generally pointed to the picture showing a concrete object; in the latter to the picture showing an action. Since then other researchers have proved that children make different hypotheses about the meaning of words depending on the syntactic environments in which the words appear (see Katz, Baker, and Macnamara 1974; Waxman and Gelman 1986; Taylor and Gelman 1989; Waxman and Kosowski 1990; Waxman 1994; Bloom 1994b for further applications of this idea). In the same vein, Gleitman and collaborators argue that the syntactic context in which a verb occurs gives hints about its meaning.

The hypothesis that syntax cues verb meaning rests on the plausible assumption that there is a correlation between syntax and semantics and that children are biased to expect this correlation to hold. Verbs have an argument structure (or a subcategorization frame) that specifies the number of their arguments. For example, transitive verbs, like *break*, take two arguments (or are associated with a transitive frame); intransitive verbs, like *laugh*, take one argument (or are associated with an intransitive frame). Arguments define participants in the event described by the verb and can be distinguished in terms of the role they play in that event: the so-called thematic roles agent, patient, theme, goal, and so on. Moreover, each argument in a sentence has a grammatical function (subject, object, etc.). Simplifying somewhat, the hypothesis that syntax cues verb meaning holds that by listening to a sentence like (21a), children remark that the verb *break* has two arguments (or has a transitive frame), as is apparent in the argument structure in (21b). They identify the arguments' grammatical functions, subject and object.

(21) a. John broke a glass.
     b. break: [Arg_1, Arg_2]

To infer the meaning of the verb *break*, children exploit the innate expectation that syntax and semantics are correlated in conjunction with the extralinguistic context in which sentence (21a) is uttered. Given that the verb in (21a) has a transitive frame, children will be biased to seek an agent/theme interpretation of the scene, because such a frame is generally associated with this interpretation. Thus, they will link the subject (Arg_1, *John*) with the agent role and the object (Arg_2, *glass*) with the theme role; and they will infer that the verb *break* has a causative meaning since the thematic roles agent and theme generally lexicalize such a meaning (for more specific discussion and different views about the organization of the lexicon, see, e.g., Grimshaw 1990; Levin and Rappaport Hovav 1996). By contrast, the child cannot infer that the verb *laugh* has a causative meaning since it has only one argument (it does not involve an agent acting upon something).

(22) John laughs.

This is a simplification, because Gleitman's actual hypothesis (see, e.g., Landau and Gleitman 1985) is that children may learn aspects of verb meaning not from a single frame, but from a set of argument structures associated with a given verb. However, it gives an idea about how children use syntactic context to get at verb meaning.

   Syntactic structures are a projection of lexical properties. Therefore, by observing the structural environment in which a novel verb is embedded (e.g., transitive or intransitive frame), one can guess certain aspects of its meaning. Consider the following examples with nonce verbs:

(23) a. John gorped that Mary came.
     b. Bill sibbed.
     c. John stog from Milan to Naples.

By looking at these three sentences, one can guess that *gorp* is more likely to mean something like *say* or *think* than *laugh*, because it takes a clausal complement; that *sib* is more likely to mean something like *laugh* than *say*; and that *stog* implies some movement along a path. Syntactic information alone does not inform the child of the *exact* meaning of words. It narrows the range of interpretations available for a given situation by having the child focus on the interpretations that are compatible with the structural environments in which the verb is used. The exact meaning must then be fixed by observing the extralinguistic context. For example, *stog* in (23c) is compatible with several meanings (e.g., *fly*, *drive*, *walk*); its exact meaning can only be assessed through inspection of the extralinguistic context in which (23c) is used.

Because one can exploit only those aspects of meaning encoded syntactically (e.g., number of arguments, their grammatical function, their case marking or position in the clause), syntactic cueing can only reveal global properties of verb meaning: whether a verb is causative, in which case it has a transitive frame (e.g., (21)); implies transfer, in which case it must be accompanied by three arguments (*John gives a book to Mary*); or expresses a mental/perceptual state and thus takes clausal complements (*John thinks that Mary left*). The information that can be gleaned from syntax is a precondition for efficiently exploiting the information provided by the extralinguistic context to establish a unique interpretation for a verb. In other words, syntactic cues help toddlers to "zoom in" on one of the many interpretations consistent with a scene.

The hypothesis that syntax cues verb meaning is very appealing. But is there any actual evidence that children exploit syntactic information to arrive at the meaning of verbs?

3.3.3   Children Use Syntax to Determine the Meaning of Novel Verbs

Several experiments have tested the hypothesis that syntax cues verb meaning. Their results show that from the age of 2 years learners do rely on syntax to make hypotheses about the meaning of novel verbs. Most of these studies have focused on the syntax-semantics correlation between the transitive verb frame and the causative meaning, on the one hand, and the intransitive verb frame and the noncausative meaning, on the other. Using the **preferential looking paradigm**, Naigles (1990) has established that, when children hear a sentence like (24) in which the nonce verb *gorp* is inserted in a transitive frame, they look longer at a picture displaying a causative action in which one person acts upon another (e.g., A hitting B) than at a picture displaying a noncausative action involving the same two characters (e.g., A and B playing together).

(24) The duck is gorping the bunny.

Conversely, when children hear a sentence like (25) in which *gorp* is inserted in an intransitive frame, they look longer at the noncausative action than at the causative one (see also Naigles and Kako 1993).

(25) The duck and the bunny are gorping.

Notice that to respond differently to sentences (24) and (25), children do not need to have a complete syntactic structure. They could rely on the linear order of constituents or on the co-occurrence of verbs with certain kinds of nouns. How do researchers establish children's preference for the scene that matches a sentence that they hear?

In the preferential looking paradigm children are seated on a blindfolded parent's lap in front of two side-by-side video screens, each displaying a different event. A hidden speaker utters an auditory stimulus (e.g., sentence (24) or sentence (25)), which matches the image on one of the displays. A typical setting is depicted in figure 3.5. The child's task is to look at one of the two video screens. Preference is established in terms of the length of time children watch one screen or the other. (A light bulb mounted atop the speaker attracts infants' attention between trials to ensure that they choose afresh which video screen to look at on each new trial.) Usually, children tend to look longer at the video screen matching the auditory stimulus. For example, in the case of sentence (24) they look longer at the video screen displaying a causative action than at the video screen displaying a noncausative action (see Hirsh-Pasek and Golinkoff 1996 for a more detailed discussion of the methodology).

In Naigles's (1990) experiment described above the verb is presented in a single syntactic frame. Although this information helps the child in making the correct conjecture, it is often insufficient, even in combination with extralinguistic information. For example, the nonce verb *gorp* in (26) can mean either 'carry' or 'bring'.

(26) John gorped a cake to Mary.

To decide which meaning is correct, we need to look at the other syntactic frames in which the same verb occurs. For example, if we hear (27) in addition to (26), we can deduce that *gorp* is more likely to mean 'bring' than 'carry', since *carry* cannot be used in the double object construction (**John carried Mary a book*).

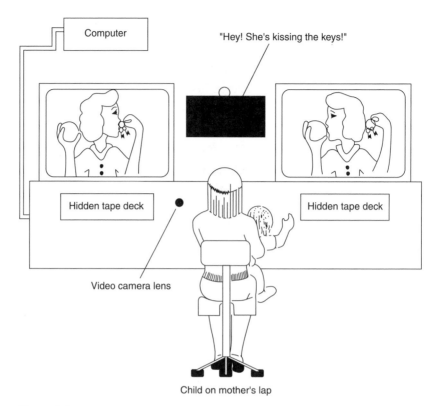

Figure 3.5
A depiction of the experimental setting for the preferential looking paradigm. The child sits on a parent's lap facing two video screens, one displaying a scene that matches an auditory stimulus ("Hey! She's kissing the keys!") and one displaying a scene that does not. Stimuli are delivered by a concealed audio speaker midway between the two video screens. (Reprinted from Hirsh-Pasek and Golinkoff 1996, 60. Used with permission from the MIT Press.)

(27) John gorped Mary a cake.

Apparently, then, to glean the meaning of a verb, one must look at a range of syntactic frames. Are children capable of using multiple frames to deduce the meaning of verbs? The answer is yes. Naigles (1996) showed that 2;2- to 2;6-year-old children can appreciate the presence of multiple frames and make conjectures about the meaning of novel verbs that depend on the frames in which these verbs are heard. Specifically, she tested children's ability to distinguish contact verbs like *touch*, *bite*, and *scratch* from causative verbs like *break* and *open*. Contact verbs depict an action in which an agent enters into contact with a patient. Causative verbs depict an action in which an agent causes something to happen. Both classes of verbs share the transitive frame. However, causative verbs enter the causative alternation (CS), illustrated in (28) (see Levin and Rappaport Hovav 1996), while contact verbs enter a type of alternation in which the object is omitted (OO), illustrated in (29).

(28) *Causative alternation (CS)*
    a. John broke the glass.
    b. The glass broke.

(29) *Object omission alternation (OO)*
    a. John was painting the picture.
    b. John was painting.

As the examples show, in the CS alternation the object of the transitive verb becomes the subject of the intransitive verb. By contrast, in the OO alternation the subject is the same in both the transitive and intransitive frames. If children have access to the two frames in (28) and (29), then, they can infer whether a particular verb has a causative or a contact meaning.

Naigles's experiment included familiarization and experimental phases. In the familiarization phase children watched a videotaped scene including two simultaneous actions—one causative, the other contact—accompanied by a sentence introducing the nonce verb. For example, one scene displayed a duck grasping a frog's shoulder with one foot, causing the frog to bend over (causative action), and contacting the frog's head with the other foot (contact action). While children were watching this scene, they listened twice to the sentence in (30a) followed by either (30b) or (30c).

(30) a. The duck is sibbing the frog.
    b. The frog is sibbing.
    c. The duck is sibbing.

By listening to (30a) followed by (30b), children were exposed to the two frames associated with the causative meaning; by listening to (30a) followed by (30c), they were exposed to the two frames associated with the contact meaning. The goal of the familiarization phase was for children to learn the meaning of the new verbs from the syntactic and the extralinguistic contexts. If children use the syntactic environments in which a verb occurs to zoom in on an aspect of the videotaped scene, then children who have heard the CS alternation should conjecture that *sib* means something like 'cause to bend over' and those who have heard the OO alternation should conjecture that it means something like 'touch'.

To test this prediction, during the experimental phase the causative and contact actions were separated and presented on two video screens: one showed the duck grasping the frog's shoulder, causing the frog to bend over, and the other showed the duck contacting the frog's head. While watching the picture, children listened to the sentence, "Where is sibbing?" It was found that children's looking preference depended on whether they had previously heard the CS alternation ((30a) and (30b)) or the OO alternation ((30a) and (30c)). Children who had heard the CS alternation during familiarization gazed longer at the picture displaying the causative action, while children who had heard the OO alternation watched the causative action much less.[7] According to Naigles, this result must have come about because during the familiarization session children used the frames in which they heard the verb (either the CS or the OO alternation) to zoom in on either the causative or the contact meanings; that is, they must have conjectured that *sibbing* had a causative or a contact meaning, depending on the syntactic contexts in which they heard it. This mapping explains the responses in the experimental phase.

The outcome of this experiment supplies the first piece of evidence that children are capable of using the multiple frames in which a verb occurs to target its meaning, as the syntactic-cueing-of-verb-meaning hypothesis maintains. This ability is particularly striking because it shows that children are capable of performing some structural analysis on the sentences and of relating the different structures. They must have figured out that in the CS alternation the object of the transitive sentence becomes the subject of the intransitive, while in the OO alternation the subject remains the same. In order to do so, they cannot just exploit the co-occurrence of verbs with certain kinds of noun; instead, they must be able to build some sort of structural representation. The experiment shows, then, that cross-sentential observation is crucial in language acquisition and more importantly that children can perform it (see also note 9).

3.3.4 Is Syntactic Cueing of Verb Meaning an Option in Real Life?

We have seen that children have the capacity to recruit the argument structure associated with a verb for determining its meaning. But the hypothesis that children systematically use argument structure to figure out global aspects of meaning can be realistic only if one can show that such information is available to them. Do the utterances to which children are exposed include such information, and if so, how useful is it? An answer comes from a study on blind children's acquisition of the meaning of perception verbs. Landau and Gleitman (1985) noticed that, in spite of their different perceptual experience, sighted and congenitally blind 3-year-old children have very similar semantic representations of vision-related terms like *see* and *look*. Blind children know that *look* is active (it involves a deliberate intention to see something) and *see* is not. When asked to touch a chair, but not to look at it, they merely tap on it, but do not explore it; and when asked to look at the chair, they explore it. Unlike sighted children, blind children take vision terms to refer to haptic perception, when these terms are applied to themselves. However, they are aware that for sighted people *see* and *look* involve visual perception. When a blind child facing an experimenter is asked to show the back of her pants, she turns around and shows her back. This response suggests that blind children know that the experimenter can see an object only if that object is in her visual field.

How can blind children correctly determine the meaning of vision verbs, despite their perceptual deficiency? Landau and Gleitman (1985) presume that blind children use structural information in combination with the extralinguistic context to figure out the meaning of *see* and *look*. If this conjecture is correct, the linguistic input should include the relevant structural information. To test this hypothesis, Landau and Gleitman analyzed the speech used by a mother when she was talking to her blind child. They found that the syntactic environments in which she used *see* and *look* were different from those in which she used other verbs. For example, *see* and *look* were followed by clausal complements, while verbs of motion like *come* and *go* were not (*Look how I do it* vs. **I come that you do it*). The syntactic environments for *see* and *look* themselves also differed: *look* was used for commands (*Look at this*), while *see* was not (**See this table*). In addition, both *see/look* and the other verbs were used in a range of different syntactic frames. Clearly, then, the relevant syntactic information is readily available to children. This conclusion has been further confirmed by Naigles and Hoff-Ginsberg (1995), who found that in child-directed speech mothers use most verbs in multiple syntactic frames. Another especially interesting finding was that children themselves more frequently used those verbs that mothers employed in different syntactic frames. From these outcomes, then, we can conclude that syntactic information associated with verbs is available to learners and that this information facilitates learning what they mean.

3.3.5   Intermediate Summary

The syntactic environments in which verbs are inserted, together with the extralinguistic context in which they are used, provide reliable clues about certain global properties of the verbs' meaning.

3.4   BOOTSTRAPPING OF SYNTAX

The idea that children can use syntactic information to acquire verb meanings rests on a number of premises. Children must be able to build some kind of structural representation, parse sentences, categorize words, and figure out the grammatical function of arguments. Only in this way can they map grammatical functions to thematic roles and infer a plausible meaning for a verb. But how can children acquire all this knowledge? This question in turn raises another: how do children break into syntax? The answer is important for understanding how children acquire verb meanings and how they can access the kind of structural representation that linguists attribute to sentences. This topic belongs both to a chapter dedicated to the lexicon and to one dedicated to syntax. We will take it up here to complete the discussion of how children fix the meaning of verbs.

3.4.1   Overview

The input to the language learner consists of sequences of sounds, which the learner has to parse into structural representations, using abstract notions such as grammatical categories (noun, verb, etc.), grammatical functions (subject of, object of, etc.), and the X-bar schema or something equivalent. In this task children are assisted by innate constraints on the form of possible grammars provided by UG. These constraints limit the hypotheses that children can entertain to those that are compatible with the human language architecture. Children unconsciously know that there are nouns, verbs, subjects, and objects, and that sentences have a structure expressed by the X-bar schema. But this is not enough: they still have to identify which sequences of sounds in the language they are exposed to are nouns, which are verbs, and so on (see Fodor 1966). Having no language-specific syntactic knowledge, how do children break into the system? That is, how can they build a structural representation for sentences if they do not know which words belong to which syntactic category? Clearly, they face another bootstrapping problem: the problem of bootstrapping of syntax.

Researchers have proposed various solutions, mentioned briefly here and discussed in more detail in sections 3.4.2–3.4.4. Under any theory of how syntactic bootstrapping works, it seems that a preliminary step for breaking into syntax consists in locating linguistically relevant units in the speech stream, that is, breaking the input into chunks that correspond to linguistic constituents (e.g., clauses). One hypothesis is that children accomplish this by phonological bootstrapping; that is, they exploit phonological cues for singling out linguistic constituents in the input. In sections 3.1.1 and 3.1.2 we invoked this hypothesis to explain how children build a prelexical representation segmented into prosodic units. Researchers suggest that this same representation can be useful for discovering aspects of the syntactic representation—a hypothesis called **phonological bootstrapping of syntax**.

Once learners have made a first-pass analysis of the incoming sound stream, they face the problem of discovering grammatical categories, relations between structural units, and so on. According to Pinker (1994a, 385), children exploit "certain contingencies between perceptual categories and syntactic categories, mediated by semantic categories" to bootstrap into syntax. This hypothesis is called **semantic bootstrapping** (see Grimshaw 1981; Macnamara 1982; Pinker 1984). An alternative is suggested by Fisher et al. (1994) and further developed by Gillette et al. (1999). According to these scholars, different layers of information become available at different times and develop on the basis of the preceding ones. Children start syntactic acquisition with a partial sentential representation including the nouns that they know. This flat representation is the basis for constructing a more structural representation.

3.4.2   Phonological Bootstrapping of Syntax

As we have seen, the phonological bootstrapping hypothesis holds that an acoustic analysis of the speech stream provides learners with a prosodically segmented prelexical representation that can be exploited to find word forms. It turns out that this representation can also be exploited to bootstrap into syntax. In fact, it supplies learners with prosodically segmented units that roughly correspond to syntactic units (recall section 3.1.2.2; see also, e.g., Gleitman and Wanner 1982; Peters 1983; Gleitman et al. 1988). Between 6 and 9 months infants become sensitive to the prosodic coherence of units of different size. By 7 months infants can parse the ongoing speech stream into clause-sized units (see section 3.1.2.2) and by 9 months into phrase-sized units (see Gerken, Jusczyk, and Mandel 1994).[8] Thus, the structural information that children can glean from phonological information is sentence segmentation and the major phrase bracketing—resulting in a representation that looks like (31), where *XP* and *YP* stand for major phrases and *ZP* stands for a clause. This is not a hierarchical representation, but a flat one.

(31) [$_{ZP}$[$_{XP}$ the dog] [$_{YP}$ chased the cat]]

The phonological bootstrapping hypothesis does not hold that syntactic organization can be directly read off from the phonological representation, or that there is a one-to-one mapping between phonological cues and syntactic units.[9] It merely claims that an initial segmentation and partial bracketing of the speech input may get the child started on the process of discovering syntactic structures by limiting the possibilities (for discussion of this issue, see Morgan 1986; Morgan, Meier, and Newport 1987).

3.4.3   Bootstrapping of Syntax from a Partial Sentential Representation

Fisher et al. (1994) retain the idea that the phonological bootstrapping procedure provides some information useful in acquiring syntax. Specifically, children get from phonology the kind of representation given in (31). From this representation they can recover word forms using the procedures discussed earlier in this chapter, and then they can map the recovered word forms onto meanings. Fisher at al. propose that children fix the meaning of certain nouns through the word-to-world mapping procedure. Phonology and the word-to-world mapping procedure enable the learner to build a **partial sentential representation**, which includes known nouns and an unknown word that the learner takes to be a verb because learners expect sentences to convey predicate-argument structures. Consider a child who hears *The dog pushes the cat*. Suppose that this child knows the nouns *dog* and *cat* but not the word *pushes*. As just described, the child takes *pushes* to be a verb. Then, on the basis of phonological information and the word-to-world mapping procedure, the child builds a representation like (32).

(32) [[... dog] [pushes ... cat ...]]

Learners take nouns to stand for arguments and the unknown word to stand for the predicate, a verb. The information contained in (32) (meaning of nouns, co-occurrence of nouns with a verb), coupled with the extralinguistic context, can be used for fixing global aspects of verb meaning (see Gillette et al. 1999). By inspecting the number of arguments in a representation like (32), children conclude that the verb encodes a binary relation or is associated with a transitive frame. This information, modulated by certain biases, urges them to zoom in on a causative interpretation of the scene, in which an agent acts upon a patient. In fact, various experiments indicate that children and adults have biases to linguistically describe certain aspects of an event. For example, given a nonce verb in isolation paired with two possible events, subjects' preferred guess is that the verb refers to a causative action involving an agent and a patient/theme (see Fisher et al. 1994; Naigles 1996); that is, learners take the verb to encode a causative action performed by the agent. Furthermore, children can elaborate the representation in (32) as in (33) and obtain a **partial structural representation** (which, however, does not yet conform to the X-bar schema).

(33)   push

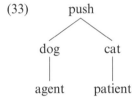

Because the first argument in (33), *dog*, satisfies two quasi-universal properties of the category "subject of a transitive verb"—it is an agent and it occupies the leftmost position of the sentence—children infer that it has the grammatical function subject. Thus, the subject-agent link is derived from a procedure that requires knowledge of the number of arguments in a partial structural representation of the kind in (33). The reference to the number of arguments is crucial because it is only transitive sentences whose agent usually surfaces as subject. Finally, from (33) children will eventually build the kind of phrase structure representation described by current linguistic theories (the X-bar theory).

In summary, children can bootstrap into syntax by exploiting information supplied by the phonological bootstrapping procedure. Then, equipped with a basic scaffolding of nouns, they can build partial sentential representations, determine the number of arguments in a given representation, and decide whether the verb encodes a unary or a binary relation. For example, if the verb encodes a unary relation, it will be incompatible with a causative meaning. By contrast, if it encodes a binary relation, a causative meaning is likely to be correct (see Pinker 1994a for criticism of this view). Once children have fixed the meaning of a few verbs in this way and have bootstrapped phrase structure from the partial structural representation, they can proceed to acquire more verbs, exploiting more complex syntactic properties.

3.4.4 Semantic Bootstrapping of Syntax

An alternative view, proposed by Pinker (1984, 1994a), is that children can bootstrap into syntax by using semantic/conceptual information. This hypothesis, called *semantic bootstrapping*, is inspired by the observation that semantic entities are structurally realized in certain canonical ways (see Grimshaw 1979). For example, in the vast majority of cases objects are expressed by nouns, actions are expressed by verbs, and so on.

Pinker argues that children innately have access to semantically transparent notions such as person, thing, action, agent, patient.[10] These are elements of the semantic representation of sentences that children hear, and they form the inductive basis for deriving the sentences' syntactic counterparts (e.g., the syntactic category of words). Children assume that a word for a thing belongs to the category Noun, a word describing an action belongs to the category Verb, an attribute of an object belongs to the category Adjective, and a word indicating spatial relations belongs to the category Preposition. Similarly, via semantic bootstrapping children can discern the grammatical functions of arguments in sentences. Given a sentence and a co-occurring event, they build a semantic representation of the sentence, which, among other things, encodes the thematic relations that the arguments bear to the verb. By inspecting the thematic roles of arguments in sentences, children infer their grammatical function. Children assume that a word referring to an agent of the action described by some sentence has the grammatical function subject, that a patient or a theme has the grammatical function object, and so on.

The syntactic categories Noun and Verb are used to project the various phrases according to the X-bar schema, shown in (34), where X is a variable over the set of lexical (and functional) categories (N(oun), V(erb), A(djective), P(reposition), I(nflection), etc.) and XP is a phrase with head X.

(34) XP $\rightarrow$ Spec X$'$
      X$'$ $\rightarrow$ X^0 YP

Phrases are then connected by noting the "semantic relations of words and exploiting the canonical association between logical/semantic relations and phrase structure configurations" (Pinker 1987, 409). For example, if X is a V, an NP having the thematic role patient will be an object and as such will be attached as sister of V^0, replacing the YP in (34) ($V' \rightarrow V^0$ NP). (The direction of attachment, to the right or the left of V^0, is subject to parametric variation and must be decided by looking at the input.) If X is an I (an inflectional item; e.g., the auxiliary in (35)), an NP having the thematic role agent (e.g., *John* in (35)) will be a subject and as such will be attached as sister to I', replacing *Spec* in (34) (IP $\rightarrow$ NP I').

(35) John has scratched the bear.

Once children have induced syntactic notions, they can learn the lexical category of words and the grammatical function of arguments that are not semantically transparent by performing a structure-dependent distributional analysis. To see how this works, let us examine the grammatical function "subject" (see Pinker 1984). "Subject" is just a symbol that is manipulated by different syntactic processes that tend to be correlated across languages. "Subject" is

(36) a. the agent of action verbs (e.g., *hit*),
   b. the argument that occupies the leftmost position in the sentence,
   c. the function that an object assumes in passive sentences,
   d. the constituent whose grammatical features are encoded by agreement affixes on verbs and so on.

Thus, children can establish on the basis of (36a) that a given argument is a subject. For example, they might hear a sentence like *John is hitting Bill*, paired with a situation in which an action is occurring that involves someone who is hitting and someone who is being hit. They thus establish that *John* is the agent. Since they know (36a) that agents of action verbs are subjects, they conclude that *John* is the subject of the sentence. Note that under this view the link between agent and subject is established by means of an asyntactic procedure, while under Fisher et al.'s (1994) view it is based on inspecting the argument structure, that is, whether the verb has a transitive frame or not.

   Once children have established the agent-subject link, because of the phenomena correlated with (36a), they then expect subjects to satisfy the properties in (36b), (36c), and (36d). For example, by noting that in (37) *this idea* occupies the leftmost position of the sentence and determines the choice of agreement affixes on the verb, as *John* does in *John is hitting Bill*, they may infer that it is a subject, although it is not an agent.

(37) This idea is scaring me.

The semantic bootstrapping hypothesis holds that children can profit from semantically transparent notions to deduce syntactic notions that form the vocabulary with which grammatical constraints are expressed. Armed with these notions, they can learn the lexical category and grammatical function of semantically nontransparent words. The semantic bootstrapping hypothesis presents some problems, however. For example, Bloom (1994a) points out that the kind of mapping it posits from semantically transparent notions to syntactic notions has no counterpart in the adult language; that is, this mapping is not part of the mature competence, but is specifically posited to solve the problem of acquisition. It would be desirable to appeal to mechanisms that are not specifically devised to solve the acquisition problem, but are used by the adult system as well.

3.5   SUMMARY AND CONCLUDING REMARKS

In this chapter we have examined the problem of how children acquire a lexicon. On the one hand, children have to find word forms in the continuous stream of speech, something they start to do from 6 months of age. On the other hand, they have to map sounds onto meaning, a skill they exhibit by about 10–12 months of age. For extracting word forms from the speech stream, infants rely on various sources of language-specific information: the prosodic shape of words, distributional regularities, phonetic information, and phonotactic constraints. By using these sources of information, infants show that they are good at keeping track of frequent patterns in the speech stream that are linguistically significant—that is, relevant for finding linguistic units. These highly sophisticated speech perception abilities are prerequisites for learning the native-language lexicon.

Acquiring the meaning of words is a complex task involving various factors, among them the child's conceptual system. In accomplishing this task, children probably rely on different kinds of information. Children innately know that words refer and that others use them with a referential purpose. They can use nonverbal cues to establish word meaning; for example, they can note where a speaker's attention is focused when the speaker utters a word. They can also fix the meaning of a limited stock of nouns by relying on the extralinguistic context, that is, by exploiting a word-to-world mapping procedure. The hypotheses they entertain about the meaning of a noun may be constrained by certain biases. However, for fixing the meaning of verbs toddlers must adopt a sentence-to-world mapping procedure; that is, they must have access to the syntactic context in which a verb is inserted. The fact that the word-to-world mapping procedure is not helpful in determining the meaning of verbs may explain why children initially learn more nouns than verbs; the meaning of (at least some) nouns can be learned even without mastering syntax, but the meaning of verbs cannot. However, notice that even for nouns the word-to-world mapping procedure is limited; it can help at the beginning, but it cannot account for the acquisition of all nouns. In more advanced stages children must rely on other sources of information. For example, the meaning of abstract nouns cannot be fixed by observing the external contingencies for their use.

As soon as children begin to combine words, their lexicon starts to grow exponentially (see Gillette et al. 1999, 139, and references cited there). It is possible that the emergence of syntax speeds up the acquisition of the lexicon: children start to use verbs, whose meaning is fixed by inspection of the syntactic context, and the acquisition of nouns is accelerated because syntax provides children with another procedure for determining their meaning.

The idea that children use syntactic information to glean the meaning of verbs raises the question of how they bootstrap into syntax. It seems unavoidable that some sort of phonological bootstrapping procedure is responsible for a rudimentary parsing of the input into linguistically relevant units (e.g., words, constituents, clauses). This phonological representation must be the input to further analysis: categorizing words, assigning a label to relevant constituents, and fixing their grammatical function. One hypothesis is that children start off with a basic scaffolding of nouns (learned through a word-to-world mapping procedure), on which they then build a partial sentential representation. Another hypothesis is that children induce syntactic notions from semantically transparent notions; for example, they conjecture that words for things or individuals belong to the category Noun and that words for actions belong to the category Verb. As Gleitman (1990) suggests, it may be that these two hypotheses about how children break into syntax (bootstrapping from a partial sentential representation and semantic bootstrapping) are both implicated in acquisition and that they act in a complementary manner; that is, they may be used for different goals.

Summary of Linguistic Development

1. At birth infants can perceive acoustic cues marking prosodic boundaries.
2. Between 6 and 8 months infants
   a. are sensitive to the prosodic coherence of clauses,
   b. prefer lists of bisyllabic words from their native language, this preference being based on prosodic properties of words.
3. At 8 months infants
   a. can compute distributional regularities,
   b. can recognize words in continuous speech after having been familiarized with these words.
4. At 9 months infants
   a. can use phonotactic and phonetic constraints to discriminate between lists of words from their native language and from a foreign language,
   b. are sensitive to the prosodic coherence of major phrases.
5. At 9 months infants learning English prefer to listen to bisyllabic words respecting the trochaic pattern.
6. Between 10 and 12 months children start to pair words with meanings.
7. At 20–24 months children
   a. experience a vocabulary spurt,
   b. begin to produce multiword utterances,
   c. use syntactic information to infer word meaning.

Further Reading

For papers on various aspects of the acquisition of the lexicon, see Gleitman and Landau 1994. Gordon 1985 deals with how children handle lexical rules of word formation. Pinker 1989 discusses the acquisition of argument structure—in particular, how children decide which verbs enter into certain alternations (e.g., *I gave a book to John*, *I gave John a book*) and which do not (*I donated a book to John*, **I donated John a book*). Waxman 1998 discusses how words help children in forming categories (animals, food, etc.). Waxman, Senghas, and Benveniste 1997 explores, from a crosslinguistic perspective, the role of structural contexts in deciding word categorization. Bloom 1999 discusses associationist theories of word learning and points out alternatives. For a proposal that intentional considerations play a role in the acquisition of meaning, see Bloom 1997.

Several works discuss production of words, a topic we have not addressed in this chapter. Boysson-Bardies and Vihman 1991 takes up the relation between babbling and first word production. Locke 1983, Gerken 1994b,c, 1996b, and Demuth 1996 discuss the properties of the first words that children produce. Smolensky 1996 offers a proposal to deal with the mismatch between production and perception of words: although children simplify words they utter by deleting or substituting certain segments, they do perceive these segments.

The phonological bootstrapping hypothesis is discussed in two collections of papers, Morgan and Demuth 1996a and Höhle and Weissenborn 2001. The relation between the development of children's highly sophisticated speech perception abilities and the onset of word learning is taken up in Stager and Werker 1997 and Werker and Tees 1999.

Key Words

Biases on word meaning
Distributional regularities
Hypothesis formation and testing procedure
Mutual exclusivity bias
Partial sentential representation
Partial structural representation
Phonological bootstrapping of lexical acquisition
Phonological bootstrapping of syntax
Phonotactic constraints
Preferential looking paradigm
Problem of induction
Semantic bootstrapping
Sentence-to-world mapping procedure
Syntactic cueing of verb meaning
Taxonomic bias
Transitional probability
Two-step model of lexical acquisition
Typical word shapes
Whole object bias
Word-to-world mapping procedure

Study Questions

1. What factors conspire to make the acquisition of words difficult?

2. What developmental changes are related to the acquisition of words? (See also chapter 2.)

3. How are early nouns and verbs acquired? What is their role in the early acquisition of the lexicon? What differences have been noted between the early acquisition of nouns and the early acquisition of verbs?

4. How can syntactic context help in fixing the meaning of words?

5. Is information from a single syntactic frame sufficient for children to learn the meaning of verbs? Explain your answer.

6. How do we know that infants have access to prosodic and to segmental information at different points in development?

7. Try to design an experiment that would establish whether children use syntactic/morphological information to fix the category of words, for example, nouns versus adjectives, nouns versus verbs (see, e.g., Waxman, Senghas, and Benveniste 1997).

Chapter 4

The Emergence of Syntax

INTRODUCTION

At around 2 years children start to combine words. Although the first multiword utterances have a telegraphic character, they are not a mere simplification of the adult language. Under closer scrutiny they reveal quite sophisticated knowledge; and although deviating from the adult language, they show features of a grammatical, rule-governed system.

As noted earlier, children are surprisingly quick to capture the properties of the language they are exposed to. Languages differ syntactically—for example, in the order of constituents and in the morphosyntactic properties of verbs. These variations are expressed as parameters, to which children must assign a value based on their linguistic experience. The data gathered since the 1990s clearly show that some of these parameters have been set to the correct value by the time children produce their first word combinations.

Section 4.1 briefly discusses the order of constituents in early clauses and deals with the parameter governing the order of constituents across languages. Section 4.2 considers aspects of children's clausal architecture, first introducing assumptions concerning adult clause structure and then presenting two hypotheses about the structure of early clauses, the small clause hypothesis and the full competence hypothesis. Section 4.3 takes up the subject-agreement relation, presenting evidence for regarding it as a structure-dependent relation even in early systems. Section 4.4 discusses a salient deviation of early languages from the adult target: the phenomenon of root infinitives or optional infinitives in early systems, that is, children's use of infinitive verbs in main clauses.

4.1 WORD ORDER IN CHILDREN'S PRODUCTIONS

Languages vary with respect to the order of their heads and complements.[1] English heads have their complements to the right; that is,

English is head initial. Turkish heads have their complements to the left; that is, Turkish is head final. This parametric variation is governed by the **head direction parameter** or word order parameter.

(1) *Head direction parameter*
    Is the language head final or head initial? (Values to be chosen: head initial, head final)

To build a phrase structure conforming to the X-bar schema given in (2), the learner has to know whether a complement attaches to the left or to the right of the head.

(2) $XP \rightarrow Spec\ X'$
    $X' \rightarrow (YP)\ X^0\ (YP)$

In other words, the learner has to figure out through exposure to the ambient language which of the two possibilities in (1) is instantiated in that language.

Children's early multiword utterances hardly deviate from their target language with respect to the order of heads and complements (see Bloom 1970; Brown 1973): complements follow the head in head-initial languages (English, French, Italian) and precede it in head-final languages (Japanese, Turkish). Moreover, even before children start combining words, they can detect and use the order of words in comprehending multiword utterances. Hirsh-Pasek and Golinkoff (1996) tested 17-month-old single-word speakers with the preferential looking paradigm (see section 3.3.3) to see if they rely on word order to comprehend active reversible sentences of the type in (3). In reversible sentences the two NPs can change places without yielding a semantically implausible sentence. Thus, to understand them one must pay attention to the order of the NPs.

(3) Big Bird is washing Cookie Monster.

Children were seated in front of two television screens, each featuring the same two characters involved in an action—in this case Big Bird and Cookie Monster involved in a washing action. While one screen showed Big Bird washing Cookie Monster, the other showed Cookie Monster washing Big Bird. Simultaneously a loudspeaker uttered the sentence in (3). It was found that children prefer to watch the matching screen (in this case the one depicting Big Bird washing Cookie Monster) rather than the nonmatching one. Since the sentences they heard were reversible, knowledge of how things may stand in the world cannot have helped children in deciding which picture to look at in response to each stimulus sentence. It must be concluded that they relied on word order.

These findings indicate that from the onset of multiword utterances (or even earlier) children are sensitive to word order phenomena, and in particular that they have already correctly fixed the value of the parameter in (1); that is, they have discovered by listening to the language around them whether it is head initial or head final. Along with the results discussed in previous chapters, this finding suggests that the language capacity is tuned to discover the regularities of the ambient language at a startling pace. In the following sections we will see that children are highly sensitive to morphosyntactic properties related to the order of constituents within clauses.

4.2 THE STRUCTURE OF EARLY CLAUSES

In this section we will look at the structure of clauses in the speech of 2- to 3-year-old children. To set the stage, let us consider how adult clauses are structured. (For more details, see Haegeman 1994, chaps. 2 and 12; Webelhuth 1995; Radford 1997, chap. 2.)

4.2.1 The Adult Clause Structure

Under current approaches the structure of an English declarative sentence like (4a) is (4b). The same structure is valid for French and Italian (non-verb-second languages). For concreteness it will be assumed that nouns project up to DP (although the term *NP* will often be used).

(4) a. John has eaten an apple.

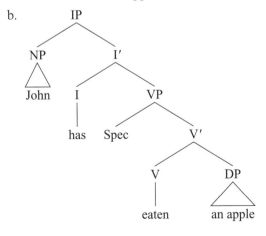

The structure of the clause in (4b) minimally includes the lexical projection VP that reflects the argument structure of the verb and one or more functional projections, which encode the features [±agreement] and [±tense] specified on the verb. Although in most popular approaches each feature heads a distinct projection—AgrP, TP, AspP (see, e.g., Pollock 1989; Cinque 1998)—for simplicity we will assume that there is just one functional projection above VP—namely, IP—unless a more articulated structure is required to explain relevant acquisition data.

Verbs are all generated in VP and move overtly or covertly to inflectional projections. By looking at word order phenomena (position of verbs with respect to other clausal constituents such as negation), one can establish whether or not the verb has moved overtly. In general, finite and nonfinite verbs behave differently within a language. Let us start with finite verbs. *Overt* movement takes place in languages such as French, Italian, Dutch, and German. *Covert* movement takes place in English, but only for lexical verbs—verbs from the class that includes auxiliaries, modals, the copula *be*, and the dummy auxiliary *do* all either move to I overtly or are directly generated there. A separate class of auxiliaries that exhibit special movement properties does not exist in other languages (e.g., French, Italian, Dutch, German), where all finite verbs behave alike with respect to verb movement: namely, they move overtly to I (or to C). Nonfinite verbs generally remain in V or move to a projection just above VP, say, AspP. Italian infinitives are an exception, because they raise as far as I, like finite verbs. Thus, by and large, across languages finite and nonfinite verbs are distinguished in terms of their movement properties.

In verb-second (V2) languages (Dutch, German, Norwegian, Swedish) the finite verb of root clauses occupies the second position in the clause and a phrasal constituent (a subject or any other clausal element) occupies the first position. In the German sentence (5a) the first position is filled with the object, in (5b) with the subject.

(5) a. Ein Buch kaufte Johann.
       a   book bought Johann
    b. Johann kaufte ein Buch.
       Johann bought a   book

Root or matrix clauses in V2 languages are CPs: the verb moves from V to I to C, and a phrasal constituent (the subject, the object, or an adverb) moves to Spec CP (see Haegeman 1994, chap. 11, for an introduction).

Tree (6a) illustrates the structure of sentence (5a), and tree (6b) the structure of sentence (5b).

(6) a.

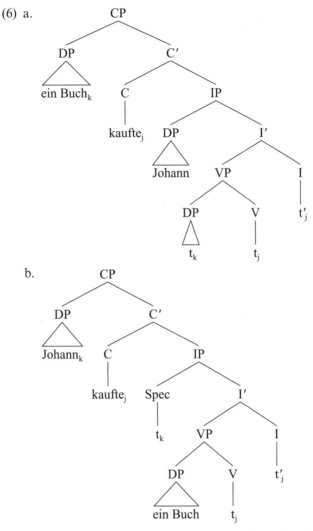

b.

Table 4.1 summarizes the verb movement (or verb-raising) privileges in different languages.

4.2.2   The Small Clause Hypothesis

It has long been noted that from their first word combination up to about 3 years English-speaking children often produce sentences like (7a–d),

Table 4.1
Verb movement possibilities in various languages

Movement type	Verb type	Language(s)
Move to C	Finite verbs	V2 languages (Dutch, German, etc.)
Move to I	Finite verbs	French
	Finite and infinitive verbs	Italian
(or are generated there)	Auxiliaries, modals, *do*, *be*	English
Do not move to I	Infinitives	French, V2 languages
	Lexical finite and nonfinite verbs	English

in which either the third person singular inflection *-s* or the past tense marker *-ed* is missing and the verb surfaces as a bare or uninflected form.[2]

(7) a. Papa have it.   (Eve, 1;6)
  b. Cromer wear glasses.   (Eve, 2;0)
  c. Marie go.   (Sarah, 2;3)
  d. Mumma ride horsie.   (Sarah, 2;6)

Other typical sentences are shown in (8), where an auxiliary (either the perfective *have* or the progressive *be*) is lacking (indicated in square brackets) and only the participle form of the verb is expressed.

(8) a. Eve gone [has].   (Eve, 1;6)
  b. Eve cracking nut [is].   (Eve, 1;7)
  c. Mike gone [has].   (Sarah, 2;3)
  d. Kitty hiding [is].   (Sarah, 2;10)

In children's earliest multiword utterances, modals and the copula *be* are also frequently absent, as (9a,b) illustrate.

(9) a. That my briefcase [is].   (Eve, 1;9)
  b. You nice [are].   (Sarah, 2;7)

Similarly, the dummy auxiliary *do* is missing from negative sentences (10a,b) and questions (10c) (for a discussion of *wh*-questions, see chapter 6).

(10) a. Fraser not see him.   (Eve, 2;0)
  b. He no bite ya.   (Sarah, 3;0)
  c. Where ball go?   (Adam, 2;3)

In summary, all functional elements, listed in (11), are usually absent in children's early clauses, with the result that children's speech strongly resembles telegraphic speech (see Bloom 1970; Brown 1973).

(11) Grammatical morphemes (e.g., third person singular -*s*, past tense -*ed*)
Auxiliaries (perfective *have*, progressive *be*)
do
Copula *be*

The functional elements listed in (11) share a common property: all express the feature content of the I node. Because children rarely use these elements, Radford (1990) has proposed that early clauses lack the corresponding inflectional category IP. Their representation includes only the lexical category VP. The structure of an early declarative clause like (7d) is shown in (12).

(12)

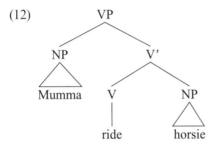

The VP hosts the verb and all its arguments: the complement as a sister of V and the subject as a sister of V′. Hence, an early clause is a projection of the lexical properties of the verb and thus encodes the thematic relationships between the verb and its arguments. In (12) the V (*ride*) assigns the thematic role theme to its complement and the V′ assigns the role agent to its subject (see Haegeman 1994, chap. 1, for discussion of the relevant notions).

The hypothesis that children's clauses are VPs is also called the **small clause hypothesis**, a label that emphasizes the similarity between early clauses and some adult structures that have also been viewed as lexical projections of the predicate (see Stowell 1983; see also Cardinaletti and Guasti 1995 for a critical discussion of the notion of small clause in relation to acquisition). An example of an adult small clause is the verbal complement following a verb of perception (see (13a)). This complement cannot include functional elements (see (13b,c)), and its verb cannot be inflected for tense or agreement. Therefore, such clauses have often been analyzed as bare VPs.

(13) a. I saw Mary eat an apple.
     b. *I see Mary have eaten an apple.
     c. *I saw Mary could eat an apple.

Thus, according to the small clause hypothesis, the early grammar is a lexical-thematic system, in which lexical items project according to the X-bar structure and in agreement with the Projection Principle (which states that lexical information is syntactically represented). Although functional categories are part of Universal Grammar (UG), their availability is subject to maturation; that is, they are programmed to emerge and become operative around age 3 (see Radford 1990; see also section 4.4.4 for a discussion of maturation).

Evidence for the small clause hypothesis comes principally from English. Crosslinguistic investigations have not supported the view that the initial grammar includes no functional categories. Most researchers instead agree that functional categories are present even in the earliest multiword utterances, though they may not agree how much functional structure should be granted to children's clauses at a given period of development. In the next section we evaluate evidence against the small clause hypothesis coming from early languages other than English.

4.2.3   Functional Categories in Children's Grammar

The small clause hypothesis has had the merit of bringing children's telegraphic speech into the purview of recent linguistic and psycholinguistic theories, but its claims have proven to be too strong. As already illustrated for English, there is no doubt that some of children's earliest multiword utterances are impoverished in comparison with the adult target. Learners of other languages (e.g., Danish, Dutch, French, German, Swedish) also deviate from the adult target by producing main clauses with infinitive verbs instead of finite ones (Here and throughout in examples of child speech, square brackets indicate material missing from children's utterances.)

(14) a. Hun sove.   (Jens, 2;0)
         she   sleep-INF
     b. Earst kleine boekje lezen.   (Hein, 2;6)
         first little   book   read-INF
         'First (I/we) read little book.'

   c. Dormir petit bébé.   (Daniel, 1;11)
      sleep-INF little baby
      'Little baby sleep.'
   d. S[ch]okolade holen.   (Andreas, 2;1)
      chocolate   get

However, these deviations do not entitle us to conclude that children's grammar does not include functional categories. Crosslinguistic studies have shown that learners of Danish, Dutch, French, German, and Swedish also produce a fair number of finite clauses, examples of which are given in (15).

(15) a. Kann ikke see.   (Anne, 2;0)
        can   not see
        '(I) cannot see.'
     b. Hij doet 't niet.   (Hein, 2;4)
        he makes it not
        'He does not make it.'
     c. Dort bébé.   (Daniel, 1;11)
        sleeps baby
        'Baby sleeps.'
     d. Da is[t] er.   (Andreas, 2;1)
        here is   he
        'He is here.'

A defender of the small clause hypothesis might still argue that for children finite verbs are unanalyzed chunks. If this claim were sound, finite clauses could be represented as bare-VP small clauses in which the finite verb stays in V, as nonfinite verbs do. This conjecture allows us to formulate a clear and falsifiable prediction. We know that in adult languages the position of finite and infinitive verbs differs as summarized in table 4.1. If finite and nonfinite verbs do not differ formally in children's grammar, as the small clause hypothesis holds, then they should display the same distribution and the same structural positions. This prediction has been tested by extending to children's language the same procedure used to study adult language: examination of word order phenomena.

4.2.3.1   The Distribution of Verbs with Respect to the Negation   Although initially children use finite and infinitive verbs to form their matrix clauses, they treat them differently. Consider the relative positions of verb and negation illustrated in (16). In Danish, Dutch, German, and French the finite verb precedes the negation (16a,b), while the infinitive follows it (16c,d). Examples (16a,c) are from German, a V2 language; examples (16b,d) are from French, a non-V2 language.[3]

(16) a. Johann isst nicht. (V_{fin} Neg)
       Johann eats not
       'Johann does not eat.'
   b. Marie ne *mange pas*. (V_{fin} Neg)
       Marie NEG eats   not
       'Marie does not eat.'
   c. um   *nicht zu essen* (Neg V_{inf})
       in order to not   to eat-INF
   d. pour   ne *pas manger* (Neg V_{inf})
       in order to NEG not eat-INF

Interestingly, in children's speech the placement of a verb with respect to the negation depends on whether it is finite or nonfinite (see Weissenborn 1990; Pierce 1992b; Déprez and Pierce 1993): children place a finite verb before the negation and a nonfinite one after the negation. This finding is very robust in French (see the contingency table 4.2) and has been replicated for German and Dutch (De Haan and Tuijnman 1988; Weissenborn 1990; Verrips and Weissenborn 1992; Poeppel and Wexler 1993). The following are samples from early French and German (German data cited in Weissenborn 1990).

(17) a. Pas manger la poupée. (Nathalie, 1;9)
       not eat-INF the doll
       'The doll does not eat.'
   b. Elle roule pas. (Grégoire, 1;11)
       it   rolls not
       'It does not roll.'

Table 4.2
Finiteness versus verb placement with respect to the negation in the speech of three French learners. Data from Philippe, Nathalie, and Daniel (age range 1;8–2;3).

	+Finite	−Finite
Verb-Neg	173	2
Neg-Verb	9	122

Source: Based on Pierce 1992b
$\chi^2 = 263.02$, $p < .001$

c. Kann ma[n] nich[t] essen.   (Simone, 2;1)
   can   one   not   eat-INF
   'One cannot eat (this).'

d. Das macht der Maxe nicht.   (Simone, 2;1)
   this makes the Maxe not
   'This, Maxe does not make.'

Clearly, children tacitly know the distribution of verbs with respect to the negation and distinguish finite from infinitive verbs.

4.2.3.2 Verb Placement in Early V2 Languages In adult Dutch and German matrix clauses, finite verbs appear in second position in the clause, whereas infinitives appear clause-finally. This is illustrated by the German examples in (18).

(18) a. Simone *braucht* das.
     Simone needs   that
   b. Simone wird das *lesen.*
     Simone will that read-INF
     'Simone will read that.'

Do learners of V2 languages respect this distributional pattern? To answer this question, researchers have looked at utterances including at least three words. (Two-word utterances cannot be used, of course, because the second position is also the final position.) They have found that children reserve second position for finite verbs and final position for infinitives. Recall, for example, the early Dutch and German utterances (15b,d), repeated here.

(15) b. Hij doet   't niet.   (Hein, 2;4)
     he makes it not
     'He does not make it.'
   d. Da is[t] er.   (Andreas, 2;1)
     here is   he
     'He is here.'

Quantitative evidence comes from the contingency analysis conducted by Poeppel and Wexler (1993) on the utterances of a German child, shown in table 4.3 (see Clahsen, Penke, and Parodi 1993/1994; also De Haan and Tuijnman 1988 and Jordens 1990 for early Dutch and Wexler 1994 for other early V2 languages).

Table 4.3
Finiteness versus verb placement in the speech of a German learner. Data from
Andreas (age 2;1).

	+Finite	−Finite
V2	197	6
Verb-final	11	37

Source: Based on Poeppel and Wexler 1993
$\chi^2 = 150.25,\ p < .001$

4.2.3.3 The First Clausal Constituent in V2 Clauses   There is an interesting asymmetry in the speech of learners exposed to a V2 language. Clause-initial position can be occupied by a subject regardless of whether the clause is finite or infinitive.

(19) a. Hij doet   't niet.   (Hein, 2;4)
         he makes it not
         'He does not make it.'
     b. Hij op kussens slapen.   (Hein, 2;6)
         he on cushions sleep-INF
         'He sleep on cushions.'

By contrast, only in finite clauses can a nonsubject constituent (an object or an adverb) occur clause-initially; that is, finite clauses may also exhibit the order XP V S, as seen in (20) from German and Swedish (Swedish example cited from Santelmann 1998).

(20) a. Eine Fase hab ich.   (Andreas, 2;1)
         a   vase have I
         'I have a vase.'
     b. Daer bodde de.   (Anders, 2;1)
         there lived they
         'There, they lived.'

For early German, the contingency between the finiteness or nonfiniteness of the verb and the nature of the first clausal constituent is evident in table 4.4. For early Swedish, Santelmann (1998) shows that the order XP V S is found from the earliest transcripts (child age 1;11) and is limited to finite clauses.

Table 4.4
Finiteness versus type of clause-initial constituent in the speech of a German learner. Data from Andreas (age 2;1).

	+Finite	−Finite
SV(O)	130	24
XPV(O)	50	0

Source: Based on Poeppel and Wexler 1993, tables 7 and 8
$\chi^2 = 8.83$, $p < .005$

4.2.4   The Full Competence Hypothesis

Finite and infinitive verbs are distributed differently in children's clauses with respect to other clausal constituents. This discrepancy is unexpected under the small clause hypothesis, which holds that all verbs should behave alike—that is, stay in the VP and thus follow the negation, occur in clause-final position. If the small clause hypothesis is not correct, as the data discussed so far appear to suggest, what *is* the structure of early clauses? To address this question, let us evaluate the data presented so far in the light of the current theory of adult clausal structure summarized in section 4.2.1. We will see that children's finite clauses are adultlike, a conclusion supporting the hypothesis that children have **full competence** (see Poeppel and Wexler 1993). (Infinitive clauses will be discussed in section 4.4.)

4.2.4.1   Finite Clauses in Early Non-V2 Languages   Let us start by evaluating the syntactic implications of the data examined so far. Concentrating first on non-V2 languages (e.g., French), we will see that the functional category IP is present in early grammar. As a first step, we need to look at some assumptions about the structure of negative sentences in the adult language (for an introduction, see Haegeman 1994, chap. 11).

Negative sentences contain a NegP located between IP and VP. Its specifier hosts the negation, *pas* in French. The structure of the French finite negative sentence (16b), repeated here, is given in (21).

(16) b. Marie ne   mange pas.
　　　　Marie NEG eats   not
　　　　'Marie does not eat.'

(21)

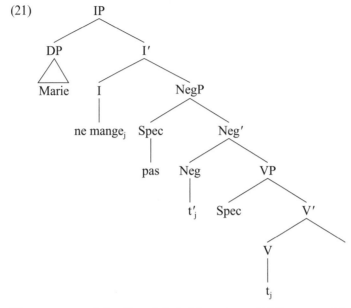

The structure of the French infinitive phrase (16d), repeated here, is given
in (22).

(16) d. (pour)   ne   pas manger
            in order to NEG not eat-INF

(22)

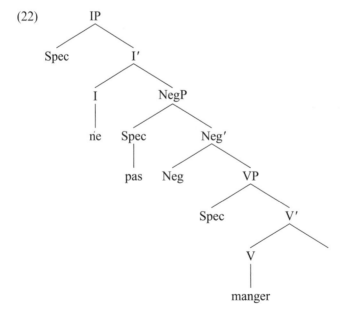

The structural interpretations of the relative order of the verb and the negation in (21) and (22) show that finite verbs raise from V to I, past the negation *pas*, while infinitives remain below the negation in the VP.[4] The order V Neg indicates that the verb has moved and the order Neg V that it has not.

In section 4.2.3.1 we saw that children's finite verbs are positioned to the left of the negation (V_{fin} Neg), while their infinitives are positioned to the right (Neg V_{inf}). Since lexical verbs are all generated in VP, their different distribution with respect to the negation tells us that in children's grammar, as in adults' grammar, finite verbs raise to a functional projection, past (and thus preceding) the negation, while infinitives remain in VP (thus following the negation).[5] Two conclusions follow. First, besides the lexical projection VP, the early grammar must contain the functional projection IP, to accommodate raising of finite verbs; consequently, early clauses are at least IPs. Second, children, like adults, express the morphosyntactic distinction between finite and infinitive verbs in terms of verb raising. These conclusions are schematized as follows:

(23) a. The grammar of early non-V2 languages includes functional categories.

    b. Children learning non-V2 languages distinguish finite and infinitive verbs in terms of verb raising.

    c. Finite clauses are at least IPs in early non-V2 languages.

4.2.4.2 Finite Clauses in Early V2 Languages The conclusions reached for early non-V2 languages are valid for early V2 languages as well. Under the assumption that negative sentences contain a NegP, located between VP and IP, the fact that (for finite sentences) children use the order V_{fin} Neg shows that they move the finite verb out of the VP into a position higher than the negation. Since (for infinitive sentences) children use the reverse order, Neg V_{inf}, they must know that infinitives remain in VP. This conclusion is further confirmed by the occurrence of finite verbs in second position in the clause and of infinitives in clause-final position. Since Dutch and German are SOV languages, the presence of the infinitive in clausal-final position is an indication that children have not moved it (see Donati and Tomaselli 1997 for a defense of this view and Zwart 1997 for an alternative position). In turn, the fact that in children's speech the finite verb occurs in second position in the clause means that it has moved out of VP to a functional projection. These data lead to the following conclusions:

(24) a. The grammar of early V2 languages includes functional
projections.
   b. Children learning V2 languages distinguish finite and infinitive
verbs in terms of verb raising.

Can we also conclude that in early V2 languages finite verbs move to C
and that finite clauses are CPs, as adult clauses are? It is often assumed
that in German I is head final and consequently takes its VP complements
to the left, as shown in (6). Given this assumption, if finite verbs in early
German moved only to I, finite clauses should display the order SOV$_{fin}$;
that is, children should produce sentences like (25), with the representation given in (26).

(25) *Johann ein Buch kaufte.
      Johann a   book bought

(26)

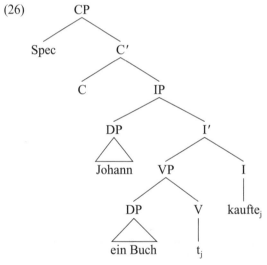

However, this order is rarely attested in early finite clauses; instead, children place the verb in second position. Thus, if we adopt the hypothesis
that I is head final, then we can accommodate the finding that finite verbs
occur in second position in early German and Dutch by assuming that
these verbs have moved from I to a higher functional projection, C.

The head-final status of I has been challenged (see Zwart 1997). If I
were head initial (i.e., took its VP complement to its right), then a verb in
second position could very well be in I rather than in C. In other words,
the order SVO could be accommodated by saying that the verb raises to I,

the subject occupies Spec IP, and the object resides in VP. Under this view the structure of (5b) would not be (6b), but (27) (the structure in (27) assumes that V is head initial in Germanic languages, as in Kayne 1994).

(27)

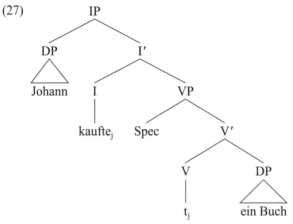

It is thus desirable to have further evidence for rejecting the hypothesis that finite verbs raise only as high as I rather than moving to C. One piece of unambiguous evidence that can be accommodated only by a CP structure is the order of clausal constituents. While the order SVO is common to both V2 and non-V2 languages, clauses with a nonsubject constituent in first position are unique to V2 languages. From the internal organization of sentences in early V2 languages discussed in section 4.2.3.3, we know that in root finite sentences the clause-initial constituent can be the subject or any other clausal constituent; that is, in addition to the order SVO, children produce root finite sentences with the order XP V S ... (where XP can be a complement or an adverb), as shown in (20) for German and Swedish. This finding, which has been confirmed for early Dutch, German, and Swedish, allows us to definitely reject the view that finite verbs raise only to I. We can account for the order XP V S ... only by assuming that the subject is in Spec IP; the verb that precedes the subject must then be in C and the XP in Spec CP. The structure of (20a) is therefore (28).

(28)

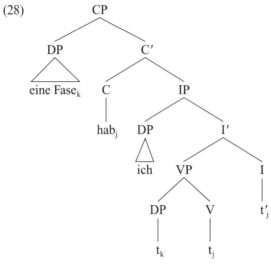

We can then infer that in addition to VP and IP, children's clauses in V2 languages include CP.[6] This is necessary to accommodate movement of a nonsubject (and also of a subject) constituent to its specifier and movement of the finite verb to its head. We reach the following conclusion:

(29) Early V2 clauses are CPs.

Notice that the order XP V S proves that the early clausal representation includes the CP, regardless of whether we assume that I is head final or head initial. Under both assumptions the subject must be in Spec IP and the verb that precedes it must be in a higher position, precisely CP.

4.2.4.3   Finite Clauses in Early English   Do English learners also know that lexical verbs in their language do not move overtly? There is evidence that they do. Harris and Wexler (1996) have shown that English learners almost never raise a lexical verb past the negation. That is, they do not produce sentences like (30a); instead, they move auxiliaries past the negation and produce sentences like (30b,c).

(30) a. *John eats not.
      b. I can't see you.   (Eve, 1;10)
      c. I don't want soup.   (Eve, 1;11)

These findings suggest that

(31) English learners distinguish between lexical verbs and auxiliaries
     and know that lexical verbs do not move overtly to I, while
     auxiliaries do (or are base-generated there).

(See Stromswold 1990 for more arguments in favor of this conclusion.)

The evidence from this and previous sections weakens the small
clause hypothesis. However, Radford (1996) points out that it is still possible that just as they begin to produce multiword utterances, children
go through a small clause stage, in which they do not employ functional
projections. This stage, he claims, may not be evident in all children and
may be very short. For example, he notes that in one transcript Nathalie,
a French learner (age 1;9), uses only infinitive verbs and thus does not
display knowledge of inflection. These infinitive clauses are likely to be
analyzed as small clauses. Thus, for a short period Nathalie may be going
through a small clause stage. Radford also reports data from Spanish-
and Welsh-speaking children indicating that they may be going through
this stage as well.

4.2.5 Intermediate Summary

The fact that 2- to 3-year-old children do not consistently use inflectional
morphology, especially in English, has motivated the formulation of
the small clause hypothesis. This asserts that early clauses encode only
lexical-thematic information and that functional categories are subject to
maturation. The dearth of morphological manifestations of functional
categories is a partial index of children's competence. Distributional facts
are relevant clues. Although children use nonfinite and finite verbs in
main clauses, they do not treat the two verb forms alike. The distribution
of these verbs with respect to other clausal constituents indicates that
children formally distinguish them in terms of verb movement: finite verbs
move to I or C (in V2 languages), while infinitives do not. Whether or not
a verb raises to I (or to C) in the overt syntax is subject to parametric
variation, the relevant parameters being the **verb movement parameter**
(32a) and the **V2 parameter** (32b) (see table 4.1). In French and Italian
verbs move overtly to I, in V2 languages they move to C, and in English
they remain in VP (except for auxiliaries, modals, *be*, and *do*, which either
move to or are generated in I).

(32) a. *Verb movement parameter*
        Do finite verbs raise overtly to I?
     b. *V2 parameter*
        Do finite verbs raise overtly to C?

The data examined here suggest that Dutch, English, French, German, and Swedish learners have fixed the correct value of the parameters in (32) from about the age of 2 years. Children obey the structural restrictions that govern the distribution of verbs in the adult grammar.

Since finite verbs move to I in early grammars, we must postulate that functional categories are present in these grammars. Consequently, we must conclude that children's representations of finite clauses encode not only lexical but also functional information; that is, the structure of early clauses must be as shown in (4) or in (6). Radford (1996) has pointed out that children may indeed go through a small clause stage, which may however be very short and not always detectable. The fact that there is overwhelming evidence for early use of functional categories and that not all children display evidence for a small clause stage may indicate that learners are very quick at detecting the regularities of their language. Be that as it may, either children start directly by producing clauses with functional projections or they do produce small clauses but only for a short time.

4.3   THE SUBJECT AGREEMENT RELATION

We have established that children know the morphosyntactic properties of verbs. Finite verbs are usually associated with agreement and tense features. Are these features present in the initial grammar? In other words, is I specified for these features? Focusing here solely on agreement, does children's speech offer evidence for the presence of agreement features?

4.3.1   The Morphological Expression of Agreement

We start exploring the acquisition of verbal agreement by asking if children use verbal agreement morphemes appropriately and consistently. Answering this question is hard if one looks at languages with considerable syncretism (e.g., French, where the first, second, and third singular and third plural endings are homophonous in the present tense). By contrast, it becomes fairly easy if one looks at languages with a rich inflectional paradigm (e.g., Italian, Catalan, and Spanish). Investigations on the acquisition of verbal agreement in these languages have uncovered the following generalizations:

(33) a. Italian, Spanish-, and Catalan-speaking children use singular
        agreement morphemes with the appropriate subject.

b. Contexts for the use of plural agreement morphemes are initially absent and thus plural agreement morphemes appear some months after singular ones.

c. Errors are rare and mostly found with plural subjects.

From their initial multiword productions, around 1;8–1;10, Italian-, Catalan-, and Spanish-speaking children do use first, second, and third person singular morphemes (see Hyams 1986; Pizzuto and Caselli 1992; and Guasti 1993/1994 for early Italian; Torrens 1995 for early Catalan and Spanish). According to Pizzuto and Caselli (1992), this use amounts to 90% correct in obligatory contexts at around age 2 in early Italian. Since contexts for the use of plural inflections are initially lacking, plural person markers appear later (by some months) than singular ones (a phenomenon that is not limited to plural verbal inflection, but seems to reflect a more general delay in the use of plurality). Agreement errors are rare, about 3–4% in early Italian (Guasti 1993/1994; Pizzuto and Caselli 1992), 1.72% in early Catalan and Spanish (Torrens 1995). These rare errors mostly consist of using a singular third person morpheme with a plural subject or a third person morpheme with a first person subject. These findings have been replicated for early German: Poeppel and Wexler (1993) found that their child subject, Andreas (2;1), used the first and third singular agreement morphemes accurately; the three plural morphemes and the second singular morpheme were rare or absent in his speech; and errors were rare.[7]

To the quantitative evidence, we can add a qualitative analysis of verbs in children's speech. Italian-speaking children use different verbs with the same agreement morpheme. For example, they use the third person, second conjugation marker -*e* with different roots (*cad-e* 'fall-3sg', *pang-e* 'cry-3sg'; Martina, 1;8); they also use the three singular agreement markers with the same verbal root (*mett-o, mett-i, mett-e* 'put-1sg/2sg/3sg'; Diana, 1;11). These data suggest that children analyze a verb into a root and an inflectional affix and have started to build a verbal paradigm; in other words, they do not learn verb forms by rote, but apply a productive rule in comprehending and producing them (see Guasti 1993/1994; see Pinker 1994b regarding a model for the learning of morphological paradigms; and see section 1.5.3).

The fact that the full verbal agreement paradigm is not fully instantiated in children's speech is hardly evidence that children do not know agreement: lack of use does not imply lack of knowledge. The only evidence that would entitle one to conclude that children's grammar lacks agreement would be a substantial number of agreement errors or nonadherence to the structural restrictions imposed by the presence of agreement; but the available evidence shows that children are accurate when they do use agreement morphemes. We can then conclude that the agreement feature is included in children's grammar from the earliest multiword productions.

4.3.2 Subject Types

Although we cannot hear overt agreement morphemes in certain early languages, as in their adult target, we may infer their presence from their structural reflexes.

Learners of French use subject clitic pronouns, such as *je* 'I', *elle* 'she', and *il* 'he', only with finite verbs. Pierce (1992b) reports that in early French 96% (605/632) of all subject clitics occur with finite verbs (see also Verrips and Weissenborn 1992). For example:

(34) a. Il est pas là.   (Nathalie, 2;2)
        he is not there
    b. Elle tombe.   (Philippe, 2;2)
        she falls

By contrast, French learners use nonclitic pronouns, such as *moi* 'me', with both finite and infinitive verbs, according to Pierce. For example:

(35) a. Bois   peu moi.   (Daniel, 1;8)
        drink-1SG little me
        'Me drink little.'
    b. Moi fais   tout seul moi.   (Grégoire, 2;1)
        me make-1SG all   alone me
        'Me make all by myself.'
    c. Aller   dedans moi.   (Grégoire, 2;3)
        go-INF inside me
        'Me go inside.'
    d. Moi dessiner la mer.   (Daniel, 1;10)
        me draw-INF the sea
        'Me draw the sea.'

Haegeman (1995a) reports an analogous discrepancy among types of subjects in early Dutch. Investigating the speech of a Dutch-speaking child from age 2;4 to age 3;1, she found that phonologically reduced subject pronouns such as *'k* 'I' and *ze* 'she' (cliticlike pronouns, called weak pronouns) occurred only in finite clauses, while strong subject pronouns such as *ik* 'I' and *zij* 'she' occurred both in early finite and in early infinitive clauses (for discussion of these pronouns, see Cardinaletti and Starke 1999). Haegeman found 472 weak subject pronouns with finite verbs, but not a single weak subject pronoun with an infinitive. Thus, clitic subjects in early French and weak subject pronouns in early Dutch are restricted to finite clauses.

It is generally assumed that subject clitics and weak pronouns are licensed by the agreement feature. From this assumption and the selective distribution of pronouns observed in early French and Dutch, we can infer that the agreement feature is positively specified in finite clauses, but not in infinitive clauses. In other words, subject clitics and weak pronouns occur in early finite clauses because only in these clauses is the agreement feature positively specified (as it is in the adult grammar).

In section 4.2.4 we posited that children's finite clauses include a functional projection, IP, to accommodate verb raising. The data we have just discussed lead us to assume that I includes the agreement specification needed to license subject clitics and weak pronouns or (in a framework in which each feature heads a distinct projection) that the structure of early clauses includes AgrP.

In sum, we have seen that

(36) a. children distinguish between types of pronouns (clitic/weak versus nonclitic/strong pronouns),
  b. they are sensitive to the different feature content associated with finite and infinitive clauses, and that
  c. only finite clauses include the feature needed to license subject clitics and weak subject pronouns.

4.3.3 Subject Agreement as a Structure-Dependent Relation

In adult grammars IP is the projection where subject agreement is realized in a structural configuration involving the head of I (containing agreement features specified on the verb) and its specifier (hosting the structural subject). In other words, **agreement** is a **structure-dependent relation** between a constituent in Spec IP and the head I, as illustrated in (37).

(37)

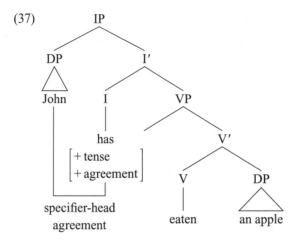

Children can handle agreement relations, witness their ability to realize subject agreement. However, this does not suffice to conclude that agreement is a structural relation in children's grammar. We must first discard two alternatives: that agreement is a linear relation between two adjacent elements, and that it is a semantically based notion. These two alternatives are schematized in (38).

(38) a. The inflected verb agrees with the NP (DP) immediately to its left.

b. The inflected verb agrees with the NP (DP) representing the agent of the sentence.

4.3.4 Subject Agreement as a Relation Based on Linear Adjacency

4.3.4.1 Postverbal Subjects   A rule of the type in (38a) saying that the verb agrees with the NP to its immediate left works very well for Italian sentences such as (39a): the verb agrees with the NP to its left, *i bambini* 'the kids'. However, it fails to account for Italian (Spanish, Catalan) sentences such as (39b) with a postverbal subject.[8]

(39) a. I   bambini lo regaleranno   a Gianni.
the kids   it will offer-3PL to Gianni
'The kids will offer it to Gianni.'

b. A Gianni lo regaleranno   i   bambini.
to Gianni it will offer-3PL the kids
'It is the kids that will offer it to Gianni.'

Italian learners whose speech has been studied use postverbal subjects in about 30% of their sentences with overt subjects and make no agreement errors (see Guasti 1993/1994, fn. 16). Some examples are given in (40).

(40) a. L'ap[r]o   io.   (Diana, 1;10)
        it open-1SG I
        'It is me that open it.'
    b. Chiudo   io.   (Martina, 1;11)
        close-1SG I
        'It is me that close.'
    c. [Al]   mare andavo   io.   (Raffaello, 2;0)
        to the sea   go-PAST-1SG I
        'It is me that went to the sea.'

If children regarded subject agreement as a linear relation, subject to the rule in (38a), their sentences with postverbal subjects should display agreement errors; but they do not.

4.3.4.2 Coordinate Subjects Further evidence against viewing agreement as a linear relation may come from coordinate subjects. Consider the examples in (41).

(41) a. Gaia e   Giulia [si]   danno   un
        Gaia and Giulia [each other] give-3PL a
        bacino. (Diana, 2;0)
        little kiss
        'Gaia and Giulia give each other a little kiss.'
    b. *Gaia e   Giulia si   da   un bacino.
        Gaia and Giulia each other give-3SG a   little kiss
    c. Che erano Orazio e   Gaspare. (Guglielmo, 2;10)
        that were Orazio and Gaspare

If agreement were a linear relation, the inflected verb in (41a) should agree with the first NP to its left, *Giulia*, and be affixed with the third singular morpheme, as in (41b); similarly for *erano* 'were' in (41c). However, although no systematic investigations have been carried out, examples such as (41a) and (41c) found in the CHILDES database show that children do not make mistakes with coordinate subjects. Therefore, in their grammars the two coordinate NPs must form a constituent that enters into an agreement relation with the inflected verb.

The findings from sentences with postverbal subjects and with coordinate subjects therefore suggest that children's rule for subject agreement is not based on linear adjacency.

4.3.5   Subject Agreement as a Semantic Notion

4.3.5.1   Nonagent Subjects   In addition to the thematic role agent, subjects can have the role experiencer or theme.

(42) a. John wants an apple.
     b. John fears snowstorms.

If children applied a rule such as (38b) stating that the inflected verb agrees with the NP bearing the agent role, they should be unable to perform subject agreement or should make more agreement errors when the subject is not an agent. To test these predictions, let us examine the speech of the Italian-speaking children investigated in Guasti 1993/1994. Although (Italian-speaking) children use quite a few agent subjects, they also use nonagent subjects—for example, experiencers with verbs like *want*, *see*, *sleep*, *remember*, *fear*, *like*, *have* (in the sense of 'possess'). In the vast majority of cases, agreement with nonagent subjects is accurate. As we saw in section 4.3.1, the rate of agreement error in early Italian is quite low and even the few reported errors are by no means confined to verbs occurring with nonagent subjects. Of the 19 errors reported in Guasti 1993/1994, only 3 occur with nonagent subjects. Two of these were produced by Martina. This child used 131 nonagent subjects and in 2 cases (1.5%) she failed to produce the correct agreement. Since the overall rate of agreement errors in early Italian is around 3%, this 1.5% error rate with nonagent subjects is well within the overall limit. Hence, the expectation that children make more agreement errors with nonagent subjects than with agent subjects is not fulfilled. Since children are equally accurate in computing agreement regardless of the thematic role of the subject, it is very unlikely that they are applying a rule of the type in (38b).

4.3.5.2   Copular Constructions   Another piece of evidence against a rule like (38b) is provided by copular constructions. The copular verb *be* does not assign a thematic role (see Moro 1995); consequently, rule (38b) is of no help in establishing agreement between the copula and the structural subject. Italian learners use many copular constructions. Frequently the verb occurs with a third person singular subject and is correctly inflected (43a); some examples with a plural subject (in postverbal position) are also found, and all display agreement between the grammatical subject and the copular verb (43b,c).

(43) a. Chetta è la papera.   (Martina, 1;11)
         this   is the duck
     b. Sono   galli. (Martina, 2;2)
        (they) are cocks
     c. Ci   sono m[a]iali?   (Guglielmo, 2;3)
        there are   pigs
        'Are there pigs?'

Apparently rule (38b) cannot have helped the child in spelling out the correct agreement morphemes in such utterances.

4.3.5.3 Impersonal Constructions   A third piece of evidence against a semantically based notion of agreement in children's language comes from Italian impersonal sentences. These contain a third person singular verb and the clitic *si*, as shown in (44a). Despite the presence of a singular verb, the understood subject of these sentences may refer to a plurality, which in English is rendered by the first person plural pronoun. An Italian-speaking child, Diana, produces these sentences frequently; although she understands that the subject refers to a plurality, she uses a third person singular verb, as shown in (44b).

(44) a. Si mangia la pizza.
        SI eats   the pizza
        'We eat the pizza.'
     b. Si va   al   mare. (Diana, 2;0)
        SI goes to the sea
        'We go to the sea.'

If Diana computed agreement on a semantic basis, in terms of the referents of the action, she could not perform agreement correctly in (44b).

4.3.6   Intermediate Summary

In this section we have seen that the agreement feature is positively specified in children's finite clauses. Morphological evidence comes from languages such as Catalan, Italian, and Spanish, in which children use agreement morphemes appropriately and abundantly. The presence of agreement is also evident from the structural requirements it imposes on the distribution of clausal constituents. A case in point is the distribution of subject clitics and weak subject pronouns in early finite French and Dutch clauses.

Children's knowledge of subject agreement is knowledge of a structure-dependent relation involving a constituent in Spec IP and the head of IP hosting the inflected verb. Other ways of computing agreement cannot explain the child data. First, agreement cannot be captured by a linear rule ("The verb agrees with the NP immediately to its left"), witness correct agreement in early Italian sentences with postverbal and coordinate subjects. Second, agreement is not semantically driven ("The verb agrees with the agent"). In children's speech agreement is insensitive to the subject's thematic role; can be established in the absence of a thematic relation between the verb and its subject, as in copular constructions; and is not determined by the person and number of the referent, as impersonal constructions show.

4.4   ROOT INFINITIVES

As we have seen, children demonstrate quite refined syntactic knowledge, in spite of certain deviations from the target adult grammar. One widely studied deviation, presented in section 4.2.3, consists of producing main clauses containing an infinitive verb, rather than a finite one. This phenomenon has been observed in a wide variety of languages including Danish, Dutch, French, German, Russian, and Swedish (see Platzack 1992; Wexler 1994; Haegeman 1995b; Hamann and Plunkett 1998). It is peculiar to the earliest multiword productions and lasts until about 3 years. Some examples reported in (14) are repeated here.

(14) a. Hun sove.   (Jens, 2;0)
        she   sleep-INF
     b. Earst kleine boekje lezen.   (Hein, 2;6)
        first   little   book   read-INF
        'First (I/we) read little book.'
     c. Dormir   petit bébé.   (Daniel, 1;11)
        sleep-INF little baby
        'Little baby sleep.'
     d. S[ch]okolade holen.   (Andreas, 2;1)
        chocolate   get

In early English there is no infinitive marker and children produce uninflected verbal forms, as shown in (7) and repeated here.

(7) a. Papa have it. (Eve, 1;6)
    b. Cromer wear glasses. (Eve, 2;0)
    c. Marie go. (Sarah, 2;3)
    d. Mumma ride horsie. (Sarah, 2;6)

For a long time the status of these English uninflected verbs was poorly understood. However, the discovery that children learning Danish, Dutch, French, and so on, use infinitives in main clauses has prompted an analysis of early English uninflected verbs: they are the English variant of infinitives in other early languages. The claim that bare forms in early English are infinitives brings English into line with other early languages.

The occurrence of infinitives in main clauses was first noted by Wexler (1994). The terms applied to this phenomenon, **optional infinitive** (OI) and **root infinitive** (RI), emanate from different theories, although now (as in this book) they are often used without any theoretical burden.

So far we have discussed evidence in favor of a **continuity view of language development**—namely, that children's grammars include the same functional projections as adults' grammars, and the early clausal representation is couched in the same vocabulary as the adult one. The presence of RI clauses in early speech challenges this view: since these clauses are not acceptable in the adult language, they represent a discontinuity. How can we make sense of them? Various researchers have proposed that RI clauses originate from grammatical deficits due to lack of maturation of relevant grammatical principles (see Rizzi 1993/1994; Wexler 1999). It is assumed that, although the principles in question are part of UG, they are under the control of a biological program that makes them available at given points of development. Only when these principles mature do RI clauses cease to be an option in the early grammar. A maturational approach is compatible with a continuity view of language development, because the differences between the child and adult systems are assumed to be constrained by UG (see Borer and Wexler 1987; Wexler 1999; see also section 4.4.4).

4.4.1 Properties of Root Infinitives

Root infinitives are attested in a wide variety of early languages. There are some notable exceptions, however: in early Catalan, Italian, and Spanish RIs are extremely rare (see Guasti 1993/1994; Torrens 1995) and

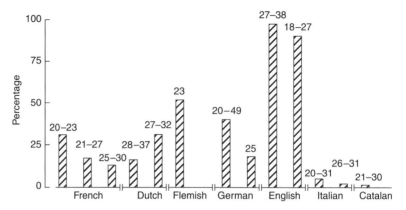

Figure 4.1
Percentage of root infinitives (RI) in early languages. Each bar shows the overall percentage of RIs produced by a single child in the age range (given in months) indicated above the bar. Data taken from Rasetti 2000 (French: Daniel, Nathalie, Philippe); Haegeman 1995b (Dutch: Hein); Phillips 1995, crediting Krämer 1993 (Dutch: Thomas; Flemish: Maarten); Phillips 1995, crediting Beherens 1993 (German: Simone); Poeppel and Wexler 1993 (German: Andreas; English: Eve, Sarah); Guasti 1993/1994 (Italian: Martina, Guglielmo); Torrens 1995 (Catalan: Guillem).

infinitives are used in an adultlike way from the start, that is, in governed contexts like those in (45) from early Italian.

(45) a. *pe[r]* c[u]ocere   (Martina, 1;8)
         to   cook-INF
         'in order to cook'
     b. *Voglio*   bere.   (Martina, 1;10)
         want-1SG drink-INF
         '(I) want to drink.'

In (45a) the infinitive is selected by a preposition and in (45b) by a matrix verb.

The crosslinguistic dimension of the phenomenon is evident in figure 4.1, which reports the overall rate of main clause infinitives produced by children speaking various early languages. The percentage of RIs is calculated by dividing the number of RIs by the total number of verb forms uttered (imperatives excluded). For English the counts include only verbs with third person subjects (overt or null), because for other persons the bare form is homophonous with the finite form (e.g., *speak/you speak*).

Verb forms inflected with the *-ing* morpheme and not introduced by an auxiliary (e.g., *you speaking*) are also not included in the counts. Figure 4.1 clearly shows that RIs are robustly attested in French, Dutch, Flemish, German, and English, but they are nonexistent in Catalan and Italian. (Notice that languages displaying RIs are non-pro-drop languages and languages lacking RIs are pro-drop languages.)

RIs are morphosyntactically infinitive verbs; and like them, they do not raise to I. In section 4.2.3.1 we saw that infinitive verbs, unlike finite verbs, follow the negation in French, Dutch, and German, as illustrated in (17a) for French and repeated here.

(17) a. Pas manger la   poupée.   (Nathalie, 1;9)
       not eat-INF the doll
       'The doll does not eat.'

Under the assumption that NegP is located between IP and VP, the order Neg V$_{inf}$ indicates that infinitives remain in VP. This conclusion is also supported by the observation that in V2/SOV languages infinitives surface at the end of the clause (section 4.2.3.2), as illustrated in (46).

(46) a. Ditte nu   opeten.   (Hein, 2;5)
       this   now up-eat-INF
       'This eat up now.'
     b. Du das haben.   (Andreas, 2;1)
       you that have-INF
       'You have that.'

VP being head final in such languages (see (6b)), clause-final position is the position where infinitives are generated. This entails that in RI clauses the verb remains in VP. RI clauses differ from finite clauses in other respects. Unlike first position in a finite clause, first position in an RI clause in early Germanic languages cannot be occupied by a nonsubject constituent (section 4.2.3.3). Moreover, clitic and weak pronoun subjects are incompatible with RIs (section 4.3.2). Beyond these structural restrictions, RIs display a limited distribution: they are found in declarative sentences, but not in *wh*-questions (see Weissenborn 1990; Rizzi 1993/1994). Table 4.5 illustrates this fact for early Dutch (see Haegeman 1995b); Crisma (1992) reports a similar result for early French. Finally, lexical verbs but not auxiliaries can show up in RI clauses; that is, children do not produce sentences like (47) with an infinitive auxiliary (Poeppel and Wexler 1993; Wexler 1994).

Table 4.5
Distribution of infinitives in declaratives and *wh*-questions in the speech of a Dutch child. Data from Hein (age range 2;4–3;1).

	+Finite	−Finite
Declaratives	3768	721
Wh-questions	80	2

Source: Based on Haegeman 1995b, table 4, and p. 226
$\chi^2 = 11.22$, $p < .005$

(47) *Marie avoir   mangé la   pomme.
      Marie have-INF eaten   the apple

In sum, RIs have the following properties:

(48) a. RIs do not occur in pro-drop languages.
     b. RI clauses are not introduced by nonsubject XPs in V2 languages.
     c. RIs are incompatible with clitic and weak pronoun subjects (French and Dutch, respectively).
     d. RIs occur in declarative sentences, but not in *wh*-questions.
     e. RIs are incompatible with auxiliaries.

A child who produces RIs knows that

(49) a. finite and nonfinite verbs are distinct in terms of verb movement, with infinitives not raising to I, and that
     b. finite clauses include functional projections.

Then the occurrence of RIs in children's speech raises the following questions:

(50) a. What factor allows RIs in early systems?
     b. What is the structure of RI clauses?

4.4.2 Sources of Root Infinitives

We have seen that children know a lot about the morphosyntactic properties of finite and infinitive verbs. What they do not appear to know is that infinitives cannot be used in main declarative sentences. To explain this apparent deviation from the adult target, researchers have elaborated two main families of theories. Schematically, one asserts that RIs arise from the option of leaving some functional feature underspecified. The other views RI clauses as reduced structures that result from the option of truncating structures at different levels of the clausal architecture.[9] In this section we will look at the leading ideas of the two families of approaches and discuss the pros and cons of each.

4.4.2.1 An Underspecification Account: The Tense Omission Model   In finite clauses the inflectional node I is positively specified for a bundle of features, among them the agreement and tense features, which express finiteness. When a feature is positively specified, it is generally morphologically expressed. **Underspecification** accounts hold that a feature that is usually present in a finite clause (e.g., tense) fails to be specified or is missing in a given syntactic representation. When this happens, the morpheme expressing that feature cannot surface and the syntactic processes for which the feature is responsible do not occur. The choice of leaving a feature underspecified must be optional, since children in this particular developmental stage produce both infinitive and finite clauses. Hence, the name *optional infinitive* was coined to refer to infinitive main clauses.

There are two types of underspecification theories, diverging chiefly in their claims about which feature remains underspecified in the child's clausal representation: number (Hoekstra and Hyams 1995; Hyams 1996) or tense (Wexler 1994). The latter view has been further refined by Schütze (1997) and Wexler (1999), who claim that either tense or agreement or both can be left underspecified. For simplicity, we will look at only one of these approaches: the **tense omission model**, summarized in (51). (In this section the term *optional infinitive (OI)* is used because this is the term coined by proponents of the tense omission model.)

(51) *The tense omission model*
    An OI clause arises when the child leaves the tense feature
    underspecified in a given clausal representation.

According to the tense omission model, children, like adults, know the so-called **Tense Constraint**.

(52) *Tense Constraint*
    A main clause must include a specification of tense.

They also know that the specification of the tense feature imposes certain constraints. When they choose this feature, they express the morphemes encoding it. However, unlike adults, children may choose to omit the tense feature from the representation. In English tense is encoded by the past tense marker *-ed*, the third person present marker *-s* (which also encodes agreement), the copula, *do*, modals, and auxiliaries. When tense is underspecified, none of the morphemes that express it can be present and the lexical verb surfaces as a nonfinite form, or a bare form—an OI.

To explain why children can omit tense from the clausal representation, Wexler (1999) proposes an account couched in the minimalist vocabulary (Chomsky 1995) and requiring a more articulated clausal structure than we have assumed so far, one that includes TP and AgrP (for an introduction to the minimalist framework, see Radford 1997). Wexler (1999) adopts the widely held hypothesis that subjects are base-generated in VP and that they move from there first to Spec TP and then to Spec AgrP (for discussion of the VP-internal subject hypothesis, see Haegeman 1994, chap. 6; Radford 1997, chap. 8; see also section 7.3.1). To explain why the subject moves from Spec VP to Spec TP and then to Spec AgrP, Wexler proposes the **Checking Constraint** in (53).

(53) *Checking Constraint*
Both Agr and T have a D-feature, which must be eliminated by being checked against the D-feature of a DP subject that raises to Spec TP and Spec AgrP.

According to this constraint, Agr and T are endowed with an uninterpretable D-feature that needs to be checked, and thereby eliminated, by the interpretable D-feature associated with the DP subject.[10] If the uninterpretable D-feature of Agr and T is not checked and eliminated, the representation is ill formed. Therefore, the DP subject must raise to participate in the checking operation.

Wexler (1999) further assumes that children's grammar includes the **Uniqueness Constraint**, stating that the D-feature of a DP can check the D-feature of either T or Agr, but not both.

(54) *Uniqueness Constraint*
A subject can check the uninterpretable feature of either T or Agr, but not both.

Subjects are generated in Spec VP, and in the adult language they raise from there first to Spec TP and then to Spec AgrP, to eliminate the D-feature of both functional projections. In other words, in adults' grammar a subject enters into a specifier-head relation with both T and Agr. In children's grammar a representation in which the subject checks the D-feature of both T and Agr violates the Uniqueness Constraint. To avoid this violation, children can leave T underspecified. Consequently, TP is removed from the clausal representation and the subject needs to check only the D-feature of Agr. However, if children's speech were exclusively under the control of the Uniqueness Constraint, we would expect them to produce only OI clauses. Yet in the period when children produce OI clauses, they also produce clauses with finite verbs, including both TP and AgrP, apparently violating the Uniqueness Constraint. To account for the fact that OI clauses are merely optional, Wexler proposes that there is another constraint, present in both children's and adults' grammar, that interacts with those introduced so far: **Minimize Violations**.

(55) *Minimize Violations*
Given two representations, choose the one that violates as few grammatical constraints as possible. If two representations violate the same number of constraints, then either one may be chosen.

Now let us see how the Tense, Checking, and Uniqueness Constraints and Minimize Violations interact. (Notice that Wexler's (1999) use of the term *constraints* differs from its use in the principles-and-parameters model (adopted here). In Wexler's account constraints are soft and violable, much as in Optimality Theory (see, e.g., Barbosa et al. 1998); in the principles-and-parameters model they are not violable.) OI clauses violate one constraint in children's grammar, the Tense Constraint, which requires that tense be present in a clause. But finite clauses also violate another constraint in their grammar, the Uniqueness Constraint, which requires that the D-feature of only one functional head (Agr or T) be checked. Recall that in the adult grammar the subject in a finite clause must raise and check the D-feature of both T and Agr. The options available to the child are schematized in (56) and (57) for finite and OI clauses, respectively.

(56) *Finite clause (with T)*
a. John runs.

b.

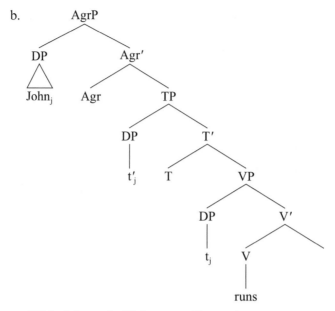

c. (56b) violates the Uniqueness Constraint.

(57) *OI clause (with no T)*
  a. John run.

b.

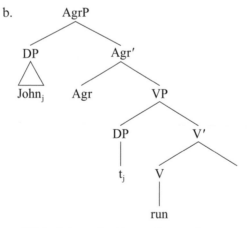

c. (57b) violates the Tense Constraint.

In (56b) the subject, generated in Spec VP, has raised to Spec TP and Spec AgrP to check the uninterpretable features of T and Agr, violating the Uniqueness Constraint. In (57b) the TP layer has been omitted, violating the Tense Constraint. Children's grammar allows two representations, one of which violates the Tense Constraint and one of which violates the Uniqueness Constraint. Since representations (56b) and (57b) each violate the same number of constraints, either one can be chosen, according to Minimize Violations. Consequently, early main clauses can surface either as finite clauses or as OI clauses. In adults' grammar the Uniqueness Constraint does not hold. Therefore, representation (56b) incurs no violation and, in compliance with Minimize Violations, it is chosen. Thus, the difference between adults' and children's grammar consists in the absence versus the presence of the Uniqueness Constraint.

Wexler's (1999) proposal accounts for the properties of OIs as follows. OIs are nonfinite verbs, something that children know very well since they do not raise them out of the VP (section 4.4.1). Lacking tense, OI clauses display certain restrictions that finite clauses do not. One is that in early V2 languages OI clauses, unlike finite ones, do not allow a non-subject constituent in clause-initial position (section 4.2.3.3). This asymmetry hinges on the limited movement abilities of nonfinite verbs. In finite clauses the verb moves to C and licenses a nonsubject initial constituent in Spec CP. Since infinitives do not raise to C, they cannot license a non-subject constituent in Spec CP.

Aspectual auxiliaries do not appear in OI clauses, precisely because of their aspectual nature. Auxiliaries need to be licensed by tense: they either are generated in T or need to raise to T (see Guasti 1993). Consequently, in a representation lacking the tense specification auxiliaries cannot be licensed.

The lack of OIs in Italian and Catalan can be traced to the properties of Agr, the licensing head for null subjects (see section 5.1.1). The essential idea is that because Agr in pro-drop languages licenses a null subject, it does not have an uninterpretable D-feature to be checked. Therefore, a lexical DP subject does not need to raise to Spec AgrP to check a feature of Agr. Instead, learners of pro-drop languages need to raise the DP subject as far as Spec TP to check the uninterpretable D-feature of T. In this way, their finite clauses simultaneously satisfy the Uniqueness Constraint and the Tense Constraint. A finite clause in a pro-drop language has the representation shown in (58b); a potential Italian OI clause in which tense is underspecified has the representation shown in (59b).[11]

(58) *Finite clause (with T)*
    a. Corre Lia.
       runs   Lia

b.

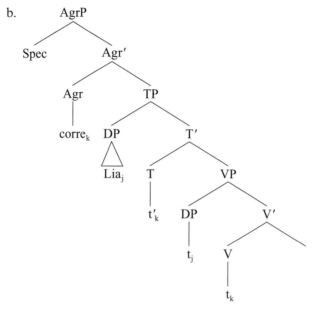

c. (58b) does not violate constraints.

(59) *OI clause (with no T)*
   a. Correre Lia.
      run-INF Lia

   b.

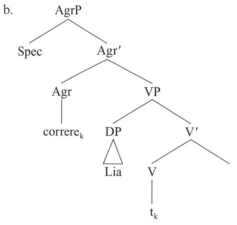

c. (59b) violates the Tense Constraint.

In (58b) the subject has raised to Spec TP and the verb to Agr. In (59b) TP is absent and the infinitive has moved to Agr, as infinitives do in Italian. The subject does not raise because Agr in Italian does not have an uninterpretable D-feature that needs to be checked. While (58b) does not violate any constraints, (59b) violates one, the Tense Constraint. Since by Minimize Violations, learners must choose the representation that involves fewer violations, they choose (58b) and thus never produce OIs. This explanation presupposes that learners know that the language they are exposed to is a pro-drop language (and that Agr has certain properties in their language). As we will see in section 5.1.5, there is evidence that from the age of 2 Italian learners have fixed the pro-drop parameter to the value valid in their language.

The incompatibility of OI clauses with clitic and weak pronouns might be difficult for the tense omission model to explain. It is generally assumed that clitics and weak subject pronouns are licensed by Agr. Therefore, in a clause in which Agr is present, but tense is not (as in an OI clause), one would expect to find clitics and weak subject pronouns. But this does not occur.

The tense omission model also falls short of explaining the lack of infinitives in *wh*-questions. The fact that tense is underspecified should not prevent OIs from occurring in *wh*-questions. In fact, proponents of the tense omission model dispute the observation that OIs are forbidden in *wh*-questions. They point out that bare verbs appear in *wh*-questions in early English, as shown in (60) (see Roeper and Rohrbacher 2000; Bromberg and Wexler 1995).

(60) Where train go?   (Adam, 2;4)

Since bare verbs are the English variant of OIs in other early languages, (60) is held to prove that OIs can be used in *wh*-questions. However, any firm conclusion about the structure of (60) must be viewed in the light of crosslinguistic investigations. No language studied so far allows OIs in *wh*-questions. Why should early English differ? There are two possibilities. One might seek an independent reason for why no early language but English allows OIs in *wh*-questions (for discussion, see Phillips 1995; Rizzi 2000). Or one might challenge the OI status of the verb in (60). As we will see in section 6.2, questions like (60) have been analyzed as involving a null auxiliary in C, the null counterpart of *do*, selecting the bare verb; that is, (60) is the counterpart of (61), which differs from it in the overt expression of *do* (see Guasti and Rizzi 1996; Guasti 2000).

Table 4.6
How the tense omission model, according to which optional infinitive (OI) clauses are clauses with tense underspecified (i.e., without TP), explains restrictions on optional infinitives

Restriction	Explanation
OI clauses are not introduced by nonsubject XPs in V2 languages.	Failure of infinitives to raise to C
OIs are incompatible with clitic and weak pronoun subjects.	Problematic
OIs do not occur in pro-drop languages.	Properties of Agr
OIs do not occur in questions.	Disputed
OIs are incompatible with auxiliaries.	Lack of tense feature and thus of TP

(61) Where does the train go?

If this analysis involving a null auxiliary is tenable, then the bare verb in (60) need not be regarded as a genuine OI and the absence of OIs in *wh*-questions is still in need of an explanation.

Table 4.6 summarizes how each restriction on OIs is explained within the tense omission model.

In the tense omission model the underspecification of a feature results in the absence of the projection hosting this feature. Under the split-I hypothesis, according to which tense and agreement features head separate projections (TP and AgrP, with AgrP higher than TP), an OI clause ends up with the structure in (62). Here the TP level has been stripped away, as indicated by the gray box.

(62)

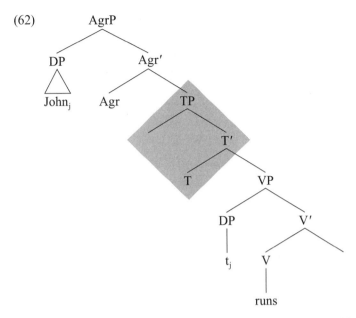

The absence of the functional layer including the underspecified feature is not common to all underspecification accounts of OI clauses. Hoekstra and Hyams (1995) argue that an OI clause has the same structural shape as a finite clause and includes the same functional projections. It differs from a finite clause in its feature content: some features are not specified. It is difficult to decide on empirical grounds which of the two approaches is correct since their predictions do not seem to differ.

4.4.2.2 The Truncation Model   An alternative account of the RI phenomenon is proposed by Rizzi (1993/1994). The starting observation is that in adult languages infinitives are generally used in subordinate contexts, while finite verbs are present in both main and subordinate contexts. This asymmetry is often traced back to the fact that the tense of infinitive clauses is anaphoric; that is, the temporal interpretation of infinitive clauses is ensured through the connection between their tense and the tense of the matrix verb. The requirement that the anaphoric tense of infinitives be identified by the tense of a matrix clause can be expressed as the **Constraint on the Identification of Anaphoric Tense**.

(63) *Constraint on the Identification of Anaphoric Tense*
      An anaphoric tense must be identified sentence-internally.

This constraint justifies the absence of infinitives in main clauses in adult languages. Since children use infinitives precisely in main clauses, the constraint must somehow be overridden in early systems. Elaborating on Wexler 1994, Rizzi assumes that tense can be removed in early clauses, but he offers a structural implementation of this idea that differs from Wexler's.

Rizzi proposes the **axiom on clausal representation**: namely, that all clauses, declaratives included, have a uniform representation: they are CPs, even in non-V2 languages.

(64) *Axiom on clausal representation*
    CP is the root of all clauses (finite and infinitive).

This assumption is tantamount to saying that all finite declarative clauses, even in non-V2 languages, have a CP layer even if it is not filled by lexical material. While the axiom is always operative in adults' grammar, it applies optionally in children's grammar. Therefore, in children's speech some clauses are CPs, while others can be less than CP; that is, functional projections can be truncated below CP, and a category that is lower than CP—that is, AgrP, TP, or VP—can be the root of a clause, as shown in (65). (Arcs indicate truncation sites, and the clausal structure has been enriched for explanatory purposes.)

(65)

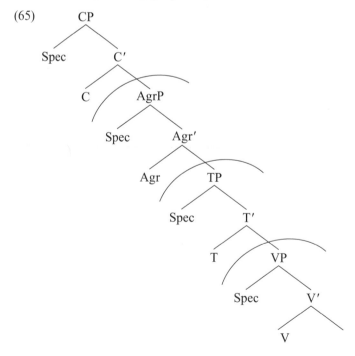

The **truncation mechanism** works as follows. Truncation operates at the top level of the structural hierarchy and strips away every projection above the truncation site. However, it cannot remove projections from the middle of the tree; for example, in (65) it is not possible to omit TP while projecting CP, AgrP, and VP. In other words, every projection dominating the truncation site is missing and every projection dominated by the truncation site must be present. In this respect, the truncation model differs from Wexler's underspecification approach, according to which functional projections can be stripped away from the middle of the tree (compare (65) with (62)).

RI clauses are structures truncated below TP; that is, they are VPs or may include some functional layer immediately above VP.[12] Truncation at the VP level is possible for nonfinite verbs, because these do not raise to I (recall section 4.4.1), or, equivalently, their morphosyntactic feature can be satisfied within the VP. Since RI clauses are VPs, they lack the TP layer and the Constraint on the Identification of Anaphoric Tense cannot be invoked: there is no anaphoric tense in RI clauses that needs to be identified. The temporal interpretation of RI clauses is not grammatically determined, but is fixed by the context. In fact, Harris and Wexler (1996) found that English RI clauses display a variety of temporal meanings determined by the context; English-speaking children use RIs to refer to present, past, and future events. By contrast, they employ finite verbs affixed with a present (*-s*) or past (*-ed*) morpheme only for referring to present or past events, respectively.

The truncation mechanism can apply in finite clauses as well. A finite clause may be truncated below CP or even below AgrP, at least in languages in which verbs do not raise to Agr (see section 5.2.3 regarding the former option; see Ingham 1998 regarding the latter). Finite truncated clauses do not violate the Constraint on the Identification of Anaphoric Tense even if they include a TP layer, because their tense is not anaphoric.

The fact that RI clauses are structures truncated below TP explains their restricted distribution. If a given projection is cut off from the clausal representation, none of the morphosyntactic processes involving this projection can apply. First, since clitics and weak subject pronouns must be licensed by Agr (recall section 4.3.2), they cannot occur in an RI clause, where AgrP is missing. In the same vein, the fact that a nonsubject constituent cannot occupy first position in an RI clause in early V2 languages is explained by the absence in these structures of the CP level necessary to accommodate initial nonsubject constituents. By contrast, subjects *can* occur in RI clauses, because they can stay in the VP, where they are generated. Similarly, the lack of auxiliary RI clauses can be explained by the absence of TP under the assumption that auxiliaries are licensed by T (they either are generated in T or raise to T).

The absence of RIs in pro-drop languages hinges on the movement properties of infinitives in these languages (see table 4.1). Truncating an infinitive clause above TP and merely projecting a VP is possible in early non-pro-drop languages, because infinitives do not raise to I. In pro-drop languages, instead, infinitives must raise to TP and AgrP, and these projections must be present to accommodate the properties of infinitive verbs. Since TP is present, the Constraint on the Identification of Anaphoric Tense is enforced. Because a sentence-internal identifier for the anaphoric tense is not available, RI clauses in pro-drop languages violate this constraint.

Finally, since RI clauses are VPs, they do not include any projection above VP and in particular they do not contain CP to host *wh*-movement of a fronted *wh*-element. Hence, RIs are not found in *wh*-questions.

Table 4.7 summarizes how each restriction on RIs is explained within the truncation model.

Like the underspecification account, the truncation account of RIs incorporates the idea that tense is somehow deficient in children's grammar. In the former case this deficiency is traced back to the Uniqueness Constraint in (54), stating that a DP subject can check the D-feature of only one functional projection; in the latter it is tied to the hypothesis that different nodes can count as the root of the clause in children's gram-

Table 4.7
How the truncation model, according to which root infinitives (RIs) are truncated structures, explains restrictions on root infinitives

Restriction	Explanation
RIs are not introduced by nonsubject XPs in V2 languages.	Lack of CP
RIs are incompatible with clitic and weak pronoun subjects.	Lack of AgrP
RIs do not occur in pro-drop languages.	Infinitives raise to AgrP and include TP, thus enforcing (63)
RIs do not occur in questions.	Lack of CP
RIs are incompatible with auxiliaries.	Lack of TP

mar. Although under both approaches the TP projection is missing, an RI clause has a different structure, a fact that has empirical consequences. Under the tense omission model RIs are expected in *wh*-questions; under the truncation model they are not.

Under both the truncation and tense omission models an RI or OI clause is a reduced structure that lacks certain functional layers. In this respect, both theories retain some insights of Radford's (1990) small clause hypothesis (section 4.2.2): some early clauses may lack functional projections. They crucially differ from this hypothesis in claiming that functional categories are part and parcel of children's grammar from the earliest multiword utterances.

4.4.3   Open Problems

While there is ample agreement that RIs represent a grammatical phenomenon with specific properties, the status of bare verbs in early English is still widely debated. Usually these bare verbs are taken as the English variant of infinitives in other early languages. As noted, bare forms may occur in early English *wh*-questions (*What he eat?*). This is very striking since no other early language studied so far allows infinitives in *wh*-questions. One hypothesis is that the bare form used in English questions is not a true RI. Guasti and Rizzi (1996) suggest that they are forms selected by a null auxiliary (see sections 4.4.2.1 and 6.2). That even in declarative clauses some bare forms are not RIs is supported by findings discussed by Hoekstra and Hyams (1999). These authors have identified an asymmetry between early English bare forms and RIs in other early languages. While RIs in French, Dutch, and so on, are restricted to verbs that describe events (*run*, *eat*, etc.), in early English they can describe both events and states (*want*, *love*, *know*, *see*). Suppose that verbs surfacing as RIs *must* describe events; then the fact that English bare forms do *not* all describe events may be a clue that they are not all RIs. The ones that are not RIs must be analyzed in some other way. Guasti and Rizzi (2002) suggest that some bare forms are finite forms missing the *-s* or the *-ed* morpheme. Evidence for this claim comes from English learners' production of sentences like *He don't hear me* (Sarah, 3;5), where a finite verb (*do*) is used, but it fails to be affixed with the third person marker.

Crosslinguistic investigation has been very fruitful for analyzing early English bare forms, which until the discovery of RIs were poorly understood. Certain differences remain between early English bare forms and

RIs in other early languages, as the findings discussed above show. It is to be hoped that crosslinguistic considerations will shed light on these differences.

4.4.4 Maturation and Root Infinitives

RI clauses are not acceptable in the adult language and disappear from children's speech at around age 3. How do they disappear? Some authors have appealed to maturation, a biological mechanism that surely underlies the development of certain features of biological systems (see Rizzi 1993/1994; for extensive discussion of the maturational view, see Borer and Wexler 1987, 1992; Wexler 1999; Felix 1987, 1992). For example, humans start to walk at about 12–18 months of age; at 2 years they have a set of teeth doomed to be lost at 5 years and replaced by a new set. Maturation is likely to control some aspects of language development —for example, the fact that infants start to babble orally or manually around 6–8 months. According to the maturational view, a genetic program also controls the development of syntax (i.e., the development of grammatical objects—features, principles) and determines the timing by which components of UG become available to the child. Under this view RIs occur because principles of UG have not matured. The maturational course is relatively independent of experience, in that whether or not a component of UG is available depends almost exclusively on the biological schedule. It is not until age 3 that the Uniqueness Constraint disappears from children's grammar or that the axiom in (64) that CP is the root of the clause is genetically programmed to become fully operative. When this happens, RI clauses disappear from children's speech.

4.5 SUMMARY AND CONCLUDING REMARKS

When children start to combine words, they already know a good deal about the morphosyntactic properties of their target grammar. They know the order of constituents valid in their target language; that is, they have set the head direction parameter to its correct value. French learners produce clauses featuring the order VO, and Dutch and German learners produce infinitive clauses featuring the order OV. From their earliest multiword utterances, children also seem to have set the verb movement parameter. Children know whether or not verbs in their native language raise and which verbs raise (finite), as the distribution of verbs with respect to other clausal constituents shows. English learners never say *John speaks not* (Harris and Wexler 1996), because they know that lexical verbs do not raise in their language. By contrast, French, German, and Dutch learners, who know that finite verbs move in their language, do say the counterpart of *John speaks not*. Learners of V2 languages (Dutch, German, Swedish) know that finite verbs move to second position in the clause.

Thus, from the earliest syntactic productions there is evidence that children have assigned the correct value to the parameters that govern clausal structure (head direction parameter, verb movement parameter, V2 parameter) (see Wexler 1999). The fact that children correctly fix the value of parameters early on again demonstrates how rapidly they discover the regularities of the ambient language. They are guided in this task by UG, which directs their attention to those properties that have linguistic import.

Children also demonstrate knowledge of grammatical relations and constraints. They know that agreement is a structure-dependent relation between a head and a constituent in a specifier (which implies that they also know that words are grouped together into phrases).

These findings indicate that children's grammar is couched in the same vocabulary as adults' grammar, thus supporting a continuity view of language development.

Despite the striking similarities between children's and adults' grammars, though, children's speech does deviate from the adult target. Along with finite verbs, children produce root or optional infinitive clauses. RIs are most likely not a simplification of adult finite clauses, verbal forms that children use when they do not know the finite form. RI clauses are subject to grammatical constraints. For example, they are found in declaratives, but not in *wh*-questions; they can occur with certain clausal elements, but not others (e.g., subject clitics).

We have examined two accounts of RIs: the tense omission model and the truncation model. According to the tense omission model, RIs result from the underspecification of the tense feature. The properties of RI clauses follow from the interactions of various constraints: the Tense, Uniqueness, and Checking Constraints and Minimize Violations. According to the truncation model, RI clauses are structures truncated below TP. Truncation at this level ensures absence of TP and thus avoidance of the constraint requiring identification of an anaphoric tense. Properties of RIs follow from the absence of structural layers.

Summary of Linguistic Development

Between 2 and 3 years children know

a. the value of the head direction parameter in their native language,
b. the value of the verb movement parameter in their native language,
c. the value of the V2 parameter in their native language,
d. that subject agreement is a structure-dependent relation,
e. that clauses include the agreement feature,
f. (if they are English learners) that lexical verbs and auxiliaries belong to distinct classes with different formal properties,
g. the morphological properties of verbs,
h. lexical and functional categories.

Further Reading

Regarding the case system in early grammars, see Rispoli 1994 and Vainikka 1994. Schütze 1997 discusses the relation between Case and root infinitives. For specific studies on negation, see Déprez and Pierce 1993, Drozd 1995, Harris and Wexler 1996, and Stromswold and Zimmermann 1999/2000. Penner and Weissenborn 1996, Bohnacker 1997, and Eisenbeiss 2000 discuss the omission of determiners. Relevant to the debate about maturation of grammatical constructs are two studies on the early second language acquisition of functional categories, Paradis and Genesee 1997 and Prévost and White 2000.

Key Words

Agreement as a structure-dependent relation
Axiom on clausal representation
Checking Constraint
Constraint on the Identification of Anaphoric Tense
Continuity view of language development
Full competence hypothesis
Head direction parameter
Minimize Violations
Optional infinitive
Root infinitive
Small clause hypothesis
Tense Constraint
Tense omission model
Truncation mechanism
Underspecification
Uniqueness Constraint
Verb movement parameter
V2 parameter

Study Questions

1. As shown in section 4.4.1, Italian-speaking children use infinitives in governed contexts as adults do. Establish whether or not this is also true of early languages that display root infinitives. Choose some files from the CHILDES database that include utterances by children up to age 3 and analyze whether infinitives appear in verb-governed contexts and after prepositions when root infinitives are used.

2. In languages such as Catalan, Italian, and Spanish, clitics are placed to the left of finite verbs, but to the right of infinitives, as exemplified in (i) from Italian.

(i) a. Gianni lo mangia.
        Gianni it eat-3SG
        'Gianni eats it.'
    b. Maria ha promesso di mangiarlo.
        Maria has promised of eat-INF-it
        'Maria has promised to eat it.'

Guasti (1993/1994) and Torrens (1995) have found that children speaking these languages consistently place clitics in the correct position; they do not misplace them. What can one infer from this fact?

3. In Italian, negative adverbs follow both finite and nonfinite verbs, as shown in (i), a pattern respected by learners of this language.

(i) a. Gianni non beve   più.
        Gianni not drink-3SG more
        'Gianni does not drink anymore.'
    b. per non bere   più
        to not drink-INF more

Assuming that negative adverbs occupy Spec NegP, how can one interpret this fact about the relative position of verbs and negative adverbs in Italian learners' speech? (See Guasti 1993/1994.)

4. Harris and Wexler (1996) have found that English learners produce (i) but not (ii).

(i) John not speak.

(ii) John speaks not.

How can (i) be analyzed under the tense omission model and the truncation model?

5. What is the evidence for attributing a CP analysis to early finite clauses in Germanic languages?

6. On the basis of what evidence can one discard the hypothesis that children compute agreement on a semantic basis?

7. What are the properties of root infinitives?

8. What is the major structural difference between the tense omission model and the truncation model?

9. Children produce root infinitives in main declarative clauses but not in subordinate clauses. For example, French-speaking children produce sentences like (i) but not ones like (ii).

(i) Jean partir.
    Jean leave-INF

(ii) Marie a   dit   que Jean partir.
     Marie has said that Jean leave-INF

How can one account for this discrepancy by adopting the truncation model? (See Rizzi 1993/1994.)

10. A prediction that follows from the truncation model is that root infinitives should not appear in subordinate clauses, whose structure includes the CP layer (see Rizzi 1993/1994). Verify this prediction by looking at transcripts from the CHILDES database.

11. Discuss evidence in favor of the view that subjects raise from Spec VP to Spec IP. For example, look at distributional facts (see also section 7.3.1; see Wexler 1999).

12. According to the small clause hypothesis, not only I but all functional categories are initially absent from children's grammar. Therefore, elements that instantiate these categories are expected to be absent from children's speech. Discuss this statement (see Radford 1990).

Chapter 5

Null Subjects in Early Languages

INTRODUCTION

In the previous chapter we looked at a peculiar feature of early clauses, the use of infinitives in root declarative clauses. In this chapter we turn to another peculiar aspect of children's clauses between 2 and 3 years: the optional omission of the sentential subject. Children learning to speak a variety of languages (e.g., Danish, Dutch, English, French, German) optionally omit the subject of sentences, though their target language requires it to be lexically expressed. Examples from Danish, English, and French are reported in (1).

(1) a. Se, blomster har.   (Jens, 2;2)
       look flowers   have/has
       'Look, (I/you/she/we) have/has flowers.'
    b. Tickles me.   (Adam, 3;6)
    c. Mange du   pain.   (Grégoire, 2;1)
       eat-3SG some bread

The early null subject is one of the most studied topics in the acquisition of syntax. Scholars have taken two basic positions on this phenomenon. One holds that the early null subject reflects an aspect of children's competence. The other tackles the problem by appealing to limitations on children's performance.

This chapter is organized as follows. Section 5.1 presents and evaluates two competence-based approaches to the early null subject (which have now been abandoned). Both attribute the phenomenon to an incorrect setting of the parameters governing the lexical expression of subjects across languages. One assimilates the early null subject to null subjects in

Italian, and the other assimilates it to null subjects in Chinese. Section 5.2 presents a new competence-based approach holding that the parameter(s) responsible for the phonological omission of subjects is/are correctly set; the early null subject reflects a grammatical option available in the early grammar, namely, the option of truncating structures. (This is the same mechanism claimed to be responsible for another early phenomenon, root infinitives, discussed in section 4.4.) Finally, section 5.3 discusses some performance-based accounts.

5.1   PARAMETRIC ACCOUNTS OF EARLY NULL SUBJECTS

Parametric approaches hold that children start with a default value of a given parameter and that if this is not the value expressed in their target language, they will change the value on the basis of their linguistic experience. These approaches are very appealing because they claim that children can attain the adult grammar by relying on positive evidence, without invoking other developmental mechanisms (see Atkinson 1982 for an introduction to such approaches). Approaches to early null subjects based on parameter missetting enjoyed widespread popularity in the 1980s but have now been abandoned. Empirical discoveries concerning the structural properties of early null subjects have set these apart from null subjects in adult languages like Italian and Chinese and have made the missetting view highly implausible. To lay the groundwork, we will look briefly at the parameters governing the distribution of lexical subjects across languages.

5.1.1   Parameters Governing the Omission of Subjects across Languages

There are typologically different adult languages that allow the subject of a sentence to be phonologically null. Although the matter is still controversial, for purposes of clarity we will assume here that two types of null subjects can be found: one present in languages like Catalan, Italian, and Spanish, and the other present in languages like Chinese, Japanese, and Korean (see Jaeggli and Safir 1989 for various approaches to null subjects; also see Harbert 1995).

Null subjects of the Italian kind are somehow linked to a morphologically rich agreement system. This intuition has been formalized by saying that this kind of null subject is a phonologically silent pronoun licensed by I and identified by ϕ-features (person, number) expressed by agreement morphemes on verbs (see Rizzi 1986). A language that allows null subjects of this type is said to have a positive setting for the **pro-drop parameter**. (2a,b) are examples of Italian subjectless sentences. Notice that phonologically null subjects are merely optional, not obligatory. A subject pronoun can be used, as (2c) illustrates.

(2) a. Vedo   un aereo.
       see-1SG an airplane
       'I see an airplane.'
    b. Chi hai   visto?
       who have-2SG seen
       'Who have you seen?'
    c. Io ho   visto un aereo,   lei una nave.
       I have seen an airplane she a   boat
       'I saw an airplane, she a boat.'

Thus, the grammar of Italian allows subject pronouns to remain phonologically silent. Whether a pronoun *is* lexically expressed or not depends on discourse conditions. For example, in (2c) overt pronouns are employed to express a contrast. In general, overt pronouns require some sort of emphasis.

The representation of an Italian subjectless sentence like (2a) is (3). (For simplicity, the subject appears directly in Spec IP, rather than being moved there from Spec VP. Unless otherwise necessary, this practice is adopted throughout. Also, representations have just one functional projection above VP.)

(3)

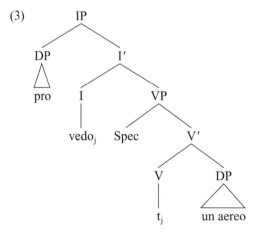

Under suitable discourse conditions null subjects are also allowed in Chinese, Japanese, and Korean. Unlike in Italian, the existence of these null subjects cannot be linked to a rich agreement system since verbs in these languages carry no agreement affix. A subjectless Chinese sentence (from Huang 1984) is shown in (4).

(4) —   Kanjian ta le.
    (he) see   he ASP
    'He saw him.'

In Chinese, Japanese, and Korean, unlike in Italian, Catalan, and Spanish, objects as well as subjects can be dropped (Chinese example from Huang 1984).

(5) Ta kanjian —   le.
    he see   (him) ASP
    'He saw him.'

It has been proposed that null subjects and null objects in Chinese (and similar languages) are not pronominal elements, but variables (or Ā-bound elements) created by movement of an empty operator (Op) to Spec CP. The structure of (4) and (5) is shown in (6a) and (6b), respectively. (For simplicity, the aspectual morpheme *le* is not represented in these trees, and it is assumed that the verb does not raise to I.)[1]

(6) a.

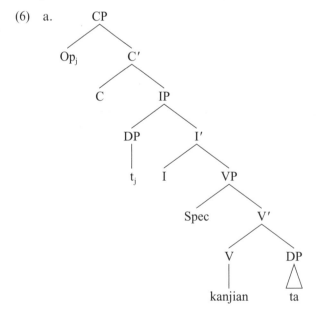

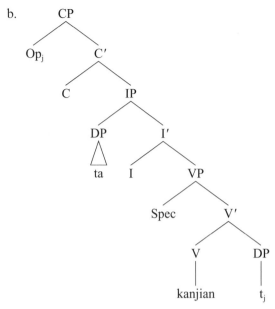

The empty operator is generated in subject or object position and is then moved to Spec CP. It leaves a trace in the base position (a trace being an empty category that receives case and is Ā-bound by an operator—here, the empty operator itself). Since the empty operator is null, it needs to be identified. Its identification is ensured in the discourse by a previously established discourse topic. For example, suppose the speaker is talking about Paul and says (5). Then *Paul* identifies the empty operator. Since the empty operator is identified in the preceding discourse, it is said to be *discourse bound*. Subject and object omission in Chinese depend on the availability of an empty discourse-bound operator. Null subjects and null objects in Chinese are known as *dropped topics* (see Huang 1984; Lillo-Martin 1986, 1991). Their occurrence is governed by the **topic-drop parameter** (or the *discourse-oriented parameter*).

Thus, there are thought to be two parameters governing the distribution of null subjects across languages: the pro-drop and topic-drop parameters.

(7) *Pro-drop parameter*

Are null pronominal subjects identified by ϕ-features (person, number) on I?

(8) *Topic-drop (or discourse-oriented) parameter*
Is a discourse-bound operator available to bind null subject (and object) variables?

5.1.2   The Pro-Drop Hypothesis

In an initial attempt to account for subject omission in early English, Hyams (1986) proposed that parameters in Universal Grammar (UG) have an unmarked value and that for the pro-drop parameter this value is positive. Because of this, children initially omit subjects. Under this view early subjectless sentences would have the same representation as subjectless sentences in (adult) Italian; subject position would be occupied by pro. The representation of (1b) would be (9).

(9)

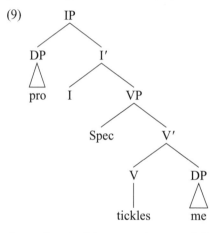

According to this account, around the age of 3 English learners discover that the value of the pro-drop parameter is not positive in their target language. They change the value of the parameter to negative and cease to omit subjects.

5.1.3   The Topic-Drop Hypothesis

An important theoretical question for Hyams's (1986) view is how the content of early null subjects is recovered. In pro-drop languages null subjects are identified by the ϕ-feature expressed on the verb. Such a mechanism is not available in early non-pro-drop languages like English, because these do not display a rich agreement system. For this reason, Hyams (1992) retracted her pro-drop proposal and claimed instead that early null subjects are of the Chinese kind since, like these, they do not

depend on φ-features for their identification. This is tantamount to saying that early null subjects arise from the positive setting of the topic-
drop parameter. Given these assumptions, this claim can be interpreted
by assuming that in early systems, as in Chinese, a null discourse-bound
operator is available that binds a variable left in subject position. Thus,
under this view the structure of an early subjectless sentence would look
like that of a null subject sentence in Chinese, and the representation of
(1b) would be (10).

(10)

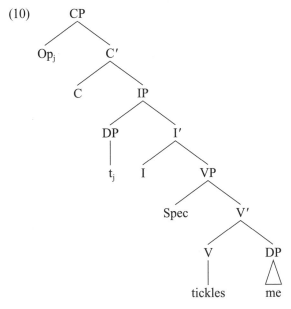

The null discourse-bound operator has moved from Spec IP to Spec CP,
and from there it Ā-binds the subject variable in Spec IP. The null operator is identified by a topic previously established in the discourse.

5.1.4   Evaluation of the Topic-Drop Hypothesis

Although the topic-drop analysis solves the problem of identifying
early null subjects, it faces other difficulties. As noted earlier, in discourse-
oriented languages objects can be dropped as well as subjects, as shown
in (5), repeated here.

(5) Ta kanjian —   le.
    he see   (him) ASP
    'He saw him.'

Table 5.1
Subject and object omission in early English and Chinese

	Age range	MLU range	Rate of subject omission	Rate of object omission
English	2;5–4;5	2.69–4.80	33.11%	3.75%
Chinese	2;0–4;4	2.41–5.98	46.54%	22.53%

Source: Data from Wang et al. 1992

If subject drop in early systems were the expression of the positive setting for the topic-drop parameter, English learners should drop objects as well. However, object drop is not an option in early English. Hyams and Wexler (1993) report that English-speaking children omit subjects at a rate of 48%, but omit objects at a significantly lower rate: 9%. This discrepancy makes the assimilation of early null subjects to null subjects in Chinese quite suspect (for responses to this criticism, see Hyams 1992; Hyams and Wexler 1993).

The viability of a topic-drop analysis of early null subjects is further undermined by a comparative study of early English and Chinese. Wang et al. (1992) offer evidence that both subject and object drop are possible in early Chinese (see also Lee 1996 and references cited there). By examining the speech of Chinese- and English-speaking children in the same age and mean-length-of-utterance (MLU) ranges, they also show that the rates of subject and object drop in early Chinese and English differ markedly (see table 5.1).

These data show convincingly that object drop is not an option in early English, but is a well-established option in early Chinese. Similar findings have been replicated for other discourse-oriented languages such as Japanese (see, e.g., Mazuka et al. 1986; Kim 1997). The differences between early English and Chinese reflect the role of the target language.[2] Chinese-speaking children have correctly set the topic-drop parameter and know that a discourse-bound operator is available in their language for identifying both null subjects and null objects. By parity of reasoning, we can conclude that English-speaking children know that their language does not have such a discourse-bound operator: they do not omit objects. Consequently, their omission of subjects cannot be reducible to an incorrect setting of the topic-drop parameter (see Weissenborn 1992 for further criticism).

5.1.5   Evaluation of the Pro-Drop Hypothesis and Structural Properties of Early Null Subjects

Hyams's (1986, 1992) contribution was invaluable, for it brought language acquisition within the realm of the principles-and-parameters approach and opened the possibility of generating precise predictions about the properties of early null subjects, which have been very fruitful for researchers' understanding of the phenomenon.

However, during the 1990s various structural and distributional differences between early null subjects and null subjects in adult pro-drop languages emerged, which cast doubt on the adequacy of a parameter-missetting analysis of early null subjects (see Valian 1990). It was found that early null subjects are impossible or highly infrequent in the following contexts:

(11) a. questions with a fronted *wh*-element (Valian 1990; but see Bromberg and Wexler 1995; Roeper and Rohrbacher 2000),
   b. subordinate clauses (see Valian 1990; Weissenborn 1992),
   c. matrix clauses with some fronted XP other than the subject (but see Haegeman 1995a).

By contrast, in adult pro-drop languages null subjects are allowed in all these contexts, as shown by the Italian data in (12), (13), and (14). These observations carry over to topic-drop languages as well, like Chinese, modulo the lack of overt *wh*-movement in these languages.

(12) Wh-*questions*
   Cosa hai   detto?
   what have (you) said

(13) *Subordinate clauses*
   Gianni ha detto che verrà.
   Gianni has said that (he) will come

(14) *Matrix clauses with a fronted adverb*
   Ieri   ho   parlato a Carlo.
   yesterday (I) have spoken to Carlo

In section 5.1.4 we saw that the null subject used by Chinese learners is qualitatively different from early English null subjects. Now we will see that the null subject used by Italian learners also has different properties from early null subjects in non-pro-drop languages. In early non-pro-drop languages null subjects are not found in *wh*-questions. By contrast, Italian learners omit subjects in a way consistent with the adult language—for example, in *wh*-questions (see Rizzi 1994). Guasti (1996, 2000) reports that null subjects are found in 56.1% of the *wh*-questions produced by 5 Italian-speaking children ranging in age from 1;7 to 2;10 (for discussion of early *wh*-questions, see chapter 6). Evidently, Italian learners must have correctly set the pro-drop parameter. As noted earlier, null subjects are identified via the φ-features expressed by the agreement morphemes on the verb (see (7)). The hypothesis that Italian learners have correctly set the pro-drop parameter predicts that these learners have command of agreement, to ensure the recovery of null subjects. Indeed, children speaking a pro-drop language demonstrate a firm knowledge of verbal agreement early on, as shown in section 4.3.1. This makes the hypothesis that Italian learners can identify null subjects through the mechanism adopted in the adult grammar highly plausible.

The distributional properties of early null subjects further support the conjecture that they are null subjects neither of the Italian type nor of the Chinese type.

5.1.6   Intermediate Summary

The influence of the target language is evident very early in children's speech. Null subjects in early Italian and Chinese exhibit the same structural privileges as null subjects in the adult languages. By contrast, null subjects in early English (Danish, French) share neither the properties of Italian null subjects nor those of Chinese null subjects. From these facts, we conclude that

(15) a. Italian learners have correctly set the pro-drop parameter
      (positive value),
   b. Chinese learners have correctly set the topic-drop parameter
      (positive value), and
   c. English learners have correctly set both the pro-drop and
      topic-drop parameters (negative value).

These conclusions force us to depart from a parameter-missetting approach and to examine the status of null subjects in early systems.

5.2   ROOT NULL SUBJECTS

In this section we will look in more detail at the properties of early null subjects, some of which we have touched upon earlier.

5.2.1 Structural Contexts of Early Null Subjects

As noted above, subject omission tends not to occur in the three environments listed in (11), repeated here:

(11) a. questions with a fronted *wh*-element,
     b. subordinate clauses, and
     c. matrix clauses with some fronted XP other than the subject.

A generalization that seems to emerge from (11) is that early null subjects are restricted to clause-initial position and are thus incompatible with constructions in which some other constituent must occupy this position, hence the term **root null subjects**.[3] Of the contexts in (11), here we will consider *wh*-questions more extensively, because they have been widely investigated. Haegeman (1996b) has shown that Dutch-speaking children rarely omit subjects from *wh*-questions (see table 5.2). Notice that Haegeman's data include just 10 counterexamples (2%) to the generalization in (11a). Evidence from early German also supports this generalization (Clahsen, Kursawe, and Penke 1995), as do transcripts from a French child, Philippe (Crisma 1992) (see table 5.3).

Table 5.2
Clause type and overtness of subjects in the speech of two Dutch learners. Data from Thomas (age range 2;3–2;11) and Hein (age range 2;4–3;1).

	Null subjects	Lexical subjects
Declaratives	1012	3238
Wh-questions	10	464

Source: Based on Haegeman 1996b
$\chi^2 = 118.46$, $p < .005$

Table 5.3
Clause type and overtness of subjects in the speech of a French learner. Data from Philippe (age range 2;1–2;7).

	Null subjects	Lexical subjects
Declaratives	488	1125
Wh-questions	2	311

Source: Based on Crisma 1992
$\chi^2 = 121.20$, $p < .005$

Crisma's outcomes are disputed by Phillips (1995) on the grounds that they are an artifact of verb type and not of clause type (*wh*-question vs. declarative). Noting that all verbs in Philippe's *wh*-questions are auxiliaries, Phillips concludes that the reluctance to use null subjects in *wh*-questions is a by-product of the reluctance to use null subjects with auxiliaries. He then points out that in early English null subjects seem to be rare with auxiliaries and modals. For example, in a cross-sectional study of 21 children Valian (1990) found from 1% to 6% subjectless declarative sentences with modals. Hamann and Plunkett (1998) observe a similar trend in the speech of Danish learners, reporting a 9% overall rate of null subjects with the copula 'be' and a 25% rate with finite lexical verbs. However, the paucity of null subjects with auxiliaries is not replicated in other early languages. Hamann and Plunkett (1998) report that Augustin, a French learner, omits more subjects with auxiliaries (34%) than with finite verbs (22%) (see Hamann, Rizzi, and Frauenfelder 1996; Rasetti 2000), although other French learners reverse this pattern.

In sum, then, null subjects do not occur in equal proportions with lexical verbs and with auxiliaries. However, some children omit subjects more often with lexical verbs than with auxiliaries, and other children show the reverse pattern. Rizzi (2000) points out that Phillips's proposal that lack of subject drop in *wh*-questions is a side effect of the use of auxiliaries would be sound only if children avoided null subjects with auxiliaries regardless of clause type. But because subjects are omitted in declarative clauses including auxiliaries, Phillips's proposal cannot be correct. Let us therefore accept as a significant generalization the idea that subject drop does not occur in *wh*-questions in early non-pro-drop languages. This situation contrasts sharply with the overwhelming frequency of null subjects in early Italian *wh*-questions (section 5.1.5). This is not surprising, since the early Italian null subject has the same properties as the adult Italian null subject and arises from the positive setting of the pro-drop parameter.

While evidence for the lack of null subjects in questions is abundant, there have been few systematic studies on subject omission or lack thereof in subordinate clauses. One exception is the study by Valian (1990), who found no null subjects in 123 examples of subordinate clauses in early English.

In early V2 languages such as Dutch and German, subjects tend to be expressed when a constituent other than the subject occupies clause-initial position. Although Haegeman (1995a) has found some noninitial null subjects, their proportion is very low. However, further studies are needed to better establish the proportions of null subjects in subordinate clauses and in noninitial positions of root clauses.

In conclusion, the early null subject obeys a strong structural constraint: it is bound to occur in clause-initial position. Equivalently, one can say that the early null subject is a root phenomenon.

5.2.2   Null Subjects and Root Infinitives

Subjects are omitted with finite verbs as well as with root infinitives (RIs). Some examples are reported in (16).

(16) a. Est   trop gros . . .   (Philippe, 2;2)
         (it) is too big
     b. Tourner dans l'autre   sens.   (Philippe, 2;2)
         turn-INF in   the other direction

Figure 5.1 plots the percentage of finite and nonfinite subjectless clauses in some early languages. Three notes are in order regarding this figure. (1) In the calculations the denominator is the sum of overt (nominal and pronominal) and null subjects. (2) For English the counts were limited

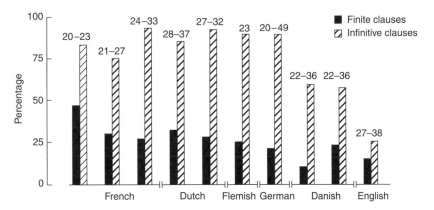

Figure 5.1
Percentage of subject omission in finite declarative clauses and infinitive clauses across languages. Each pair of bars shows the overall percentage of subject omission in the speech of a child in the age range (given in months) indicated above the bars. Data taken from Rasetti 2000 (French: Daniel, Nathalie, and Augustin); Haegeman 1995b (Dutch: Hein); Phillips 1995, crediting Krämer 1993 (Dutch: Thomas; Flemish: Maarten); Phillips 1995, crediting Beherens 1993 (German: Simone); Hamann and Plunkett 1998 (Danish: Anne, Jens); English (Sarah).

to verbs occurring with third person singular subjects, since English lexical verbs can be classified unambiguously as finite or nonfinite only when they occur in third person singular contexts. Although auxiliaries are marked overtly in other contexts besides third person singular, for uniformity the counts were limited to auxiliaries used with third person singular subjects. Finally, verbs marked with *-ing* but not accompanied by an auxiliary (e.g., *you speaking*) were not included. (3) Adult Dutch and German are topic-drop languages, but they exhibit some restrictions that Chinese does not. Nevertheless, data from early Dutch and German are included in the figure, because there is evidence that early null subjects in Dutch cannot all be the expression of the positive setting of the topic-drop parameter; at least some of them are like null subjects in other early languages, a claim to which we return in section 5.2.5.

The figure clearly shows that subject omission is a widespread phenomenon across early languages. Since it is not an option in the adult languages, we must conclude that (like other deviations of child language) it is not input driven.

Note that the rate of null subjects is much higher in infinitive clauses than in finite ones, although the null subject is clearly an option even with finite verbs. Hence, the available data do not warrant the conclusion that null subjects are limited to RIs (for discussion of this issue, see Rasetti 2000 and references cited there; also see Ingham 1992; O'Grady, Peters, and Masterson 1989).

Note also that the developmental trend for subject omission parallels the developmental trend for RIs. One might attribute this parallel development to the fact that subject omission occurs more frequently with infinitive than with finite clauses. If this view were correct, though, the observed parallelism would be a trivial fact: RIs require null subjects. However, the parallel development is observed even if we only consider subject omission in finite clauses. Hamann and Plunkett (1998) and Rasetti (2000) have compared the developmental curves of RIs with those of missing subjects in finite clauses only. Figures 5.2 and 5.3 illustrate such a comparison based on the speech of two children, one learning French (Philippe) and the other Danish (Anne). It is apparent from these figures that the developmental curves of RIs and of subject omission in finite clauses are parallel. Hamann and Plunkett report a high level of correlation between the rate of subject drop in finite clauses and the rate of RIs (Spearman's rank correlation: $\rho = 0.90$, $p < .0001$). The omission of subjects in finite clauses and the use of RIs are attested in child speech

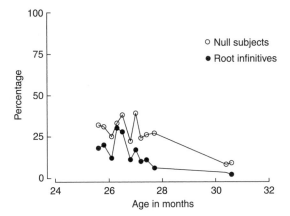

Figure 5.2
Percentage of missing subjects in finite clauses and of root infinitives in the speech of a French learner, Philippe (age range 2;1–2;6). Data taken from Rasetti 2000.

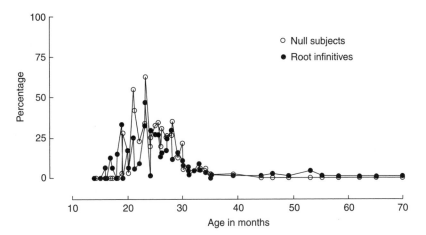

Figure 5.3
Percentage of missing subjects in finite clauses and of root infinitives in the speech of a Danish learner, Anne (age range 1;1–5;10). A similar figure appears in Hamann and Plunkett 1998; the data used here were kindly made available by the authors.

from the first multiword utterances and exhibit parallel development. Moreover, there is no period during which RIs are produced but null subjects are not. We can express this state of affairs as an implication.

(17) RIs → null subjects

This implication says that whenever a child's grammar allows the production of RIs, it also allows the omission of subjects. It is a one-way implication since null subjects may still be attested, at least for a short period, when RIs have disappeared from children's speech. The implication suggests that RIs and subject drop are somehow related, an observation that underlies the analysis of early null subjects to which we now turn.

5.2.3   The Truncation Analysis of Root Null Subjects

We have established that early null subjects have the following properties:

(18) a. They are a root phenomenon.
   b. Their development matches the development of RIs.

Rizzi (1993/1994) has proposed a unified account of early null subjects and RIs, claiming that these two phenomena arise from the same mechanism: the possibility of truncating clausal structures in early systems (for an alternative view, see Hoekstra and Hyams 1995). Recall that according to the **truncation hypothesis** (section 4.4.2.2), the following axiom holds in the adult grammar:

(19) *Axiom on clausal representation*
   CP is the root of all clauses (finite and infinitive).

In other words, any clause, main clauses included, starts with a CP, the highest projection, and thus includes all the phrasal projections that CP dominates.

   Early grammars differ from adult grammars in offering the option of clausal truncation; that is, in child grammars clauses may be truncated at levels lower than CP. As a result, some or all layers of functional projections can be omitted and several kinds of root clauses (e.g., VP, IP) can be produced. In other words, in child language VP or IP can become the root of a main clause. The truncation site cannot be arbitrarily chosen, however. Where truncation can apply depends on the morphosyntactic properties of the verb in the clause. RI clauses can be truncated at the VP level or at the projection above this (say, AspP), since infinitives do not overtly raise very high. Finite clauses may be minimally truncated at the IP level, since finite verbs in non-V2 languages generally raise to I in the overt syntax (an exception is English). In this way IP, rather than CP, can be the root of a finite clause. A finite subjectless sentence in child language, like (1b), would then be represented as in (20).

(20)

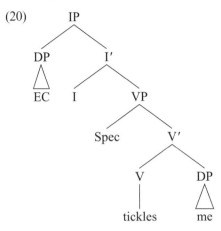

Temporarily the null subject is represented as an empty category (EC) in Spec IP, the specifier of the root; its nature will be made precise in the next section. The finite verb overtly raises to I or not, depending on language-particular properties (see section 4.2.1, table 4.1).

In conclusion, the occurrence of RIs indicates that the mechanism of clausal truncation is available in child grammar; it can operate at different structural levels and make different categories the root of the clause. When IP is the root of the clause, a null subject is legitimate in its specifier.

5.2.3.1 The Nature of the Empty Category

What kind of empty category is the null subject in (20)? To answer this question, Rizzi (1994) proposes to enrich the typology of empty categories by adding a new feature to the familiar [±anaphoric], [±pronominal]: namely, [±variable] (see Haegeman 1994, chap. 8, for a characterization of empty categories in terms of features). This allows a distinction between two types of Ā-bound empty elements: one with the feature content [−a, −p, +v] and the other with the feature content [−a, −p, −v]. The former is called *variable* and the latter **null constant** (NC). This partition between Ā-bound elements is motivated by certain so-called crossover effects brought to light by Lasnik and Stowell (1991) (see Haegeman 1994, sec. 7.7.2, for discussion of crossover). These effects are potentially found when an operator, moving from its base position to a surface position, crosses over a pronoun. For example, in (21) *who*, moving from the object position indicated by the trace to its surface position at the front of the sentence, crosses over the pronoun *his*.

(21) Who does his boss dislike t?

There are two types of crossover: weak and strong. True variables like the trace in (21) are subject to weak crossover (WCO) effects. Question (21) is well formed, but it cannot be interpreted as asking for which x, does x's boss dislike x. This interpretation would correspond to the representation in (22), where the pronoun *his* is coindexed with the trace of the *wh*-operator, a variable (and with the *wh*-operator as well). (The asterisk here indicates that the question is ungrammatical if *who*, *his*, and the trace are coindexed, that is, if it is interpreted as just described.)

(22) *Who$_i$ does his$_i$ boss dislike t$_i$?

(22) is an example of a weak crossover violation; the *wh*-operator crosses over the pronoun, but the pronoun does not c-command the trace of the operator, a variable.

By contrast, NCs are not subject to WCO effects. Consider (23a,b).

(23) a. The man$_i$, who$_i$ his$_i$ brother dislikes NC$_i$, is John.
      b. This$_i$ book, Op$_i$ I would never ask its$_i$ author to read NC$_i$.
          (from Lasnik and Stowell 1991)

(23a) may mean that the man x such that x's brother dislikes x is John (i.e., the man whose brother dislikes him is John); and (23b) may mean that this book x is such that I would never ask x's author to read x (i.e., as for this book, I would never ask its author to read it). These readings correspond to the representations in (23). In (23a) the pronoun *his* is coindexed with the trace of the *wh*-operator, an NC (and with the operator as well).[4] In (23b) the pronoun *its* is coindexed with the trace of the empty operator (and with the operator as well). Unlike in (22), in (23) the trace of the moved operator can be coindexed with the pronoun and with the trace as well, although it crosses the pronoun.

Being R-expressions, both true variables and NCs are subject to strong crossover (SCO) effects. Consider (24a–c) (where again the asterisks mean that the sentences are ungrammatical under the reported coindexation).

(24) a. *Who$_i$ does he$_i$ dislike t$_i$?
      b. *The man$_i$, who$_i$ he$_i$ dislikes NC$_i$, is John.
      c. *This child$_i$, he$_i$ wants to invite NC$_i$.

(24a) cannot be interpreted as asking for which x, x dislikes x (i.e., who dislikes himself). (24b) cannot mean that the man x who x dislikes x is John (i.e., the man who dislikes himself is John). And (24c) cannot mean that this child is such that he wants to invite himself. These interpretations are prohibited because in all these structures (a *wh*-question, a nonrestrictive relative clause, and a topicalization structure) the pronoun cannot be coindexed with the *wh*-expression or with the empty operator (and thus be Ā-bound by them). (24a–c) are all examples of strong crossover; the *wh*-operator or the other operators cross over the pronoun that c-commands the trace of the moved elements. The adjective *strong* is meant to convey that (24a–c) are much more sharply ungrammatical than (22).

In sum, Ā-bound empty categories are of two types: true variables and NCs. Variables are subject to WCO and SCO effects, (22) and (24a), while NCs are subject only to SCO effects, (24b,c). For our discussion, this distinction is sufficient (for more details, see Lasnik and Stowell 1991).

With this background let us return to the original question: which kind of empty category is the early null subject? In the adult language the NC is the trace of a moved operator (e.g., a relative operator as in (23a) or an empty operator as in (23b)). Rizzi (1994) argues that the NC can also arise as a base-generated empty category, not derived by movement of an operator, and that the early null subject is in fact an antecedentless NC located in Spec IP. Under these assumptions the representation of a subjectless sentence such as (1b) in child language is (25), with the NC in Spec IP.

(25)

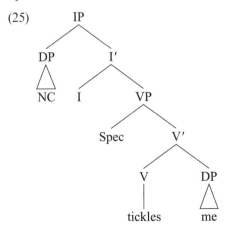

5.2.3.2 The Identification Requirement Nonpronominal empty categories need to be identified by an antecedent. The NC in (25) apparently violates this requirement: it cannot be identified sentence-internally. However, the NC can survive in a configuration like (25) if we adopt Rizzi's (1994) reformulation of the identification component of the Empty Category Principle (ECP) given in (26) (for a presentation of the ECP, see Haegeman 1994, sec. 8.2.1; also see Hornstein and Weinberg 1995).

(26) *Empty Category Principle (ECP) (revised)*
A nonpronominal empty category must be identified by an antecedent *if it can.*

The constraint requiring a nonpronominal empty category to be identified applies if a c-commanding antecedent is available for the empty category. If no such antecedent is available, an NC can survive without a sentence-internal identifier and without violating (26). Therefore, the NC is legitimate if it is in a position that is not c-commanded by a potential antecedent. Being highest in the clause and therefore obviously being dominated by nothing else, the specifier of the root qualifies as this position. Early null subjects are NCs in the specifier of the root, where the root is IP owing to clausal truncation.

To recapitulate:

(27) a. In child language the mechanism of clausal truncation allows projections other than CP to function as the root of a clause.
b. Clausal truncation allows early null subjects to occupy the specifier of the root.
c. Early null subjects are base-generated antecedentless NCs.
d. Since early null subjects occupy the specifier of the root, they have no potential antecedent and are thus exempted from the identification requirement in (26).

Different languages exhibit different types of null subjects. Null pronominal subjects (pro) are identified by ϕ-features expressed on the verb (section 5.1.1). These null subjects typically occur in languages with a rich agreement system, such as Italian, Spanish, and Catalan. In Chinese the null subject is a variable generated by movement of, and identified by, an empty discourse-bound operator.[5] In both cases the null subject is identified sentence-internally. Child language (as well as a special register of adult language; see section 5.2.4) presents a third type of null subject: an NC whose content is not identified sentence-internally, but is recovered directly through the discourse.[6]

5.2.3.3 Properties of Early Null Subjects The truncation hypothesis accounts as follows for the restrictions we have noted on the distribution of early null subjects.

Structural restrictions. NCs cannot survive in *wh*-questions, because these require the CP projection to accommodate movement of the *wh*-operator, as shown in (28b), the representation of (28a).

(28) a. What drinks?

b.

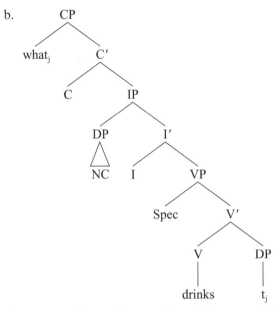

In (28b) Spec IP is not the specifier of the root, CP being present and serving as the root of the clause. The identification principle in (26) must be invoked: an antecedent identifying the NC is then required. Since there is no appropriate identifier, structure (28b) is ruled out. The same explanation carries over to embedded clauses and to clauses with a fronted XP. In all these cases the option of clausal truncation at the IP level cannot be exercised because CP is needed to accommodate clausal material. Thus, in such structures the NC cannot occupy the specifier of the root and (26) cannot be escaped.

Subject/object asymmetry. We have seen that while subjects can be omitted in child language, objects cannot. The explanation just offered for the nonoccurrence of subjectless *wh*-questions is also valid here. In the representation of a sentence with a null object, the NC would be in the base object position, as shown in (29b), the representation of (29a).

(29) a. John saw —.

b.

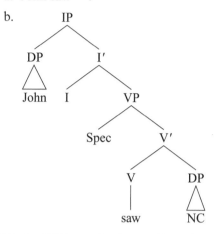

In (29b) the NC is not in the specifier of the root; hence, the identification principle in (26) becomes fully operative and the structure is ruled out because there is no suitable identifier for the NC.

5.2.4   Root Null Subjects in Adult Registers

Antecedentless NCs are not unique to early grammars. The closest analogue in adult language is the null subject in diaries (illustrated here with English and French examples from Haegeman 2000).

(30) a. Cried yesterday morning: as if it were an hour for keening: why is crying so pleasurable. (Plath 1983, 288)
   b. Elle est alsacienne. Paraît intelligente. (Léautaud 1989, 48)
      'She is Alsatian. Seems intelligent.'

This adult null subject in **diary style** presents the same structural characteristics as early null subjects: it is restricted to the specifier of root clauses and is therefore incompatible with *wh*-questions and embedded clauses (a few null subjects are found in clauses with a fronted adverb; see Haegeman 2000).

   In diaries, as in child language, only subjects can be dropped; objects cannot. Given these structural similarities, it has been proposed that the grammar of diaries also includes the mechanism of clausal truncation, allowing IP to be the root of the clause and allowing an NC to survive in Spec IP without violating (26).[7]

The existence of adult grammars that include a formal device allowing an antecedentless empty category in the specifier of the root is evidence for the continuity between child and adult grammars (see Rizzi 2000). The child grammar is couched in the vocabulary of an adult system; it includes the same grammatical objects and the same grammatical mechanisms, since both systems express options made available by UG.

5.2.5   Topic Drop and Early Null Subjects in V2 Languages

We have seen that topic drop is an option in languages like Chinese, Korean, and Japanese. Topic drop is also possible in the colloquial variety of some V2 languages, such as Dutch and German (but not others, such as Flemish and Danish). (31a) illustrates subject drop and (31b) object drop in German.

(31) a.   Hat Klaus gesehen.
             (he) has Klaus seen
             'He has seen Klaus.'
       b. Hat er   gesehen.
           has he (him/her/it) seen
           'He has seen him/her/it.'

In Germanic languages, unlike in Chinese, topic drop must occur clause-initially; that is, null topic clauses are verb-first clauses. Topic drop cannot occur clause-internally (e.g., in *wh*-questions and embedded clauses), as shown in (32). The symbol *( ) indicates that the material between parentheses cannot be omitted; if it is, the sentence becomes ungrammatical.

(32) a. Was hast *(du) gesehen?
         what have (you) seen
       b. Ich glaube dass *(er) ein Buch gelesen hat.
           I   believe that (he) a   book read   has
       c. Heute habe *(ich) ein Buch gelesen.
           today have (I)   a   book read

Topic drop in these Germanic varieties is analyzed in much the same way as it is in Chinese, modulo the restriction to clause-initial position. Topic drop is seen as the expression of the positive setting of the topic-drop parameter, given in (8). In these varieties an empty discourse-bound operator is available that moves to Spec CP from either the subject or the object position, where it leaves a trace. Accordingly, the structure of (31a,b) is as shown in (33a,b).[8]

(33) a.

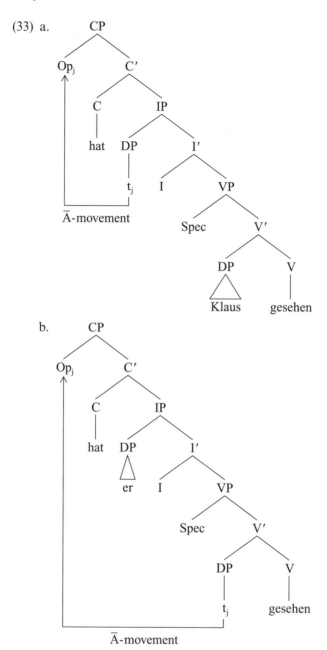

The existence of topic drop in colloquial Dutch and German raises the question of the status of null subjects in early Dutch and German. So far

we have simply assumed that they are like null subjects in other early
languages, that is, antecedentless NCs in Spec IP. It is time to look at
evidence for this assumption.

It is a matter of debate whether null subjects in early German and
Dutch are true dropped topics, analyzed as in (33a), or antecedentless
NCs, as in other early languages. De Haan and Tuijnman (1988) and
Verrips and Weissenborn (1992) take the first stance, while Haegeman
(1995a) takes the second. Analyzing data from early Dutch, Haegeman
points out that

(34) a. early null subjects, but not dropped topics, can be quasi
arguments or expletives; and that
    b. developmentally, in Dutch learners' speech the decrease in null
subjects parallels the decrease in RIs.

In adult Germanic languages, quasi arguments and expletives cannot
be dropped. This is exemplified in (35a,c) for Dutch and in (35b,d) for
German.[9]

(35) a. *(Er) werd gedanst.
    b. *(Es) wird getanzt.
       (there) is   danced
    c. *(Het) regent.
    d. *(Es) regnet.
       (it)   rains

By contrast, quasi arguments and expletive null subjects can be omitted in
early Dutch. Children's transcripts include both (36a), with a subject, and
(36b,c), without subjects.

(36) a. 't regent. (Hein, 2;7)
       it rains
    b. Regent beetje? (Niek, 3;6)
       (it) rains a little
    c. Was   heel donker. (Thomas, 2;4)
       (it) was very dark

However, as Haegeman (1995a) herself notes, the omission of expletive
subjects is not robustly attested. The three children she studied (Hein,
Niek, and Thomas) produced only 19 sentences requiring a quasi-
argumental subject. Of these 7 had an overt quasi-argumental subject and
12 lacked it.

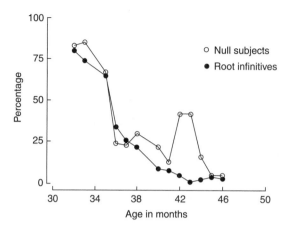

Figure 5.4
Percentage of missing subjects in finite clauses and of root infinitives in the speech of a Dutch learner, Niek (age range 2;8–3;10). Data from Haegeman 1995a.

A more compelling argument comes from the observation that RIs and null subjects display similar development. As in the speech of the French and Danish learners examined in section 5.2.2, subject omission and RIs decline in parallel fashion in early Dutch. Figure 5.4 illustrates this fact in the speech of Niek, which at first exhibits a high percentage of RIs and null subjects and then a decrease.

This pattern suggests a distinction between null subjects in adult and early Dutch. In adult Dutch null subjects are null topics analyzed as in (33a). Haegeman (1995a) concludes that in early Dutch (and by extension in early German) null subjects originate from the option of clausal truncation and are NCs occupying the specifier of the root (i.e., Spec IP), as in other early languages. This view explains the parallel developmental course of null subjects and RIs.

Although Haegeman's (1995a) arguments are sound, her claims are too strong. Proponents of the other view, that null subjects in early Dutch are dropped topics, explain the decrease in null subjects by appealing to a gradual mastery of the pragmatic conditions for dropping subjects; they fail, however, to capture the similarity between missing subjects and RIs. As a result, their view may also not be defensible in its strong form. Nonetheless, it is likely that it can be maintained in a weaker form compatible with a weaker version of Haegeman's (1995a) proposal. We have seen that at least some parameters are fixed to the correct value early in children's linguistic experience. For example, learners assign the positive (Italian and Chinese) or negative (English, French, etc.) value to the parameters responsible for missing subjects in their language. It would be surprising if Dutch learners did not set the topic-drop parameter (to the positive value). However, a more viable hypothesis is that they indeed set the topic-drop parameter, but like children speaking English or French, they have access to another option, the antecedentless NC. Therefore, from their first multiword utterances, Dutch and German learners produce subjectless clauses that can be either truncated structures with a null subject in Spec IP or full clauses with an empty discourse-bound operator in Spec CP binding the subject trace in Spec IP. In other words, a Dutch or German subjectless sentence like (37a) can have one of the structural representations in (37b,c), at least if the null subject is not an expletive or a quasi argument, in which case only the representation in (37b) would be valid. Notice that this solution forces one to assume that I is head initial in Dutch, at least in structures such as (37b,c), an assumption that is not without consequences (see also section 4.2.4.2). (In (37b) V is also head initial.)

(37) a. Trinke   Apfelsaft.
      (I) drink apple juice

    b.

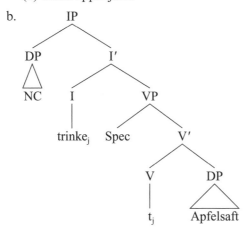

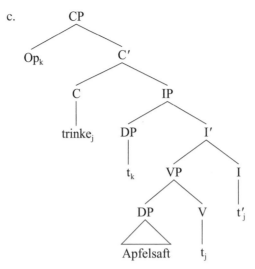

Around 3 years the structural option in (37b) disappears, and only the option in (37a) remains valid. As a result, the rate of null subjects declines; still, some null subjects remain because they are dropped topics, as in the target language.

5.2.6   Null Subjects in Root Infinitive Clauses

So far we have been dealing with null subjects in finite clauses. However, as figure 5.1 shows, subjects are omitted from children's RI clauses as well. RIs are structures truncated at the VP level. Therefore, the null subject in RI clauses is in Spec VP, or in some higher functional specifier —but in any event, in the specifier of the root. What kind of empty category is this null subject? Nothing prevents us from analyzing it as an NC, like the null subject in finite clauses. However, with infinitive clauses other options are open as well. In the adult language nonfinite verbs license PRO subjects (see chapter 10). If we want to minimize the difference between the adult and child grammars, the more plausible assumption is that null subjects in RI clauses are PRO. Hence, the structure of a subjectless RI clause like (38a) is (38b).

(38) a. Have two crackers.   (Eve, 1;8)

b.

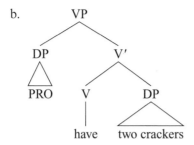

Thus, early clauses exhibit two types of null subjects: PRO in RI clauses and the NC in finite clauses. Notice that the assumption that RI clauses include PRO presents a problem. In adult languages PRO either is controlled by an antecedent and refers to some specific individual or is uncontrolled and can refer to anyone. In RI clauses PRO is uncontrolled; however, it cannot refer to just anyone, instead picking out some individual through the context—a process that is hard to capture formally (but see section 10.2.2). (To pursue the pros and cons of this hypothesis further, see Rasetti 2000 and Rizzi 2000.)

5.2.7 Intermediate Summary

Around 2 years of age, when they start to combine words, children have correctly set the parameters that govern the distribution of null subjects across languages. Early finite subjectless sentences in non-pro-drop and non-topic-drop languages do not arise from an incorrect setting of the relevant parameters. Instead, they arise from another option governing the projection of functional categories in child grammar: the mechanism of clausal truncation. Early null subjects are antecedentless NCs licensed in the specifier of the root. RI clauses also include null subjects, which can be either NCs or PROs.

5.3 PERFORMANCE ACCOUNTS

In this section we turn to other approaches to early null subjects, which view them as the expression of performance limitations.

Like competence-based accounts of subject omission, performance-based accounts posit that the child grammar is like the adult grammar; that is, children know that subjects are obligatory. These accounts attribute subject omission not to a grammatical option, but to processing deficits, whose nature, in general, is extralinguistic. They claim that the language processor operates under the processing demands of the various cognitive systems (e.g., memory) and that these are more severely constrained in children than in adults. Consequently, in producing sentences, children omit subjects to alleviate the processing load and to release resources for planning and uttering the most informative parts of sentences. Various sorts of processing accounts have been proposed; here we will consider two. One sees early null subjects as the processing system's response to risks of overload; the other attributes them to difficulties in producing certain phonological structures. (For additional discussion, see Bloom 1970; Bloom 1990; Valian 1990; Valian, Hoffner, and Aubry 1996. For criticism of these accounts, see Hyams and Wexler 1993; Lillo-Martin 1994; Rizzi 2000.)

5.3.1   The Sentence Length Account of Subject Omission

Bloom (1990) claims that early null subjects arise from a performance limitation on **sentence length**. The longer a planned utterance, the more processing resources it demands. It is conjectured that children's processing capacities are limited and that the processing load is greatest at the beginning of an utterance. Consequently, elements at the start of a clause are more likely to be dropped than elements at the end (see also Bloom 1970; Valian, Hoffner, and Aubry 1996). Subjects, which generally come first in a sentence, are more frequently omitted than clause-internal arguments. This approach explains why subjects are more frequently omitted than objects and why subjects are not omitted in *wh*-questions: in neither case would the missing element occupy first position.

One criticism of this proposal is that subjects are omitted more frequently in nonfinite than in finite environments. Yet finite environments are morphologically more complex than nonfinite ones: in English they require the presence of an extra morpheme that nonfinite verbs do not have (Schütze 1997). Other things being equal, the processing demands should be greater for producing a finite than a nonfinite clause; thus, more subjects should be omitted in finite clauses.

Bloom (1990) points out that children's subjectless sentences are longer than their sentences with subjects, because by dropping the subject children can allocate resources for planning longer sentences (but see Hyams and Wexler 1993; Hamann and Plunkett 1998). There is little doubt that a correlation between sentence length and subject omission exists; as Hyams and Wexler (1993) note, the same correlation is even present in adult Italian, a pro-drop language. However, this certainly does not imply that the adult Italian null subject has its roots in processing limitations. The correlation between sentence length and subject omission, then, is a very disputable piece of evidence. Processing considerations may very well affect children's production, as they affect adults' production, but they can hardly override grammatical competence (see Rizzi 2000). The observed correlation between subject omission and sentence length can be integrated into a competence-based analysis of subject omission by claiming that processing constraints may favor subject omission, but this option must be first of all grammatically sanctioned.

5.3.2   The Metrical Account of Subject Omission

Another performance-based account of subject omission is Gerken's (1991) **metrical account**. Unlike other performance-based accounts, it locates children's difficulty in a language-specific mechanism, the speech production system. English-speaking children's subjectless sentences are said to arise from a preference for the trochaic foot, a metrical unit formed by a strong syllable (S) followed by a weak one (W). This preference, which likely stems from the fact that the trochee is the most common foot in English (and across languages), is observed in experiments with English learners (see section 3.1.2.4). According to the metrical hypothesis, children apply a metrical template, the trochaic foot, to their intended utterance; they align the strong syllable of the template with the strong syllable of the intended utterance and omit all weak syllables that do not fit the template. This strategy has the effect that, for example, children are more likely to drop the first syllable of *giraffe*, which is weak, than they are to drop the second syllable of *zebra*, which is also weak. In other words, they are more likely to say *raffe* than *ze*. Let us see in detail how this strategy works. Consider (39) and (40).

(39) a.   gi-raffe
      b. Metrical structure   W S
      c. Trochaic template   S(W)

(40) a.   ze-bra
      b. Metrical structure   S W
      c. Trochaic template   S W

The first syllable of *giraffe* is weak. Therefore, it cannot be aligned with the strong syllable of the trochaic template, and it is dropped. Then the second syllable of *giraffe*, which is strong, is aligned with the first (strong) syllable of the template, and the child says *raffe*. By contrast, the first, strong syllable of *zebra* is aligned with the strong syllable of the trochaic template, and its second, weak syllable with the weak syllable of the template. The metrical structure and trochaic templates being perfectly aligned, no syllable is omitted (see also Gerken 1994a,b, 1996b).

The trochaic template also applies in children's multiword utterances. Simplifying somewhat, suppose the child plans a sentence like (41a), whose metrical structure is (41b).

(41) a.   She kissed him.
     b. Metrical structure   W   S   W
     c. Trochaic template   S   W

The subject pronoun *she* is a weak syllable that is dropped since it does not fit the trochaic template. *Kissed* being a strong syllable, it is aligned with the strong syllable of the trochaic template; *him* being weak, it is aligned with the weak syllable of the template. Thus, the child produces *Kissed him*, which fits the trochaic template.

Under this view missing subjects must be pronouns, which are omitted because they are prosodically weak syllables that do not fit the trochaic template. Object pronouns, which at the metrical level are also weak syllables, are not omitted because they can be footed into the trochaic template, as shown in (41): the pronoun *him* is the second syllable of the trochee. This proposal accounts for why subjects are omitted more frequently than objects: subjects, being the first element of a clause, are weak syllables that do not fit the trochaic template, while objects are often footed with the strong syllable of the preceding verb. It also explains why early null subjects occur in clause-initial position. Under Gerken's approach this follows from the fact that a weak syllable in first position does not fit the trochaic foot and thus tends not to be pronounced. By contrast, object pronouns (or even subject pronouns) in sentence-internal positions can form a trochaic foot with a preceding strong syllable and thus do tend to be pronounced.

The metrical hypothesis has been formulated primarily to account for English data; whether it can be extended to account for subject omission in other early languages remains to be determined. In part, this depends on whether the preference for the trochee is language specific or universal. In any event, there is one fact the metrical hypothesis does not capture;

namely, the correlation between null subjects and RIs (see section 5.2.2). How can metrical factors be held responsible for RIs? One can hardly deny that metrical factors may play a role in children's production, since there is overwhelming evidence that children are very sensitive to prosodic properties. Still, the view most consistent with the data again seems to be the one mentioned in the previous section: prosodic preferences may favor the omission of subjects, but this omission is governed by syntactic constraints.

5.4 SUMMARY AND CONCLUDING REMARKS

Since Hyams's (1986) seminal work researchers have pursued the notion that the null subject is a grammatical option of early systems. In the 1980s subject omission was attributed to a missetting of the parameters governing the lexical expression of subjects across languages. In the 1990s this approach was abandoned under the pressure of new evidence that early null subjects have their own structural properties distinguishing them from null subjects in pro-drop and topic-drop languages. These null subjects cannot be modeled after the adult targets (French, English, Danish) because the latter do not include null subjects. They are instead the expression of a rule-governed mechanism whose source is UG: namely, clausal truncation. More precisely, they are antecedentless empty categories, NCs, occupying the specifier of the root (clause-initial position). Like any empty category in natural language, they are subject to licensing conditions that are not unique to child language. The diary style, an adult register, manifests null subjects with the same structural properties as early null subjects, providing evidence for a continuity view of child and adult language. Children pick up options that UG makes available.

The influence of the target language is evident in children's subject omission. Chinese and Italian learners omit subjects in the same structural environments in which adults omit them. We have interpreted these facts as evidence that Chinese and Italian learners have correctly fixed the value of the relevant parameter (positive value). By parity of reasoning, we have concluded that learners of languages that do not allow subject omission must also have correctly fixed the value of the relevant parameters (negative value). Otherwise, it would be mysterious why they do not behave like Chinese or Italian learners. Along with other parameters (see section 4.5), the pro-drop and topic-drop parameters are correctly set early on, showing once again that children are very quick at detecting the regularities of their target language. We conjecture that this is because they know which regularities they have to pay attention to, since UG guides them in their search.

Besides grammatical accounts, a number of performance-based accounts of the early null subject have flourished, viewing it as the response of a severely limited cognitive system to processing demands. Evidence suggests that by themselves these performance-based accounts are unlikely to explain children's production. A more plausible view is that processing demands may orient certain grammatical options and favor some of them over others when processing demands are excessive. However, they cannot supplant a grammatical option, either in child language or in adult language.

Although theorists have reached a certain level of well-grounded knowledge about the properties of early null subjects, some problems deserve further investigation. One is the presence of null subjects in early English *wh*-questions (see note 3; also see Bromberg and Wexler 1995; Roeper and Rohrbacher 2000). At first sight this phenomenon contradicts the claim in (11a) that null subjects do not occur in *wh*-questions. However, closer inspection reveals other facts. In all English *wh*-questions in which the subject is omitted, the verb is bare or inflected with *-ing*; that is, it is a nonfinite form. By contrast, null subjects in English declarative sentences are found in both finite and nonfinite contexts (recall figure 5.1). Although present understanding of the phenomenon is still poor, this asymmetry casts doubt on attempts to equate null subjects in declaratives and in *wh*-questions, especially because early English is the sole language where the latter case is found. One conjecture about how to make sense of these findings is offered by Rizzi (2000). He proposes that early English displays two kinds of null subjects. One is the NC, which is found in all the other early non-pro-drop (or non-topic-drop) languages and can only occur in the root of the clause. The other, which is likely to be PRO, can occur in *wh*-questions. Although it seems reasonable to assume that there are two types of null subjects in early English, it is less obvious how to explain why only early English displays this property. Granting that there is another kind of null subject in early *wh*-questions solves some problems, but raises others, answers to which depend on the analysis of subjectless *wh*-questions. This is a puzzle that future research may try to address.

Summary of Linguistic Development

Between 2 and 3 years children

a. omit sentential subjects,
b. have correctly fixed the value of the topic-drop and pro-drop parameters.

Further Reading

Prévost and White 2000 examines subject drop in the speech of French and German young L2 learners. Hamann 1996 discusses sentence-internal null subjects in the speech of 3-year-old German learners, treating them as distinct from early root null subjects. Müller, Crysmann, and Kaiser 1996 analyzes object drop in the speech of a French-German bilingual child.

Key Words

Diary style
Metrical account of subject omission
Null constant
Pro-drop parameter
Root null subject
Sentence length account of subject omission
Topic-drop parameter
Truncation hypothesis

Study Questions

1. Although subjects cannot be omitted from *wh*-questions (with a fronted *wh*-), they are omitted from yes/no questions. Between 2;1 and 2;2 Philippe, a French learner, was found to omit 25% of subjects from yes/no questions and 42% from declarative sentences (Crisma 1992). How can this fact be explained within the truncation approach?

2. Why was the idea that children misset the pro-drop or topic-drop parameter abandoned?

3. What are the structural restrictions on the occurrence of early null subjects?

4. What is the major difference between null subjects in early Italian and, for example, early French?

5. What arguments favor the idea that early Dutch, like other early languages, includes the antecedentless NC?

6. What is the relation between early null subjects and root infinitives?

7. Discuss the nature of null subjects in infinitive clauses.

Chapter 6
Acquisition of *Wh*-Movement

INTRODUCTION

Having dealt in chapter 4 with children's formation of declarative sentences, we now turn attention to structures derived by movement of some constituent of the clause: *wh*-questions (based on main clauses and embedded clauses) and relative clauses. In English and in other languages *wh*-questions are derived by preposing a *wh*-word in front of the clause. The standard analysis of relative clauses holds that they also arise via *wh*-movement of an overt or covert operator. By looking at these two constructions, we will investigate the emergence of *wh*-movement in children's grammar. We will see that from their early productions children obey the demands of a universal constraint governing question formation, the *Wh*-Criterion. Moreover, they set the correct value of the parameters encoding crosslinguistic variations on the way the *Wh*-Criterion is satisfied. This general picture is valid for most early languages that have been studied (e.g., German, Italian, Swedish); from the beginning, *wh*-questions are target consistent. Although data from early English are compatible with this conclusion, some deviations from the adult target are observed. For example, English learners produce many *wh*-questions lacking an auxiliary (*What you eat?*) and sometimes, although not often, fail to invert the auxiliary (*What he can eat?*). We will see that this discrepancy is only apparent: English learners also master the basic ingredients of question formation, the nonadult structures being attributable to language-specific factors.

With regard to relative clauses, we will concentrate on two issues: the structure children assign to relative clauses and the mechanism they use to derive them. Although it was once believed that children treat relative clauses as coordinate structures, more recent evidence suggests that this view is not correct. Instead, early relative clauses have a hierarchical structure that involves the mechanism of recursion. A source of debate is whether early relative clauses are derived by *wh*-movement or not. We will examine arguments favoring the view that they are—a hypothesis that allows us to maintain a continuity view of child and adult grammar.

This chapter is organized as follows. Section 6.1 deals with the formation of *wh*-questions in early systems. Section 6.2 discusses one kind of nonadult *wh*-question: auxiliary-lacking ("auxless") questions in early English. Section 6.3 considers application of *wh*-movement from an embedded clause (long-distance *wh*-movement) and section 6.4, early relative clauses.

6.1   QUESTION FORMATION IN EARLY SYSTEMS

In this section we will examine *wh*-question formation in early systems. (We will not consider questions having a potentially formulaic pattern (*What's that?*, *What's this?*), concentrating instead on productive questions.) As background, let us look at the constraints governing question formation in the adult language.

6.1.1   The *Wh*-Criterion

In English, nonsubject constituent questions feature the fronting of a *wh*-operator and **subject-auxiliary inversion** (SAI), as (1) illustrates.

(1) a. What can he eat?
    b. Where does he go?

SAI results in a configuration in which the fronted *wh*-operator and the verb are adjacent. The same two elements are also adjacent in questions in other languages, such as Italian. Unlike in English, however, in Italian adjacency is obtained by placing the subject in a left- or right-peripheral position or by using a null subject. The three possibilities are illustrated in (2).

(2) a. *Subject in left-peripheral position*
       Gianni cosa fa?
       Gianni what makes
       'What does Gianni make?'
    b. *Subject in right-peripheral position*
       Cosa fa   Gianni?
       what makes Gianni
       'What does Gianni make?'

   c. *Null subject*
     Cosa fa?
     what makes
     'What does (he) make?'

Rizzi (1996) has interpreted the adjacency requirement between the *wh*-operator and the verb in (1) and (2) in terms of a well-formedness constraint on question formation, the ***Wh*-Criterion** (see also May 1985).

(3) Wh-*Criterion*
   a. A *wh*-operator must be in a specifier-head relation with a head carrying the *wh*-feature.
   b. A head carrying the *wh*-feature must be in a specifier-head relation with a *wh*-operator.

The *Wh*-Criterion is a universal constraint on question formation that may be satisfied overtly or covertly. This aspect of crosslinguistic variation is encoded by parameters that we will look at shortly.

Consider the representation in (4).

(4)

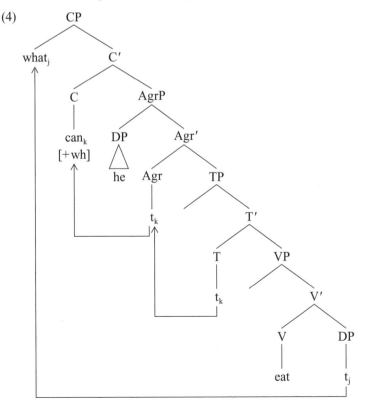

Suppose that the *wh*-feature is generated in T (under the hypothesis that a clausal representation includes AgrP and TP). If nothing happened, the *Wh*-Criterion would not be satisfied since the *wh*-operator and the *wh*-feature, each in its base position, would not be in a specifier-head relation. To satisfy the *Wh*-Criterion, the *wh*-operator must move to Spec CP and the *wh*-feature to C, as depicted in (4). Since lexical verbs do not move in English, they cannot carry the *wh*-feature to C. Instead, if an auxiliary or a modal is present in T, it carries the *wh*-feature to C; otherwise, the carrier is the pleonastic verb *do*. By contrast, in Italian all verbs move and thus can carry the *wh*-feature to C.[1] Movement of the *wh*-operator and of the *wh*-feature yields the surface forms in (1) and (2).[2]

Overt fronting of the *wh*-operator is not a universal property of *wh*-questions. In languages such as Chinese, Japanese, and Korean the *wh*-element stays in situ, as in (5) (Japanese, from Haegeman 1994).

(5) John-wa   naze kubi-ni natta no?
    John-TOPIC why was   fired QUESTION MARKER
    'Why was John fired?'

In this type of language the *Wh*-Criterion is satisfied at LF by covert movement of the *wh*-element to Spec CP and of the *wh*-feature to C. Thus, the *Wh*-Criterion holds universally, but its satisfaction is governed by the parameters in (6) (see Haegeman 1994, chap. 7, for discussion of *wh*-movement).

(6) *P1:* Overt movement vs. in-situ placement of the *wh*-element
    P2: Application or nonapplication of I-to-C movement

(*I-to-C movement* is a more technical term referring to what was long known as *subject-auxiliary inversion* (SAI). The term *head component of the* Wh-*Criterion* also refers to SAI. For convenience, the three terms will be used interchangeably.)

With this background, let us look now at whether children's questions satisfy the *Wh*-Criterion and how children handle the parameters governing *wh*-movement.

6.1.2   Crosslinguistic Evidence for Early Acquisition of *Wh*-Movement

The *Wh*-Criterion includes both a specifier component and a head component. Although Rizzi (1996) views these components as two sides of the same coin, we will examine them separately, as if they were independent. In this section we will deal with the specifier component.

For the sake of argument, let us suppose that the specifier component of the *Wh*-Criterion were inoperative in certain early languages. If English, Italian, and German learners disregarded the specifier component and did not set the parameter P1 governing placement of the *wh*-element, we would expect them to produce *wh*-questions in which the *wh*-element had not moved to clause-initial position, that is, structures like these, with the auxiliary/verb moved (7d–f) or not (7a–c) (remember that German is an OV language and thus the unmoved *wh*-element precedes the verb, like any other complement):

(7) a. *John has eaten what?   (English)
    b. *Gianni ha mangiato cosa?   (Italian)
       Gianni has eaten   what
    c. *Johann hat was gegessen?   (German)
       Johann has what eaten
    d. *Has John eaten what?   (English)
    e. *Ha mangiato cosa Gianni?   (Italian)
       has eaten   what Gianni
    f. *Hat Johann was gegessen?   (German)
       has Johann what eaten

Guasti (2000) examined the transcripts of 4 English-speaking children aged between 1;6 and 5;1 (Adam, Eve, Sarah, Nina). She found that over-all these children asked 2,809 *wh*-questions, 41 of which (1%) had a *wh*-element in situ (*wh*-in-situ). From context, she established that most of these 41 questions, perhaps even all, were echo questions. They lacked an auxiliary and were scattered throughout the period investigated (i.e., not limited to the earliest transcripts). These echo questions are target consistent, since echo questions do not involve *wh*-movement even in the adult grammar. We can conclude that *wh*-in-situ does not take priority over *wh*-movement in the English grammar, even though echo questions may be a source of conflicting evidence for the English-learning child. English-learning children do observe *wh*-movement in standard questions, and they avoid it in echo questions. (Roeper and de Villiers (1992) suggest that to explain why children are not confused by this conflicting evidence, we need to add to the parametric theory the assumption that if *wh*-movement occurs in a particular language, the counterevidence is consid-ered to be exceptional. Since *wh*-movement occurs frequently in English, echo questions, which feature *wh*-in-situ, are taken to be exceptions.)

The conclusion that children apply *wh*-movement whenever it is required is corroborated by analyses of questions in early Italian and early Swedish (see Guasti 2000; Santelmann 1998). Other studies that have looked at *wh*-questions in early languages do not report failures to apply *wh*-movement (see Haegeman 1995a for Dutch; Clahsen, Kursawe, and Penke 1995 for German). Notice that there is no intrinsic prohibition against *wh*-in-situ in the early grammar; if the adult language features it, so does the early language. According to Hamann (2000), French-speaking children, like French-speaking adults, produce both *wh*-in-situ questions and questions with a fronted *wh*-operator. These facts allow us to conclude that children set the parameter governing the placement of *wh*-elements, P1 in (6), very early, and that the specifier component of the *Wh*-Criterion is operative from the earliest productions. *Wh*-movement always occurs in questions whenever it is required in the target system.

6.1.3   Crosslinguistic Evidence for Early Acquisition of Verb Movement in Interrogatives

Now let us look at the head component of the *Wh*-Criterion. As a first step, consider early Italian. If Italian learners did not adhere to the head component of the *Wh*-Criterion, they would be expected to produce questions in which adjacency between the fronted *wh*-element and the verb is interrupted by the subject, as in (8).

(8) *Cosa Gianni fa?
     what Gianni makes

To test this prediction, Guasti (1996, 2000) investigated the production of 5 Italian learners (age range 1;7–2;10). She counted 130 questions with an overt subject, in all but 5 of which the subject appeared in left- or right-peripheral position. The 5 exceptions displayed the order Wh S V, and all were questions introduced by the *wh*-operator *perchè* 'why'. Since *perchè* appears in constructions with this order even in the adult grammar, even these questions cannot be considered ungrammatical. Italian learners never place the subject between the *wh*-operator and the verb, producing ungrammatical structures like (8). One can conclude, then, that the head component of the *Wh*-Criterion is in place in early Italian.

Investigation of early V2 languages reveals that the head component of the *Wh*-Criterion is in place here as well. As in declarative sentences in V2 languages (see section 4.2.4.2), in *wh*-questions the finite verb moves to second position in the clause, preceding the subject. In addition, an XP,

Table 6.1
Questions displaying or not displaying I-to-C movement in early German, Italian, and Swedish

Language	Number of subjects	Age range	Questions displaying I-to-C movement	Questions not displaying I-to-C movement
German	9	1;7–3;8	703	6
Italian	5	1;7–2;10	125	5
Swedish	13	1;9–3;0	—[a]	5 (1%)

Source: Data from Clahsen, Kursawe, and Penke 1995; Guasti 1996; Santelmann 1998
[a] The source does not give the number of questions displaying I-to-C movement, but the instances in which I-to-C movement fails represent 1% of the total.

the *wh*-operator, raises to Spec CP, as illustrated by the German example in (9a) and its representation in (9b).

(9) a. Was isst Julia zum Frühstück?
   what eats Julia for breakfast
   'What does Julia eat for breakfast?'
   b. [$_{CP}$ Was [$_C$ isst] [$_{IP}$ Julia zum Frühstück]]?

The analysis of *wh*-questions proposed above naturally extends to questions in V2 languages: the *wh*-element raises to Spec CP and the verb carries the *wh*-feature to C. Santelmann (1998) looked at questions in the speech of 13 Swedish learners (age range 1;9–3;0) and found only 5 questions (1%) in which the verb was not moved. Similarly, Clahsen, Kursawe, and Penke (1995) found only 6 noninverted finite verbs in 709 questions in the speech of 9 German learners (age range 1;7–3;8).

   The data showing that children apply I-to-C movement in questions are summarized in table 6.1. Clearly, there is a fair amount of crosslinguistic evidence that children raise the verb to C so that it can enter into a specifier-head relation with the *wh*-operator in Spec CP. This shows that they do obey the head component of the *Wh*-Criterion.

   Let us now look at English. If English learners did not respect the demands of the head component of the *Wh*-Criterion, they would be expected to produce questions like (10), with a noninverted auxiliary (recall that in English only auxiliaries can move to C).

(10) *What John has done?

This expectation has been extensively investigated since Bellugi's (1971) seminal work. After studying the natural speech of Adam, Eve, and Sarah, Bellugi proposed that the acquisition of the head component, more popularly known as the acquisition of SAI, proceeds in a piecemeal fashion. Before achieving the adult grammar of question formation, children pass through the following stages:

(11) *Stages of the acquisition of SAI*
       a. SAI is performed in yes/no questions, but not in *wh*-questions.
       b. SAI is performed in positive questions, but not in negative
          questions.

Since 1971 a number of researchers have investigated these stages, with conflicting results (see Stromswold 1990 for a critical discussion of the literature; see Radford 1994 for an analysis of Bellugi's stages from the point of view of the principles-and-parameters framework). The evidence for the first stage is very controversial. For the second, the data show not only that SAI lags in negative questions, but also that the presence of the negation evokes different kinds of nonadult structures.

When English learners start to use auxiliaries in questions, they generally perform SAI. (In the initial stage children produce questions with auxiliaries and questions without auxiliaries. Obviously the latter cannot be included in the counts for assessing whether children fail to perform SAI, since no auxiliary is present.) Investigating the speech of 12 children whose transcripts are included in the CHILDES database, Stromswold (1990) found that in positive questions including an auxiliary these children inverted the auxiliary 93.4% of the time (with individual rates ranging from 54% to 98% and a median inversion rate of 95%; see Stromswold's table 5.5). With the exception of the child whose inversion rate was 54%, the children inverted the auxiliary at least 90% of the time. Five children failed to invert the auxiliary for a brief time, but this occurred after a period of near-perfect performance. The other 7 children inverted at a constant rate. Figures 6.1 and 6.2 depict the developmental trends of SAI in the *wh*-questions of two English-speaking children (sessions in which the child produced fewer than 4 instances of *wh*-questions were discarded). Apparently, from the beginning English learners move the auxiliary to C in their questions, although they do not do so all the time, unlike what researchers have found in the speech of German, Ital-

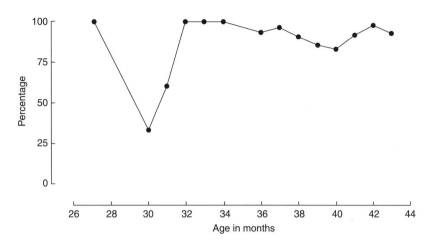

Figure 6.1
Developmental trend of subject-auxiliary inversion (SAI) in Adam's *wh*-questions

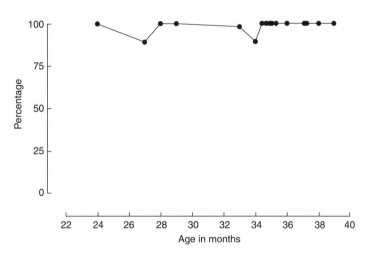

Figure 6.2
Developmental trend of subject-auxiliary inversion (SAI) in Nina's *wh*-questions

ian, and Swedish learners. For some English-speaking children SAI drops slightly and then increases again; for others it occurs constantly in 90% of the cases.

The existence of a stage in which SAI is performed in yes/no questions but not in *wh*-questions is a matter of debate. The transcripts of the 12 children investigated by Stromswold show that the overall inversion rate is 93% in *wh*-questions and 93.7% in yes/no questions. Three children inverted more in yes/no questions than in *wh*-questions, 4 displayed the reverse pattern, and 5 inverted at the same rate in both kinds of question. In addition, Stromswold reports that the children who inverted more in yes/no questions were not the youngest and that the advantage of yes/no questions over *wh*-questions was not great. Other researchers who have investigated this stage report mixed results. Some found a higher percentage of inversion in yes/no questions than in *wh*-questions, others found the reverse, and still others found an equal proportion in both structures (Erreich 1984; Tyack and Ingram 1977; Kuczaj and Maratsos 1975; also see the summary in Stromswold 1990). Thus, rather than speaking of a stage in which SAI occurs in yes/no questions but not in *wh*-questions, it is more appropriate to speak of a preference for inversion in some structures over others, likely due to extragrammatical factors, as Stromswold (1990) suggests.

In sum, the findings from studies on early English lead to these conclusions:

(12) a. Research reveals *optional* failure to perform SAI in early
        English, but not necessarily in the earliest stages.
    b. The evidence for a stage in which SAI occurs in yes/no questions
        but not in *wh*-questions is debatable. More likely, this advantage
        reflects a preference due to extragrammatical factors.

Although failure to perform SAI is observed in the speech of English learners, it is optional, as are many child language phenomena we have observed so far. Given this optionality, and given the crosslinguistic data, it is hard to conclude that English learners do not know I-to-C movement or do not respect the head component of the *Wh*-Criterion. It is more likely that they optionally produce nonadult questions because of some language-specific factor involved in satisfying the *Wh*-Criterion. One candidate worth exploring is the morphosyntactic status of English verbs. In Italian, German, and Swedish all finite verbs have the same syntactic privileges: they can all raise to I and to C. By contrast, English distinguishes two classes of verbs: auxiliaries and lexical verbs. The former can raise to I and to C. The latter cannot; they remain in V. Although English learners distinguish these two classes of verbs and never raise lexical verbs to I (recall section 4.2.4.3), learning the properties of auxiliaries may somehow pose problems that may in turn be responsible for the difficulties these learners experience in forming questions (see Guasti 1996 for an attempt to formalize this suggestion).

6.1.4   Negative Questions

Negative questions in early English often do not have the adult shape. As mentioned earlier, Bellugi (1971) suggested that SAI lags in negative questions, a proposal confirmed by other researchers (see Labov and Labov 1978). Investigating the spontaneous speech of 11 children, Stromswold (1990) found that they performed SAI in 90.7% of positive questions, but in only 55.6% of negative ones. Guasti, Thornton, and Wexler (1995) extended this result. They elicited negative questions from 4- to 5-year-old American English–speaking children and found that when introducing negation into questions, the children produced different structures. As Bellugi anticipated, they failed to apply SAI and instead produced questions like (13a), the noninverted structure; but they also produced other nonadult structures, the aux-doubling structure (13b) and the *not*-structure (13c).

(13) a. *Noninverted structure*
    Where he couldn't eat the raisin?   (Kathy, 4;0)
  b. *Aux-doubling structure*
    What did he didn't wanna bring to school?   (Darrell, 4;1)
  c. Not-*structure*
    Why can you not eat chocolate?   (Darrell, 4;1)

In (13b) an auxiliary has raised to C and a copy has remained in the IP to support the clitic negation. In (13c) the auxiliary has inverted and the negation *not* has remained in the IP. This structure is acceptable in the adult language, but it is not the structure an adult would use in the context set up for the experiment; consequently, Guasti, Thornton, and Wexler (1995) designate it as nonadult. A breakdown of the children's responses by structure is given in table 6.2 on page 199.

Bellugi (1971) described this stage of early English by saying that SAI lags in negative questions. However, a better characterization is that children's grammar obeys the following constraint:

(14) Avoid raising the negation (or negative auxiliaries) to C.

In adult English negative questions take the form in (15a), where the
auxiliary plus the clitic negation *n't* raises to C as illustrated in (15b)
(where it is assumed that the negation heads its own projection, NegP,
located between VP and IP).

(15) a. What don't you eat?

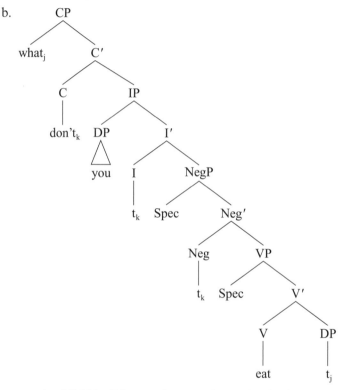

By contrast, in child English negative questions take the form in (13a–c),
where the negation does not raise to C, but remains in the IP, as the representation of these sentences in (16) makes clear. If something raises to
C, it is a positive auxiliary.[3]

(16) a. *Noninverted structure*
        [CP Where [IP he couldn't eat the raisin]]?
     b. *Aux-doubling structure*
        [CP What [C did [IP he [I didn't wanna bring to school]]]]?
     c. Not-*structure*
        [CP Why [C can [IP you not eat chocolate]]]?

Table 6.2
Negative *wh*- and yes/no questions in early English

Subject/ Age	Number of noninverted structures	Number of aux-doubling structures	Number of *not*- structures	Number of adult-like structures
KI 4;7	2	25	5	4
LI 4;5	6	9	3	24
AN 4;3	5	10	5	1
MA 4;3	1	29	1	8
EM 4;2	1	6	2	9
DA 4;1	3	21	23	
KA 4;0	10	11		
CH 3;10	7	13	2	26
AL 3;8	41	5		
RO 3;1	21	37		

Source: Data from Guasti, Thornton, and Wexler 1995

The failure of negation and negative auxiliaries to raise to C in early English cannot be attributed to processing difficulties inherent in the use of negation, since children learning Italian form adultlike negative questions (see Guasti 1996). Examples are shown in (17).

(17) a. Perchè non vuole andare a scuola la bambina?   (D., 4;7)
        why   NEG wants to go   to school the girl
        'Why doesn't the girl want to go to school?'
    b. Cosa non ta [sa] fare il   bambino?   (D., 3;11)
        what NEG can   do   the child?
        'What can't the child do?'

Under the approach adopted so far, in (17b) the *wh*-operator occupies Spec CP and the negation plus the verb occupy C, as shown in (18). (For simplicity, the postverbal subject in (18) is attached to the right of VP. Notice that the negation in Italian is analyzed as a clitic head that has attached to the verb (see Belletti 1990).)

(18)

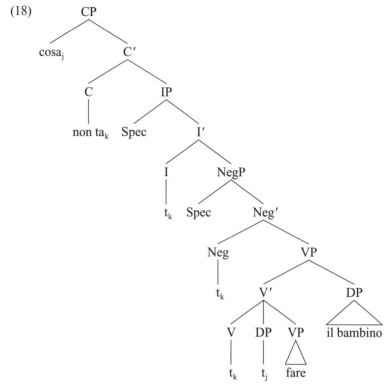

Hence, like failure to perform I-to-C movement of auxiliaries or modals in positive questions, failure to raise the negation, negative auxiliaries, or negative modals to C in early English negative questions may result from some language-specific factor, such as the presence in English of two classes of verbs with distinct movement possibilities: auxiliaries and lexical verbs (see Guasti 1996 for a possible account of these findings). Finite auxiliaries can raise to I and, when necessary, to C, while lexical verbs do not move from V in the overt syntax (see section 4.2.1; Haegeman 1994, chap. 11).

In addition to child English, certain adult languages fall under the generalization in (14), or under whatever subsumes its effects. According to Poletto (1993), Paduan, a dialect of Italian, allows raising of the verb to C only in positive questions (19a). In negative questions I-to-C movement is forbidden (19b); to express negative questions, Paduan uses cleft structures (19c).

(19) a. Cosa galo   fato?
         what has-he done
     b. *Cosa no galo   fato?
         what not has-he done
     c. Cosa ze che nol   ga fato?
         what is that not-he has done

It is unclear whether movement of a negative verb to C is blocked for the same reason in Paduan and early English. Nevertheless, the fact that an adult language exhibits a close analogue to children's negative questions lends support to the view that early grammars exploit options within the space defined by Universal Grammar (UG).

In sum, English learners have difficulty with negative questions and use different structures to express them, all sharing the property that the negation is not raised to C.

6.1.5 Intermediate Summary

In adult grammars question formation is governed by the *Wh*-Criterion, a universal constraint stating that a *wh*-operator and the head endowed with the *wh*-feature must enter into a specifier-head relation. Under the assumption that the *wh*-feature is generated in T, the required configuration is obtained by moving the *wh*-operator to Spec CP and a verb carrying the *wh*-feature to C. Children invariably front the *wh*-operator and invert the lexical verb or an auxiliary, showing that their grammar includes the *Wh*-Criterion and that English, Italian, and V2-language learners have correctly set the parameters governing *wh*-movement from the time of their first *wh*-questions.

(20) *Setting of the parameters governing* wh-*movement in English, Italian, and V2 languages*
     P1: Overt *wh*-movement
     P2: Application of I-to-C movement

English learners apply SAI in their questions (although not entirely consistently). No stage is systematically found in which SAI occurs in yes/no questions but not in *wh*-questions; by contrast, a stage in which children have difficulties with negative questions is attested.

It is thus uncontroversial that English learners, unlike Italian and V2-language learners, produce some nonadult questions in which the auxiliary fails to be inverted or in which negation or negative auxiliaries do not occupy C. Rather than reflecting lack of knowledge of SAI, these deviations may express a difficulty with certain language-specific properties, possibly the presence of two classes of verbs with distinct morphosyntactic properties. These facts are consistent with the view that innate components (universal constraints) manifest themselves early in development, while language-specific aspects involved in these components may take some time to be fully mastered.

6.2   AUXLESS QUESTIONS IN EARLY ENGLISH

Children learning English produce another type of question that deviates from the adult pattern: the **auxless question**, which (as its name implies) lacks an auxiliary (see Brown 1968; Bellugi 1971; Stromswold 1990; Guasti and Rizzi 1996; Hoekstra and Hyams 1998; Guasti 2000). Auxless questions take the two forms illustrated in (21): the verb is either a bare verbal root (21a,b,c) or inflected with -ing (21d,e).[4]

(21) *Bare lexical verbs*
    a. Where Daddy go?   (Adam, 2;3)
    b. Where Daddy put the window?   (Sarah, 2;11)
    c. What Papa have?   (Eve, 1;11)
    Verbs inflected with -ing
    d. What dat train doing?   (Adam, 2;4)
    e. What I doing?   (Eve, 2;0)

Auxless questions of the type in (21) are present from the time children first start producing nonformulaic *wh*-questions and are attested along with questions in which SAI has applied. Table 6.3 gives a breakdown of auxless questions and of the total number of questions produced by 4 English learners (age range 1;6–5;1) (data taken from Guasti 2000).[5] Only positive nonsubject *wh*-questions with an overt subject were counted. The

Table 6.3
Frequency of two types of auxless questions (bare verb, Wh S V; verb inflected with -ing, Wh S V -ing) and total number of questions produced in the speech of 4 English learners

Subject/Age range	Wh S V	Wh S V -ing	Total
Adam 2;3–4;3	469	268	1824
Eve 1;6–2;3	42	44	149
Sarah 2;3–5;1	127	23	441
Nina 1;11–3;3	14	19	354

Source: Data from Guasti 2000

data show that children make extensive use of auxless questions. In section 6.1 we saw that *wh*-movement and SAI are part of children's grammar. The data in table 6.3 raise the following questions: How is the *Wh*-Criterion satisfied in auxless questions? What is the source of these questions?

6.2.1 The Null Auxiliary Hypothesis

In keeping with the conclusion that children adhere to the *Wh*-Criterion, Guasti and Rizzi (1996) and Guasti (2000) propose the **null auxiliary hypothesis**—namely, that the structure of the questions in (21d,e), where the verb is inflected with *-ing*, includes a null auxiliary, the counterpart of the lexical *be*. Like its overt counterpart, this null element selects a verb inflected with *-ing* and carries the *wh*-feature from T to Agr to C. The structure of (21d) is given in (22), where 0_{aux} stands for the null auxiliary.

(22)

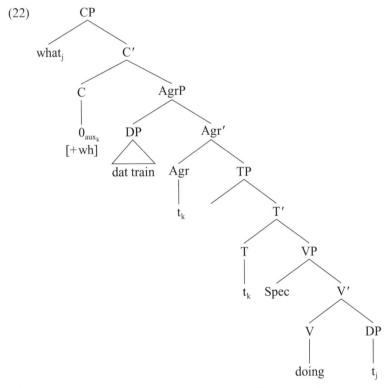

This hypothesis can be extended very naturally to questions containing a bare verbal form, as in (21a) (*Where Daddy go?*). In these questions the null auxiliary is the counterpart of *do*; and like *do*, it selects a bare verb and carries the *wh*-feature from T to Agr to C.

This proposal handles children's questions in a uniform way.[6] Despite surface differences, questions with an overt auxiliary and auxless questions are the outcome of the same underlying mechanism: the *Wh*-Criterion, which in both cases is satisfied by moving the *wh*-operator to Spec CP and by carrying the *wh*-feature from T to Agr to C through a null or an overt auxiliary. Children's deviation from the adult target thus depends on the availability of a null auxiliary.

6.2.2   A Root Null Auxiliary

Why it should be possible to posit a null auxiliary for early English, when it does not exist in the standard grammar of adult English, deserves explanation. Guasti and Rizzi (1996) draw a parallel between the null auxiliary and the early null subject (see section 5.2.3). They claim that, like the early null subject, the null auxiliary must occur in the root of a clause.

Recall that, according to Rizzi (1994), early null subjects are legitimate only in the specifier of the root, because this is the only position where they can survive without enforcing the Principle of Clause-Internal Identification, the ECP in section 5.2.3.2. This is a universal principle of grammar, according to which null nonpronominal elements must be identified by being connected to a clause-internal antecedent. This principle cannot be enforced for elements in the root, the highest position of the clause, since the root lacks a position for hosting a potential clause-internal identifier. Similarly, a null auxiliary is possible in questions because it is located in C, the head of the root. In this position it need not be identified clause-internally, because there is no higher position to host a potential identifier.

As it stands, this proposal is too permissive. Since C is the head of the root in adult languages as well, it would predict that the null auxiliary could occur in all varieties and registers of adult English. While some varieties and registers indeed allow this option, others do not (see Akmajian et al. 2001; Labov 1995). Consequently, there must be some difference between the child and adult grammars. This difference is located in the internal structure of the CP system. Rizzi (1997) proposes that the CP system, like the IP system, is layered. ForceP is the highest projection, which determines the clausal type (a question, an exclamative, etc.); it dominates various projections, among which is FocP (Focus Phrase), whose specifier is the landing site for *wh*-operators and whose head hosts inverted auxiliaries (FocP is what has so far been called CP). Thus, adult questions require the projection ForceP to determine the clausal type (question) and FocP to host the *wh*-operator and the carrier of the *wh*-feature. This elaboration of the CP system leads to revising the **axiom on clausal representation** (sections 4.4.2.2 and 5.2.3) asserting that CP is the root. Under this revision ForceP becomes the root of the clause.

(23) *Axiom on clausal representation* (revised version of (64) in chapter 4)
     ForceP is the root of all clauses (finite and infinitive).

   With this background we can return to children's auxless questions and spell out the parallel between the null auxiliary and early null subjects. Recall that subject omission has been traced to the availability of clausal truncation in child grammar (section 5.2.3; Rizzi 1994; see also section 4.4.2.2 for a truncation account of RIs). In keeping with that analysis, Guasti and Rizzi (1996) argue that children's auxless questions are structures truncated below ForceP, as shown in (24), the structure of (21d).[7]

(24)

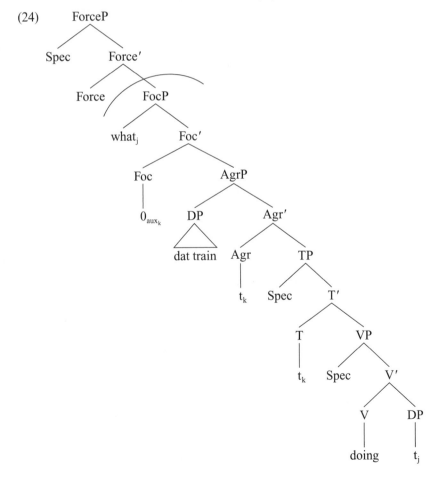

Truncation below ForceP ensures that children have enough of the C system to accommodate the *wh*-operator and invert the null auxiliary, which can then occupy the head of the root. In this position a null auxiliary is legitimate since the Principle of Clause-Internal Identification given in (25) is not enforced.

(25) A null auxiliary must be identified clause-internally *if it can.*

In the adult system ForceP is the necessary endpoint of any syntactic representation and must therefore always be projected. Consequently, a null auxiliary in Foc will never occupy the head of the root since Force dominates it. The usual requirement of clause-internal identification is invoked in this case and rules out auxless questions in the adult grammar.

Thus, the null auxiliary, like other early phenomena, has its source in the mechanism of clausal truncation.

6.2.3   Support for the Null Auxiliary Hypothesis

Since null auxiliaries are possible only in the head of the root, they should not be found in contexts where I-to-C movement does not occur because in such contexts they would *not* occupy the head of the root. Consequently, the Principle of Clause-Internal Identification would be enforced and would rule out the structure. A context where this prediction can be tested is subject questions. According to Rizzi (1997), there is no I-to-C movement in subject questions, as the impossibility of inserting unemphatic *do* in (26a) shows.

(26) a. *Who does read books?
     b.   Who reads books?

The absence of *do* in (26b) and the fact that lexical verbs do not raise in English indicates that I-to-C (or I-to-Foc) movement has not occurred.[8] Lack of I-to-C movement in turn means that null auxiliaries are banned in early subject questions, because it would not occur in the head of the root. Therefore, subject questions like (27b), which would include the null counterpart of *be* in (27a), should not be attested in child speech.

(27) a. Who is laughing?
     b. Who laughing?

Guasti and Rizzi (1996) report that examples like (27b) represent 2% of Adam's, Eve's, and Sarah's subject questions. For nonsubject questions with verbs inflected with *-ing* (e.g., (21d), *What dat train doing?*), this rate

rises to 16%, a statistically significant difference ($\chi^2 = 40.25$, $p < .005$).[9]
This sharp contrast between subject and nonsubject *wh*-questions can be
interpreted as the expression of a grammatical constraint present in the
child grammar, likely the principle in (25) requiring a null auxiliary to be
identified. The structure of (27a,b) is (28a,b). In (28a) the auxiliary *is* stays
in Agr and the *wh*-operator in Spec CP (more correctly, FocP). (28b) differs from (28a) in that the auxiliary in Agr is null (indicated as 0_{aux}).

(28) a.

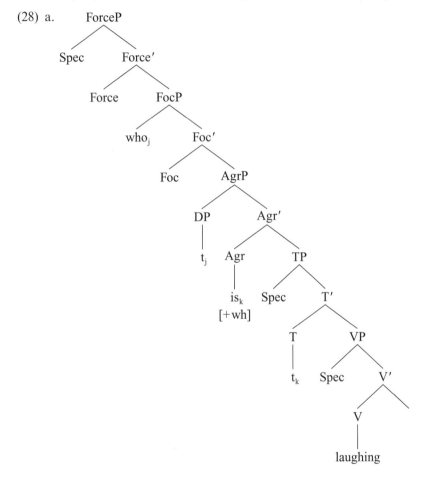

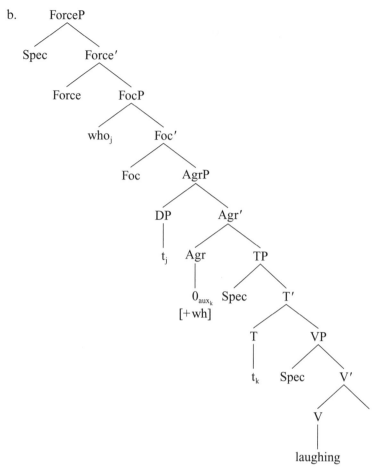

In (28b) the null auxiliary in Agr is subject to the principle in (25), because a position (Foc) for a potential antecedent is available. But no such antecedent is present; consequently, the null auxiliary fails to be identified and the sentence is ruled out.

6.2.4   Intermediate Summary

Although English learners respect the requirements imposed by the *Wh-*Criterion, some of their early questions deviate from the adult target: they frequently omit the auxiliary and produce questions with the order Wh S V. These auxless questions have been analyzed as truncated structures (below ForceP) involving a null auxiliary in the head of the root. Such a move is tantamount to assimilating the null auxiliary to other phenomena peculiar to children's language (e.g., the null subject). Given the availability of truncation, a null element can occur in the root of the clause, a position from which the Principle of Clause-Internal Identification cannot be invoked.

6.3   LONG-DISTANCE *WH*-MOVEMENT

As we have seen, children master *wh*-movement out of main clauses, an instance of short-distance (SD) movement. Let us now look at *wh*-movement out of embedded clauses, an instance of long-distance (LD) movement.

6.3.1   Adult Long-Distance *Wh*-Questions

A question like (29) instantiates LD *wh*-movement.

(29)   What did she say [that John cooked t]?

The *wh*-element is extracted from the embedded clause (indicated by square brackets), where it has left a trace. LD extraction questions are subject to grammatical constraints. Consider the sentences in (30).

(30)   *Object extraction*
    a.   What do you think (that) monkeys eat t?
    Subject extraction
    b.   *Who do you think that t eats bananas?
    c.   Who do you think t eats bananas?

While the complementizer can be present when an object is extracted from an embedded clause, as in (30a), for most speakers it cannot be present when a subject is extracted, as the contrast between (30b) and (30c) shows.[10]

    From the viewpoint of language acquisition, LD extraction raises these questions: Do children produce and comprehend LD extraction questions? If so, are children's LD questions subject to the same constraints operating in the adult language?

6.3.2   Comprehension of Long-Distance Questions

First let us look at whether children comprehend LD questions extracting from different positions. Using a comprehension experiment, de Villiers, Roeper, and Vainikka (1990) have investigated this issue in early English. After presenting 3;5- to 6-year-old children with a story, they asked questions about the story that allowed both an LD and an SD answer. Examples of argument and adjunct extraction questions used in this experiment are given in (31) (—— marks the possible extraction sites).

(31) a. *Argument extraction question*
    Who did the boy ask —— to call ——?
                        gap₁   gap₂

  b. *Adjunct extraction question*
    When did he say —— he hurt himself ——?
                      gap₁   gap₂

De Villiers, Roeper, and Vainikka reasoned that if children have mastered LD extraction questions, they should sometimes answer (31a) by indicating the person who was called and (31b) by indicating the time he hurt himself (gap₂). By contrast, if they have not mastered LD movement, they should systematically answer (31a) by indicating the person who was asked and (31b) by indicating the time when he spoke (gap₁). The main finding (confirmed by Thornton and Crain (1994) using a different method) was that children gave both LD and SD responses. We can conclude that children have access to LD movement at least from about 3;5 years of age.

6.3.3   Production of Long-Distance Questions

Children's LD questions have been extensively investigated by Thornton (1990); a discussion of the data can also be found in Thornton and Crain 1994 and Crain and Thornton 1998.

Working with 21 English-speaking children (age range 2;10–5;5), Thornton (1990) conducted an elicited-production experiment designed to evoke LD questions extracting from subject and object position. As table 6.4 indicates, most children produced adultlike subject and object LD questions, but they also produced various kinds of nonadult questions. Thirteen children asked subject or object questions with the complementizer *that* (32a); 10 formed subject or object extraction questions that included an extra *wh*-word in the intermediate CP (32b,c)—so-called **medial-*wh* questions** (examples from Thornton 1990; see also McDaniel, Chiu, and Maxfield 1995 for evidence that children judge medial-*wh* questions acceptable).[11] (For simplicity, in what follows all nonadult questions will often be referred to as medial-*wh* questions.)

(32) a. What do you think that Ninja Turtles like to eat?   (SR, 3;11)
  b. What do you think what Cookie Monster eats?   (Katie, 5;5)
  c. Who do you think what babies drink ... to grow big?
     (Matthew, 3;3)

Thornton's findings were replicated by van Kempen (1997) for early Dutch. This author found medial-*wh* questions in the spontaneous and

Table 6.4
Frequency of different types of questions in children's speech (with *that* in intermediate CP; medial-*wh*; adultlike)

Subject/ Age	Object *wh*-questions			Subject *wh*-questions		
	That	Medial-*wh*	Adult	*That*	Medial-*wh*	Adult
KM 5;5	1	1		2	1	3
MI 5;5			4		1	3
CA 5;4	1		5			5
SO 5;3	1		7			6
JI 5;1			8			4
PM 5;1	2		6	1		10
KP 5;0			4	1		9
TI 4;9		3	2	1	9	
AM 4;6	3		6	2	2	6
KE 4;4			6	1		6
GA 4;0			5			4
KL 3;10	1		6			7
TT 3;9	4		1	4		
KR 3;9			5	1	2	6
MO 3;9	2	1	1	3		
RE 3;9			2			6
MC 3;7		1				1
CA 3;7	—			—		
JE 3;6	—			1	3	
MA 3;3		3	2	4		
PI 2;10	—				3	

Source: Adapted from Crain and Thornton 1998, table 22.1

elicited production of two Dutch-speaking children up to the age of 7 and 8 years. For example:

(33) a. Wat denk je   wat ik zie? (S., 5;1)
         what think you what I see
         'What do you think what I see?'
     b. Welke pen denk je   welke ik ga kopen? (L., 7;10)
         which pen think you which I   will buy
         'Which pen do you think which I will buy?'

In sum, children not only comprehend but also produce LD questions. However, some of these questions deviate from the adult target. We can gain some understanding of these deviant constructions and their source by looking more closely at their structural properties.

6.3.4   Properties of Children's Medial-*Wh* Questions

Thornton notes that subject questions with *that* and medial-*wh* questions share certain properties. Both contain material in the intermediate CP that is not found in the adult language. Both occur when children extract from a finite embedded clause (extraction from infinitival clauses features neither *that* nor a medial *wh*-word: *Who_i do you want t_i to see?*). The developmental course of questions with *that* and with medial *wh*-words is also peculiar. Initially children use these structures when they extract from either the subject or the object position (see table 6.4); later they restrict this option to subject questions. In medial-*wh* questions the fronted and medial *wh*-words are usually the same (see (32b), (33a)). Out of 21, only 2 of the English-speaking children studied by Thornton (1990) produced questions with a medial *wh*-word that did not match the fronted one (examples from Thornton 1990).

(34) a. What do you think where the marble is?   (Kelly, 3;11)
       b. Who do you think what babies drink . . . to grow big?
           (Matthew, 3;3)

In questions introduced by a *wh-phrase* the intermediate CP is invariably filled with a *wh-word*, as seen in (35a,b) from Dutch and (35c) from English (from van Kempen 1997 and Thornton 1990, respectively).

(35) a. Hoe laat   denk je   wanner die komt?   (L., 8;2.19)
           at what time think you when   he comes
           'At what time do you think when he comes?'
       b. Op welke manier denk je   hoe Douwe praat?   (L., 8;3.8)
           in   which way   think you how Douwe talks
           'In which way do you think how Douwe talks?'
       c. Which Smurf do you think who has a roller skate on?
           (Tiffany, 4;9)

In sum, all children's nonadult questions in Thornton's (1990) and van Kempen's (1997) studies have the following properties:

(36) a. The intermediate CP is filled.
       b. Such questions are restricted to extraction from finite embedded clauses.
       c. The medial element is always a *wh*-word (never a *wh*-phrase).

The development of these questions may include two stages:

(37) a. *Stage 1*
     Production of subject and object medial-*wh* questions
   b. *Stage 2*
     Production of subject medial-*wh* questions

Children do not necessarily go through both stages, but if they do, then stage 1 precedes stage 2 and never the reverse.

The properties in (36) and the developmental pattern in (37) suggest that LD extraction questions with a medial *that* and those with a medial *wh*-word are related. Therefore, they deserve a unified account. Thornton proposes that the medial element is the overt expression of *wh*-movement through the intermediate CP. Let us look at this analysis in detail.

6.3.4.1   Agreement in the Intermediate CP in Adult Languages   Thornton (1990) points out that there are adult languages that manifest agreement in the intermediate CP, as does early English. In Irish, for example, the complementizer *go* found in declarative sentences changes to *aL* when a *wh*-element is extracted from an embedded clause (McCloskey 1990). This change in the form of the complementizer is quite general and occurs in both subject and object LD extraction questions. An example of object extraction is given in (38) (from McCloskey 1979, cited in Crain and Thornton 1998).

(38) Cén   t-úrscéal aL   mheas mé aL   dúirt sé aL   thuig
     which novel   COMP thought I   COMP said he COMP understood
     sé?
     he
     'Which novel did I think he said he understood?'

A similar phenomenon is attested in French, but is limited to questions extracting from subject position. Here the declarative complementizer *que* changes to *qui*.

(39) a. Je crois   que Marie est partie.
         I   believe that Marie is   left
         'I think that Marie left.'
     b. *Qui crois-tu   qu'est (= que est) parti?
         who believe you that(*que*) is   left
         'Who do you think that left?'
     c. Qui crois-tu   qui   est parti?
         who believe you that(*qui*) is   left
         'Who do you think left?'

Rizzi (1990) proposes that the French *que/qui* alternation is the manifestation of specifier-head agreement in the intermediate CP. In LD questions extracting from subject position, the *wh*-element moves through the specifier of the intermediate CP, leaving a trace that agrees with the head of CP. The results of these processes are illustrated in (40), the structure of (39c). Specifier-head **agreement in CP** is represented with indices and phonologically expressed by *qui* (for simplicity, the layered representation of CP introduced in section 6.2.2 is not used here).

(40)

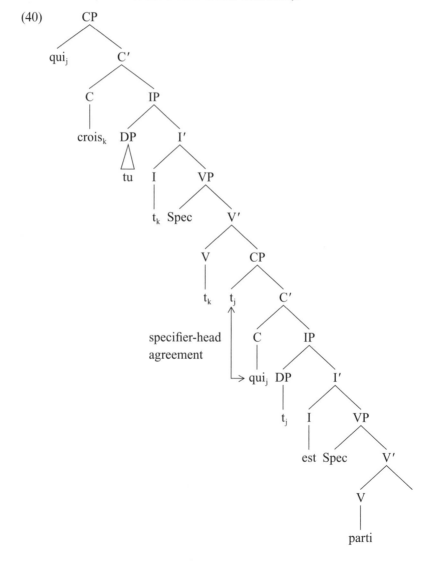

In French, movement through the intermediate CP and the ensuing process of specifier-head agreement occur when the subject is extracted; these processes are expressed by the *que/qui* alternation. The presence of *que* in (39b) is a sign that the intermediate trace has *not* moved through the intermediate CP and agreement has not occurred; thus, the sentence is ruled out. In Irish, movement through the intermediate CP applies to questions extracting from both subject and object position; therefore, both types of questions involve specifier-head agreement, expressed by the overt complementizer *aL*. In English, as in French, movement through the intermediate CP is limited to subject extraction questions; agreement in CP also occurs, but is manifested covertly, according to Rizzi (1990). Consider (30b,c), repeated here.

(30) *Subject extraction*
    b. *Who do you think that t eats bananas?
    c.   Who do you think t eats bananas?

Like its French counterpart *que* in (39b), the complementizer *that* does not express agreement in CP. Instead, this process is signaled in English by a phonologically null complementizer, indicated as *0* in (41), the representation of (30c).

(41)

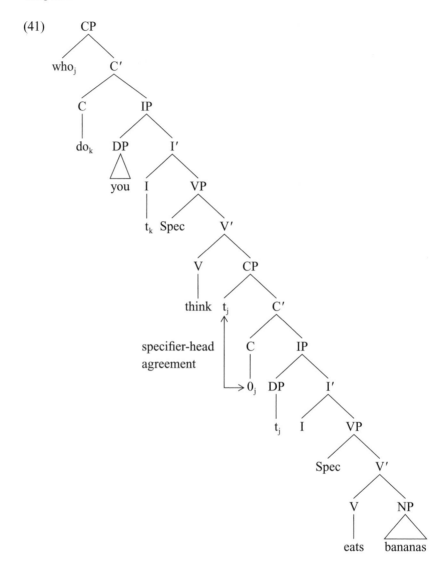

6.3.4.2　Agreement in the Intermediate CP in Early Languages　Rizzi (1990) claims that agreement in CP is an option made available by UG, manifested overtly in some languages and covertly in others. Since it is inborn, children have access to this option, but must find out

(42) a. whether it is restricted to subject extraction questions or applies in object extraction questions as well, and
　　b. how it is signaled in their language.

This framework provides an explanation for children's medial-*wh* questions and questions with *that*. (For expository purposes the explanation that follows refers to early English, but it is meant to be valid for Dutch as well, modulo language-particular properties.)

Thornton (1990) proposes that children initially conjecture that movement through CP and agreement in CP occur in both subject and object extraction questions, as in Irish; then they limit this option just to subject extraction questions (for other approaches to children's medial-*wh* questions, see de Villiers, Roeper, and Vainikka 1990; McDaniel, Chiu, and Maxfield 1995; van Kempen 1997). Thornton assumes that the intermediate *wh*-element in medial-*wh* questions is a complementizer like *that*, and she takes both *that* and the intermediate *wh*-word as the overt manifestation of specifier-head agreement in CP. Support for the conjecture that the intermediate *wh*-element is a complementizer comes from the absence of intermediate *wh*-phrases. Unlike *wh*-words, *wh*-phrases are XPs and thus could not be located in a head. Since some children also produce questions without an overt complementizer—namely, the adult structure in (30c)—it ought to be the case that they take the null complementizer as another manifestation of agreement in CP. Thus, they have three forms of agreeing complementizers: *that*, a *wh*-element, and the null complementizer.

According to this view, then, children have incorrectly categorized *that* and *wh*-words as agreeing complementizers. In part, this might have happened because they are misled by the input—specifically, by relative clauses. There is a close similarity between subject relatives and LD questions extracting from subject position. Relative clauses involve *wh*-movement (see section 6.4), and in French the complementizer *que* used in object relatives (see (43a)) becomes *qui* in subject relatives (note the contrast between (43b) and (43c)).

(43) a. la fille que Paul a   vue
         the girl that Paul has seen
     b. *la fille **que** parle
         the girl that speaks
     c. la fille **qui**   parle
         the girl that+Agr speaks

Rizzi (1990) interprets the subject/object asymmetry in French relative clauses by assuming, as for questions, that *qui* is the manifestation of agreement in CP. The structure of (43c) is (44), where Op is an empty operator (for simplicity it is assumed that the complex phrase including the relative clause is an NP rather than a DP).

(44)

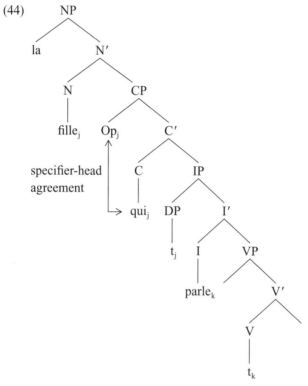

In English the situation is different. The complementizer *that* is optional in object relatives but obligatory in subject relatives, as shown in (45).

(45) a.   the girl (that) Paul saw
     b.   *the girl t came
     c.   the girl that t came

In keeping with previous assumptions, Rizzi (1990) proposes that in subject relative clauses *that* is the overt realization of specifier-head agreement in CP. Thus, while in French the agreeing complementizer has the same form both in LD questions extracting from subject position and in relative clauses, in English the null complementizer expresses agreement in LD questions extracting from subject position, while *that* plays the same role in relative clauses.

Because relative clauses and *wh*-questions in English involve two different agreeing complementizers, children may be confused and may initially assume that both *that* and the null complementizer are agreeing complementizers in *wh*-questions.

English learners first use *that*, the null complementizer, and a *wh*-word to express agreement in CP and assume that this process occurs in all questions, as in Irish. Then they restrict the process to subject extraction questions, as in adult English, but still use the three forms of agreeing complementizers. Finally they realize that in subject questions only the null form expresses agreement in CP.

One prominent property of medial-*wh* questions is their restriction to extraction from finite embedded clauses. LD questions extracting from an infinitival clause display neither *that* nor a medial *wh*-element. Thornton (1990) evoked questions like (46) from the 21 children she tested who produced medial-*wh* questions.

(46) Who do you want to come to the party?

The lack of a medial *wh*-element or of *that* when children extract from the infinitival clause here depends on knowledge of the properties of the verb *want*: its complement is an IP with the subject trace in the embedded Spec IP. Since this verb takes an IP as complement, there is no intermediate CP position for performing agreement in CP, as (47) illustrates.

(47) Who$_i$ do you want [$_{IP}$ t$_i$ to come to the party]?

6.3.5   Intermediate Summary

We started with two questions: (1) Do children produce and comprehend LD questions? (2) If so, are children's LD questions subject to the same constraints operating in the adult language? Children comprehend and produce LD questions from about 3;5 years. Their productions do not wholly conform to the adult target, however; they sometimes produce medial-*wh* questions when they extract from subject and object position of an embedded clause, and they sometimes use *that* in their LD subject extraction questions. These structures are the outcome of a process allowed by UG: movement through the intermediate CP with the ensuing process of agreement in CP. Languages vary as to whether agreement in the intermediate CP occurs in both subject and object extraction questions or is limited to subject extraction questions. This variation is one factor responsible for children's errors. Learners must discover whether agreement in the intermediate CP applies consistently or only in a limited set of structures. Initially children assume that their language is like Irish and apply agreement in CP in questions extracting from both subject and object position. Then they restrict this process to just subject questions, as in the adult grammar. Learners must also figure out how agreement in CP is (lexically) expressed in their language. Initially English learners take agreement in CP in LD questions to be expressed by three forms of complementizer: *that*, *wh*-words, and a null complementizer.

6.4   RELATIVE CLAUSES

We now turn to another construction involving *wh*-movement: the restrictive relative clause (see Haegeman 1994, sec. 7.6.3, for a more detailed discussion). After looking briefly at the adult grammar of relative clauses, we will consider two issues: the structure children assign to relative clauses and the mechanism they use to derive them.

6.4.1   Adult Relative Clauses

A restrictive relative clause in English takes the form in (48).

(48) the girl to whom Kostas will give a book

As (49) illustrates, the relative clause is a CP. The whole PP—including the *wh*-operator or relative pronoun *whom*—is raised to Spec CP and coindexed with its trace, a variable, within IP.

(49) [$_{CP}$ to whom$_i$ [$_{IP}$ Kostas will give a book t$_i$]]

The relative clause introduced by the *wh*-operator *whom* modifies the head noun, *girl*, as the coindexation between the head and the relative pronoun indicates. Restrictive relatives have the structure in (50) (for simplicity, relatives are shown as NPs, although under current approaches it would be more appropriate to say that they are DPs).

(50)

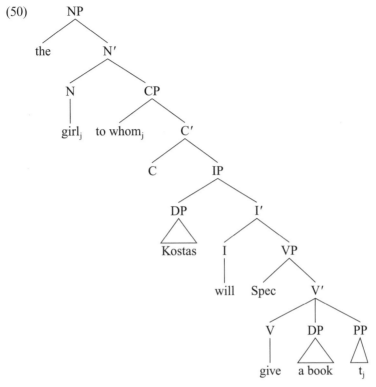

In English it is also possible to move the *wh*-operator alone, stranding the preposition.

(51) the girl who Kostas will give a book to

Preposition stranding is not allowed in, for example, Romance languages, where prepositional pied-piping is instead obligatory, as the French contrast in (52) illustrates.

(52) a. la fille à qui   Kostas va donner le livre
         the girl to whom Kostas will give   the book
     b. *la fille qui Kostas va donner le livre à
         the girl who Kostas will give   the book to

By analogy with relative clauses with overt *wh*-operators, it is assumed that the relative clauses in (53a,b), which display no overt *wh*-operator, include a nonovert *wh*-operator moved to Spec CP, as illustrated in (54a,b).

(53) a. the man (that) you saw
     b. the man that laughed

(54) a.

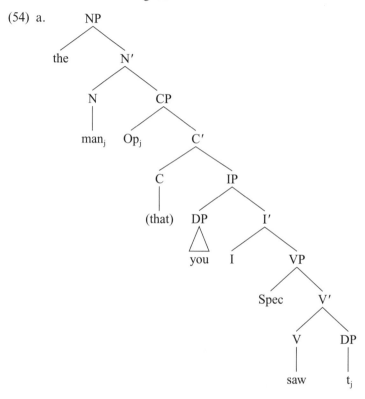

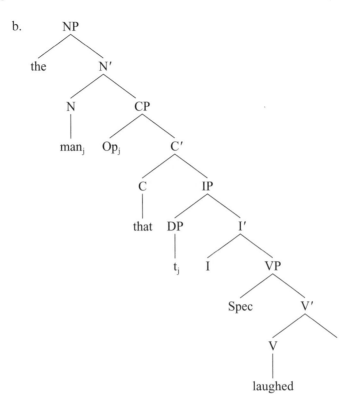

6.4.2 Children's Errors in Comprehending Sentences with Relative Clauses

Several studies carried out in the 1970s and early 1980s probed children's knowledge of relative clauses and demonstrated that these structures are difficult for children to comprehend even after 6 years of age. In a pioneering work Sheldon (1974) presented English-speaking children with the four types of sentences illustrated in (55).

(55) a. SS [The dog that t jumps over the pig] bumps into the lion.
    b. OO The dog stands on [the horse that the giraffe jumps over t].
    c. SO [The lion that the horse bumps into t] jumps over the giraffe.
    d. OS The pig bumps into [the horse that t jumps over the giraffe].

These sentences vary according to

(56) a. the grammatical function of the relativized NP inside the main clause (S = subject or O = object),
    b. the grammatical function of the relative gap inside the relative clause (S = subject or O = object).

For example, (55c) is an SO relative in which the relativized NP is the subject of the main clause and the gap (or trace) is the object of the relative clause.

In Sheldon's experiment children were asked to enact the events described by sentences like (55a–d). These enactments revealed that children find certain relatives (SS and OO) easier to interpret than others (OS and SO). They also showed that children make a number of errors in interpreting relative clauses, replicated in subsequent studies on the acquisition of relative clauses in English, French, and Japanese (see Ferreiro et al. 1976; de Villiers et al. 1979). One of the most frequently cited errors, which we will focus on here, is that English and French learners take the relative clause in an OS sentence as a modifier of the subject of the main clause rather than of its object.

Children's errors in comprehending sentences with relative clauses have motivated two classes of explanations. One holds that children's poor performance in experimental tasks reflects lack of adult competence (see Tavakolian 1981). It is argued that children use processing strategies that refer to the linear arrangement of syntactic categories or that they assign relative clauses a flat structure. A second line of explanation maintains that children's competence is intact and attributes their errors either to the complexity of the structures being tested or to the infelicity of the pragmatic conditions in which relative clauses have been probed. In the next sections we will look at both classes of explanations.

6.4.3   The Nonadult Competence Hypothesis

Consider (55d), repeated here.

(55) d. OS The pig bumps into the horse [that t jumps over the giraffe].

Children take the relative clause in this sentence as modifying the matrix subject, *the pig*, and not the matrix object, *the horse*. Tavakolian (1981) argues that this error comes about because children have no access to the recursive rules for building relative clauses; hence, they fall back on a "flat" structure—specifically, a coordinate structure. This amounts to saying that children take *that* in (55d) as a coordination marker, on a par with *and*; that is, for children (55d) is parallel to (57), in which the subject of the second clause is not phonologically expressed.

(57) The pig bumps into the horse and t jumps over the giraffe.

According to this view, the child's structure for sentences including relative clauses is not the adult one, with the relative clause embedded within the NP, as in (54a). Rather, it is the structure found in conjoined clauses, as in (58) (see Crain and Thornton 1998, chap. 18, for criticism of the conjoined-clause analysis).

(58)

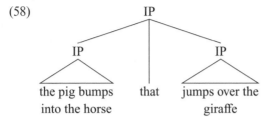

This analysis of relative clauses forces children to interpret the phonologically null subject of the second conjunct as picking out the individual denoted by the subject of the main clause, as in the coordinate structures exemplified in (59) (see Lebeaux 1990 for another nonadult analysis of early relative clauses).

(59) The pig bumps into the horse and —— jumps over the giraffe.

One major drawback of this analysis is a learnability problem (see Crain and Thornton 1998). Children have to unlearn the conjoined-clause analysis for relative clauses and its interpretation, which is not like the adult one. If children are to get rid of the wrong interpretation, they need to have access to what a sentence cannot mean. For example, because children assign (55d) a conjoined-clause analysis, they take the pig to be jumping over the giraffe, while for adults it is the horse that jumps over the giraffe. To get rid of the wrong interpretation of this sentence, children must be informed that it cannot mean what sentence (59) means. This information, called negative evidence, is hardly available in the linguistic environment since children are rarely if ever told what a sentence cannot mean (see Marcus 1993; also see section 1.1.2).

6.4.4 The Adult Competence Hypothesis

The hypothesis that children misinterpret sentences with relative clauses because their grammar is defective has been challenged by Goodluck and Tavakolian (1982) and by Hamburger and Crain (1982). These authors have shown that once disturbing factors are removed, children's comprehension of relative clauses improves significantly. Goodluck and Tavakolian offer a processing account of children's errors, while Hamburger and Crain attribute them to pragmatic factors involved in the experimental procedure.

6.4.4.1   A Processing Account of Children's Errors in Interpreting Relative Clauses   We have seen that children often interpret the relative clause of an OS sentence as modifying the matrix subject rather than the matrix object. Goodluck and Tavakolian (1982) showed that the frequency of this error is a function of the complexity of the relative clause. Children's rate of correct responses significantly increases when the relative clause includes an intransitive verb, as in (60), instead of a transitive one.

(60) OS The pig bumps into [the horse that t hops up and down].

While 4- to 5-year-old children correctly act out OS sentences like (55d) only 49% of the time, they correctly act out OS sentences like (60), in which the verb in the relative clause is intransitive, 76% of the time. This discrepancy is a hint that a factor bearing on children's incorrect interpretation of OS sentences is the complexity of the relative clause—specifically, the number of arguments present. Once the relative clause is simplified, children interpret the sentence accurately.

An analogous finding was obtained by Lee (1992) for Chinese. In Chinese, relative clauses occur to the left of the relativized noun and are introduced by the morpheme *de*, as shown in (61) (from Lee 1992).

(61) [Bao zhe xiaoxiong] de   neige baitu shui le.
      hug ASP teddy-bear NOM that   rabbit sleep ASP
      'The rabbit that is hugging the teddy bear has fallen asleep.'

Chinese learners were successful (75% correct responses) in comprehending SS and SO sentences from 4 years of age when the verb in the relative clause was intransitive. They had more difficulty when the verb was transitive.

These data point to the conclusion that children can analyze relative clauses as adults do. Thus, lack of competence cannot be the cause of the difficulties that children encounter with more complex relative clauses; these difficulties are likely due to some processing factor.

6.4.4.2   A Pragmatic Account of Children's Errors in Interpreting Relative Clauses   The conclusion that children's errors in handling relative clauses are not due to lack of competence is further confirmed by Hamburger and Crain's (1982) study. Hamburger and Crain established that children's performance significantly improves when the felicity conditions for the use of relative clauses are met. The term *felicity conditions* refers to the fact that what is being asserted during a conversation must be appropriate to the goals of the conversation (see Grice 1989). For example, if you are asked, "Is it raining?" and you answer, "I'm drinking juice," you are asserting something that may be true, but your answer is not appropriate to the goals of the conversation. Similarly, the use of a sentence with a relative clause like (62) in a situation in which there is only one ball does not meet felicity conditions.

(62) Give me the ball that is on the table.

If we are faced with a set of objects and we need to single out one of them, it is sensible to use a restrictive relative clause. If there is just one object around, the use of a relative clause is redundant. It is, then, felicitous to use (62) only if there is more than one ball in the context. The existence of a set to restrict is a presupposition that relative clauses bear, that is, something the hearer takes for granted when the speaker uses a relative clause. Hamburger and Crain point out that in the experiments testing children's comprehension of sentences with relative clauses this presupposition was not met. Typically, in experiments that evoked nonadult responses for (55d), repeated here, children were given (besides a pig and a giraffe) only one horse, a situation that makes the use of the relative clause superfluous (see Crain and Thornton 1998 for further discussion of flaws in experimental settings testing children's comprehension of relative clauses).

(55) d. The pig bumps into [the horse that t jumps over the giraffe].

To circumvent this infelicitous situation, Hamburger and Crain made a minor change in their experiments: they gave children more than one object of the kind referred to by the head of the relative (e.g., more horses when the experimental sentence was (55d)). The outcome was that 5-year-olds gave 95% correct responses, and even children younger than the ones tested in previous experiments (3-year-olds) performed well (69% correct responses). These findings indicate that when the pragmatic context makes the use of a relative clause felicitous or relevant to the situation, children perform in an adultlike way. Therefore, Hamburger and Crain conclude, the errors that children made in previous experiments do not reflect their lack of knowledge of the relative clause structure; rather, they reveal their attempt to overcome infelicitous conditions for the use of relative clauses.

Children's mastery of the relative clause structure is further demonstrated by the results of several elicited-production experiments with children as young as 2;8 speaking a variety of languages: English (Hamburger and Crain 1982), Italian (Crain, McKee, and Emiliani 1990), and French (Labelle 1990; Guasti et al. 1996). Examples of relative clause structures these children produced are given in (63a) and (63b) (from Crain and Thornton 1998 and Guasti et al. 1996, respectively).

(63) a. Point to the guy that's eating the strawberry ice cream.   (3;11)
   b. Viens toucher la   tomate qu'on   coupe.   (A., 6;3)
      come to touch the tomato that we cut
      'Come touch the tomato that we are cutting.'

6.4.5   Intermediate Summary

Children's difficulties in interpreting relative clauses were originally explained by saying that they analyze these structures differently than adults do—for example, as coordinate structures (the conjoined-clause analysis). It was believed that children do not have access to the rule of recursion and thus cannot build embedded structures. However, later studies revealed that children's difficulties in comprehending relative clauses were artifacts of the experimental situation. Once the disturbing factors were removed, children displayed no difficulty in correctly understanding relative clauses. It ought to be, then, that children's grammar includes the rule of recursion—and as we will see, children produce relative clauses that are indeed compatible with an analysis involving recursion.

6.4.6   The Nonmovement Analysis of Relative Clauses

As we have seen, in the adult grammar relative clauses arise by *wh*-movement of an overt *wh*-operator or an empty operator to Spec CP. Labelle (1990) contends that this operation is responsible for the formation of early relative clauses on the grounds that early French relative clauses deviate from the adult target, in two respects:

(64) a. **Pied-piping in relatives** is absent.
   b. Resumptive pronouns are used abundantly.

6.4.6.1   Pied-Piping in Relative Clauses   In standard French only oblique relatives display overt *wh*-movement of a *wh*-operator, which pied-pipes the preposition (see (52)). Relativization of the object does not involve *wh*-operators. Instead, the relative clause is introduced by the complementizer *que* 'that', as in (65).

(65) l'homme que Jean a   vu
     the man that Jean has seen
     'the man that Jean saw'

Out of 1,348 relative clauses produced by 3- to 6-year-old Canadian French–speaking children interviewed by Labelle (1990), not one was a relative with prepositional pied-piping. Labelle's findings have been replicated in several studies on early Continental French (see Guasti et al. 1996; Labelle 1996; and references cited in these works). For example, out of 17 children tested (age range 4;5–7;3), Guasti et al. (1996) found a single 6-year-old French learner who used pied-piping in relative clauses. Early French relatives are generally introduced by the complementizer *que*, as shown in (66). (The *wh*-operator that should have been used appears in square brackets.)

(66) a. T'as   qu'à toucher çui-là   que [à qui]   quelqu'un
        you have but to touch the one there that [to whom] someone
        a   pris l'argent. (N., 7;0)
        has taken the money
        'You have but to touch the one there from whom someone has stolen the money.'
     b. Est-ce que tu veux toucher le couteau que [avec lequel]
        is it   that you want to touch the knife   that [with which]
        le monsieur coupe le   sapin? (A., 5;1)
        the man   cuts   the fir-tree?
        'Do you want to touch the knife with which the man is cutting the fir-tree?'
     c. Touche le pirate que [dont] le frère
        touch   the pirate that [whose] the brother
        est en train d'aller en vélo. (N., 7;1)
        is riding a bicycle
        'Touch the pirate whose brother is riding a bicycle.'

As we have seen, relatives displaying pied-piping tend to be avoided in production and are rejected in comprehension by 3- to 6-year-old English learners, according to McDaniel, McKee, and Berstein (1998). These children instead opt for relatives with preposition stranding, a possibility allowed in their target language (see (51)). There is one exception to this avoidance of pied-piping: according to Goodluck and Stojanovic (1996), Serbo-Croatian learners aged between 5 and 6 years produce and comprehend relatives featuring pied-piping.

In sum, pied-piping in relative clauses is not a natural option in child language; it either does not occur or occurs very rarely. Notice that the problem must not reside in pied-piping per se since children produce pied-piped interrogatives, as shown by Labelle (1990) and illustrated in (67).

(67) Sur quoi on pèse? (2;0)
    on what one weighs
    'On what do we weigh?'

Since pied-piping unequivocally involves *wh*-movement, as the *wh*-operator is overtly represented in (52a), repeated here, Labelle takes the failure to pied-pipe as an indication that children do not form relatives through *wh*-movement.

(52) a. la fille à qui   Kostas va donner le livre
       the girl to whom Kostas will give   the book

6.4.6.2 Resumptive Pronouns in Relative Clauses As Labelle (1990) reports, French-speaking children produce many relatives with resumptive pronouns (**resumptive relatives**) (example from Labelle 1990).[12]

(68) celle-là   que le papa lui   montre un dessin (JF, 5;0)
    that-one there that the father to-her shows a   drawing
    'that one there whose father shows her a drawing'

Other studies have confirmed the massive use of resumptive pronouns in early relative clauses in Continental French (Guasti et al. 1996), Spanish (Pérez-Leroux 1995) and Serbo-Croatian (Goodluck and Stojanovic 1996).[13] English-speaking children use a small number of resumptive pronouns, as discussed by Pérez-Leroux (1995) and exemplified in (69) (examples from Pérez-Leroux 1995, 122).

(69) a. the one that he lifted it   (Lia, 4;5)
    b. the one that the little girl is taking a bath with it   (Callie, 3;5)

The use of resumptive pronouns is not unique to child language. Hebrew, Irish, Palestinian Arabic, Welsh, nonstandard English, and many spoken varieties of Romance (e.g., French, Italian, Spanish, northern Italian dialects) all allow resumptive relatives (see, e.g., McCloskey 1990; Shlonsky 1992). Examples from French, Brianzolo (a northern Italian dialect), Spanish, and nonstandard English are given in (70) ((70a) from Zribi-Hertz 1984; (70c) from Suñer 1998; (70d) from Prince 1990, cited in Suñer 1998).

(70) a. Voici l'homme que Marie lui   a   parlé.
        here-is the man that Marie to-him has talked
        'Here is the man that Marie has talked to him.'
     b. el bagai che g'hoo   da   el liber
        the child that (I) to-him have given the book
        'the child that I gave the book to him'
     c. Hay   personas que no les   interesa nada.
        there-are persons that not to-them interests nothing
        'There are people that nothing interests them.'
     d. You get a rack that the bike will sit on it.

The standard view takes the presence of resumptive pronouns in these adult languages as an indication that no *wh*-movement has occurred;[14] at LF the resumptive pronoun is interpreted as a variable bound by a base-generated operator located in Spec CP (see Chomsky 1982; Shlonsky 1992). The LF structure of a resumptive relative such as (69a) is shown in (71).

(71)

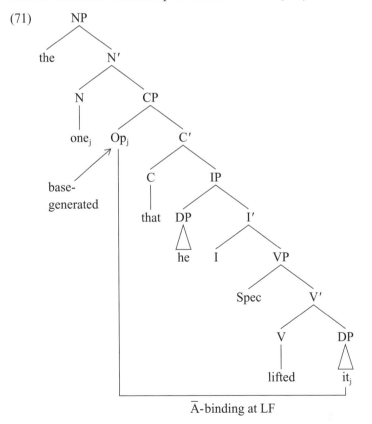

$\overline{\text{A}}$-binding at LF

We see, then, that languages display two kinds of relative clause, one derived by *wh*-movement (recall section 6.4.1) and one derived by LF Ā-binding of a resumptive pronoun. Thus, the use of resumptive pronouns in early relative clauses is consistent with Labelle's (1990) view that relative clauses do not arise through *wh*-movement.

6.4.6.3 Hypotheses about the Derivation of Early Relative Clauses
Early French relative clauses do not display pied-piping but do display the use of resumptive pronouns. Pied-piping is overt evidence that *wh*-movement has occurred in relative clauses, and the use of resumptive pronouns is generally seen as a clue that movement has not occurred. These two pieces of data are at the core of Labelle's (1990) hypothesis that *wh*-movement does not occur in early relative clauses. Labelle grounds her proposal in the belief that early systems include semantic constructs derived by conceptual categories that are later replaced by syntactic constructs (see, e.g., Macnamara 1982). She proposes that early relative clauses are formed exclusively by a semantic mechanism. This proposal raises a strong discontinuity problem since, to converge on the adult target, children would have to give up a semantically based analysis of relative clauses in favor of a syntactic analysis (see Pérez-Leroux 1995). Moreover, the data at hand need not be interpreted as Labelle did. An alternative can be offered that retains some insights of Labelle's proposal yet minimizes the gap between child and adult grammars.

Let us start with early resumptive relatives. The null hypothesis is that early resumptive relatives are like adult ones; they involve base generation in the syntax of an empty operator in Spec CP that binds the pronominal variable at LF.

Children also produce relative clauses with gaps introduced by a complementizer, as in (72), about 50% of the time (see Labelle 1990). (72a) is an oblique relative and (72b) a direct object relative (both are from Guasti et al. 1996). (The correct form of the relative pronoun appears in square brackets.)

(72) a. (Touche le garçon) que [à qui]   la dame a   montré le
        touch   the boy   that [to whom] the lady   has showed the
        trésor ——.   (A., 6;3)
        treasure
     b. celle-ci   qu'elle coupe — (A., 6;3)
        this-one here that she cuts

While resumptive relatives may very well not involve *wh*-movement, adult relatives with gaps are commonly taken to do so. To maintain the hypothesis that early relative clauses with gaps do not feature *wh*-movement, one can say, following Labelle (1996), that the empty category in (72) is a base-generated null resumptive pronoun. On this view relatives with gaps, even object and subject relatives, would be derived like resumptive relatives, the only difference being that in this case the resumptive pronoun is null. The LF structure of (72a) would be (73) (compare with the LF structure in (71) where the resumptive pronoun is overt).

(73)

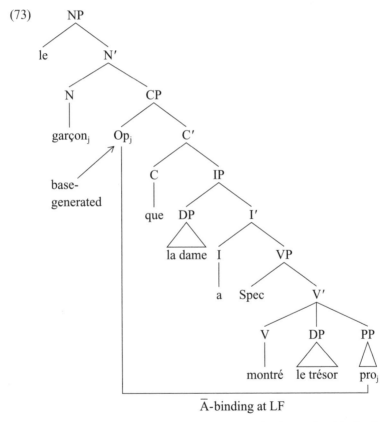

Ā-binding at LF

At LF the base-generated empty operator in Spec CP binds the null resumptive pronoun (indicated with *pro*). In (73) Ā-binding is indicated through coindexation between the empty operator and pro. Thus, resumptive relative clauses and relative clauses with gaps are not derived by movement, but involve base generation of an empty operator in Spec CP that Ā-binds a resumptive pronoun, be it lexical or null.

An alternative is also conceivable. In this case we assume that all early relative clauses with gaps (not featuring pied-piping) are indeed derived by *wh*-movement of an empty operator to Spec CP. Generally, the empty operator is present in subject and object relative clauses, as outlined in section 6.4.1 (see the structure in (54a), repeated here).

(54) a.

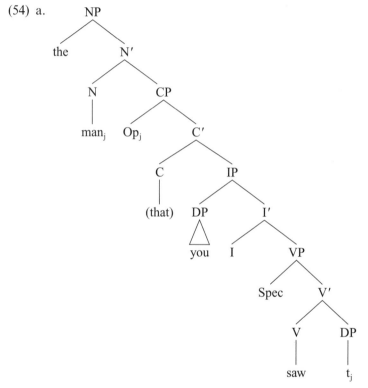

Our assumption amounts to saying that in children's grammar the use of the empty operator is more widespread. Not only subject and direct object relatives but also relatives on oblique arguments would involve movement of a null operator, as shown in (74), the structure assigned to (72a) under this new hypothesis about early relative clauses with gaps.

(74)

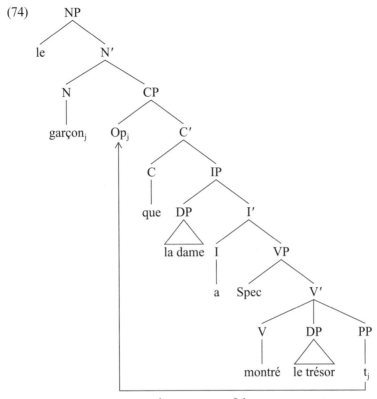

wh-movement of the empty operator

Notice that, unlike in (73), where the *wh*-operator is base-generated in Spec CP, here it is moved to that position, and the empty category in the base position is a variable left by movement (and not a resumptive base-generated null pronoun). This is tantamount to saying that, unlike in the adult grammar, in the child grammar the null operator can be used to derive any relative clause, whatever the function of the relativized argument.

The hypotheses considered so far concerning how early relative clauses are derived can be summarized as follows:

(75) a. *Resumptive relatives*
        Ā-binding at LF of resumptive pronouns by a base-generated empty operator

b. *Relatives with gaps*
   H1: Like resumptive relatives, the gap being a null resumptive
   pronoun
   H2: Wh-movement of a general-purpose empty operator

(75a) (or whatever analysis one adopts for adult resumptive relatives) seems to be fairly uncontroversial. For one thing, French and Spanish learners hear resumptive relatives in the adult speech around them, so it is not surprising to find them in child speech as well. The hypothesis in (75a) has the merit of not creating a discontinuity between the child and adult systems, since it holds that children derive resumptive relative clauses through the same syntactic mechanisms used in adult grammar.

Relatives with gaps are open to two analyses, given in (75b). The idea that relative clauses with gaps do not involve *wh*-movement rests essentially on the absence of pied-piping in relatives in early languages (see section 6.4.6.1). Evidence for the hypothesis that relatives with gaps *do* involve *wh*-movement is discussed in the next section.

6.4.7   *Wh*-Movement in Children's Relative Clauses

What evidence supports a *wh*-movement analysis of early relative clauses?

6.4.7.1   Subject Relatives   Both child and adult French speakers produce subject relatives like (43c), repeated here.

(43) c. la fille qui parle
        the girl that speaks

Qui 'that' is the overt manifestation of a process of specifier-head agreement in CP. In subject relative clauses an empty *wh*-operator moves from the embedded subject position to Spec CP, as shown in (44), repeated here. The moved empty operator agrees with the head of CP, and this agreement process is manifested by *qui*.

(44)

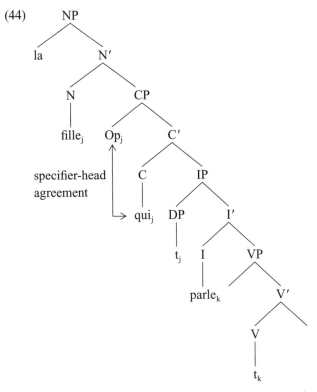

Relative clauses of the kind in (76) are not grammatical; the presence of *que* is taken to indicate that the empty operator has not moved to CP and consequently that agreement in CP has not taken place.

(76) *la   fille que t parle
       the girl that speaks

If early subject relative clauses were not derived by *wh*-movement, but, as suggested in section 6.4.6.3, by base generation of an empty operator in Spec CP Ā-binding a null resumptive pronoun (pro) in subject position, examples such as (76) would have to be licit. They would have the structure in (77), parallel to the structure of oblique relatives in (73).

(77) *[$_{NP}$ la   fille [Op$_j$ que [pro$_j$ parle]]]
        the girl   that   speaks

The relative clause would have a null resumptive pronoun in subject position bound by a base-generated empty operator. The nonexistence of examples like (76) in child French is a hint that *wh*-movement is indeed involved in the derivation of early subject relative clauses.[15]

6.4.7.2 Relatives on Locative Arguments The Canadian French–speaking children studied by Labelle (1990) produced some relatives on locative arguments, introduced (as in the adult language) by the *wh*-element *où* 'where'. This finding was replicated by Guasti et al. (1996), who in fact found that all relatives on locative arguments produced in their study (71 instances) conformed to the adult target. Examples are given in (78).

(78) a. Touche la chaise où   la petite fille s'est assise. (N., 7;1)
        touch   the chair where the little girl SE-REFL is sitting
        'Touch the chair where the little girl is sitting.'
    b. Touche la chaise où   il y a   le garçon. (A., 6;3)
        touch   the chair where there is the boy
    c. Touche la luge où   la fille saute dessus. (V., 6;0)
        touch   the sled where the girl jumps over

One might analyze these constructions by saying that the *wh*-element, an operator, moves to Spec CP by *wh*-movement. Labelle (1996) contests this proposal on the grounds that children overgeneralize *où* 'where' to relatives other than locative relatives, a finding replicated by Guasti et al. and illustrated in (79).

(79) a. Tu dois toucher le garçon où   [dont]   son chariot
        you must touch   the boy   where [whose] his hand-cart
        roule. (A., 6;3)
        goes
        'You must touch the boy whose hand-cart is going.'
    b. Tu veux toucher le couteau où   [avec lequel] le monsieur
        you want to touch the knife   where [with which] the man
        est en train de couper l'arbre? (S., 4;4)
        is cutting   the tree
        'Do you want to touch the knife with which the man is cutting the tree?'

However, it is possible to interpret this overgeneralization otherwise: namely, by saying that children take *où* 'where' as another general-purpose relative operator and use it for all kinds of relative clauses. Labelle rejects this possibility, but it cannot be overlooked given that there are adult languages, such as Swiss German dialects, in which the counterpart of *où* is used to form all types of relative clauses, such as the one in (80).

(80) dr Maa wo   i em   s'Büch   ghä   ha
     the man where I to-him the book given have
     'the man to whom I gave the book'

6.4.7.3   *Wh*-Movement or Not?   It is time to evaluate the evidence for
and against *wh*-movement in early relative clauses. Children produce
relatives with gaps. For subject relatives an analysis in terms of *wh*-
movement of an empty operator cannot be discarded. If this is valid for
subject relatives, there is nothing that precludes extending the same
analysis to early object relatives, which are target consistent. In this way,
subject and object relatives are both derived by *wh*-movement of an
empty operator that leaves a trace in the base position. *Wh*-movement
might also be involved in the derivation of early locative relatives. By
assuming that *wh*-movement is responsible for the construction of subject, object, and locative relatives, we do not introduce an unwanted difference between the child and adult systems. As a matter of fact, in
children's speech these three types of relatives are generally adult in form.
If we had to assume that they received different representations in the
child and adult grammars, we would run into a learnability problem. How
could children discover that a given sequence that they had analyzed in a
certain way needed to be reanalyzed in another way? What kind of positive evidence would be available to trigger the reanalysis? The hypothesis
that subject, object, and locative relatives are derived via *wh*-movement
avoids this problem and ensures continuity between the child and adult
grammars.

What about relative clauses on oblique arguments, which are introduced by the complementizer *que* or by the *wh*-operator *où* 'where'? If we
want to maintain that these are also derived by *wh*-movement, we must
assume that they involve a general-purpose null operator or a general-
purpose *où* operator, respectively. This brings us to the following revision
of the hypotheses in (75b):

(81) b. *Relatives with gaps*
        Wh-movement of a general-purpose null or *où* 'where' operator

We continue to assume that unlike relatives with gaps, which are derived by *wh*-movement, resumptive relative clauses are derived by base
generation of an empty operator in Spec CP that binds the resumptive
pronoun at LF. That there are two ways of deriving relatives in early
systems should not come as a surprise since the same holds for the
adult targets, although in the latter case these two options seem to belong

to two distinct registers, at least to some extent. Suñer (1998) points out that Spanish speakers of all socioeconomic levels use resumptive relatives, although this use is condemned by prescriptive grammarians. Similarly, resumptive relatives are found in nonstandard/spoken French. By adopting the hypothesis in (81), we considerably reduce the difference between the child and adult grammars; what needs to be explained is why children use general-purpose operators and avoid prepositional pied-piping. The problem cannot reside in pied-piping per se since children do apply pied-piping in interrogatives (see section 6.4.6.1). Pied-piping in relative clauses involves the use of a set of relative pronouns. Children's deviations are likely due to their ignorance of relative pronouns, a lacuna that one must assume is filled in during the school years through explicit teaching since the 7-year-old French-speaking children investigated by Guasti et al. did not use prepositional pied-piping in relatives (see Guasti and Shlonsky 1995 for an alternative explanation). Under this view the null operator or *où* 'where' replaces the more specific forms of relative pronouns or *wh*-operators that take some time to enter children's lexicon. Following a suggestion by McKee, McDaniel, and Snedecker (1998), we can take the null operator and *où* 'where' as defaults that children avail themselves of until they have learned the more specific forms. These default forms might be "flagged" (see Pinker 1984 for this notion), that is, marked in the lexicon as unsure forms that give way to more specific forms as soon as these are learned. Under this view children have the same grammar for relative clauses as adults have. The deviations from the target are a matter of lexical learning: children need to learn the full range of *wh*-operators.

Still, an interesting question that remains to be answered is why children avoid pied-piping in the first place. One possibility suggested by McDaniel, McKee, and Berstein (1998) in a study on early English is that pied-piping is a more costly operation than preposition stranding or, it might be suggested, than the operations involved in the formation of resumptive relatives or of relatives with general-purpose *wh*-operators.

6.5   SUMMARY AND CONCLUDING REMARKS

Children form *wh*-questions from their first multiword combinations. They respect the requirement of the *Wh*-Criterion and know the values of the parameters involved in question formation. Whenever the target language requires overt *wh*-movement, so does the early language. Learners of English know that their language requires subject-auxiliary inversion. Nevertheless, their negative *wh*-questions often take nonadult forms, and often they omit the auxiliary. One way of looking at these questions is that they involve the presence of a null auxiliary in C.

As for relative clauses, we have discarded the idea that children misinterpret relative clauses in experimental studies because they initially do not have access to the mechanism of recursion and consequently assign these clauses a flat structure. Rather, children do manifest adultlike competence when experimental stimuli are simplified and the setting is made felicitous for the use of relative clauses. In their production of relative clauses children deviate somewhat from the adult target. French and Spanish learners frequently use resumptive relatives and avoid prepositional pied-piping. The fact that children produce resumptive relatives is not surprising since these are abundantly attested in the linguistic environment. These resumptive relatives are derived by base generation of an empty operator in Spec CP, in both adult and child grammars. Children also produce relatives with gaps, but they avoid prepositional pied-piping. The claim that these early relatives are also not derived by *wh*-movement is controversial. On the one hand, by producing subject relatives, French learners adopt a structure that is generally assumed to involve *wh*-movement. On the other hand, it is true that children have a general tendency to avoid prepositional pied-piping, a fact that Labelle (1990) interpreted as evidence against occurrence of *wh*-movement in early relatives. However, avoidance of prepositional pied-piping can be viewed in another way. English learners avoid prepositional pied-piping and prefer preposition stranding, an option that is perfectly acceptable in the adult language. French and Spanish learners avoid prepositional pied-piping and use resumptive relatives, which are also acceptable in the adult language. Thus, avoidance of prepositional pied-piping in some cases results in structures that are perfectly acceptable in the adult language. However, it may also lead children to produce structures that are not adultlike, in which a gap, rather than a resumptive pronoun, is used. It is possible, then, that relatives with gaps are derived by *wh*-movement of general-purpose *wh*-operators. Children's deviation from the target can be attributed to lack of lexical knowledge: children do not know the relative operators that are used in relatives featuring prepositional pied-piping and instead use a nonspecific relative operator (the empty operator or *où* 'where').

In this chapter we have discussed four main kinds of deviation from the adult target: English matrix *wh*-questions lacking inversion, English auxless questions, English and Dutch medial-*wh* questions, and relative clauses lacking pied-piping and featuring general-purpose operators. Researchers have hypothesized that the deviations observed in early

English matrix *wh*-questions arise from a language-specific property that needs to be learned: the existence in English of two classes of verbs (auxiliaries and lexical verbs) with distinct morphosyntactic properties. For auxless questions researchers have invoked the mechanism of clausal truncation that allows a null auxiliary to survive in the specifier of the root. Ultimately, the presence of such a null auxiliary in early English may also depend on the existence of the two classes of verbs: the null auxiliary can be viewed as a default used until children become more confident in the use of specific auxiliaries. Medial-*wh* questions originate from the combination of two factors. On the one hand, by producing medial-*wh* questions, children exploit an option present in UG (occurrence of specifier-head agreement in CP); on the other hand, they manifest uncertainty about the appropriate lexical form of the agreeing complementizers. Finally, children use general-purpose *wh*-operators in forming relative clauses. These operators may also be considered defaults that are replaced later by the appropriate forms that need to be learned.

It seems that children often deviate from their target language because they need to learn language-specific aspects, a process that takes time. By contrast, the innate component seems to emerge rapidly, witness the fact that universal constraints are manifest from the earliest productive use of structures involving *wh*-movement. The *Wh*-Criterion is obeyed early on, and early relative clauses have a hierarchical structure (involving recursion).

Summary of Linguistic Development

1. Children between 2 and 3 years of age have set the parameters governing question formation, the one governing overt movement or in-situ placement of the *wh*-element and the one regulating the application or nonapplication of I-to-C movement.
2. German-, Italian-, and Swedish-speaking children between 2 and 3 years of age move the verb from I to C in questions.
3. English learners also move the verb from I to C, but on occasion they deviate from the adult target (producing nonadult negative questions and auxless questions up to 4–5 years).
4. Children comprehend and produce long-distance *wh*-questions around age 3.
5. By 3 years children have access to the rule of recursion and form relative clauses as adults do, through *wh*-movement (relative with gaps) or through $\bar{\text{A}}$-binding at LF of resumptive pronouns.
6. Children speaking Romance languages use resumptive pronouns and avoid prepositional pied-piping until at least 7 years of age.

Further Reading

The idea that subject-auxiliary inversion reveals that children's knowledge of grammar is structure dependent is discussed in Crain and Nakayama 1987. Further discussion of long-distance extraction and the subjacency condition that operates in this case is to be found in Goodluck, Foley, and Sedivy 1992, Roeper and de Villiers 1992, 1994, de Villiers and Roeper 1995. A subject/object asymmetry in the production of *wh*-questions is discussed in Stromswold 1995: namely, that on average English learners produce more subject than object *who*-questions, although some children produce object *who*-questions before subject *who*-questions. Tyack and Ingram 1977 reports better comprehension of subject than of object questions. Volume 4, issue 1–2, of the journal *Language Acquisition* is dedicated to *wh*-movement.

Key Words

Agreement in CP
Auxless questions
Axiom on clausal representation
Medial-*wh* questions
Null auxiliary hypothesis
Pied-piping in relatives
Resumptive relatives
Subject-auxiliary inversion (SAI)
Wh-Criterion

Study Questions

1. Discuss the stages of subject-auxiliary inversion.

2. What kind of evidence supports the null auxiliary hypothesis for questions like *What John eating?*

3. Compare early German/Italian/Swedish questions with early English questions. What conclusions can you draw?

4. Discuss the data that motivated the proposal that children's medial-*wh* questions involve agreement in CP. Can you think of an alternative analysis?

5. How can one show that children's failure to comprehend OS relatives does not have its source in their linguistic competence?

6. Discuss arguments against the conjoined-clause analysis of early relative clauses.

7. What problems face Labelle's (1990) proposal that early relative clauses are derived by a semantic mechanism?

8. What data suggest that French-speaking children derive relative clauses by *wh*-movement?

9. Design an experiment aimed at eliciting (from children) relative clauses based on different syntactic positions (see Crain and Thornton 1998).

Chapter 7

Acquisition of NP-Movement

INTRODUCTION

In this chapter we will look at another instance of movement, NP-movement. In particular, we will look at NP-movement in passive sentences, although we will also discuss an occurrence of this kind of movement in active sentences: namely, movement of the subject from its base-generated position, Spec VP, to its surface position, Spec IP (see Haegeman 1994, sec. 6.5).

Early experiments found that children's passive sentences display some peculiar properties. These led researchers to assume that at least until age 5–6 learners do not have access to the transformational mechanism involved in the formation of verbal passives, a limitation that was imputed to immaturity. More recently it has been shown that children's difficulties are essentially limited to passive sentences based on nonactional verbs and including a *by*-phrase, such as *Aladdin was seen by Jasmine*.

This finding has promoted a different account of early passive sentences, according to which children's difficulty is located not in the transformational mechanisms for forming verbal passives, but in the mechanism responsible for integrating the *by*-phrase associated with a nonactional passive verb.

This chapter is organized in four sections. Section 7.1 surveys basic properties of passive sentences in adult grammar and presents earlier findings showing that children have difficulties with passive sentences. Section 7.2 discusses a maturational account of children's difficulties with passive sentences. Section 7.3 outlines some problems for this account. Section 7.4 presents new data and discusses another proposal about children's difficulties with passives that capitalizes on the role of the *by*-phrase.

7.1 PASSIVE CONSTRUCTIONS IN ADULT AND CHILD GRAMMAR

In this section we will consider aspects of the analysis of passive sentences in adult language that are relevant for evaluating the child data. Then we will look at results from various experiments showing that children do not seem to have full mastery of passive constructions.

7.1.1 Passive Constructions in Adult Grammar

Consider the active and passive sentences in (1).

(1) a. Aladdin scratched Horace.

    b. Horace was scratched by Aladdin.

Passivization prompts a reorganization of the grammatical functions found in active sentences. The object of the active verb (the internal argument; *Horace* in (1a)) becomes the subject of the passive sentence. The subject of the active sentence (the external argument; *Aladdin* in (1a)) is optionally expressed in a prepositional phrase introduced with the preposition *by* in the passive sentence.

Movement of the object to subject position is an instance of A-movement: the NP object moves to Spec IP, an A-position. In this position it triggers agreement on the inflected verb. The internal argument leaves behind a coindexed trace, as seen in (2), through which it receives a thematic role.

(2)

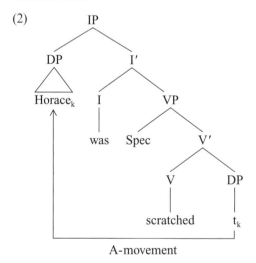

A-movement

More precisely, the A(rgumental)-chain formed by $\langle\text{Horace}_k, t_k\rangle$ is assigned a thematic role by the verb *scratched*.

The NP that plays the role of the subject of the active clause or the external argument of the verb *scratch*—namely, *Aladdin*—need not be expressed. It is assumed that the thematic role that is normally assigned to this NP in (1a) is assigned to the passive morpheme, affixed to the verb in (1b). Since this role is assigned to some element in the syntactic representation, it remains syntactically active. The syntactic presence of the external argument is evident from the following examples (for arguments that the external argument is indeed syntactically present, see also Baker, Johnson, and Roberts 1989; Baker 1988).

(3) a. Food should never be served only for oneself.
    b. The ship was sunk [PRO to collect the insurance money].

In (3a) the anaphor *oneself* must be bound in compliance with Principle A of the binding theory (see section 8.1). The binder is the passive morpheme (which receives the thematic role of the external argument of *serve*). (3b) says that someone sank the ship so that that person could collect the insurance. This meaning is captured by saying that the passive morpheme, which is assigned the thematic role of the external argument of *sink*, functions as an argument: it can control PRO in the adjunct clause.

Because the thematic role of the external argument is assigned to the passive morpheme, it cannot be assigned again to another NP; to express it, English speakers use an adjunct PP headed by the preposition *by*, as in (4).

(4) Horace was scratched by Aladdin.

The PP *by Aladdin* is clearly related to the verb: it is the agent of the active sentence (see Marantz 1984 for further evidence). To capture this intuition, it is assumed that the agent role, which is assigned to the passive morphology, is transmitted to the NP in the *by*-phrase, an operation expressed by coindexing the passive morpheme and the *by*-phrase as in (5) (see also Jaeggli 1986).

(5)

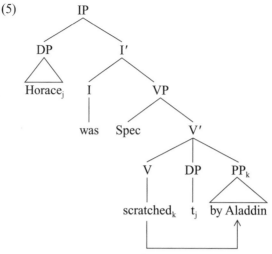

transmission of the thematic role

In summary, passive constructions involve (among other things) the following processes:

(6) a. NP-movement of the object (of the active sentence) to Spec IP,
   b. assignment of the thematic role of the external argument to the passive morpheme,
   c. optional transmission to the NP in the *by*-phrase of the thematic role assigned to the passive morpheme.

Also important for understanding children's passive is the distinction between **adjectival** and **verbal passives**. A short passive in English, like (7), is ambiguous: it can be an adjectival or a verbal passive.

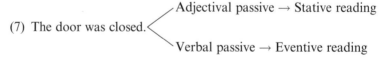

(7) The door was closed. Adjectival passive → Stative reading

Verbal passive → Eventive reading

(7) can refer either to the state of the door's being closed or to the event of the door's being closed. These different interpretations reflect different syntactic structures that this sentence receives. Under the **stative reading** (7) is an instance of adjectival passive and *closed* heads an adjectival phrase. Under the **eventive reading** (7) is an instance of verbal passive and *closed* heads a VP.

If the *by*-phrase is added to (7) to obtain (8), there is no longer any ambiguity; (8) is a verbal passive and is interpreted as describing the event of the door's having been closed by Aladdin.

(8) The door was closed by Aladdin.

As noted, adjectival and verbal passives are derived through different mechanisms. Verbal passives are formed through the operations summarized in (6), which occur in the syntactic component. Adjectival passives are standardly assumed to be generated in the lexicon (see Wasow 1977). For example, the verb *close* takes an agent role and a theme role. The lexical process that derives the adjectival passive *closed* involves a change of category: the passive of the verb *close* is an adjective. It also involves the elimination of the thematic role assigned to the external argument (the agent of *close*) from the argument structure and the externalization of the argument assigned the theme role (the object acted upon; here, *the door*); that is, this argument becomes the external argument in the lexicon and is directly projected into the subject position. The crucial point is that unlike in verbal passives, in adjectival passives the argument bearing the theme role is not moved into the subject position, but is generated there (see Williams 1980).[1] Because the external argument (the agent in our example) has been erased from the argument structure associated with *closed*, it cannot be assigned in the syntax to the passive morphology. Since the NP in the *by*-phrase cannot receive a thematic role by transmission, it cannot be projected. (9) summarizes the operations involved in forming an adjectival passive, and the syntactic consequences of these operations.

(9) *Formation of adjectival passives*

Active	Adjectival passive
close → *closed*	
Verb → Adjective	

a. Argument structure of *close* [+V]:
           [agent,   theme]
       (external argument; internal argument)
b. Elimination of the agent role of the external argument
c. Externalization of the internal argument
d. Argument structure of *closed* [+A]:
           [theme]
       (external argument)
e. No *by*-phrase
f. Projection of the newly externalized argument in subject position

The syntactic representation of (7) under the adjectival reading is (10a)—a representation identical to that of a sentence including a standard adjective, as a comparison between (10a) and (10b), the structure of *Aladdin is happy*, shows (see also Chomsky 1981). Notice that, unlike the representation of verbal passives (see (5)), the representation of adjectival passives does not include traces of moved elements.

(10) a.

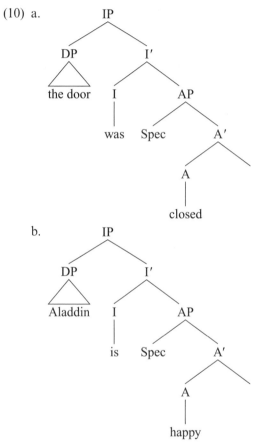

Unlike in English, in Hebrew and German adjectival passives are morphologically (and interpretively) distinct from verbal passives, and ambiguities like the one in (7) are never found in these languages. In Hebrew, verbal passives are inflected for tense and agreement, as verbs are. Adjectival passives do not take tense markers; they agree in gender and number, as adjectives do, but not in person. Tense is expressed on the copular verb *haya* 'to be'. Verbal passives allow the *by*-phrase, as in (11), while adjectival passives do not, as in (12) (examples from Borer and Wexler 1987).

(11) *Verbal passives*
Tense and agreement inflection on the verb; *by*-phrase possible
a. Ha-yalda sorka   (al-yedey 'ima   shel-a).
    the-girl combed-PASS by   mother of-her
    'The girl was combed by her mother.'
b. Ha-yalda tesorak   (al-yedey 'ima   shel-a).
    the-girl will-combed-PASS by   mother of-her
    'The girl will be combed by her mother.'

(12) *Adjectival passives*
Only gender and number inflection on the adjective; *by*-phrase not possible
a. Ha-yalda hayta mesoreket (*al-yedey 'ima   shel-a).
    the-girl was   combed-ADJ by   mother of-her
b. Ha-yalda tihiye mesoreket (*al-yedey 'ima   shel-a).
    the-girl will-be combed-ADJ by   mother of-her

7.1.2   Passive Constructions in Child Grammar

Earlier studies report that children's passives manifest certain peculiar properties.

Maratsos et al. (1985) found that before age 4–5 English learners produce and comprehend **actional passives** (passives of actional verbs such as *comb*, *scratch*, *touch*) better than **nonactional passives** (passives of nonactional verbs such as *see*, *hear*, *fear*); that is, they perform better with sentences such as (13a) than with sentences such as (13b).

(13) a. Jasmine was combed (by Wendy).
     b. Peter Pan was feared (by Captain Hook).

This asymmetry was also found by Sudhalter and Braine (1985).

Horgan (1978) observes that short passives (passives lacking the *by*-phrase) are produced and comprehended earlier than long passives (passives including the *by*-phrase). Two examples of children's short passives, produced in a task in which children were required to describe pictures, are shown in (14) (from Horgan 1978).

(14) a. Tree is broken.
     b. That was colored.

Horgan also points out that early passives describe after-the-fact observations on states; that is, they describe a state and not an event. In other words, early passive sentences are similar to sentences like *John is blond* or *Aladdin is happy* that report the state in which John or Aladdin finds himself. For example, (14a) describes the state resulting from some action that has occurred: the tree is in a broken state.

Finally, Berman and Sagi (1981) observe that Hebrew learners produce adjectival passives earlier than verbal passives (which they do not produce until 10 years). The same is reported for early German by Mills (1985).

7.1.3   Intermediate Summary

The findings discussed in this section are summarized in (15).

(15) a. Passives based on actional verbs are better comprehended and more easily produced than passives based on nonactional verbs.
  b. *By*-phrases tend to be omitted.
  c. Passives report after-the-fact observations about states.
  d. Adjectival passives appear earlier than verbal passives in early Hebrew and German.

These findings have been interpreted as evidence that children do not attain full mastery of passives until at least 5–6 years.

7.2   A MATURATIONAL ACCOUNT OF EARLY PASSIVE CONSTRUCTIONS

In this section we will look at a maturational account of children's difficulties with passives, according to which the properties of early passives are due to the unavailability in child grammar of the mechanism for connecting the moved object and its trace.

7.2.1   Early Passives Are Adjectival Passives

Borer and Wexler (1987) argue that the properties in (15) follow from the assumption that the early grammar only allows the formation of adjectival passives. In other words, at a certain stage of development children can avail themselves only of the mechanisms in (9) responsible for the formation of adjectival passives. Hebrew and German learners clearly start by producing adjectival passives; this is obvious because in these languages verbal and adjectival passives are morphologically distinct. English learners produce short passives like (7), repeated here.

(7) The door was closed.

Although (7) is ambiguous for adults, since there is no morphological distinction between verbal and adjectival passives in English, Borer and Wexler claim that it is not ambiguous for children. In early speech (7) is an adjectival passive; that is, it has the structure in (10a), repeated here.

(10) a.

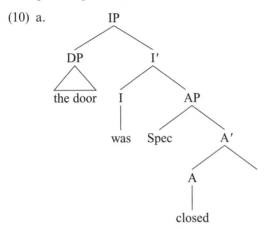

Borer and Wexler explain the properties of children's passives listed in (15) as follows. Being adjectival, children's passive sentences are incompatible with the *by*-phrase, as adult adjectival passives are. Being adjectival, children's passive sentences only report on after-the-fact observations about states, because this is the interpretation associated with adjectival passives in the adult language. Finally, because nonactional verbs usually do not lend themselves to adjectival passives, children, who only have the tools to produce adjectival passives, will be unable to form nonactional passives.

7.2.2 Maturation of A-Chains and the Properties of Children's Passives

Borer and Wexler (1987) propose that children's grammar includes mechanisms for forming only adjectival passives, not verbal passives. One crucial property distinguishing verbal from adjectival passives is that in the former the NP occupying subject position is moved there from underlying object position, whereas in the latter it is directly generated there. Borer and Wexler claim that children cannot produce verbal passives because they are unable to form A-chains and thus cannot assign the thematic role to the moved object in a structure such as (5). In other words, the displaced object cannot be connected to its trace and does not receive a thematic role. When children want to express a passive sentence, they are obliged to circumvent their limitations by forming adjectival passives in the lexicon, thus exploiting an option made available by UG.

Since the mechanism for forming verbal passives is part of UG, it need not be learned, and should be readily available to the child. Because at a certain stage it is not, we must find out why. Borer and Wexler propose that the machinery that allows the formation of A-chains is subject to maturation (sometimes called **maturation of A-chains**). Clearly certain abilities, like the ability to walk, become available at certain developmental points. Similarly, certain aspects of linguistic competence are deemed to mature at certain developmental points. The mechanism responsible for the formation of A-chains does not mature until at least age 5–6. As a consequence, children cannot produce verbal passives and resort to adjectival passives (see also Pierce 1992a regarding the acquisition of passives in early Spanish and Babyonyshev et al. 2001 for evidence from Russian).

7.2.3   Intermediate Summary

Children's passive sentences present certain peculiarities listed in (15). According to Borer and Wexler (1987), the restrictions in (15) hold because children's grammar allows the formation of adjectival passives only. Children cannot produce verbal passives because they do not have access to the mechanism for forming A-chains that is biologically determined to become available at 5–6 years. Adjectival passives are derived in the lexicon and, unlike verbal passives, do not require the formation of an A-chain. Children's passives, being adjectival, are incompatible with the *by*-phrase, and their meaning is stative, as is the case for adjectival passives in the adult language.

7.3   PROBLEMS WITH THE MATURATIONAL ACCOUNT

As we will see, the claim that the mechanism for forming A-chains matures has been challenged on both theoretical and empirical grounds.

7.3.1   A-Chains and the VP-Internal Subject Hypothesis

A potential theoretical challenge for the maturational view comes from an innovation in linguistic theory introduced around the start of the 1990s. As noted earlier (section 4.4.2.1), it is widely assumed that subjects are universally base-generated within VP and then are moved to Spec IP (see, e.g., Koopman and Sportiche 1991). Like movement of the underlying object to subject position in passive sentences, this movement is an instance of A-movement. It involves the formation of an A-chain between the moved subject and the coindexed trace in VP, as illustrated in (16b), the structure of (16a). In both cases the moved NP determines agreement with the inflected verb.

(16) a. Alice will jump.

b.

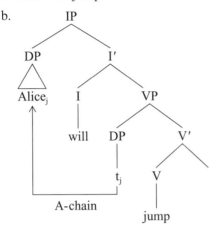

The hypothesis that subjects are generated in VP is a problem for the maturational account only if one accepts it; if the linguistic arguments in its favor are too weak, the challenge does not arise. Since this hypothesis *is* fairly well accepted, let us take it as valid and examine the consequences for the maturational account of children's passives.

We have seen (section 4.2.4) that children's finite sentences include an inflectional projection IP to which the finite verb moves. There is clear evidence that lexical subjects in finite clauses occupy Spec IP in the speech of 2- to 3-year-old learners. For example, subject clitics in early French occur in finite clauses and precede the verb, which is known to occupy I (see section 4.3.2); therefore, they must occupy Spec IP. Other lexical subjects also precede the finite verb in early French, according to Friedemann (1993). Friedemann found that out of 160 lexical subjects occurring in the speech of two French learners (Grégoire and Philippe), 49 (or 35%) preceded the finite verb (the rest followed the finite verb). Subjects precede the finite verb in other early languages as well, for example, in German and Dutch (section 4.2.4.2). Thus, early finite sentences with preverbal subjects necessarily involve an A-chain connecting the subject in Spec IP to its trace in Spec VP (for further evidence in favor of subject raising out of VP, see Harris and Wexler 1996; Pierce 1992b; Déprez and Pierce 1993).

Borer and Wexler (1992) note the problem that the VP-internal subject hypothesis poses for the view that the mechanism for forming A-chains matures, and they propose a solution compatible with their maturational view of early passives. They claim that not all A-chains are problematic for children, but only those A-chains that relate two potential theta positions. The A-chain that connects the subject in Spec IP and its trace is not that kind, because only Spec VP is a theta position; in Spec IP no thematic role is assigned. By contrast, the A-chain that arises in passive sentences includes a link that connects two theta positions. (Such A-chains are called *nontrivial A-chains*.) Fox and Grodzinsky (1998) spell out this hypothesis along the following lines: The proposal that subjects are generated within VP requires revising the analysis of passives outlined in section 7.1. In passive sentences Spec VP is a potential theta position, but the thematic role usually associated with the DP in this position is assigned to the passive morphology. The object generated as sister to V does not move directly from its base position to Spec IP; instead, it raises first to Spec VP, a potential theta position, and then to Spec IP. Under these assumptions the structure of (1b) is not (2) or (5), but (17).

(17)

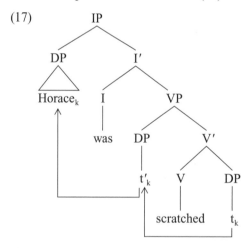

The representation in (17) is an updated version of the representation in (2). Since Spec VP is a potential theta position, the first link of the A-chain $\langle t'_k, t_k \rangle$ in (17) connects two potential theta positions.[2] It is this link of the A-chain that creates problems for children and makes them unable to build the A-chain in verbal passives. The chain from Spec VP to Spec IP, which is common to both passive and active sentences, is not problematic, because it does not connect two theta positions. With these amendments the maturational account of children's passives can still be maintained.

7.3.2 Unaccusative Verbs

A more serious problem for the maturational account comes from sentences including unaccusative verbs, like *arrive, come, go, remain, descend, climb, run, fall* (Burzio 1986; Haegeman 1994, chap. 6). These verbs have an internal argument generated in object position that, like the internal argument in passives, raises to Spec IP and behaves like a (surface) subject in that it triggers agreement on the verb. Movement of the internal argument of unaccusative verbs involves the same kind of A-chain found in passives. Under the assumptions introduced in the previous section, this means that the internal argument moves from object position first to Spec VP and then to Spec IP, as shown in (18b), the representation of (18a).

(18) a. John has arrived.

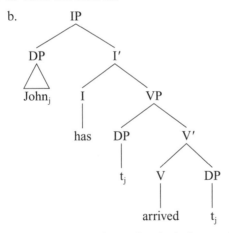

If children do not form the A-chain required for representing verbal passives, they would be expected either to avoid sentences with unaccusative verbs or to produce such sentences, but with the internal argument still in its base-generated position; that is, they would be expected to systematically produce sentences like (19a,b).

(19) a. Arrive John.
     b. Come a boy.

Sarah's transcripts in the CHILDES database show that this expectation is not fulfilled. Transcripts in the age range 2;3–2;6 contained 50 declarative sentences with unaccusative verbs; in all cases the internal argument was in preverbal position, as in the following examples:

(20) a. My teddy bear gone.   (Sarah, 2;3)
    b. Marie go.   (Sarah, 2;3)
    c. I fall down.   (Sarah, 2;6)

Other children reportedly produce unaccusative sentences with the internal argument in postverbal position, but not systematically. Déprez and Pierce (1993) offer examples such as these:

(21) a. Going it.   (Naomi, 1;10)
    b. Come car.   (Eve, 1;6)
    c. Fall pants.   (Nina, 1;11)

Pierce (1992b) and Déprez and Pierce (1993) report that in the vast majority of cases the order in (21), with the internal argument or the surface subject in postverbal position, is observed only with unaccusative verbs; with unergative verbs this is never found. The expectation that children are unable to move the internal argument of unaccusative verbs because they cannot form nontrivial A-chains is therefore not fulfilled (see also Snyder and Stromswold 1997). Even though English learners sometimes fail to raise the internal argument of unaccusative verbs, these failures cannot be taken as evidence that they cannot form nontrivial A-chains, because in most cases they do.

Babyonyshev et al. (2001) (see Borer and Wexler 1992) suggest that children do not assign the adult structure to sentences with unaccusative verbs. They propose that instead of the structure in (18b), children's unaccusative sentences have the structure in (22).

(22)

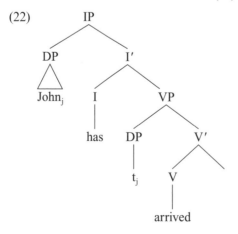

In this structure *John* is an external argument generated in Spec VP, as all subjects are, and it moves from there to Spec IP. Remember that under the amendment proposed in section 7.3.1 the chain from Spec VP to Spec IP is not problematic for children. In advancing their proposal, Babyonyshev et al. are saying that children analyze sentences with unaccusative verbs as if they included unergative verbs; that is, they classify unaccusative verbs as being unergative verbs like *sleep* and *telephone*, whose argument is generated in Spec VP.

There are two serious drawbacks to this proposal. First, in languages like Italian, unaccusative and unergative verbs select different auxiliaries: 'be' and 'have', respectively. If children took unaccusative verbs to be unergative verbs, Italian learners would be expected to choose the wrong auxiliary and to produce sentences like (23a), rather than the correct form (23b).

(23) a. *Gianni ha andato.
        Gianni has left
     b. Gianni è andato.
        Gianni is left
        'Gianni left.'

The Italian data show that this expectation is not borne out. Between 2;0 and 2;7 an Italian learner, Diana, produced 22 sentences with an auxiliary and an unaccusative verb. Of these, only 3 included the wrong auxiliary ('have' rather than 'be'); the others correctly included 'be'. Samples of early Italian sentences with unaccusatives are given in (24).

(24) a. È   caccata.   (Diana, 2;0)
        (she) is fallen down
        'She fell down.'
     b. È volato via   Titti. (Diana, 2;5)
        is flown away Titti
        'Titti flew away.'

These data are only compatible with the view that Italian learners have clear knowledge of unaccusative verbs before 3 years. A similar conclusion follows from Snyder, Hyams, and Crisma's (1995) analysis of auxiliary selection in Italian reflexive constructions. Thus, it ought to be the case that Italian learners represent sentences including unaccusative verbs as in (18b) and not as in (22); consequently, they can form nontrivial A-chains. The idea that children misanalyze unaccusative verbs as unergative is clearly inadequate for early Italian, and the findings discussed here make it suspect to claim that English learners make this mistake (but see Baby-onyshev et al. 2001 for counterarguments). Why should the unergative/unaccusative split be part of the early Italian grammar, but not the early English one?

A more serious drawback is that if English learners assigned (18a) the structure in (22), how could they correct their erroneous unergative analysis of clauses with unaccusative verbs? They would hardly receive any positive evidence that could help them to do this—that is, to figure out that (18a) has the structural representation in (18b) and not the one in (22) (see Snyder and Stromswold 1997, 294fn. 18, for discussion of this point).

In sum, the existence in child speech of adultlike sentences with unaccusative verbs poses a serious problem for the maturational account of children's passive.

7.3.3   Intermediate Summary

The maturational account of children's difficulties with passives encounters several theoretical and empirical problems. If the hypothesis that subjects are generated in the VP is correct, the claim that children cannot form A-chains, as the maturational account holds, cannot be maintained as such. In fact, Borer and Wexler (1992) have amended their proposal by assuming that children cannot form certain types of A-chains, nontrivial A-chains. Empirical problems come from the observation that children have a quite sophisticated knowledge of unaccusative verbs, whose argument generated in object position raises to subject position, a movement that gives rise to an A-chain of the same type found in passive constructions. Children move the argument of unaccusatives to preverbal position. Moreover, in languages where unaccusative and unergative verbs select different auxiliaries (e.g., Italian), children do not make mistakes, and they select the correct auxiliary as a function of verb type.

7.4   NEW FINDINGS ABOUT EARLY PASSIVES

More recent findings cast further doubt on the view that children have difficulty producing and comprehending passive sentences. There is evidence that children know some aspects of the machinery involved in passivization.

First, Pinker, Lebeaux, and Frost (1987) show that from about 3 years English-speaking children spontaneously produce passives like those in (25).

(25) a. He all tied up, Mommy.   (Adam, 3;7)
    b. I don't want the bird to get eated.   (Adam, 3;7)
    c. I want to be shooted.   (Adam, 3;8)
    d. How could it go up if it's not ... if it's not flyed?   (Adam, 3;10)
    e. His mouth is splitted.   (Sarah, 5;1)

As these examples show, children produce different forms of the passive: some structures have the auxiliary *be*, others have the auxiliary *get* (called **be-passives** and **get-passives**, respectively). Some participles used in these passives are incorrect—a hint that children form passives productively. The most interesting fact is that the passives in (25) cannot have a stative reading and thus cannot be adjectival passives. In other words, children's passives are not limited to a stative reading; at least some have an eventive interpretation that is usually associated with verbal passives. Similar evidence is provided by Demuth (1989), who shows that children speaking Sesotho, a Bantu language, produce passive constructions including the *by*-phrase from about 2;8 years. A constraint holding in Sesotho prohibits a *wh*-word in subject position. To ask a subject question like English *Who bought this book?*, a Sesotho speaker must use the passive structure equivalent to *This book has been bought by who?* Sesotho learners know this constraint on subject *wh*-words: when they have to ask a subject question, they use the required passive structure. Interestingly, the passive sentences that Sesotho learners produce have an eventive interpretation and must therefore be verbal passives.

More evidence for early mastery of passives comes from a study probing children's ability to form passives with nonce verbs. Pinker, Lebeaux, and Frost (1987) carried out elicited-production and comprehension experiments using an act-out task with 4-year-old English learners. In the comprehension experiment they first taught the children nonce verbs and then tested them with active and passive sentences including these new verbs. For example, they taught children the nonce verb *pilk* with the meaning 'hit'. They then presented the children with a sentence like (26) and asked them to act out its meaning.

(26) The elephant is pilked by the kitty.

In the production experiment they presented the children with two animals involved in some action and invited them to describe what was happening to one of the animals, preceding the request with a statement that would likely elicit a passive sentence. For example, if the two animals were a kitty and an elephant, they might say:

(27) Now something is happening to the elephant.

By using (27), they made the elephant the topic of the discourse so as to elicit a passive sentence. Children were invited to say what was happening to the elephant. It was found that children could produce and comprehend passive sentences including novel verbs. Since the verbs used in the experiments were nonce verbs, children could not have been exposed to them before. This ensured that children's responses must have been based on knowing the machinery for forming passive sentences and that the passive verbs the children produced were not rote-learned forms. Thus, the data at hand show that children can form passives productively and that these passives can have the eventive interpretation usually associated with verbal passives.

Pinker, Lebeaux, and Frost's (1987) experiment proved that children comprehend not only actional passives but also nonactional passives, contrary to what was found by Maratsos et al. (1985). Moreover, they produce both actional and nonactional passives. Although children often failed to produce the *by*-phrase, in one experiment they did use it in 85% of their passives. In another comprehension experiment using the truth value judgment task, Fox and Grodzinsky (1998) found that 3;6- to 5;5-year-old English learners comprehend actional passives with or without the *by*-phrase 100% of the time and also display good comprehension of *get*-passives (e.g., *Goofy got pushed by Pippo*). These facts suggest that the *by*-phrase does not impede comprehension, and they hint that children's reluctance to produce it cannot be attributed to the lack of some piece of competence. Since the *by*-phrase appears only with verbal passives, Fox and Grodzinsky's results also indicate that children must have access to the representation underlying verbal passives, contrary to what Borer and Wexler (1987) claim.

On nonactional short passives (i.e., passives without the *by*-phrase, such as *Ariel was seen*), the children tested by Fox and Grodzinsky (1998) performed slightly worse than they did on actional passives, but well above chance; they responded correctly 86.5% of the time. However, children perform at chance level when they are presented with nonactional passive sentences including the *by*-phrase (46% correct), according to Fox and Grodzinsky's results. Table 7.1 summarizes the results from their experiment. These results clearly show that children's problems with passives are not due to the *by*-phrase or to nonactional verbs taken as isolated factors. Instead, they depend on the interaction of these two factors: children have difficulties in handling nonactional passives including the *by*-phrase.

Table 7.1
Comprehension of passive sentences by English learners ($N = 13$; age range 3;6–5;5; mean age 4;7)

Condition	Percentage of correct responses
Actional long passive *The rock star is being chased by the koala bear.*	100
Actional short passive *The rock star is being chased.*	100
Get-passive *The boy is getting touched by the musician.*	100
Nonactional long passive *The boy is seen by the horse.*	46
Nonactional short passive *The boy is seen.*	86.5
Actional active[a] *The mouse is touching the little girl.*	100
Nonactional active[a] *The pizza baker sees the buffalo.*	100

Source: Fox and Grodzinsky 1998
[a] Control sentences

In sum, the data discussed in this section lead to the following conclusions:

(28) a. Children comprehend and produce actional and nonactional *be*-passives.
   b. Children comprehend and produce *get*-passives.
   c. The *by*-phrase does not impede comprehension of actional passives, and although its use is rare, it is not nonexistent.
   d. Children have difficulties in comprehending nonactional passives including the *by*-phrase.
   e. Children's passives may have an eventive interpretation.

These findings raise two questions. First, it is apparent that the results discussed in this section conflict with the results discussed in section 7.1.2. How can we make sense of this clash? Second, how can we explain children's difficulties with nonactional passives including the *by*-phrase? In the next two sections we will look at these questions in turn.

7.4.1   Sources of the Conflicting Findings

In general, passives are very infrequent in parental speech to children. Nonactional passives are even rarer than actional ones, constituting just 10% of the verbal passives; and full passives including the *by*-phrase are very uncommon, accounting in one study for only 4 out of 85,000 sentences in caregivers' speech to children (Gordon and Chafetz 1990). These facts may shed light on children's reluctance to produce *by*-phrases and their superior performance on actional passives. Crain and Fodor (1993) point out that the paucity of full passives in adult speech is generally not interpreted as lack of knowledge of the mechanisms involved in deriving this construction. Rather, it is taken to reflect the marked character of passives, which are appropriate in special discourse situations. The same logic should apply to children. Under this view, when the pragmatic conditions are felicitous for the use of passives, children should not display any reluctance to produce them.

Crain and Fodor (1993) tested this prediction; that is, they tested whether children can produce the *by*-phrase in appropriate discourse conditions. The protocol they used to elicit full passives is reported in (29) (from Crain and Fodor 1993, 132).

(29) *Adult:*   See, the Incredible Hulk is hitting one of the soldiers. Look over there. Darth Vader goes over and hits a soldier. So Darth Vader is also hitting one of the soldiers. Ask Keiko which one.
  Child to Keiko: Which soldier is getting hit by Darth Vader?

Here, two soldiers are being hit, one by Darth Vader and one by the Incredible Hulk, and the child wants to know which one is being hit by Darth Vader. In this context, to get a correct answer, the child must use a *by*-phrase. And in fact, children in this experiment used the *by*-phrase 50% of the time. Examples of the passives elicited in this experiment are reported in (30).

(30) a. Which giraffe gets huggen by Grover?   (4;9)
  b. Which girl is pushing, getting pushed by a car?   (3;8)

Thus, under appropriate discourse conditions children can produce the *by*-phrase. In studies that reported a tendency to omit it, its expression was not appropriate or was not required in the communicative situation. A similar explanation can account for earlier studies' reports of children's superior performance with actional than with nonactional passives, since even in adult speech nonactional passives are rarer than actional ones (see

Lebeaux 1988 for an alternative explanation of children's preference for actional passives).

Horgan's (1978) finding that children's passives have a stative interpretation can be attributed to the particular task she used (description of pictures), which invites a static report of what is depicted (see Pinker, Lebeaux, and Frost 1987).

Finally, the fact that Hebrew learners use adjectival passives earlier than verbal passives finds its roots in the input, since verbal passives are very rare in parental speech to children (see Pinker, Lebeaux, and Frost 1987, crediting Borer and Wexler 1987).

In sum, there is no absolute restriction in child speech against producing and comprehending nonactional passives, against producing the *by*-phrase, or against using passives with an eventive interpretation. In other words, children can avail themselves of the machinery required to produce verbal passives, and therefore they must be able to form A-chains, which are in turn involved in forming verbal passives. The results of previous studies are likely artifacts of the experimental situations. Specific pragmatic conditions govern the use of passives. If these conditions are not met, full knowledge of the mechanisms involved in passive formation may not be manifest.

7.4.2   A Residual Advantage for Actional Passives over Nonactional Passives

The data discussed earlier in this section show that children can comprehend actional passives with or without the *by*-phrase, and that they can comprehend nonactional passives if the *by*-phrase is missing. On the basis of these results, Fox and Grodzinsky (1998) conclude that children can form A-chains, but are unable to transmit the thematic role to the NP in the *by*-phrase. Let us look at this proposal in more detail.

7.4.2.1   Mechanisms for Assigning a Thematic Role to the NP in the *By-Phrase*   As noted earlier, the standard analysis of passives holds that the thematic role of the external argument is assigned to the passive morphology and is transmitted to the NP in the *by*-phrase. The idea that the thematic role is transmitted to the NP in the *by*-phrase is motivated by the fact that the thematic role of this NP depends on the thematic properties of the passive verb, as seen in (31) (see Jaeggli 1986). In other words, the thematic role assigned to the NP in the *by*-phrase is the thematic role that the active verb would assign to its external argument: in (31a) the *by*-phrase expresses the agent of the event of pushing, in (31b) it

refers to the experiencer of the fear, and in (31c) it refers to the source of the offer.

(31) a. Aladdin is pushed by Jasmine.   (agent)
  b. Captain Hook is feared by Michael.   (experiencer)
  c. A cake is offered to Ariel by Pinocchio.   (source)

Transmission of the thematic role is not the only mechanism for assigning a thematic role to the NP in the *by*-phrase. A thematic role can also be directly assigned to the NP by the preposition *by*. This mechanism must be invoked to explain how the NP in the *by*-phrase receives a thematic role in, for example, *get*-passives (see Fox and Grodzinsky 1998). Let us see why. Recall that in *be*-passives the thematic role of the external argument of the active verb is assigned to the passive morpheme and is thus syntactically active. By contrast, in *get*-passives the thematic role of the external argument is not assigned in syntax and thus is not syntactically active. To see this difference, compare the *be*-passives in (3), repeated here, with the *get*-passives in (32) (from Fox and Grodzinsky 1998).

(3) a. Food should never be served only for oneself.
  b. The ship was sunk [PRO to collect the insurance money].

(32) a. *Food should never get served only for oneself.
  b. *The ship got sunk [PRO to collect insurance money].
  c. The ship got sunk [for John to collect insurance money].

The well-formedness of (3a) and (3b) indicates that these sentences contain a binder for the anaphor and a controller for PRO, respectively. The binder in (3a) and the controller in (3b) is the passive morpheme, which is assigned the thematic role of the external argument. By parity of reasoning, the ungrammaticality of (32a) and (32b) is a clue that, respectively, the anaphor *oneself* is not bound and PRO in the purpose clause is not controlled. Since (32c) shows that *get*-passives are compatible with purpose clauses, the ungrammaticality of (32b) cannot depend on incompatibility between purpose clauses and *get*; instead, it is due to the absence of a controller for PRO. We conclude that in *get*-passives the thematic role of the external argument is not assigned in the syntax, but is suppressed in the lexicon, much like what happens in adjectival passives (section 7.1). In *be*-passives the thematic role assigned to the passive morpheme is transmitted to the NP in the *by*-phrase. Since in *get*-passives this thematic role is not assigned, it cannot be transmitted to the NP in the *by*-phrase. In *get*-passives it is the preposition *by* itself that assigns a thematic role to its

NP complement—specifically, an agent thematic role (Fox and Grodzinsky 1998 call this role *affector*). While *be*-passives can be formed with a
wide variety of verbs and the NP in the *by*-phrase can therefore bear any
role, *get*-passives can be formed with actional verbs only and the NP in
the *by*-phrase can therefore bear only the role agent or causer, as (33a,b)
show (compare with (32a–c)).

(33) a. *Aladdin got seen by Michael.
     b. *Goofy got feared by Captain Hook.

In sum, there are two ways for the NP in the *by*-phrase to receive a thematic role:

(34) a. by transmission from the passive morpheme in *be*-passives,
     b. by direct assignment from the preposition *by* in *get*-passives (in
        this case only an agent or causer thematic role can be assigned).

7.4.2.2 The Transmission of a Thematic Role   Children's difficulties
with passive sentences based on nonactional verbs have to do with the *by*-
phrase. As Fox and Grodzinsky (1998) have shown, children can handle
the *by*-phrase in *get*-passives. This indicates that the mechanism of directly
assigning the agent thematic role to the NP in the *by*-phrase, the mechanism in (34b), is available to them. Fox and Grodzinsky conjecture that
children's difficulties with *be*-passives including a *by*-phrase lie in the
transmission of the thematic role from the passive morpheme to the NP
in the *by*-phrase; that is, children have trouble with the mechanism in
(34a). Children can comprehend and produce actional *be*-passives with a
by-phrase because direct assignment of the agent thematic role, (34b), can
obviate the need for thematic role transmission. This is possible since the
thematic role that the preposition *by* assigns to its complement, an agent
or causer, is compatible with the thematic structure of an actional verb.
Children cannot take advantage of the same escape hatch in the case of
nonactional passives with a *by*-phrase, because the agent role assigned by
the preposition *by* is inconsistent with the thematic representation of nonactional verbs. In this case the NP in the *by*-phrase can only be licensed
by the mechanism of thematic role transmission, a mechanism not available to children, according to Fox and Grodzinsky. Finally, children have
no difficulties in handling nonactional passives without a *by*-phrase because here there is no need to transmit the thematic role from the passive
morpheme to the NP in the *by*-phrase; that is, the mechanism in (34a)
need not be invoked in this case.

How does the mechanism of thematic role transmission become available to children? One solution consists in invoking maturation of the ability to transmit thematic roles. Fox and Grodzinsky do not endorse this solution. Rather, they speculate that children might not have problems with thematic role transmission per se; although they do not provide a full explanation, they suggest a processing solution. Essentially they speculate that the mechanism of thematic role transmission adds to other processes involved in the formation of passive sentences, such as the construction of an A-chain, increasing the processing load beyond children's capacity.

In summary, since the locus of children's difficulty is transmission of a thematic role, when this mechanism can be dispensed with, children perform in an adultlike way. This happens in *get*-passives, *be*-passives based on actional verbs, and passives based on nonactional verbs when these lack a *by*-phrase.

7.5 SUMMARY AND CONCLUDING REMARKS

Certain difficulties that children manifest in handling passive sentences have motivated a maturational account: children do not have access to the mechanism for forming A-chains until at least 5–6 years of age and thus cannot handle verbal passives. Since children *can* form passive sentences, defenders of the maturational view have claimed that these passives are instances of adjectival passives and as such are derived in the lexicon. This view was supported by earlier findings that in certain languages (Hebrew and German) children produce adjectival passives before verbal passives, that children avoid *by*-phrases, and that children's passives have a stative reading and are mostly based on actional verbs.

More recent findings cast doubt on the hypothesis that children cannot form A-chains and thus cannot handle verbal passives. Children distinguish between unaccusative and unergative verbs and have no trouble with unaccusative sentences, which involve the formation of an A-chain. Moreover, when the pragmatic context is felicitous, children can produce *by*-phrases and can form passives that have an eventive reading, typically associated with verbal passives. Children comprehend passives of actional and nonactional verbs. All these facts argue that children can avail themselves of the machinery involved in forming passives—specifically, they can form nontrivial A-chains. The discrepancy between earlier and more recent findings is likely due to the inadequacy of the contexts set up in earlier experiments.

However, an asymmetry has been discovered between comprehension of actional and nonactional passives when the *by*-phrase is present. Children perform perfectly in the former case (*Horace was scratched by Aladdin*), but at chance level in the latter (*Aladdin was seen by Jasmine*). These data have been interpreted as evidence that children have trouble with the transmission of the thematic role from the passive morpheme to the NP in the *by*-phrase. Possibly this mechanism is not accessible to children, being biologically determined to become available only at a certain point in development; or possibly the mechanism of thematic role transmission is indeed available to children, but its use exceeds their processing resources.

Summary of Linguistic Development

1. By 2–3 years of age children know the properties of unaccusative verbs (as shown by, e.g., auxiliary selection in Italian).
2. By at least 3;6–4 years of age children comprehend and produce passives based on actional verbs and including the *by*-phrase.
3. Children have trouble with passives based on nonactional verbs and including the *by*-phrase. By 3;6 years of age they comprehend passives based on nonactional verbs only if the *by*-phrase is absent.
4. Children can form trivial and nontrivial A-chains by 2–3 years of age (see unaccusative sentences).

Further Reading

The position occupied by the sentential subject is discussed in Pierce 1992b, Déprez and Pierce 1993, Friedemann 1993, 2000, and Labelle and Valois 1996.

Key Words

Actional passives
Adjectival passives
Be-passives
Eventive reading
Get-passives
Maturation of A-chains
Nonactional passives
Stative reading
Transmission of the thematic role
Verbal passives

Study Questions

1. What kind of evidence is compatible with the hypothesis that children's passive sentences are adjectival passives?

2. Why have nonactional passives been claimed to be difficult for children to comprehend and produce?

3. How does the VP-internal subject hypothesis bear on the question of whether or not children can form A-chains?

4. If children were unable to form A-chains, which constructions besides passives should they find difficult to handle?

5. While in early French the orders VOS and VSO are found in transitive constructions, in early English these orders are never attested. (Occasionally the order VS is found with an unaccusative verb, where S is really the internal argument (which usually raises to Spec IP and behaves like a subject).) Comment on this contrast in light of the VP-internal subject hypothesis. (Consult Pierce 1992b, chap. 2; Déprez and Pierce 1993; Friedemann 1993; Labelle and Valois 1996.)

6. As discussed in the text, English learners occasionally fail to raise the argument of unaccusative verbs to Spec IP, but never do so with the subject of unergative verbs. This may be taken as evidence that English learners have knowledge of the unaccusative/unergative split. Comment on this claim in light of the hypothesis that subjects are generated in VP. (Consult Déprez and Pierce 1993, 42–43.)

7. According to Larson (1988), the ordinary prepositional dative construction (e.g., *John gave a book to Sue*) is derived through A-movement from the double object construction (e.g., *John gave Sue a book*). If the construction of A-chains is problematic for children, their production and comprehension of the double object construction should be delayed. Try to verify this expectation by consulting the relevant literature (e.g., Groepen et al. 1989; Snyder and Stromswold 1997), and discuss the findings.

8. Design an experiment aimed at eliciting double object and prepositional dative constructions.

9. What kinds of difficulties do children display with the *by*-phrase in passive sentences?

Chapter 8

Acquisition of the Binding Principles

INTRODUCTION

In this chapter we turn to the emergence of the binding principles, one of the most widely investigated areas in the generative approach to language acquisition.

The binding theory deals with some aspects of the anaphoric relations holding between nominal and pronominal expressions in sentences, that is, relations in which the interpretation of the latter hinges on the interpretation of the former. It consists of several constraints taken to hold universally and thus to be part of the human genetic endowment. This feature makes the binding theory particularly attractive for acquisition research and an important testing ground for the principles-and-parameters model: it is expected that, being innate, constraints are operative early, at least as soon as children master the structures in which these constraints manifest themselves. Acquisition studies on binding are very relevant for linguistic theory in another sense as well: they have proven the relevance of certain linguistic distinctions and have the potential to discriminate between different versions of the binding theory.

Indeed, it has been found that children master the binding principles around age 3–4. Nevertheless, certain aspects of the interpretation of nonreflexive pronouns are not adultlike until age 6, at least in some languages. In particular, English, Dutch, and Icelandic learners sometimes take the nonreflexive pronoun *him* (or its equivalent in the other languages) in *Paul hit him* (or its counterpart in the other languages) as picking out *Paul*; that is, they seem to interpret the sentence as meaning 'Paul hit himself'. The evidence suggests that children's errors are not due to unavailability of the binding principles, but are likely related to a procedure used for interpreting nonreflexive pronouns.

This chapter is organized as follows. Section 8.1 reviews basic notions of the binding theory that are relevant for later discussion of the acquisition data. The particular approach to the binding theory adopted here incorporates aspects of Reinhart's view of binding with the classical view. (For an introduction to the most popular version of the binding theory, see Haegeman 1994, chap. 4; Harbert 1995. For an introduction that incorporates Reinhart's approach, see Heim and Kratzer 1998, chaps. 9 and 10. For an introduction that emphasizes the semantic side of the binding theory, see Chierchia and McConnell-Ginet 2000, chaps. 1 and 3. For detailed discussion, see Reinhart 1983; Reinhart and Reuland 1993.) Sections 8.2–8.4 discuss the acquisition of Principles A, B, and C of the binding theory, respectively.

8.1 THE BINDING THEORY

Let us begin by looking at aspects of the binding theory that are relevant for understanding the acquisition results.

8.1.1 Syntactic Binding

The binding theory specifies the legitimate *syntactic binding* relationships between nominal and pronominal expressions in clauses, which are embodied in the following three principles:

(1) a. *Principle A*
       A reflexive pronoun must be bound in its local domain.[1]
    b. *Principle B*
       A (nonreflexive) pronoun must be free in its local domain.
    c. *Principle C*
       An R(eferential)-expression must be free everywhere.

(2) An expression A binds an expression B iff
    a. A and B are coindexed and
    b. A c-commands B.

To see how the principles of the binding theory work, let us first look at examples that include quantifiers and pronouns. (Later we will consider referential NPs, like proper nouns or definite descriptions such as *the boy*.) Let us assume that at the level of Logical Form (LF) quantifiers raise from their base position and adjoin to some suitable site, a process necessary for their interpretation (see Haegeman 1994, chap. 9, for an introduction; also see chapter 9 regarding quantification). This particular kind of adjunction is known as Quantifier Raising (QR). Like the movement of *wh*-elements, QR is an instance of Ā-movement: the quantifier is adjoined in an Ā-position, and from there it Ā-binds its trace. Consider sentence (3a). Its LF representation is given in (3b), where QR has applied. The trace t_j is construed as a variable bound by the raised quantified expression *every Smurf*, that is, as an empty category bound by an element in an Ā-position. (Binding is indicated by coindexation.)

(3) a. Big Bird admires every Smurf.

b.

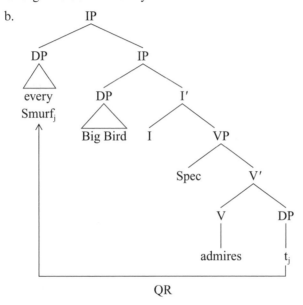

Principle A states that reflexives (and reciprocals), such as *himself* and *herself*, must be coindexed with a c-commanding antecedent within a certain kind of local domain. Principle A rules out the LF representation (4b) for (4a), since *himself* is not coindexed with anything in the local domain. It rules in the LF representation (4c), in which the reflexive is coindexed with a c-commanding antecedent (the trace of the raised quantifier) within this domain; that is, the reflexive is locally bound.

(4) a. Every Smurf scratches himself.

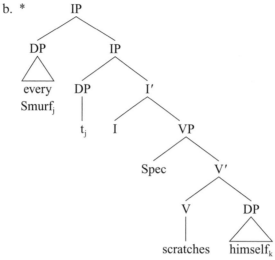

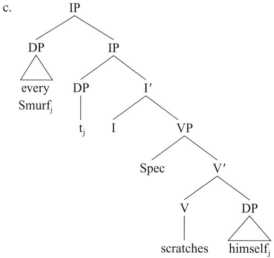

A semantic procedure takes LF representations as input and interprets them. For example, given (4c) as input, it gives the truth conditions of sentence (4a), which are shown in (5), where x is a variable.

(5) for every x, such that x is a Smurf, x scratches x

(5) says that for every x, if x is a Smurf, then x scratches x; that is, x scratches himself. To establish whether (4a) is true or false, we have to consider the set of Smurfs in our domain. Suppose it includes Smurfs A,

B, and C. Then we replace *every Smurf* in (4a) with A, B, and C to obtain the three sentences in (6). Sentence (4a) is true in our domain if every sentence in (6) is true—that is, if, for every specific Smurf we choose, it is true that this Smurf scratches himself.

(6) A scratches himself.
    B scratches himself.
    C scratches himself.

The semantic rules of interpretation (see Chierchia and McConnell-Ginet 2000, chap. 3) treat pronouns as variables (like the variables left by *wh*-movement or QR). Pronouns syntactically bound by the trace of a raised quantifier, as in (4c), are interpreted as variables bound by the raised quantifier.

In the case of (4a) the semantic procedure cannot operate on the LF representation in (4b), because this LF representation is ruled out by Principle A. If it could operate on (4b), sentence (4a) would be interpreted as meaning that every Smurf scratches another individual.

Principle B requires that nonreflexive pronouns (or simply pronouns) be free in some kind of local domain. Consider (7a–c).

(7) a. Every Smurf scratches him.
    b. *

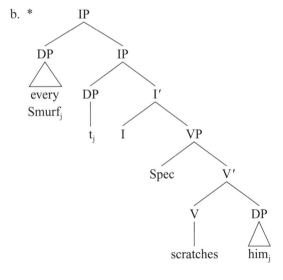

c.

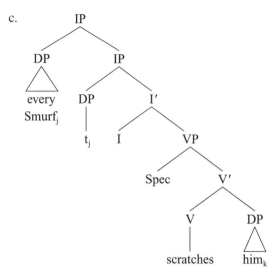

The LF representation of (7a) given in (7b) is ruled out by Principle B, because the pronoun *him* is bound in the local domain by the (trace of the) raised quantifier. The legitimate LF representation of (7a) is (7c), where the pronoun is free in the local domain in compliance with Principle B. In other words, *every Smurf* (and hence its trace as well) and *him* must carry different indices, as in (7c). This accounts for our intuition that (7a) cannot mean that every Smurf scratches himself.

In the LF representation in (7c) the pronoun is not coindexed with any other expression. The rules of interpretation specify that it is interpreted *deictically* or *exophorically*; that is, it picks up its value from the context and refers to some salient character in the discourse. Now consider (8a) and its LF representation (8b).

(8) a. Every Smurf said that Big Bird scratched him.

b.

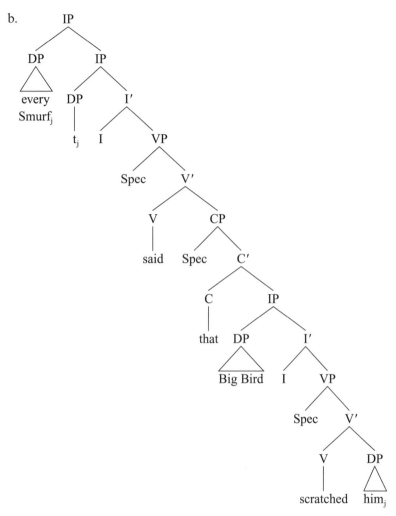

In (8b) the pronoun is locally free; nothing prevents it from being bound outside the local domain by the subject of the main clause, that is, by the trace of the raised quantifier.

This LF representation will be interpreted by the semantic procedure, which will assign it the truth conditions in (9).

(9) for every x, such that x is a Smurf, x said that Big Bird scratched x

In (8b) the pronoun carries the same index as the quantifier (and its trace) and is thus interpreted as a variable bound by the quantifier. This interpretation of pronouns is often called *anaphoric interpretation* of pronouns. An expression is an *anaphor* (or is *anaphorically linked* to another expression) if its interpretation depends on the interpretation of another expression, its antecedent. Binding by a trace of a quantifier is one kind of **anaphoric relation**. (In section 8.1.2 we will look at another kind of anaphoric relation, which does not involve binding.) Reflexive pronouns are always interpreted as anaphorically linked to an antecedent; for this reason they are often called anaphors. Nonreflexive pronouns are interpreted as anaphorically linked to an antecedent if they are bound. If they are not bound, they are generally interpreted deictically or exophorically; that is, they refer to some salient character in the extralinguistic context in which the utterance is used. (One should keep in mind that in this book (as in, e.g., Heim and Kratzer 1998) *anaphor*, *anaphoric relation*, and *anaphoric interpretation* (or *use*) *of pronouns* are broad descriptive terms that are used in an informal way.)

Now consider (10a) and the two LF representations in (10b,c).

(10) a. He scratches every Smurf.

     b. *

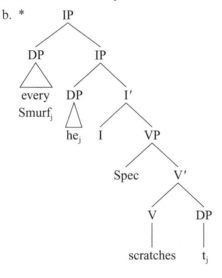

c.

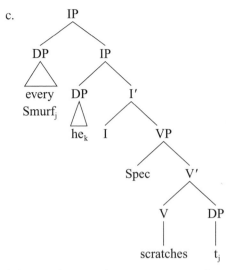

Principle C rules out the LF representation of (10a) given in (10b), because the trace of the quantifier, which is an R-expression under present assumptions, is bound by a pronoun. This captures the intuition that (10a) does not mean that every Smurf scratched himself. An LF representation that is sanctioned by Principle C and is thus a possible input to the semantic procedure is (10c), in which the relevant expressions carry distinct indices. (10b) is a case of strong crossover since the quantifier, an operator, has crossed over the pronoun (see section 5.2.3.1).

The observations made so far can be straightforwardly extended to sentences including *wh*-operators, which for the purposes of the binding theory operate in the same way.

(11) a. Who admires himself?
     b. Who$_i$ t$_i$ admires himself$_{i/*j}$?

(12) a. Who admires him?
     b. Who$_i$ t$_i$ admires him$_{j/*i}$?
     c. Who said that Big Bird scratches him?
     d. Who$_i$ t$_i$ said that Big Bird scratches him$_i$?
     e. I know who he admires.
     f. I know who$_i$ he$_{j/*i}$ admires t$_i$.

In (11b), the syntactic representation of (11a), the reflexive must be bound, in compliance with Principle A. In (12b), the syntactic representation of (12a), the nonreflexive pronoun must be locally free. (12d), a possible representation of (12c), shows that a pronoun can be bound outside the local domain and therefore be interpreted as a bound variable. (12f) is a potential case of strong crossover: the *wh*-operator crosses over the pronoun. The pronoun and the *wh*-operator must have different indices; otherwise, the pronoun would end up binding the trace of the raised *wh*-operator, an R-expression, thus violating Principle C.

So far we have considered only examples with quantifiers (or *wh*-operators). What about proper nouns? We will assume that they, like quantifiers, may undergo QR (see Heim and Kratzer 1998, chap. 9, for arguments in favor of extending QR to proper nouns; see also Chierchia and McConnell-Ginet 2000, chap. 3). Then, we are by and large in the same situation as before. Consider (13), (14), and (15).

(13) a. Goofy admires himself.
     b. *[Goofy$_j$ [t$_j$ admires himself$_i$]]
     c. [Goofy$_i$ [t$_i$ admires himself$_i$]]

(14) a. Goofy admires him.
     b. *[Goofy$_i$ [t$_i$ admires him$_i$]]
     c. [Goofy$_j$ [t$_j$ admires him$_i$]]

(15) a. He admires Goofy.
     b. *[Goofy$_i$ [he$_i$ admires t$_i$]]
     c. [Goofy$_j$ [he$_i$ admires t$_j$]]

Proper nouns are adjoined to a suitable site, an Ā-position. Principle A rules out the LF representation in (13b), as it did the one in (4b), because the reflexive is not bound. Principle B rules out (14b), because the pronoun is locally bound. Principle C rules out (15b), because the trace of the moved noun, an R-expression, is bound. The legitimate LF representations of (13a), (14a), and (15a) are (13c), (14c), and (15c), respectively. In (13c) the reflexive is coindexed with a local c-commanding antecedent. In (14c) and (15c) the NP and the pronoun bear distinct indices; the pronoun is not bound and takes its value from the context. (For sentences including referential NPs as antecedents, the interpretation of free pronouns raises interesting problems, to be addressed in the next section.)

In summary, the binding theory filters out illegitimate coindexation and feeds the semantic procedure with legitimate LF representations. In so doing, it contributes to determining what truth conditions are allowed or disallowed for a given sentence. The binding theory governs syntactic binding, the formal relation between nominal, quantified, and pronominal expressions in a syntactic structure. Syntactic binding is interpreted as *semantic binding*, the relation holding in standard quantification theory between a quantifier and occurrences of variables. A pronoun that is syntactically bound by the trace of a quantifier (or of a raised noun) is interpreted as a variable bound by that quantifier.[2] Reflexives are always syntactically and semantically bound; nonreflexive pronouns can be syntactically and semantically bound, or they can be free. The term *binding* is used in the specific sense just described. **A bound pronoun** can also be said to be anaphorically linked to its binder. A free pronoun in the context of a quantifier is always interpreted deictically or exophorically. Finally, keep in mind that variable binding use of pronouns is just one kind of anaphoric use of pronouns, as we will now see.

8.1.2   Binding and Coreference

Look again at (14), repeated here.

(14) a.   Goofy admires him.
 b.   *[Goofy$_i$ [t$_i$ admires him$_i$]]
 c.   [Goofy$_j$ [t$_j$ admires him$_i$]]

Recall that Principle B rules out the LF representation in (14b) for a sentence like (14a), since the pronoun is locally bound. (14c) is the legitimate LF representation of (14a). Here the pronoun is not bound and takes its value from the context. Suppose that we pick out Goofy as the referent of the pronoun *him* in (14c). Nothing prevents this choice. But then *him* would end up coreferring with *Goofy* (a case of what is often called *accidental coreference*—that is, the pronoun *him* and the nominal expression *Goofy* refer to the same individual). Contexts such as these have been widely discussed in the literature, first by Evans (1980) (see also Higginbotham 1983; Reinhart 1983, 1986); for convenience, let us call them *Evans-style contexts*. Consider sentences (16a–c), where capital letters indicate stress.

(16) a.   You know what Wendy, Ariel, and Peter Pan have in common. WENDY admires Peter Pan, ARIEL admires Peter Pan, and PETER PAN admires him too.
 b.   When Aladdin looks in the mirror, he doesn't see Jasmine. Aladdin sees HIM.
 c.   It is not true that no one has invited Michael. Michael has invited HIM [pointing at Michael].

In all these sentences Principle B blocks coindexation between the pronoun and the trace of the raised NP (*Peter Pan*, *Aladdin*, and *Michael*, respectively) and ensures that the pronoun is not bound. But nothing blocks **coreference** between the referential NP and the pronoun. *Coreference* is used here as a technical term limited to cases where two expressions corefer or refer to the same individual (as in Heim and Kratzer 1998). Pronouns that are not interpreted as bound variables can corefer with some expression in the sentence. This includes cases like (16a–c) and cases like (17) in which the pronoun is not c-commanded by the antecedent.

(17) Pinocchio's father saved him.

The pronoun *him* is free in (17), since *Pinocchio* does not c-command it. Nothing prohibits one from taking *Pinocchio* as the referent of the pronoun, in which case the pronoun and the nominal expression *Pinocchio* end up coreferring. Thus, this sentence can mean that Pinocchio's father (namely, Geppetto) saved Pinocchio. This interpretation of pronouns is also considered anaphoric. Thus, two semantically distinct phenomena fall under the descriptive term *anaphoric relation*: variable binding and coreference.

Syntactic binding only affects bound variable anaphors; it has nothing to say about coreference anaphors. If a pronoun is not syntactically bound, it is not interpreted as semantically bound (i.e., as a bound variable); however else it is interpreted, that interpretation does not depend on binding.

Although contexts such as those in (16) are common, speakers have the intuition that sentences such as (14a) are associated with a strong presupposition that the pronoun is not anaphorically linked to the nominal expression and are ready to suspend this presupposition when the context makes it clear, as in (16). The debate over how these facts should be explained is still wide open. Here we will assume the standard definition of the binding principles; and, to account for the presupposition that in (14a) the pronoun is not anaphorically linked to the nominal expression, we will say that on top of the binding principles there exists the interpretive procedure in (18), **Rule I***, taken from Guasti and Chierchia 1999/2000 and inspired by Reinhart's work (see Reinhart 1983; Grodzinsky and Reinhart 1993).

(18) *Rule I**

If a pronoun is not (semantically) bound by an NP A, it is generally interpreted as noncoreferential with A, unless it appears in an Evans-style context.

Rule I* governs coreference, the relation that can be established between an unbound pronoun and an expression with a fixed value (in a given domain); it is distinct from the binding principles. It establishes a default that is overridden in Evans-style contexts and works as follows. Consider (14a), repeated here. Principle B requires the pronoun to be unbound, and Rule I* states that an unbound pronoun is noncoreferential with the antecedent (unless it appears in an Evans-style context).

(14) a. Goofy admires him.

Rule I* is inspired by Reinhart's Rule I (without the star), which states that a coreference reading is legitimate only if an indistinguishable reading cannot be obtained with the mechanism of variable binding. For example, in (14a) a coreference reading (a reading in which the pronoun and the nominal expression pick out the same individual) is impossible, because a reading very similar to the coreference reading can be obtained through the mechanism of variable binding. That is, to express the anaphoric reading we can use a sentence like (13a), whose representation, shown in (13c), involves variable binding.

(13) a. Goofy admires himself.
   c. Goofy$_i$ [t$_i$ admires himself$_i$]

We will not assume Rule I here, in order to remain neutral about whether strong crossover can be subsumed under some version of Rule I, which is one way of interpreting Reinhart's proposal. The precise formulation of Rule I* is still a matter of debate (see Heim and Kratzer 1998 for relevant discussion). However, sorting out the binding theory effects from coreference is crucial, especially when we look at acquisition.

It has been suggested that something similar to Rule I* expresses a requirement on the rational use of language that invites speakers to be as explicit as possible (see Reinhart 1983, 1986). In the present case explicitness is achieved if a speaker uses variable binding to express an anaphoric relation, unless variable binding is not available. A speaker who wants to express that Goofy admires Goofy should not choose (14a), for the grammar makes available the variant in (13a), in which the anaphoric reading is expressed through the variable binding mechanism, as shown in (13c). (13a) is a much clearer way to express an anaphoric relation than (14a) would be; it is the unmarked or default option that the grammar makes available. Hence, whenever the binding option is available for expressing an anaphoric dependency, Rule I* exhorts speakers to choose it. However, in special circumstances, like Evans-style contexts, that may somehow be signaled to the hearer (e.g., by deixis, by stress, or through the linguistic context), Rule I*'s default can be suspended and an unbound pronoun can corefer with its local antecedent. To express the intended meaning in (16a), we cannot use a bound pronoun since we are attributing to Peter Pan not the property of admiring himself, but the property of admiring Peter Pan, which is quite different. While it may be true that everyone admires Peter Pan, as stated in (16a), it may not be true that everyone admires himself (or herself). Now, attributing the property of admiring Peter Pan to Peter Pan must be expressed with an unbound pronoun; but then Rule I*'s default must be suspended, for the pronoun must be able to pick out the same referent as its antecedent. The same observations carry over to (16b,c).

It is worth noticing that contexts such as those in (16) can never be constructed for quantified expressions; that is, it is impossible to manipulate the context so that *him* would end up being anaphorically linked to a local quantifier. Thus, for quantifiers Rule I* is irrelevant. An anaphoric relation between a pronoun and a quantifier can only be established through variable binding, while between a pronoun and a referential NP it can be established either through variable binding (if the name is raised and has the same index as the pronoun) or through coreference.

The comprehension of sentences including nominal and pronominal expressions results from the interaction of various autonomous components or modules: the lexicon, a syntactic binding component that prescribes the licit binding configurations, a semantic component that interprets syntactic binding, and the interpretive procedure in (18). As we will see in this chapter, investigations of children's interpretation of nominal and pronominal expressions strongly support the validity of this modular approach for the study of human language. In chapter 11 we will see that this approach may offer a key to explaining some aspects of the behavior of children with specific language impairment.

8.1.3   Intermediate Summary

An anaphoric relation can be created either through variable binding or through coreference. Variable binding obtains when a pronoun is syntactically and thus semantically bound. Reflexive pronouns are always syntactically and semantically bound; nonreflexive pronouns can be syntactically and semantically bound or they can be free. Generally, a pronoun that is not bound by an NP is taken to be noncoreferential with that

NP. However, there are cases in which an NP and a pronoun that carry different indexes are taken to be coreferential; that is, they refer to the same individual.

8.2 PRINCIPLE A

Under the principles-and-parameters model, the binding principles (or whatever subsumes their effects) are viewed as part of human genetic endowment and are thus expected to manifest themselves early in linguistic behavior, at least as soon as the child masters sentences of the complexity required for the expression of these principles and when the child knows the relevant lexical items. As a matter of fact, various autonomous components are implicated in binding:

(19) a. Lexicon: pronouns must be classified as reflexives or nonreflexives and NPs as referential or quantificational
   b. Syntax: the three binding principles and the various notions they presuppose (c-command, local domain)
   c. Semantics: the semantic procedure that interprets syntactic binding as semantic binding
   d. Pragmatics: (pragmatic) conditions for the interpretation of nonreflexive pronouns in some contexts

To uncover the emergence of the binding principles, children's comprehension of sentences including nouns, quantifiers, and pronouns has been tested. But since different components contribute to the comprehension of such sentences, we must take care to factor them out if we are to succeed in understanding whether or not children are guided by the binding principles. Failure to comprehend such sentences does not necessarily indicate that children lack the syntactic abilities for handling binding relations.

8.2.1 Children's Interpretation of Reflexive Pronouns

Various experiments have investigated the emergence of Principle A, mostly in conjunction with the emergence of Principle B. The rationale for this linkage is the fact that Principles A and B imply a strict complementarity between reflexives and pronouns: by and large a reflexive must be bound in those environments in which a pronoun must be free.[3]

The generalization that emerges is that children interpret sentences including reflexives in an adultlike way earlier than sentences including pronouns. Studies differ with respect to the age at which children correctly interpret reflexives—differences that are likely due to the difficulty of the experimental tasks employed. Using a yes/no judgment task, Chien and Wexler (1990) found that English-speaking children demonstrate knowledge of Principle A by 5 years. In this experiment children were presented with pictures illustrating characters involved in an action (the context) and were asked questions about these pictures in two conditions, a match and a mismatch condition. In the match condition the test sentence gave relevant information about the context; in the mismatch condition the test sentence and the context were not consistent. For example, in the match condition question (20) was posed about a picture showing Mama Bear touching herself. In the mismatch condition the same question was posed, but about a picture showing Mama Bear touching someone else, Goldilocks.

(20) This is Goldilocks; this is Mama Bear. Is Mama Bear touching herself?

Children were found to give many correct responses (around 90%) in both conditions by 5 years. Younger children displayed poorer performance: they responded accurately in the match condition, but not in the mismatch condition. This result is difficult to interpret, but it does not necessarily indicate that younger children do not know the properties of reflexives. Various factors might have been at work. One is the greater complexity of processing a mismatch (see Foster-Cohen 1994). Another might have been some inherent difficulty in carrying out the relevant experimental task. In fact, data collected by McKee (1992), using a different method (the truth value judgment task), show not only that children respond accurately in the match condition (100% correct) by 3 years, but also that they respond accurately in the mismatch condition (88% correct) as well (although clearly there is still a slight difference in performance between the two conditions).

Thus, the results from the match condition indicate that children know that a reflexive *can* have an antecedent, and the results from the mismatch condition indicate that children know that reflexives *must* have an antecedent. These findings suggest that children have the lexical knowledge of what a reflexive pronoun is (but see Koster 1994 and Deutsch, Koster, and Koster 1986 for discussion of comprehension errors).

Table 8.1
Percentage of American English–speaking children's correct responses to simple sentences including reflexive pronouns (e.g., *Mama Bear is touching herself*) in match and mismatch conditions

	Age range	Number of subjects	Match condition	Mismatch condition
Chien and Wexler 1990	2;6–4;0	48	94	60
(yes/no judgment task)	4;0–5;0	45	98	83
	5;0–6;0	44	97	95
McKee 1992 (truth value judgment task)	2;6–5;3	30	100	88

Table 8.1 summarizes the results from Chien and Wexler's (1990) and McKee's (1992) experiments.

Can we conclude from the data examined so far that Principle A is operative by age 3? No, because one might claim that children's accurate performance is due not to Principle A, but to some strategy that they adopt. One candidate is the **strategy of self-oriented action** proposed by Grimshaw and Rosen (1990).

(21) *Strategy of self-oriented action*
Take the presence of a reflexive as an indication that a self-oriented action is to be expected.

If children adopt the strategy in (21), when asked (20) they have only to make sure that the picture displays a self-oriented action. If it does, they answer "yes"; otherwise, they answer "no." Often answers based on this strategy cannot be distinguished from answers based on Principle A.

The issue of whether children use a strategy to interpret sentences including reflexives was addressed by Grodzinsky and Kave (1993). Hebrew learners were asked a question modeled on (22) about a picture in which B, rather than A, is touching himself.

(22) This is A. This is B. Is A touching himself?

In this condition children answered "no" to (22), because A was not touching himself. Notice that this answer is only compatible with the hypothesis that children are guided by Principle A. If they are guided by the strategy in (21), they should answer "yes," because a self-oriented action was indeed depicted.

Grodzinsky and Kave's result disproves the hypothesis that children use something like the strategy in (21) in comprehending sentences including reflexives. It is thus very likely that when children hear a sentence including a reflexive, they look for the local antecedent. Further evidence that children know that the antecedent of a reflexive must be in the local domain comes from another experiment by Chien and Wexler (1990). They presented children with sentences like (23), containing two potential antecedents for the reflexive (here, *Kitty* and *Sarah*), and asked them to act out the sentence.

(23) Kitty says that Sarah should give herself a car.

Since a reflexive must have a local antecedent, only *Sarah* is a legitimate antecedent in (23). Chien and Wexler found that by 5 years children know that the antecedent of the reflexive must be *Sarah*. (Younger children made anaphora mistakes by taking the reflexive to refer to the nonlocal antecedent, *Kitty*. However, in another experiment, using the truth value judgment task, McKee (1992) found that even younger learners (2;9 years old) know that the reflexive must have a local antecedent in sentences like (23) including two clauses. This result suggests that young children's poor performance in Chien and Wexler's experiment was due to the task demands.)

In sum, by 3–4 years children have command of Principle A, know what a reflexive is, and know that it must be locally bound.

8.2.1.1 Morphosyntax of Pronouns and Principle A: Crosslinguistic Evidence

Children are highly consistent in their interpretation of reflexives, no matter what language they learn. There is mounting evidence that Principle A manifests itself early, from around 3–4 years, in a variety of languages including French, Hebrew, Icelandic, Italian, Russian, and Spanish (see, e.g., Padilla 1990; Avrutin and Wexler 1992; McKee 1992; Sigurjónsdóttir and Hyams 1992; Grodzinsky and Kave 1993; Jakubowicz 1994). For example, McKee (1992) tested Italian-speaking children aged between 3;7 and 5;5 with sentences like (24) and found a high percentage of correct responses (97% and 94% in the match and mismatch conditions, respectively).

(24) Lo gnomo si   lava.
      the gnome SELF washes
      'The gnome washes himself.'

It is noteworthy that children perform so uniformly, regardless of the input language, and regardless in particular of the morphosyntactic status of reflexives, which varies across languages. For example, reflexives are expressed by a clitic form in Italian (*si*), French (*se*), and Spanish (*se*) and by a nonclitic form in English (*X-self*). In addition, in Italian, but not in English, the reflexive is invariant. As shown in (25), the same form is used with singular, plural, feminine, and masculine antecedents in Italian; and as the translations show, different forms are used in English.

(25) a. La   bambina   si lava.
        the-FEM-SG girl-FEM-SG SI wash-3SG
        'The girl washes herself.'
     b. I   bambini   si lavano.
        the-MASC-PL boy-MASC-PL SI wash-3PL
        'The boys wash themselves.'

Evidently the different morphosyntactic status of reflexives does not affect children's performance. It is reasonable to conjecture that for example gender may help in choosing the correct antecedent. It is easier to locate the antecedent in an English sentence like (26a) than in an Italian one like (26b), since in (26a) the feminine reflexive pronoun calls for a feminine antecedent. Therefore, independently of binding considerations, the gender cue on *herself* may be an indication that the antecedent must be *Mary* in (26a); by contrast, in (26b) the reflexive pronoun *si* has no gender marking.

(26) a. While John was singing, Mary was combing herself.
     b. Mentre John stava cantando, Mary si pettinava.
        while   John was singing   Mary SI was combing

Nonetheless, Italian learners perform as accurately as their English-speaking peers. Thus, the morphosyntactic status of a reflexive pronoun does not affect children's interpretation of sentences including reflexives.

8.2.1.2   Reflexive Pronouns in Production   Spontaneous production data suggest that children are aware of the properties of reflexives from age 2;3. Bloom et al. (1994) analyzed the spontaneous production of the reflexive *myself* by 3 English-speaking children from age 2;3 to age 5;1. They found that *myself* was usually correctly used; that is, it was used in sentences including the antecedent *I*. The children produced sentences like (27a), in which *myself* does not have a suitable antecedent, only 0.3% of the time, and sentences like (27b), in which *me* is used rather than *myself*, only 5.6% of the time.

(27) a. *John hit myself.
     b. *I hit me.

These data indicate that children are aware of the categorial distinction between the reflexive *myself* and the nonreflexive pronoun *me* from at least age 2;3. Similarly, Jakubowicz (1994) carried out an elicited-production experiment with French- and Danish-speaking children ranging in age from 3;0 to 3;11. These children produced about 80% correct sentences with the respective reflexive clitics *se* and *sig selv*. These data add further evidence that reflexives are appropriately categorized from the start.

8.2.2   Intermediate Summary

Children display adultlike comprehension of sentences including reflexives from about 3 years and produce such sentences spontaneously from about 2 years. Children have correctly categorized reflexives, whatever their morphological status (clitic or nonclitic); they can compute the local domain and, within this, determine the antecedent.

8.3   PRINCIPLE B

Let us now look at the acquisition of Principle B.

8.3.1   Children's Anaphoric Errors

Children's interpretation of sentences with nonreflexive pronouns (more simply: pronouns) is initially nonadult and does not improve for some years. It is not until the age of 6 that children start to reach adult levels of accuracy in interpreting sentences with pronouns. We will see that they perform poorly with pronouns not because their grammar lacks Principle B, but because they have not mastered certain aspects of the interpretation of pronouns.

Consider sentence (28).

(28) Mama Bear touches her.

Under standard circumstances, for adults, the pronoun *her* is not anaphorically dependent on the NP *Mama Bear* in a sentence like (28). That is, *her* does not pick out the same individual that *Mama Bear* does; equivalently, *Mama Bear* and *her* are taken to refer to two distinct individuals. Some children, however, allow the pronoun to be anaphorically linked to the nominal expression; that is, they interpret (28) as meaning that Mama Bear touches herself. (Recall that an anaphoric relation is not necessarily a binding relation.)

In a judgment task with pictures, Chien and Wexler (1990) presented children with pictures displaying Mama Bear and Goldilocks. In the match condition the picture showed Mama Bear touching Goldilocks, and in the mismatch condition the picture showed Mama Bear touching herself. After showing the pictures, the experimenters asked children this question:

(29) This is Mama Bear; this is Goldilocks. Is Mama Bear touching her?

Chien and Wexler found that in the mismatch condition even 5- to 6-year-old children answer this question with "no" 50% of the time. This means that they interpret the pronoun as being anaphorically linked to the local antecedent *Mama Bear* in about 50% of the cases.

Chien and Wexler's finding has been replicated in several studies using different methods. For example, McKee (1992) showed that overall English learners ranging in age from 2;6 to 5;3 take the pronoun as being anaphorically linked to the local antecedent 72% of the time. Errors in the interpretation of pronouns are evident in other languages as well—for example, early Dutch, Icelandic, and Russian (see Avrutin and Wexler 1992; Sigurjónsdóttir and Hyams 1992; Koster 1993).

Under a theory holding that constraints are innate, the results from studies on Principle B are very surprising. Recall that studies on Principle A show that children obey this binding principle, as expected, and do so from 3–4 years of age. Thus, there is a clear delay between the time children interpret reflexives correctly and the time they interpret pronouns correctly. This fact makes it difficult to interpret the responses to sentences testing Principle B. One conjecture is that children do not have knowledge of Principle B. However, this hypothesis would create an unexpected asymmetry among binding principles and would raise a learnability problem. We know that negative evidence is not available to children. Children who mistakenly take *Mama Bear touches her* to mean that Mama Bear touches herself are not told that this interpretation is incorrect. Lacking information about what a sentence cannot mean, children would have no way to acquire Principle B. But if children *do* have knowledge of Principle B, why do they respond in a nonadult way to sentences testing this principle? We will return to this issue in section 8.3.5 after examining other data bearing on the interpretation of pronouns in various contexts and in various early languages.

8.3.2 Children's Adultlike Interpretation of Pronouns

Notice that even though children incorrectly take a pronoun to be anaphorically linked to a local antecedent, they know that a pronoun can be anaphorically linked to a nonlocal antecedent. Chien and Wexler (1990) found that children accept the exophoric reading of the pronoun, in which the antecedent of the pronoun is an extrasentential character, about 90% of the time as early as age 2;6; that is, these children answer "yes" when they are asked the question in (29), repeated here, about a picture displaying Mama Bear touching Goldilocks (match condition).

(29) This is Mama Bear; this is Goldilocks. Is Mama Bear touching her?

McKee (1992) replicated this finding, testing 2;6- to 5;3-year-old children's comprehension of pronouns in both simple and complex sentences of the kind exemplified in (30). She found that children accept an exophoric reading of the pronoun in (30a) 93% of time. Moreover, she found that for (30b) children take the pronoun to be anaphorically linked to the nonlocal antecedent, *the clown*, 93% of the time.

(30) a. Smurfette washed her.
      b. While the clown was sitting down, Roger Rabbit covered him.

Children know that pronouns can have a referent provided by the extralinguistic context (exophoric reading) as in (30a) or a linguistic referent (anaphoric reading) outside the local domain as in (30b). This suggests that they do not mix reflexive and nonreflexive pronouns and know that, unlike reflexives, nonreflexive pronouns can be anaphorically linked to an antecedent outside the local domain or can be interpreted exophorically (see Sigurjónsdóttir and Hyams 1992 for similar evidence from the acquisition of Icelandic). However, it is apparent that children's knowledge about how to handle nonreflexive pronouns is somehow faulty. Is their knowledge of binding faulty? With the data accumulated so far, it is hard to answer. In section 8.2 we noted possible confusions among different components involved in binding (lexicon, syntax, semantics, pragmatics). To answer the question at hand, we must look for evidence that exclusively taps binding knowledge. It will also be helpful to expand our empirical base by investigating binding in other early languages.

8.3.3   Crosslinguistic Studies of Principle B

In a comparative study on the acquisition of Principle B, McKee (1992) found a remarkable discrepancy between the performance of Italian learners and the performance of English learners. She tested children in match and mismatch conditions with sentences like (31a,b) or their English equivalents.

(31) a. Il puffo lo lava.
         the Smurf him washes
         'The Smurf is washing him.'
      b. Mentre il puffo cantava,   Pippo lo   toccava.
         while   the Smurf was singing Goofy him was touching
         'While the Smurf was singing, Goofy was touching him.'

While in the match condition ("yes" response), in which the sentence is consistent with the context, English and Italian learners reach adult levels of performance (above 90%), in the mismatch condition ("no" response), where the sentence and the situation are not consistent, the performance of the two groups diverges significantly. For one-clause sentences, such as (31a), the rejection rate of the anaphoric reading of pronouns in Italian is 85%, but it drops to 18% in English. For two-clause sentences, such as (31b), the rejection rate of the anaphoric reading of pronouns in Italian is 80% and in English 38%. The percentage of correct responses provided by Italian and English learners is displayed in figure 8.1. Data regarding the acquisition of Principle B in Spanish replicate the results from Italian (see Padilla 1990).

Learners of languages like Italian and Spanish reject an anaphoric dependency between a pronoun and a local referential NP most of the time, while learners of languages like English, Icelandic, and Russian accept this dependency. The reason for this split must be related to the different morphosyntactic status of pronouns in the two groups of languages. In Italian (and Spanish) the pronouns are clitics, while in English (Russian, Icelandic) they are not. Unlike what we find with reflexives, the morphosyntactic status of nonreflexive pronouns appears to influence aspects of the acquisition process. Once children have categorized an element as a reflexive, they automatically know that it falls under Principle A and that it must be bound. By contrast, having classified an element as a nonreflexive pronoun only tells them that Principle B has to be invoked. This principle says that a pronoun must be free in some local domain, but

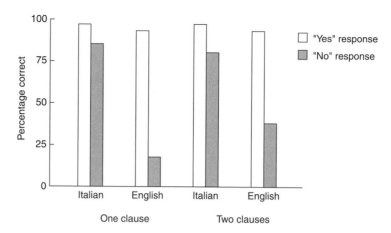

Figure 8.1
Percentage of correct responses from Italian and English learners to sentences including pronouns in the match ("yes" response) and mismatch ("no" response) conditions. The pronouns were clitics in Italian and nonclitics in English. They were located either in the main clause or in the embedded clause. (Italian learners: $N = 30$, mean age 4;8; English learners: $N = 30$, mean age 3;11). Data from McKee 1992.

does not say anything about how it can be interpreted. This aspect of interpretation does not depend on the binding theory.

8.3.4 Principle B, Quantifiers, and *Wh*-Operators

In Chien and Wexler's (1990) study English-speaking children aged between 5 and 6 years accepted an anaphoric interpretation of the pronoun in (28), repeated here, about 50% of the time, when the antecedent was a referential NP.

(28) *Name-pronoun condition*
Mama Bear touches her.

By contrast, when the antecedent was a quantifier, as in (32), the percentage of nonadult responses decreased to 16%.

(32) *Name-quantifier condition*
Every bear touches him.

The sharp asymmetry in the rate of correct responses between the name-pronoun condition and the quantifier-pronoun condition is highly significant and has been replicated in other studies with younger children. Using

Table 8.2
Percentage of children's correct responses to sentences including nonreflexive pronouns in the name-pronoun (*Mama Bear touches her*) and quantifier-pronoun (*Every bear touches him*) conditions

	Name-pronoun condition	Quantifier-pronoun condition
Chien and Wexler 1990[a]		
Match condition ("yes" response)	90	98
Mismatch condition ("no" response)	49	84
Thornton and Wexler 1999[b]		
Acceptance of anaphoric reading ("yes" response)	58	8

[a] yes/no judgment task; age range 5;0–6;0; $N = 44$
[b] truth value judgment task; age range 4;0–5;1 (mean 4;8); $N = 19$

the truth value judgment task, Thornton and Wexler (1999) found that 4-year-old English-speaking children take the pronoun to be anaphorically linked to its local antecedent 58% of the time in the name-pronoun condition, but just 8% of the time in the quantifier-pronoun condition. The results of Chien and Wexler's and Thornton and Wexler's studies are summarized in table 8.2.

A similar improvement has been observed when the possible antecedent is a *wh*-operator as in (33a) (for more detailed discussion, see Thornton 1990; Crain and Thornton 1998). Principle B rules out the LF representation in (33b), thus accounting for English speakers' intuition that (33a) cannot mean that I know the persons who scratched themselves.

(33) a. I know who scratched them.
     b. I know who$_i$ t$_i$ scratched them$_i$.

Children are highly consistent in rejecting this illicit interpretation (see also Avrutin and Wexler 1992 for evidence from Russian). This high level of performance would be unexpected if Principle B were not active in child grammar. It suggests that in the name-pronoun condition some factor obscures knowledge of binding, a factor that disappears in the quantifier/*wh*-pronoun condition. What is this factor? Given the data examined thus far, we can exclude the notion that children's errors arise from an incorrect categorization of pronouns. As a matter of fact, children are not treating nonreflexive pronouns as if they were reflexive pronouns. Another factor we can exclude is the mechanism of syntactic binding and the rules for its interpretation, because of children's responses in the quantifier-pronoun condition. The discrepancy must depend on the nature of the antecedent: a referential NP in (28) versus a quantifier in (32). Something must be special about referential NPs that makes children err.

8.3.5 The "Delay" of Principle B

Since children respond in an adultlike way to sentences including pronouns and quantifiers/*wh*-operators, they must be guided by Principle B and by the mechanism for interpreting bound pronouns (semantic binding). Hence, three of the components implicated in binding (lexicon, syntax, and semantics) are fully available to children. Consequently, the source of children's errors appears to be something like Rule I* in (18), which governs coreference. A hypothesis that in one way or another is common to most accounts of children's nonadult responses in Principle B contexts is this:

(34) Children often interpret a pronoun not bound by an NP in its local domain to corefer with that NP, even when this is not allowed in the adult language.

In the framework presented in section 8.1, (34) amounts to saying that children take a pronoun to be coreferential with a local NP even though this interpretation is not sanctioned by Rule I* or whatever subsumes its effects.

There are divergent views about why children make mistakes in interpreting pronouns, that is, why they allow a pronoun to be coreferential with a local NP in contexts that are not allowed in the adult grammar or that are not sanctioned by Rule I*'s default. (34) leaves open two avenues for exploration. In the adult language an unbound pronoun can be anaphorically linked to a local nominal expression, in Evans-style contexts (see (16)). Let us call this the *conditions making coreference readings legitimate* (or for suspending the default set up by Rule I*). The cooperative speaker signals the presence of an Evans-style context by using various devices: deixis, emphatic stress, contextual information. Let us call these the *cues signaling that a coreference reading is allowed (or intended)* (or that the default set up by Rule I* has been suspended). Children may err either because they have trouble with the conditions making coreference readings legitimate or because they cannot appreciate the cues signaling that a coreference reading is allowed. Both lines of explanation have been explored, although there are still difficulties in making them fully explicit. The following sections briefly sketch how these lines of thinking have been pursued.

8.3.5.1 Conditions Making Coreference Readings Legitimate Grodzinsky and Reinhart (1993) claim that processing limitations are responsible for children's errors in interpreting nonreflexive pronouns. Their proposal is based on slightly different assumptions than the one adopted here. Specifically, it is based on Reinhart's Rule I, which amounts to saying that "if a given message can be conveyed by two minimally different LFs one of which involves variable binding where the other has coreference, then the variable binding structure is always the preferred one" (Heim and Kratzer 1998, 271). Consider (13) and (14), repeated here. In (14a) *Goofy* and *him* cannot corefer, because the same message can be obtained through the variable binding mechanism—that is, by replacing the nonreflexive pronoun with the reflexive pronoun in (13a), where (13a) is associated with the representation in (13c), in which the reflexive is bound by the raised noun.

(13) a. Goofy admires himself.
      c. Goofy$_i$ [t$_i$ admires himself$_i$]

(14) a. Goofy admires him.
      c. Goofy$_j$ [t$_j$ admires him$_i$]

Children know Rule I, which, Grodzinsky and Reinhart claim, is innate. They also know what they have to do to apply it—namely, given sentence (14a) they have to build its LF representation, (14c), and keep it in memory. In (14c) the pronoun is free and could be interpreted as coreferential with the nominal expression *Goofy*. In order to allow the coreference reading, children have to decide whether a sentence like (14a) that conveys an anaphoric interpretation of the pronoun but with a reflexive pronoun rather than a nonreflexive pronoun might have been produced, that is, a sentence whose LF representation involves binding. In the case at hand, this sentence is (13a), with the LF representation in (13c). At this point children have to keep in memory two LF representations: (13c) and (14c). Having found that there is an LF representation that expresses an anaphoric reading of the pronoun through binding, children have to prefer that representation over one that expresses the same reading through coreference, namely, (14c). Therefore, they have to reject a coreference interpretation of the pronoun in (14a). Although children know all this, they cannot hold two LF representations in memory and thus decide which one is to be preferred, because this exceeds their processing resources. Because of their processing limitations, children are led to guess when tested on sentences like (14a); that is, they sometimes accept a coreferential reading of the pronoun.

One problem for this account is that it predicts that English and Italian learners will respond alike, a clearly false prediction (see section 8.3.3; see also Thornton and Wexler 1999 for additional criticism). While Italian learners do not accept an interpretation in which the pronoun is anaphorically linked to a local antecedent, English learners do.

A more radical stance is taken by Chien and Wexler (1990) and Avrutin and Wexler (1992). These authors propose that children cannot apply some rule very similar in outcome to Rule I*. They call it **Principle P**. Principle P prohibits coreference between two noncoindexed elements, with the notable exception of elements appearing in Evans-style contexts. Children know that two expressions with different indices can sometimes be coreferential, but they do not know the situations where this reading is legitimate and thus are led to overaccept it. On these authors' view Principle P is a pragmatic principle that cannot be applied by children, because pragmatic knowledge is acquired through experience. Many aspects of pragmatics are still poorly understood, resisting satisfactory formalization. While some pieces of pragmatic knowledge are acquired through experience, it is reasonable to think that others are innate (see Sperber and Wilson 1986). One is the principle of cooperation, which exhorts speakers to cooperate, to tell the truth, to be informative, and so on. If children did not assume that other people tell the truth, it would be hard to understand how they could learn a language. To date little is known about the development of pragmatics; thus, the hypothesis that children lack pragmatic knowledge is certainly plausible, but needs empirical testing.

In any event, notice that if pragmatic knowledge must be learned, it must be learned by Italian-speaking children as well as by English-speaking children. But then why are Italian-speaking children more adultlike than their English-speaking peers in their interpretation of pronouns? We have seen that among the cues that signal coreference is deixis. For example, in (16c), repeated here, the pronoun picks out the same referent as the NP, which the speaker makes clear by accompanying the pronoun with a pointing gesture.

(16) c. It is not true that no one has invited Michael. Michael has
         invited HIM [pointing at Michael].

Avrutin and Wexler (1992) observe that clitic pronouns such as those used
in Italian cannot be associated with a pointing gesture. Because of this,
they claim, clitics are not amenable to a coreference interpretation.

8.3.5.2   Cues for Suspending Rule I*: Emphatic Stress   McDaniel and
Maxfield (1992) take a different route. They locate children's deficiency in
interpreting nonreflexive pronouns in an inability to perceive contrastive
stress as a cue signaling that Rule I* has been overridden. However, this
proposal cannot be correct, because learners are already responsive to
prosodic features a few days after birth (see chapters 2 and 3). A more
reasonable conjecture is that children are unable to interpret stress as a
means for conveying a certain type of information. In fact, Cutler
and Swinney (1987) have shown that children under 6 years are poor at
exploiting prosodic information (stress) in comprehension as a cue to
semantic structure (see also Thornton and Wexler 1999 for a review of
studies on children's use of stress). We have seen that stress is used in
contexts in which the coreference reading of the pronoun is licit, as in
(16b), repeated here.

(16) b. When Aladdin looks in the mirror, he doesn't see Jasmine.
         Aladdin sees HIM.

Children know that a pronoun and a local antecedent can corefer, but
they are not aware of the need to stress the pronoun in this case. Thus,
they can think that *him* and *Goofy* corefer in (35), even though *him* does
not bear stress.

(35) Goofy admires him.

8.3.6   Intermediate Summary

Children know Principle B, as witnessed by their good performance when
they deal with sentences including quantifiers. However, they do not have
full understanding of the mechanism of coreference. Children are unable
to restrict coreference to contexts in which this reading is allowed in the
adult grammar; in other words, they overgeneralize, extending coreference beyond situations that permit it. This result is very important because
it shows that syntactic (and semantic) abilities emerge early, as expected
under a nativist theory; what seems to become available only with time is

something related to the implementation of Rule I* (or some equivalent rule or principle that governs coreference).

8.4   PRINCIPLE C

In earlier studies on the acquisition of anaphoric dependencies, it was argued that initially children's grammar does not include any **structure-dependent constraints** like Principle C, that is, a constraint making reference to hierarchical organization of sentences. Rather, it was argued, their grammar contains a linear constraint that prohibits a pronoun from being anaphorically linked to its antecedent when the former precedes the latter, a process called **backward anaphora** (see Tavakolian 1978; Solan 1983). The evidence for this claim was that in act-out tasks children hardly accept the licit anaphoric reading of a pronoun in sentences like (36a) and instead interpret the pronoun exophorically or as referring to an extrasentential character (see Lust 1986a for reviews; see Chomsky 1969). Under this view children also reject the anaphoric interpretation of the pronoun in (36b), not because of Principle C, but simply because of the linear constraint operative in their grammar (see Carden 1986; O'Grady, Suzuki-Wei, and Cho 1986). (The asterisk indicates that (36b) is ungrammatical when *he* binds *Goofy*.)

(36) *Backward anaphora*
    a.   When he was playing guitar, Pinocchio was dancing.
    b.   *He$_j$ washes Goofy$_j$.

On this view, for children at this stage the pronoun can be anaphorically linked to its antecedent if the pronoun follows the antecedent, as in (37), a process called **forward anaphora**. Notice that Principle C is not relevant in (37), because the pronoun does not c-command the R-expression *Pinocchio*.

(37) *Forward anaphora*
Pinocchio was dancing, when he was playing guitar.

Now if children, unlike adults, favor forward anaphoric readings of pronouns and base their anaphoric judgments on a linear constraint, then they should accept not only the licit anaphoric reading of the pronoun in (37), but also the illicit anaphoric reading of the pronoun in (38). (The asterisk means that the sentence is not acceptable when there is a binding relation between *Aladdin* and the pronoun.)

(38)   *(Illicit) forward anaphora*
        *Near Aladdin$_j$, he$_j$ saw a snake.

Several studies have investigated children's performance on forward anaphora. Some researchers report findings indicating that children interpret
the pronoun anaphorically both in (37) and in (38), supporting the hypothesis that the anaphoric reading of pronouns is governed by a linear
constraint. However, other researchers have challenged this conclusion, as
we will now see.

8.4.1   Backward Anaphora with Referential NPs

The evidence that children interpret the pronoun exophorically in (36a)
comes from experiments using the act-out task (a task in which children
act out sentences by using available toy props). For the sentence in (36a),
they generally do not choose Pinocchio as the character who is playing
guitar; instead, they choose another available character. Notice that this
response does not imply that children lack the anaphoric interpretation,
as has been argued. It merely shows that they prefer the exophoric reading
in this case (see Crain and Thornton 1998 for criticism of the act-out task).
Using a methodology that is more sensitive for testing children's available
interpretations, the truth value judgment task, Crain and McKee (1985)
were able to show that from about 3 years English-speaking children accept
the anaphoric reading of the pronoun in (36a) 73% of the time. They also
proved that children, like adults, reject the anaphoric reading in (36b)
88% of the time, when this reading is prohibited by Principle C. In both
sentences the relative order of pronoun and antecedent is the same; the
difference is structural, since in (36b) the pronoun c-commands the antecedent, while in (36a) it does not. The fact that children respond differently
to these stimuli indicates that they are guided by a structure-dependent
constraint and not a constraint based on the linear order of elements.
(Incidentally, these children also allow the exophoric reading of the pronoun in (36a) in 81% of the cases.) The data from Crain and McKee's
experiment are summarized in table 8.3.

   Thus, children can clearly discriminate between legitimate and illegitimate cases of backward anaphora, a finding observed in other studies as
well (see Lust, Eisele, and Mazuka 1992 for reviews; see also McDaniel,
Cairns, and Hsu 1990). Currently there seems to be agreement that children's grammar does not include a linear constraint for interpreting
pronouns, but instead includes a structure-dependent constraint, that is,

Table 8.3
Percentage of American English–speaking children's correct responses in backward anaphora contexts ($N = 62$; mean age 4;2)

Test sentence	Reading	Percentage of correct responses
(36a) *When he$_i$ was playing guitar, Pinocchio$_i$ was dancing.*	Anaphoric	73 (yes)
(36a) *When he$_i$ was playing guitar, Pinocchio$_j$ was dancing.*	Exophoric	81 (yes)
(36b) **He$_i$ washes Goofy$_i$.*	Principle C	88 (no)

Source: Data from Crain and McKee 1985 (truth value judgment task)

Principle C (see section 4.3.1 for discussion of another structure-dependent relation).

In the studies cited above children's interpretation of pronouns in backward contexts was tested with stimuli that included referential NPs, rather than quantifiers. It is clear by now that referential NPs are not the best candidates for testing knowledge of binding, since they may enter into an anaphoric relation either through binding or through coreference. The fact that children display adultlike behavior in judging the pair of sentences in (36) seems to suggest that when it comes to Principle C, the problems noted regarding Principle B in section 8.3.1 disappear. We will return later to this point since it deserves scrutiny.

8.4.2   Backward Anaphora with Quantified Expressions

If we want to be sure to tap knowledge of binding in an experiment, the best candidates are test sentences with quantifiers (and *wh*-operators). Recall that pronouns can enter either a local coreference or a binding relation when the antecedent is a referential NP, while they can only enter a binding relation when the antecedent is a quantifier. However, few experiments have used quantifiers and *wh*-operators in sentences testing Principle C, probably because experiments testing backward anaphora with referential NPs already showed that children abide by Principle C. A single experiment conducted with Italian learners has tested backward anaphora with quantifiers. Using the truth value judgment task, Guasti and Chierchia (1999/2000) probed children's comprehension of sentences like (39). (The phonologically null subject is rendered as *pro*; in English its position is occupied by a lexical pronoun.)

(39) Mentre (pro) ballava,   un pagliaccio suonava   la   chitarra.
     while   (pro) was dancing a   clown   was playing the guitar
     'While he was dancing, a clown was playing the guitar.'

These sentences are similar to those employed by Crain and McKee (1985), but they include a quantifier, the indefinite, rather than a referential NP.[4] In (39) the grammar allows the null subject of the temporal clause to be bound by the indefinite quantifier, *un pagliaccio*.[5] This is not possible in (40a), however. Here the null subject of the main clause c-commands and binds the trace of the raised quantifier, *un musicista* 'a musician', thus violating Principle C, as the LF representation in (40b) shows.

(40) a.   (pro) andava sul cavallo a dondolo, mentre un musicista
          (pro) was riding the rocking horse   while   a   musician
          suonava   la tromba.
          was playing the trumpet
          'He was riding the rocking horse, while a musician was playing
          the trumpet.'
     b.   *un musicista$_i$ [pro$_i$ andava sul cavallo a dondolo, mentre t$_i$
          suonava la tromba]

By age 3;10 Italian learners gave a high percentage of adultlike responses when presented with sentences like (39) and (40a). They accepted a bound reading of the pronoun 94% of the time when this reading was licit, as in (39); namely, they judged (39) appropriate in a situation in which a clown was dancing and playing the guitar. By contrast, they accepted a bound reading just 11% of the time when the grammar does not sanction this reading, as in (40a); that is, they rejected this reading 89% of the time. For children, as for adults, this sentence cannot mean that the musician was riding the rocking horse and playing the trumpet. (For completeness, note that children also accept the exophoric reading of the pronoun 89% of the time for sentences like (39).) These findings, which are summarized in figure 8.2, confirm the previous conclusion and provide unequivocal evidence that children do not uniformly reject a backward anaphoric reading of pronouns; they only do so when Principle C is violated.

8.4.3   Forward Anaphora with Referential NPs

As for instances of forward anaphora, Lust, Loveland, and Kornet (1980) and Lust and Clifford (1986) claim that children discriminate between licit and illicit cases of forward anaphora, since they accept an ana-

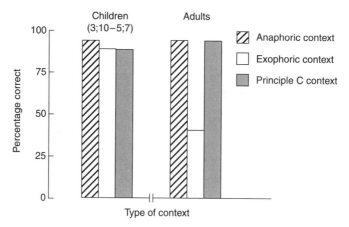

Figure 8.2
Percentage of correct responses to licit and illicit backward anaphora sentences in (39) and (40a) given by Italian-speaking children and adults. (Children: $N = 18$, age range 3;10–5;7, mean age 4;6; adults $N = 16$.) Data from Guasti and Chierchia 1999/2000.

phoric reading in sentences like (41) 66% of the time, as opposed to 18% for sentences like (38), repeated here.

(38) Near Aladdin, he saw a snake.

(41) John said that he was happy.

While the contrast between 66% and 18% is significant, in a critical evaluation of these results, Carden (1986) points out several problems that may threaten the conjecture that children are really adultlike in rejecting forward coreference in (38). Moreover, other studies report results opposite to those reported by Lust, Loveland, and Kornet (see Hsu, Eisenberg, and Schlisselberg 1989). Children may accept the forward anaphoric reading of pronouns for sentences like (38) as much as they do for sentences like (41); that is, they do not seem to discriminate between the two kinds of sentences.

The source of this disagreement may be methodological flaws in the cited experiments (see Thornton and Wexler 1999). In any event, before any conclusions can be drawn with confidence, further experimentation is needed. Another source may be that the experiments did not tap the grammar of binding (see Guasti and Chierchia 1999/2000). In all the experiments cited, the possible antecedent of the pronoun is a referential NP. Now we know that a pronoun can be anaphorically linked to a referential NP either via binding or, in certain circumstances, via coreference. We also know that children have difficulties with coreference. Hence, it might come as no surprise that children do not respond in an adultlike way when tested with sentences like (38). This might have happened if children assign this sentence the LF representation in (42) in which *Aladdin* and *he* have different indices in compliance with Principle C.

(42) [Near Aladdin$_i$, he$_j$ saw a snake].

In (42) the pronoun is unbound and its interpretation does not depend on binding. Rule I* in (18) establishes that a pronoun not bound by a local NP does not corefer with that NP. However, we know that when it comes to Rule I*, children do not behave like adults: they allow a pronoun and a local NP to corefer, where adults would not. Similarly, in (42) children may take the NP and the pronoun to pick out the same individual, Aladdin; that is, they might allow local coreference, even though they know Principle C. If this conjecture is on the right track, we need to explain why in (36b), repeated here, children never accept local coreference, although the potential antecedent is a referential expression.

(36) b. He washes Goofy.

In other words, we would like to know why children do not take *he* and *Goofy* to pick out the same individual in (36b). One possibility is that some processing factor related to the linear order of expressions is responsible for children's responses. For discussion of this possibility, see Thornton and Wexler 1999.

8.4.4   Forward Anaphora with Quantified Expressions

When we turn to sentences with *wh*-operators and quantifiers, we indeed find evidence that children perform like adults with respect to Principle C even in cases of forward anaphora. Consider the question in (43a).

(43) a.   Who does he think eats an apple?
     b.   *Who$_i$ does he$_i$ think t$_i$ eats an apple?
     c.   Who$_i$ does he$_j$ think t$_i$ eats an apple?

This question cannot be taken to mean 'for which *x*, *x* is thinking that *x* eats an apple'. That is, it cannot have the LF representation in (43b), where the pronoun is coindexed with the trace of the raised *wh*-element (and with the *wh*-element as well), since Principle C rules it out: the trace of the raised operator (an R-expression) is bound by the c-commanding and coindexed pronoun. The legitimate LF representation is (43c), in which the pronoun is unbound. This captures English speakers' intuition about the meaning of (43a), which can be rendered as follows: 'for which *x*, he (say, John) thinks *x* eats an apple'. The representation in (43b) is a case of strong crossover (see sections 5.2.3.1, 8.1). By testing children's comprehension of strong crossover questions, we can gather unequivocal evidence about children's knowledge of Principle C in forward anaphora contexts.

Using the truth value judgment task, Crain and Thornton (1998) compared children's performance on crossover questions of the kind in (43) with their performance on bound variable questions of the kind in (44a) (see also Roeper and de Villiers 1991). (The sentences used in the experiment were slightly different from those in (43) and (44).)

(44) a. Who thinks he has eaten an apple?
     b. Who$_i$ t$_i$ thinks he$_i$ has eaten an apple?

A speaker can use (44a) to ask about the *x* thinking that *x* has eaten an apple, the interpretation given in the LF representation in (44b) (another interpretation is also licit, in which the pronoun refers to some salient extralinguistic character). In (44b) the pronoun does not bind the trace of the *wh*-operator because it does not c-command it, and Principle C is satisfied. The trace of the *wh*-operator binds the pronoun (outside some local domain), and the semantic procedure discussed in section 8.1 interprets this pronoun as a variable bound by the *wh*-operator. Crain and Thornton found that English learners aged between 3;7 and 4;8 accept the bound variable reading 50% of the time in (44a). This shows that children can access the bound variable reading where the grammar of binding allows it. By contrast, they accept the same reading for (43a) only 8% of

Table 8.4
Percentage of American English–speaking children's acceptance of the bound variable reading in licit and illicit contexts

Test sentence	Reading	Percentage of correct responses
(44a) *Who thinks he has eaten an apple?*	Bound variable (licit)	50 (yes)
(43a) *Who does he think eats an apple?*	Bound variable (illicit)	8 (yes)

Source: Data from Crain and Thornton 1998 (truth value judgment task)

the time (see also McDaniel and McKee 1992; for more details and for critical discussion of experiments testing strong crossover questions, see Crain and Thornton 1998). These data, which are summarized in table 8.4, clearly show that children adhere to Principle C also in forward anaphora contexts. Similar findings, for sentences with quantifiers, have been reported by Guasti and Chierchia (1999/2000). Using the truth value judgment task, these authors tested Italian learners' comprehension of sentences like (45a,b) (*pro* is the null subject).

(45) a. Il   tesoro   di ciascun bambino, le scimmie lo nascondono
        the treasure of each   child   the monkeys it hide
        mentre (pro) dorme.
        while (pro) is sleeping
        'The treasure of each child, the monkeys hide it while (he) is sleeping.'

     b. Nel   barile di ciascun pirata con cura (pro) ha messo una
        in the barrel of each   pirate with care (pro) has put   a
        pistola.
        gun
        'In the barrel of each pirate with care (he) put a gun.'

In (45a) an NP has been preposed, but for the purposes of interpretation we assume that it is placed in its original position, as the italicized portion of the LF representation (46) indicates. Then the quantified expression *ciascun bambino* 'each child' adjoins to some suitable site, as (46) also shows (see Chierchia 1995).

(46) [[ciascun bambino]$_i$ [le scimmie lo nascondono [*il tesoro di t$_i$*]
     mentre pro$_i$ dorme]]

The raised quantified expression *ciascun bambino* 'each child' can bind the null pronoun in the temporal clause. This captures Italian speakers' intuition about the meaning of sentence (45a): 'for every child *x*, the monkeys hides *x*'s treasure while *x* is sleeping'. (In passing, note that the sentence also admits an exophoric reading of the null subject pronoun.) In (45b), too, a PP has been preposed. As we did for (45a), we assume that the PP is placed in its original position for purposes of interpretation and that the quantified expression is adjoined to some suitable site, as shown in the LF representation in (47). Now if the pronoun (pro) ended up having the same index as the raised quantified expression, it would bind its trace (an R-expression), violating Principle C.

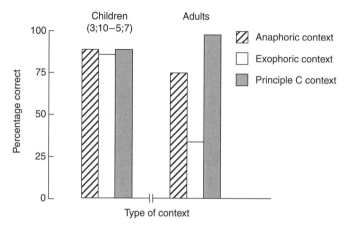

Figure 8.3
Percentage of correct responses to licit and illicit forward anaphora sentences in (45a) and (45b) given by Italian-speaking children and adults. (Children: $N = 18$, age range 3;10–5;7, mean age 4;6; adults $N = 16$.) Data from Guasti and Chierchia 1999/2000.

(47) *[[ciascun pirata]$_i$ [con cura pro$_i$ ha messo una pistola [$_{PP}$ *nel barile di t$_i$*]]]

Guasti and Chierchia found that by age 3;10 children accept the bound reading of the pronoun in (45a) 89% of the time. For sentences like (45b) children accept the bound variable reading only 10% of the time; that is, they reject this reading 90% of the time. Figure 8.3 displays these findings.

These data provide further evidence that children apply Principle C in interpreting sentences involving forward anaphora, just as they do in interpreting sentences involving backward anaphora. We can reject the hypothesis that children are guided by a linear constraint in their comprehension of anaphoric dependencies. Children instead base their judgments on a structure-dependent constraint, Principle C. This is true in both backward and forward contexts. Thus, we can conclude that all binding principles emerge around age 3–4.

8.5 SUMMARY AND CONCLUDING REMARKS

Evidence has accumulated showing that knowledge of binding is continuously operative in child grammar. This outcome is largely due to fruitful interactions between linguistic theory and acquisition theory, each posing challenging problems for the other.

Children distinguish between reflexive and nonreflexive pronouns (lexical knowledge), know the local domain in which binding conditions must be satisfied, and know the mechanism of syntactic binding and its interpretation (semantic binding). Children's knowledge of binding is couched in structure-dependent terms, that is, in terms of constraints operating on a hierarchical representation. Despite this sophisticated and highly abstract kind of knowledge, children sometimes do not correctly interpret nonreflexive pronouns in configurations governed by Principle B. They respond differently depending on whether the antecedent is a referential NP or a quantifier: they allow a pronoun and a referential NP to corefer where adults would not, as in *Goofy admired him*. In the approach adopted here this split is not surprising. The anaphoric reading in the quantifier-pronoun condition can only be obtained via binding; in the name-pronoun condition it can be obtained either via binding or via a procedure of coreference interpretation that involves Rule I* or something equivalent. Recall that this rule states that an unbound pronoun is generally interpreted as noncoreferential. Consider (36b), repeated here.

(36) b. He washes Goofy.

Principle C ensures that in this sentence the pronoun *he* does not bind the R-expression *Goofy*, and Rule I* ensures that it does not corefer with *Goofy*. However, there are cases, structurally similar to (36b), in which coreference is allowed and Rule I*'s default can be suspended. Parallel to the examples in (16) are the following examples, where the two italicized expressions refer to the same individual.

(48) a. Everyone voted for Ariel. Even *she* [pointing] has voted for *Ariel*.
   b. When Aladdin looks in the mirror, he doesn't see Jasmine. *He* sees *Aladdin*.

In (48a) *she* refers to Ariel and in (48b) *he* refers to Aladdin; that is, the pronouns end up being anaphorically linked to their antecedents. Clearly, Rule I*'s default can be overridden in these contexts. But this raises a puzzle, as recognized by Avrutin and Wexler (1992), Grodzinsky and Reinhart (1993), and Guasti and Chierchia (1999/2000), among others. Rule I* or something equivalent has been at the heart of various attempts to understand children's errors in interpreting pronouns. There is no doubt that Principle C alone is responsible for children's responses when the stimuli include quantifiers and *wh*-operators (see sections 8.4.2 and 8.4.4). When it comes to sentences including referential NPs, Rule I* becomes relevant, for it is Rule I* that forces an unbound pronoun to be interpreted as not anaphorically linked to its antecedent. If children make errors in interpreting sentences like *Goofy admires him* (see section 8.3.1) and take *him* and *Goofy* to corefer, why don't they make the same mistake in sentences like (36b) (*He washes Goofy*)? Children's adultlike behavior in backward anaphora contexts with sentences like (36b) might indicate that something is at work in these contexts that drives them away from making coreference errors. Obviously, children's rejection of the backward anaphora reading in (36b) does not guarantee that they do not make mistakes in cases of forward anaphora (e.g., *Near Aladdin, he saw a snake*). Although the evidence is controversial, it seems that in this case children do take *he* and *Aladdin* to corefer (see section 8.4.3). If further experimental evidence confirms this suggestion, we will have for Principle C something analogous to what is robustly documented for Principle B, that is, a discrepancy between responses to sentences with referential NPs and to sentences with quantified expressions. If it is not confirmed, then there must be a substantial difference between Principles B and C that linguistic and acquisition theory must uncover. These are rather speculative reflections that further research might attempt to clarify.

Summary of Linguistic Development

1. By around 3–4 years children know Principles A, B, and C of the binding theory.
2. Up to 6 years children speaking English, Icelandic, Russian, and so on, but not children speaking Italian or Spanish, have trouble with the interpretation of nonreflexive pronouns.

Further Reading

In some languages reflexive pronouns can have an antecedent outside some local domain (an instance of long-distance anaphora). This is the case in Icelandic, Chinese, and Russian (see Hermon 1994; see Harbert 1995 for a survey of problems related to long-distance anaphora). How children deal with long-distance reflexives is taken up in Hyams and Sigurjónsdóttir 1990 and in Sigurjónsdóttir and Hyams 1992 for Icelandic; in Bailyn 1992 for Russian; in Chien, Wexler, and Chang 1993 for Chinese; and in Jakubowicz 1994 for Danish.

Children's interpretation of pronouns has been claimed to be subject to a directionality effect that is discussed in detail in Lust and Clifford 1986; O'Grady, Suzuki-Wei, and Cho 1986; Lust 1986a; Lust and Mazuka 1989; and Lust et al. 1996.

Children's knowledge of binding in VP-ellipsis contexts is discussed in Thornton and Wexler 1999.

On the issue of reconstruction in Principle C contexts, see Guasti and Chierchia 1999/2000.

Key Words

Anaphoric relation
Backward anaphora
Bound pronouns
Coreference
Forward anaphora
Principle P
Rule I*
Strategy of self-oriented action
Structure-dependent constraint

Study Questions

1. What kind of evidence shows that children are not using strategy (21)—that is, simply looking for a reflexive action—when they listen to sentences including reflexive pronouns?

2. How have researchers shown that children distinguish between reflexive and nonreflexive pronouns?

3. What tells us that children know Principle B?

4. How have researchers shown that children know the binding domain for reflexive pronouns?

5. What is the contribution of crosslinguistic investigations to our understanding of Principle B?

6. What is the role of Rule I* in explaining children's errors in interpreting pronouns?

7. How have researchers challenged the claim that children reject the anaphoric reading of the pronoun in *He hit Goofy* on the basis of a linear constraint?

8. McKee (1992) tested children's comprehension of two-clause sentences like (i) after viewing a situation in which Roger Rabbit covered a clown (who was sitting down); here the antecedent of the reflexive is not in the local domain, but outside it.

(i) While the clown was sitting down, Roger Rabbit covered himself.

Children responded highly accurately, giving 91% correct responses (they rejected (i)). Does this result bear on the question of whether children use the strategy in (21) in comprehending sentences including reflexives?

Chapter 9

Aspects of the Acquisition of Quantification

INTRODUCTION

Work on the acquisition of quantification is just beginning. Since most of the research efforts have focused on children's interpretation of universally quantified sentences, we will do the same in this chapter. We have already touched on some properties of quantifiers in discussing the acquisition of binding principles in chapter 8, noting that children respond differently to sentences like *John scratches him* and *Every boy scratches him*. In this chapter we turn our attention to children's interpretation of universally quantified sentences like *Every farmer feeds a donkey*. It has long been known that children sometimes misinterpret this kind of sentence. Some authors have attributed children's errors in interpreting such sentences to nonlinguistic factors. Others have claimed that children assign such sentences an incorrect representation. By examining the strengths and weaknesses that children show in interpreting these sentences, we will try to establish whether they possess the various pieces of knowledge required for handling universally quantified sentences.

This chapter is organized as follows. Section 9.1 spells out what kind of knowledge children must have to handle quantified sentences. Section 9.2 surveys some aspects of quantification in adult language and then shows how children behave with regard to them. Section 9.3 reports comprehension errors that children sometimes make in interpreting universally quantified sentences. It also discusses two accounts of these errors: a linguistic account and a nonlinguistic account.

9.1   PREREQUISITES FOR HANDLING QUANTIFICATIONAL STRUCTURES

Natural languages use different categories to express generalizations, such as **quantificational determiners** (e.g., *every, all, few, a, three*) and **adverbs of quantification** (e.g., *always, usually*). Here we will concentrate on quantificational determiners, that is, those expressions that combine directly with a noun, have no adverbial use, and cannot modify pronouns.[1] (Where the term *quantifiers* appears in the text, bear in mind that it refers exclusively to quantificational determiners.) There are finer distinctions among quantificational determiners, but these will not be discussed; the investigation will be limited to universal quantifiers like *every* and *all*.

Quantificational determiners give speakers "the power to express generalization into language, that is, the power to move beyond talk about properties of particular individuals to saying what *quantity* of the individuals in a given domain have a given property" (Chierchia and McConnell-Ginet 2000, 113–114). A sentence like *Every girl drinks juice* conveys the idea that the quantity of individuals who drink juice in a given situation includes the totality of the girls in that situation.

If children are to properly interpret quantified sentences and use quantifiers correctly, three pieces of knowledge must be in place: they must (1) distinguish referential from quantified NPs, (2) know the syntax of noun phrases, and (3) know the semantics of noun phrases. This knowledge is articulated as follows. At the syntactic level a quantificational determiner (e.g., *every*) combines with a noun (e.g., *dog*) to form a constituent (here, *every dog*). To be interpreted, quantifiers must move and adjoin to some suitable site, a movement operation called Quantifier Raising (QR) (see Haegeman 1994 for an introduction; see also May 1985; section 8.1). Simplifying somewhat, consider the sentence in (1).

(1) Every farmer is riding a donkey.

At the level of Logical Form (LF) the quantified expressions, *every NP* (a universally quantified expression) and *a NP* (an existentially quantified expression), are moved by QR from their surface position and adjoined to some suitable site (let us assume it is IP, as shown in (2)). This operation is necessary for interpreting quantifiers.

(2)

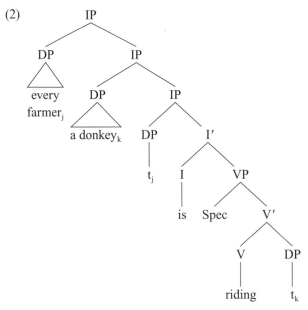

QR is an operation that allows us to define the scope of quantifiers, that is, their c-command domain. In (2) IP is the c-command domain of the quantifiers.

At the semantic level *every* is mapped onto a two-place relation holding between sets of individuals. In *Every dog barks* that relation holds between the set of dogs and the set of beings that bark. Moreover, the domain of quantification of quantified NPs is contextually or pragmatically restricted. If a sentence like *Every girl drinks juice* is uttered in a kindergarten, *every girl* will be taken to indicate the girls in the kindergarten. If the same sentence is uttered at a birthday party, *every girl* will be taken to indicate the girls at the party. In other words, a quantified sentence is generally uttered with reference to a given situation, and the entities of a particular kind that have to be considered to verify whether the sentence is true or false are not all the entities of that kind in the world, but the ones in that particular situation. This contextual restriction associated with quantificational determiners can be formally captured by saying that at the semantic level these are mapped not onto a two-place relation, but onto a three-place relation holding among the sentence's context or situation of use and two sets of individuals. For example, in *Every girl drinks juice* the relation holds between a given context, the set of girls, and the set of individuals that drink juice (see Westerståhl 1985). Under this view understanding that quantificational determiners need to be pragmatically restricted is part of the semantics of these expressions. Therefore, if children know the semantics of quantificational determiners, they also know that these are pragmatically restricted.

The requirements for interpreting quantified sentences are summarized in (3).

(3) To be able to interpret quantified sentences, one must
   a. be able to distinguish quantifiers from referential expressions,
   b. know the structure of quantified NPs and have access to a representational system (QR or something equivalent),
   c. know the mapping from syntax to semantics (quantifiers express three-place relations) and thus know that the domain of quantification is contextually restricted.

For simplicity, we will often say that quantificational determiners are mapped onto a two-place relation between sets of individuals rather than onto a three-place relation. It should be borne in mind that this is just a simplification.

9.2   THE STRUCTURE OF QUANTIFIED NPs AND THE SYNTAX-SEMANTICS MAPPING

In this section we will look briefly at some basic notions used in current formal semantic approaches to quantified sentences. The examples will consist of universally quantified sentences, since these have been widely investigated in child language. (For a more complete discussion, see Chierchia and McConnell-Ginet 2000, chaps. 3 and 9.)

Consider sentence (1), repeated here.

(1) Every farmer is riding a donkey.

Common nouns, like *farmer*, name a property that holds of objects or of individuals; we say that they *denote* the sets of objects or individuals with that property. VPs also name a property that holds of objects or individuals; in this case they denote the set of persons riding a donkey. The quantificational determiner *every* denotes a two-place relation between two sets of individuals. In this case using *every* conveys the meaning that the set of farmers bears a subset relation to the set of donkey-riders; that is, sentence (1) is true if the set of farmers is a subset of the set of donkey-riders, as shown in figure 9.1.

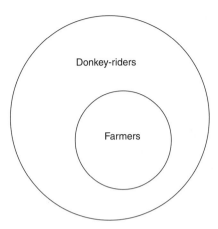

Figure 9.1
Set-theoretic representation of the relation denoted by universal quantifiers. Sentence (1) (*Every farmer is riding a donkey*) is true if the set of farmers is a subset of the set of donkey-riders.

Thus, to evaluate the truth of sentence (1), we need to check whether the set of farmers who are riding a donkey is the same as the set of farmers. One way to do this is to take every single farmer in the given context and check whether he or she is riding a donkey. We need not check every donkey. Similarly, sentence (4) is true or false depending on whether the set of cats that are waving is the same as the set of cats.

(4) Every cat is waving.

The quantifier *every* in (1) joins in the syntax with the noun *farmer*. The set of objects that *farmers* denotes is called the *restriction* of the quantifier; alternatively, the quantifier is said to *range over* the set of objects or individuals denoted by the noun *farmer*. It is a universal property of quantificational determiners that their restriction is defined by the noun they combine with syntactically.[2] This is a principle of Universal Grammar (UG). In evaluating (1) we look at the set of farmers in a given situation and ask, for every farmer, if he or she is a farmer who is riding a donkey. We disregard the set of donkeys, precisely because *donkey* does not combine syntactically with *every* and thus does not define its restriction; equivalently, *every* ranges over the set of farmers, but not over the set of donkeys.

In addition to quantificational determiners, English has adverbs of quantification like *always*. Adverbs of quantification behave in a related though different manner. They can be thought of as relations between events (or situations).

(5) John always drinks juice.

In (5) the relation holds between a set of contextually relevant events (pragmatically defined and thus subject to variation according to the situation; in the case at hand it might be the set of events in which John drinks something) and the set of events in which John drinks juice. (5) conveys the idea that the set of contextually relevant events is a subset of the set of events in which John drinks juice (see Stump 1985; Rooth 1985).

9.2.1 The Structure of Quantified NPs and the Syntax-Semantics Mapping in Child Language

As noted earlier, there are different forms of quantification, each with a different semantics. At the semantic level quantificational determiners map onto relations between sets of individuals. Adverbs of quantification like *always* map onto relations between events (or situations).

Upon encountering a quantificational expression, children must decide its semantics: is it a relation between sets of individuals or between sets of events? We might conjecture that children are guided in this task by the syntactic structure in which the quantified expression occurs. Quantificational determiners form a constituent with the noun they accompany; adverbs of quantification do not. Accordingly, children will take a quantifier + N constituent as a hint that the quantifier in question is a quantificational determiner and map it onto a relation between sets of individuals. Once they have done this, they automatically know that the restriction of the quantificational determiner is the noun it joins with in the syntax.

Is there evidence that children can restrict quantifiers to the noun they introduce? In asking this question, we are asking whether children can single out quantificational determiners and thus obey a principle of UG about how quantifiers function syntactically and semantically. This issue has been addressed by Brooks and Braine (1996) using quantified sentences containing the universal quantifier *all*. Using a picture selection task, these authors presented 4- to 10-year-old English learners with two kinds of picture displaying different numbers of characters and items involved

Figure 9.2
Picture with extra objects used in combination with test sentences (6a,b) (*All of the men are carrying a box; There is a man carrying all the boxes*). Modeled after Brooks and Braine 1996, fig. 1c.

in an action. For example, one displayed three characters, each carrying a box, and two boxes not being carried; the other displayed one character carrying three boxes and two characters carrying nothing, as seen in figures 9.2 and 9.3, respectively. Children were asked to choose the picture that matched a sentence that they heard, either (6a) or (6b).[3]

(6) a. All of the men are carrying a box.
    b. There is a man carrying all the boxes.

Even the younger children were able to match the sentence in (6a) with figure 9.2 and the sentence in (6b) with figure 9.3. The percentage of correct answers to both sentences was about 83% at age 4 and 90% or more at age 5.

Figure 9.3
Picture with extra agents used in combination with test sentences (6a,b) (*All of the men are carrying a box*; *There is a man carrying all the boxes*). Modeled after Brooks and Braine 1996, fig. 1b.

This finding was replicated by Crain et al. (1996), who used a different method (the truth value judgment task) and tested children learning different languages (English learners: age range 3;5–5;10; American Sign Language (ASL) learners: age range 4;3–8;0). They presented the children with stories acted out with toys and props. At the end of each story a puppet described what had happened in the story. The children's task was to say whether the sentence was true or false in the situation described by the story. In one story two children and a mother went skiing. They wanted to drink something and found five cups of hot apple cider and five bottles of soda. The mother drank a cup of cider, but the children wanted to drink the soda. However, the mother urged them to drink a cup of cider because it would warm them up. In the end the two children also decided to drink cider. The puppet described the story by using the sentence in (7).

(7) Every skier drank a cup of hot apple cider.

The English test sentences included the universal quantifier *every*, while at least some of the ASL test sentences included the universal quantifier *all*. Crain et al. found that English and ASL learners judged sentences like (7) true in the experimental context 88% and 89% of the time, respectively.

The results from Crain et al.'s (1996) and Brooks and Braine's (1996) experiments indicate that children know the syntax and the semantics of quantificational determiners. In particular, these findings suggest that children classify *every* and *all* as quantificational determiners and abide by the principle of UG according to which quantifiers range over the set of individuals denoted by the name they join with in the syntax. If they did not, they would have difficulty choosing the matching pictures in Brooks and Braine's experiments. Suppose they interpreted (6a) as meaning that for all men x and for all boxes y, x is carrying y; that is, suppose they took *all* to range over the set of men *and* the set of boxes. Then they could pair (6a) neither with the picture in figure 9.2 nor with the picture in figure 9.3. In both cases the sentence would be false, because there are extra men in one picture and extra boxes in the other. But this did not happen in the experiment (see section 9.3.1).

9.2.2 Do Children Have Access to Quantifier Raising?

In the LF representation of a quantified sentence the quantified constituents have been moved to a left-peripheral position by the operation of QR. Thus, the adult representation of a quantified sentence is as in (2). Do children also represent quantified sentences in this way; that is, do they apply QR to these sentences? To date this question has not been answered definitively. The most convincing evidence in favor of the view that children have access to QR would come from quantified sentences whose interpretation cannot be determined on the basis of the surface position of quantifiers. However, such sentences have rarely been used. Let us look at this argument in more detail.

In different experiments children have been tested with sentences like (7), repeated here, in suitable contexts (in this case a context in which for every skier there is a separate cup of hot apple cider that the skier drank).

(7) Every skier drank a cup of hot apple cider.

(8a) is the syntactic representation of (7) to which QR applies to obtain for example the LF representation in (8b), where it has moved and adjoined the two quantified expressions to IP.

(8) a.

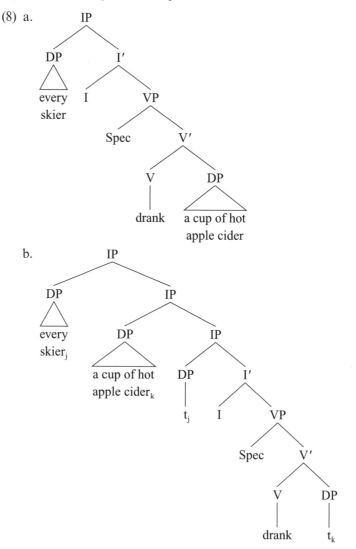

In the LF representation in (8b) the universal quantifier (*every*) has wider scope than the existential indefinite quantifier (*a*). This representation corresponds to one of the readings of sentence (7), the **universal wide scope reading**, which can be paraphrased as in (9).

(9) for every x such that x is a skier, there is a y, such that y is a cup of hot apple cider, and x drank y

However, notice that in the syntactic representation (8a), the universal quantifier in subject position already has wider scope than the existential one, even without the application of QR—specifically, it has scope over the whole sentence, including the existential quantifier, which is lower in the representation. This means that when testing children's interpretation of sentences like (7), we cannot be sure that children have applied QR. It is perfectly possible that they have relied on the representation in (8a) that corresponds to the linear order of quantifiers in (7).

Sentences with universal quantifiers can also have a reading in which the existential quantifier has wider scope than the universal one, the **existential wide scope reading**. Consider (10).

(10) Every dwarf ate a pizza.

On the existential wide scope reading (10) can be paraphrased as in (11).

(11) there is a y such that y is a pizza, for every x such that x is a dwarf and x ate y

In the adult grammar sentence (10) has the syntactic representation in (12a). The existential wide scope reading is obtained from the LF representation in (12b), in which the existential indefinite quantified expression *a pizza* has wider scope than the universal quantified expression *every dwarf*.

(12) a.

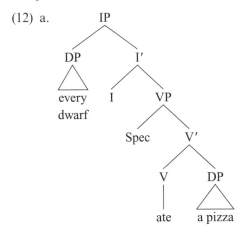

b.

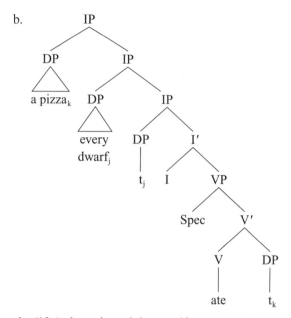

Since in (12a) the existential quantifier cannot have scope over the universal one because it is lower in the syntactic representation, the only way for it to get wide scope is to undergo raising by QR, as in (12b). Therefore, by testing sentences like (10) in a context appropriate for the existential wide scope reading—here, a context in which there is a single pizza that all the dwarfs ate—it would be possible to ascertain whether or not children apply QR to quantified sentences. Crain et al. (1996) carried out this test. They found that English learners accept the existential wide scope reading of sentences like (12) 92% of the time and ASL learners 88% of the time. Unfortunately, we cannot be sure that the learners obtained this interpretation by computing the LF representation in (12b). Let us see why. Every time (10) is true on the existential wide scope reading in (11), it is also true on the universal wide scope reading. In a situation in which there is a single pizza that all the dwarfs ate, it is also true that for every dwarf there is a pizza that the dwarfs ate; the point is that the pizza is the same one for all the dwarfs, not a different one. In other words, the existential wide scope reading in (11) entails the universal wide scope reading, because the situations that make (10) true on the existential wide scope reading in (11) are a subset of the situations that make (10) true on the universal wide scope reading. This is illustrated in figure 9.4. The moral is that children do not need to apply QR to obtain

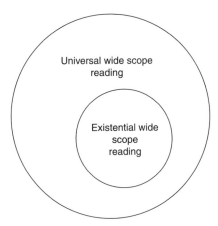

Figure 9.4
The situations that make sentence (10) (*Every dwarf ate a pizza*) true on the existential wide scope reading are a subset of the situations that make the same sentence true on the universal wide scope reading.

the existential wide scope reading in (10). This reading entails the universal wide scope reading that, as we have seen, can be obtained by relying on a syntactic representation that reflects the linear order of quantifiers, that is, on (12a). Because of the entailment relation, the existential wide scope reading can also be obtained from (12a). Therefore, on the basis of the findings discussed so far, we do not know whether children apply QR to quantified sentences. It is logically possible that they rely on linear order to obtain the relevant interpretation of the sentences tested.

Unequivocal evidence that children have access to QR would come from testing their interpretation of sentences like (13).

(13) A vase of flowers was displayed in front of every house.

The most natural interpretation of (13) is one in which a distinct vase of flowers was displayed in front of every house. This interpretation, which is paraphrased in (14), requires the universal quantifier *every* to have wider scope than the existential indefinite quantifier *a*.

(14) for every *x* such that *x* is a house, there is a *y*, such that *y* is a vase of flowers, and *y* was displayed in front of *x*

In the syntactic representation of (13), given in (15a), the universal quantifier does not have scope over the existential indefinite quantifier (or does not c-command it), because it is too deeply embedded. To have wider scope than the existential quantifier, the universal quantifier must move by QR to a left-peripheral position, where it c-commands the existential quantifier as in (15b).

(15) a.

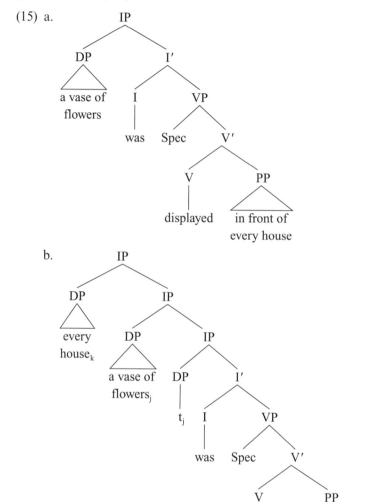

In other words, to compute the relevant reading of (13) given in (14), children cannot rely on the linear order of quantifiers, because in this case the existential quantifier has wider scope than the universal quantifier. If any, the linear order can give rise to the wide scope reading of the existential quantifier, paraphrased in (16).

(16) there is an x such that x is a vase of flowers, for all y such that y is a house, and x was displayed in front of y

But the set of situations that make (13) true on the wide scope reading of the universal quantifier is a superset of the situations that make (13) true on the wide scope reading of the existential quantifier. In other words, there are situations in which (13) is true on the wide scope reading of the universal quantifier, but false on the wide scope reading of the existential quantifier. If children have access exclusively to the linear order or to the representation in (15a) and cannot apply QR, there is no way for them to obtain the wide scope reading of the universal quantifier paraphrased in (14).

Sentences similar to (13) were used in an experiment carried out by Brooks and Braine (1996), which was not designed specifically to test the availability of QR, but to see if children attend to the position quantifiers occupy in a sentence and to lexical properties of different universal quantifiers (*all, each*). In this experiment 4- to 9-year-old children were asked to say if a sentence they heard could be matched with either of two pictures. For example, one picture displayed three boys building a boat together and another displayed three boys each building his own boat. The critical sentence was (17a); the relevant reading (the universal wide scope reading) that cannot be obtained by relying on the linear order is paraphrased in (17b).

(17) a. A boat is being built by each boy.
    b. for each x such that x is a boy, there is a y such that y is a boat, and y is being built by x

To choose the picture in which each boy is building his own boat, children have to compute the interpretation paraphrased in (17b), in which the universal quantifier *each* has wider scope than the existential quantifier *a*. Since in (17a) the universal quantifier does not have scope over the existential one, it can obtain wide scope only by being moved (through QR). Brooks and Braine found that a fair number of children preferred the universal wide scope reading of (17a), although there were differences among age groups (80% of the 4-year-olds accepted this reading, 45% of the 5-year-olds, 70% of the 6-year-olds, 73% of the 7- and 8-year-olds, and 93% of the 9-year-olds). Although more evidence is certainly necessary, this result suggests that children have access to QR (or to whatever achieves its effects).

9.2.3   Intermediate Summary

Children know the following facts about quantification:

(18) a. They distinguish referential and quantified NPs.
   b. There is suggestive evidence that they have the adult representational system for handling quantified sentences, one that includes QR or something equivalent.
   c. They can single out quantificational determiners, they know the mapping from syntax to semantics (quantifiers express relations between sets), and they know that the domain of the quantifier is contextually restricted.

The next paragraphs summarize the evidence for these claims.

We have seen (section 8.4.4) that children treat quantifiers differently from referential NPs. They interpret sentences like (19) in a nonadult way (here, as meaning that Alice washes herself).

(19) Alice washes her.

By contrast, when the referential NP is replaced by a quantified NP, as in (20), the rate of nonadult responses sharply decreases. For children, as for adults, (20) can only mean that for every x such that x is a girl, x washes some other female individual y.

(20) Every girl washes her.

Since the only difference between (19) and (20) is the type of NP, referential versus quantificational, we can interpret the different responses that children give to these sentences as an indication that they distinguish between referential and quantified NPs.

We have assumed that in order to be properly interpreted, quantifiers must undergo QR; that is, they must be adjoined to some suitable site that defines their c-command domain. In general, experiments that have tested children's interpretation of universally quantified sentences do not provide unambiguous evidence that children employ QR, because the relevant interpretations could very well be derived from a representation in which QR has not been applied. The kind of sentence that can reveal whether children make use of QR is like (13), repeated here.

(13) A vase of flowers was displayed in front of every house.

Experimental results indicate that children can assign sentences like (13) an interpretation that can only be available to them if they can apply QR to move the universal quantifier and assign it wide scope over the sentence. This is preliminary evidence that children have access to an LF representation in which quantifiers are moved.

Children can single out quantificational determiners, and they know that the restriction of a quantifier is the noun it combines with in the syntax. They also know that the domain of quantifiers is pragmatically restricted. For example, they judge that sentence (7) (*Every skier drank a cup of hot apple cider*) is true in a situation in which each skier drank a cup of hot apple cider. To give this response, children must have understood that the skiers in question were those mentioned in the story and not all the skiers in the world. If they did not understand that the domain of *every* is pragmatically restricted to the situation posed in the experiment, they would be expected to sometimes judge sentence (7) false and motivate their judgment by indicating that there might be skiers in the world who did not drink a cup of hot apple cider. But this never happened.

9.3 CHILDREN'S ERRORS WITH UNIVERSAL QUANTIFICATION

Although the conclusions reached here so far are fairly well grounded, other studies have obtained quite different results and have therefore reached quite different conclusions. It is important to examine these results.

Children's understanding of universal quantification was originally investigated by Inhelder and Piaget (1964) as a means of assessing the development of logical reasoning. Children were tested in a series of tasks for their comprehension of, for example, *all*. They were presented with four black squares, three white circles, and two black circles, as illustrated in figure 9.5, and then were asked the question in (21).

(21) Are all the squares black?

Children were unable to respond to this question correctly ("yes") until age 7 or 8. They often answered "no" and justified their response by pointing to the black circles. This response may suggest that children were interpreting the question in (21) as meaning 'Are all squares black and are all black things squares?' Their error has been taken to indicate that children are not able to form the two relevant classes of objects, "the squares" and "the black things," and to compare them, an ability that

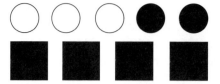

Figure 9.5
Kind of stimuli used in combination with sentence (21) (*Are all the squares black?*) to assess children's comprehension of universal quantifiers (Inhelder and Piaget 1964)

underlies the evaluation of sentences with universal quantifiers (see Bucci 1978; see also Braine and Rumain 1983 for reviews). For example, Bucci (1978) claimed that children cannot restrict the quantifier to its domain, fixed by the nominal expression *the squares*, and that they allow it to spread its domain over other parts of the sentence (see section 9.2.1). Since Inhelder and Piaget's study, this phenomenon has been observed by several researchers working on the development of reasoning (see Donaldson and McGarrigle 1973; Freeman 1985) and by linguists and psycholinguists (see, e.g., Philip 1995).

Let us survey the basic findings in more detail, examining some of Philip's (1995) experiments by way of example. In these experiments children were required to decide whether a sentence was a true or false description of a picture. In one condition, the *extra object condition*, children were shown a picture like the one in figure 9.6, displaying three farmers each riding a donkey and an "extra" donkey that is not being ridden by anyone. They were then asked the following question:

(22) Is every farmer riding a donkey?

Some 3- to 5-year-old children answer "no" to this question when shown figure 9.6; they point to the extra donkey as the reason for their rejection. In another condition, the *extra agent condition*, children were shown a picture like the one in figure 9.7, which differs from the one in figure 9.6 in that it has an "extra" farmer, but no "extra" donkey. They were then asked the following question:

(23) Is a farmer riding every donkey?

When asked this question, some children respond "no," explaining that there is a farmer not riding a donkey.

Figure 9.6
Extra object condition

Notice that in (23) the linear order of the universal quantifier *every* and the existential indefinite quantifier *a* is the reverse of the order in (22). Yet children do not seem sensitive to this difference. One claim that has been made is that children seem to disregard the relative position of quantifiers and interpret (22) and (23) to mean that every farmer is riding a donkey and every donkey is ridden by a farmer. The negative responses to (22) and (23) are called **symmetrical responses** because children's rejection seems to be motivated by lack of symmetry between farmers and donkeys in the picture. We should bear in mind that children who give symmetrical responses also give adultlike responses; they answer "yes" to the questions in (22) and (23) when they are shown the pictures in figures 9.6 and 9.7, respectively.

The evidence collected by Philip and other authors contrasts with the evidence collected in the studies discussed in section 9.2—a discrepancy that needs to be explained. One approach that has been developed is that children make mistakes because their linguistic knowledge is nonadult (see Philip 1995). We will consider this approach in the next section.

Figure 9.7
Extra agent condition

9.3.1   A Linguistic Account of Children's Errors: The Symmetrical Account

Why do children say that sentences like (1), repeated here, are false in a scenario that includes three donkey-farmer pairs and a donkey with no rider?

(1) Every farmer is riding a donkey.

Philip (1995) suggests that the right account—the so-called **symmetrical account**—should have (roughly) two components.

(24) *Component 1* (slightly simplified)
      Children take *every* in (1) to be not a quantificational determiner,
      but an adverb of quantification.

In other words, Philip claims that children treat sentences like (1) as though they contain a quantifier like *always*; namely, they treat (1) much like adults treat (25). In doing this, children seem to classify *every* not as a quantificational determiner, but as an adverb of quantification, much like *always*.

(25) John always drinks orange juice.

There is independent evidence from sentences like (25) that adult English speakers allow the context to determine what those objects are that *always* ranges over, that is, what forms the restriction of the quantifier *always*. Moreover, it has been proposed that *always* quantifies over events (see Stump 1985; but for a different approach, see Lewis 1975; Kamp 1981; Heim 1982). Sentence (25) may express the idea that any event in which John drinks something (the events that are contextually relevant) is an event in which John drinks orange juice. Here the restriction might be the events in which John drinks something. The second component of Philip's proposal amounts to this:

(26) *Component 2*
On being presented with a given scenario, children draw a certain conclusion about what the events are that the scenario or the context makes relevant. In particular, they conclude that the scenario in figure 9.6 makes the following events relevant: an event of farmer A riding donkey 1; an event of farmer B riding donkey 2; an event of farmer C riding donkey 3; an event of donkey 4 standing alone.

The relevant events form the restriction of the quantifier *every*. In other words, according to Philip, *every* functions like *always* for children; it is an adverb of quantification that ranges over events (rather than individuals). The events over which it ranges are defined by the context, and for children these events are events in which there is a farmer *or* a donkey (or both). Children judge the sentence in (1) false, because they interpret it as meaning that for any event that has a farmer or a donkey (or both) in it, it must be an event of a farmer riding a donkey, and figure 9.6 has an event that has a donkey in it, but is not an event of a farmer riding a donkey.

If this account is correct, how can we explain children's correct responses in the experiment by Brooks and Braine (1996) and Crain et al. (1996)? Philip is aware that children do not always provide symmetrical responses, because even in his own experiments children give adultlike answers in several cases. He states that children simply prefer the symmetrical interpretation, but they also have access to the adult interpretation. As support for this, he points out that when the interpretation in terms of events is not available for a sentence, children resort to the adult interpretation, in which *every* ranges over individuals. One such case is the question in (27) including a noun incorporation predicate.

(27) Is every farmer a donkey-rider?

When asked question (27) about figure 9.6, the children tested by Philip answered correctly—"yes"—in the vast majority of cases. This means that children do not interpret (27) as meaning that for any event that has a farmer or a donkey (or both) this must be an event of a farmer being a donkey-rider. Philip argues that noun incorporation predicates like the one in (27) describe more or less permanent properties of individuals and therefore cannot make reference to an event (see Kratzer 1995). Children have this knowledge and resort to the adult interpretation, which does not make reference to events, but to individuals. This proposal amounts to saying that children treat *every* both as an adverb of quantification and as a quantificational determiner; that is, for children *every* is ambiguous.

9.3.1.1 Conceptual and Empirical Problems with the Symmetrical Account The symmetrical account faces both conceptual and empirical problems (and, as we will see in section 9.3.1.2, a learnability problem as well). While it might be plausible to conjecture that children misclassify *every* and treat it as an adverb of quantification, like *always*, it is ad hoc to assign quantifiers like *every* the kind of semantics that Philip proposes. As noted earlier, Philip suggests that the relevant events that constitute the restriction of *every* have either a farmer *or* a donkey in them; that is, the restriction is defined in terms of disjunctive events, an assumption that is crucial for the symmetrical account. This is not how the restriction of adverbs of quantification is set in the adult grammar. If children really took *every* as an adverb of quantification, they should also map it onto the semantics that is assigned to these expressions in the adult language according to the standard semantic theory. In this case the relevant events that would form the restriction of the quantifier could be defined as the events in which there is a farmer riding something, or there is a farmer *and* a donkey, or there is someone riding a donkey, depending on con- textual considerations. Accordingly, the sentence could mean that any event that has a farmer riding something is an event of a farmer riding a donkey; or that any event that has a farmer *and* a donkey is an event of a farmer riding a donkey; or that any event that has someone riding a donkey is an event of a farmer riding a donkey. In all three cases sentence (1) would be true in a situation in which there is a donkey with no rider, and children would be expected to answer "yes" when they hear this sen- tence and see figure 9.6, contrary to what Philip found. Under Philip's approach children are not simply misclassifying *every*—they are also mapping it onto a semantics that does not characterize adverbs of quantification in the adult language. Therefore, it is not obvious how either component of the symmetrical account in (24) and (26) is to be derived from deeper principles. Certainly the source of children's misclassification cannot be UG, because the semantics that children supposedly assign is not part of UG.

The symmetrical account is probably also not sufficient to explain the results of the classical experiments by Inhelder and Piaget, even though it was motivated precisely by those results. Consider sentence (21), repeated here.

(21) Are all the squares black?

An interpretation in terms of events should be incompatible with the presence of the property "black" in (21) for the same reasons it was incompatible with the presence of the property "donkey-rider" in (27). However, recall that children incorrectly answer "no" to (21), because the situation they are presented with includes black circles (see figure 9.5). It is not clear how the symmetrical account can distinguish between (21) and (27).

Crain et al. (1996) point out that children preferring the symmetrical interpretation should not be able to produce sentences including a universal quantifier to describe "extra object" situations like the one portrayed in figure 9.6, at least on some occasions. Children reject sentence (1) as an appropriate description of this picture. Similarly, they should refrain from producing something like (1) to describe pictures like the one in figure 9.6. Crain et al. elicited sentences in contexts with extra objects and found that children successfully produce statements including *all* or *every*. Some examples are given in (28).

(28) a. Every girl ate a cherry.
     b. All the girls got a cherry.
     c. Everyone did.

If the symmetrical interpretation is part of children's competence, we would expect them to describe pictures with extra objects in other ways than (28), but this did not happen.

9.3.1.2 A Learnability Problem for the Symmetrical Account In addition to conceptual and empirical problems, the symmetrical account faces

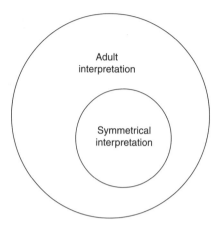

Figure 9.8
The symmetrical interpretation of *Every farmer is riding a donkey* is true in a subset of the situations in which the adult interpretation of the same sentence is true.

a learnability problem. A prominent feature of this account is that quantified sentences are ambiguous for children in a way that they are not for adults. For children, sentence (1), repeated here, has the two meanings in (29).

(1) Every farmer is riding a donkey.

(29) a. *Adult reading (universal wide scope reading)*
              for every *x*, such that *x* is a farmer, there is a *y*, such that *y* is a donkey, and *x* is riding *y*
       b. *Symmetrical (nonadult) reading*
              all events that have a farmer or a donkey (or both) are events of a farmer riding a donkey

The truth conditions of the symmetrical interpretation are more stringent than the truth conditions of the adult interpretation; that is, every time a sentence is true on the symmetrical interpretation, it is also true on the adult interpretation, but not vice versa. This can be represented as shown in figure 9.8.

The learnability problem arises because the symmetrical account claims that sentences like (1) are ambiguous for children. On this account children's grammars must undergo a drastic restructuring over the years, eliminating the symmetrical representation. However, it is hard to see how this could happen, since the input is always consistent with one of the child's interpretations. When (1) is used in a context in which there is symmetry between farmers and donkeys, the child concludes that both the meaning in (29a) and the one in (29b) can be associated with the sentence. When there is an extra donkey, they conclude that only the meaning in (29a) can be associated with (1). Therefore, even though children would keep track of the meaning associated with (1) in various situations and notice that adults often use (1) when there is no symmetry, they could not conclude that (1) cannot have the symmetrical meaning. As a matter of fact, the adult reading in (29a) is compatible with a situation in which there is symmetry between farmers and donkeys, as figure 9.8 shows. Therefore, adults sometimes might happen to use (1) in such situations.

In sum, Philip's (1995) symmetrical account holds that children's errors lie in faulty linguistic knowledge: children have a preference for an interpretation in terms of events, as in (29b), but they can also access the adult interpretation. This proposal raises conceptual, empirical, and learnability problems. Moreover, although Philip is not the only investigator to have found symmetrical responses, it is worth noting that this kind of response disappears when children are tested with other experimental tasks, as in Brooks and Braine's (1996) and Crain et al.'s (1996) studies, although in these experiments extra objects and extra agents were also present. This fact suggests, on the one hand, that children must have the relevant knowledge to handle universal quantifiers, and on the other hand, that the experimental methodology might be responsible for children's different performance across tasks.

9.3.2 A Nonlinguistic Account of Children's Errors

Crain et al. (1996) claim that children make errors with quantificational determiners not because their linguistic knowledge is defective, but because the experiments are flawed. They claim that children gave nonadult responses in Philip's (1995) experiments (and in similar ones) because the experimental situations were pragmatically inappropriate for the sentences being tested. Children think that the "extra element" present in Philip's pictures (either a farmer or a donkey) should matter. They show that they take the extra element to be relevant by responding negatively to questions like (22) or (23) when presented with pictures like those in figure 9.6 or 9.7, respectively. In Crain et al.'s view, this happens because children, who have the proper grammar to deal with quantified sentences, adopt pragmatic strategies that aim at accommodating the "infelicitous" experimental situations (see Crain and Thornton 1998 for extensive discussion of this issue). (Here and throughout *infelicitous* is used in a nontechnical sense.)

Such a view is not unique to language acquisition. Dehaene (1997) has adopted a very similar perspective to explain abnormal responses in the domain of children's numerical competence, which (contrary to Piaget's claims) is quite developed even at 5 months. Although this detour takes us away from the main topic, it is worth taking, because it shows that wrong conclusions can be reached from inadequate premises.

Dehaene reports experiments conducted by Mehler and Bever (1967) testing **number conservation** in children: the ability to see for example that when the same elements are arranged differently, the number of elements remains the same. Their first experiment was a replication of an experiment devised by Piaget. Consider figure 9.9. When 2- to 4-year-old children are shown two rows of four marbles arranged in one-to-one correspondence as in figure 9.9a and are asked the question in (30), they answer that the two rows are the same.

(30) Are these the same, or does one row have more marbles?

Thereafter the experimenter increases the space between marbles in one row, making it longer than the other as in figure 9.9b, and asks (30) again. Now children assert that the longer line has more marbles than the shorter one. This is Piaget's classical nonconservation error: children seem to be unable to conserve number under different arrangements of elements. On the basis of this result, Piaget concluded that children have poor numerical competence.

In a second experiment Mehler and Bever introduced a clever modification: they replaced marbles with candies, arranged in rows so that the longer row had fewer candies than the shorter one. This time children did not hesitate to choose the row with more candies even though the length of the row conflicted with the number, that is, when the shorter row had more candies. This result is in apparent conflict with the results obtained in the classical Piagetian experiment. It provides evidence that children's numerical competence is not poor at all.

But why did children respond differently in the two experiments? Dehaene (1997) explains children's failure in the classical Piagetian number conservation task by suggesting that children interpret the question in (30) quite differently than adults do. This question was posed twice to the children, once in the situation depicted in figure 9.9a and again in

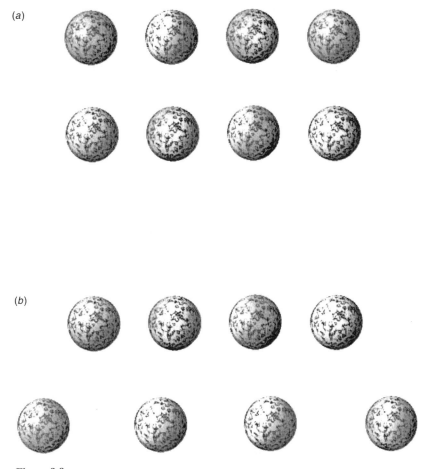

Figure 9.9
Stimuli used in number conservation tasks. In (*a*) the items in the two rows are in one-to-one correspondence. In (*b*) the bottom row has been transformed by lengthening it.

the situation depicted in figure 9.9b. "They [children] must find it quite strange that a grown-up would repeat the same trivial question twice. Indeed, it constitutes a violation of ordinary rules of conversation to ask a question whose answer is already known by both speakers. Faced with this internal conflict, perhaps children figure out that the second question, although it is superficially identical to the first, does not have the same meaning" (Dehaene 1997, 46). Perhaps they conclude that the question is not about the number of marbles but about the length of the lines and thus are biased to answer in a nonadult way.

Interestingly enough, Crain et al.'s (1996) line of explanation for children's symmetrical responses to sentences including universal quantifiers is quite similar to Dehaene's view, although it was developed independently. Crain et al. point out that in the experimental situations evoking symmetrical responses, the condition of **plausible assent** (a corollary of the condition of **plausible dissent**), a principle of pragmatic relevance, was not satisfied. What does this condition amount to? As is well known, language use is governed by **truth conditions** (semantics) and by **felicity conditions** (pragmatics) (see Grice 1989). For example, it is felicitous to use the sentence *Paul or Mary will bring a bottle of wine* only if we do not know which one is going to bring wine. If we know for certain that Mary will, the use of the sentence is not felicitous (even though, given the truth table for *or*, the sentence would be true). When felicity conditions for the use of sentences are not met, experimental subjects tend to give "erroneous" responses. If children are asked to assess whether a statement is true or false, it should be clear to them *why* it is true or false; that is, it should be clear to them when they have to dissent or assent. These are the conditions of plausible dissent (when the expected or adult answer is "no") and plausible assent (when the expected or adult answer is "yes"). To see this more clearly, consider the story about the skiers used in Crain et al.'s experiment discussed in section 9.2.2. In this story the condition of plausible assent is satisfied in the following way. In the first part of the story the mother drinks a cup of hot apple cider, while the two children consider drinking soda, but do not. This provides a *possible outcome* for the story. On this outcome sentence (7), repeated here, is false.

(7) Every skier drank a cup of hot apple cider.

In the second part of the story the mother convinces the two children to drink a cup of hot apple cider. So at the end of the story, the mother and the two children all have drunk hot apple cider. This is the *actual out-*

come. On this outcome sentence (7) is true. By creating both a possible and an actual outcome for the story, the experimenters made clear to children when sentence (7) can be true or false. Recall that at the end of the story there were two cups of hot apple cider left over; but the presence of extra objects apparently did not distract children, since they correctly answered "yes" in the vast majority of cases.

Let us return to Philip's (1995) experiment and to the reason why children occasionally gave symmetrical responses. Crain et al. (1996) claim that in Philip's experiment the condition of plausible assent was not satisfied; that is, it was not clear to children under what circumstances statement (1), repeated here, is true or false under the adult interpretation.

(1) Every farmer is riding a donkey.

Yes/no questions ask which of two statements hold in a given circumstance. Thus, it is natural to ask a yes/no question when two propositions are (possible/actual) outcomes of a trial. For example, question (22), repeated here, can be answered with either (31a) or (31b).

(22) Is every farmer riding a donkey?

(31) a. Yes, every farmer is riding a donkey.
     b. No, not every farmer is riding a donkey.

Thus, it is natural to ask question (22), a yes/no question, when the propositions expressed by (31a) and (31b) are (possible/actual) outcomes of the trial. In felicitous circumstances, then, one possible outcome would involve every farmer riding a donkey, and another would involve some farmer riding a donkey and at least one other farmer riding a different animal. This possibility was not considered in the experimental situations devised by Philip, since the pictures depicted only one outcome (the one expressed by (31a)). In other words, in this experiment children were asked yes/no questions in contexts that were not pragmatically appropriate, because only the "yes" answer was associated with the adult interpretation; the "no" answer was not. To put it yet another way, it was not made clear to children why question (22), posed with respect to figure 9.6, could be false. Even though these features conspired to make the situation infelicitous for asking a yes/no question, the child was faced with just such a question. The child thus had to infer a context in which a yes/no question would be felicitous, that is, in which the two outcomes could plausibly be under consideration. One way for children to recover from the pragmatic infelicity was to conjecture that the meaning of (22) is not about the choices in (31), but about something else. The child might infer that the question was about the symmetry between farmers and donkeys. In this way, the possible answers to question (22) are these:

(32) a. Yes, there is symmetry.
     b. No, there is no symmetry.

On this view children answer "no" to question (22) because they think the experimenter is asking them to compare two groups of things. That is, for children the yes/no question is more felicitous when interpreted in this fashion than in the adult fashion. Thus, the source of children's occasional errors is their attempt to accommodate pragmatic infelicity by resorting to an alternative interpretation of the question that makes sense given the circumstances. Essentially, children make errors because they misunderstand the experimenter's intention. They cannot make sense of the question in (22) under the readings in (31), because of its infelicity.[4]

In this connection it is worth going back to children's numerical competence. Dehaene (1997) discusses an experiment carried out by McGarrigle and Donaldson (1974) aimed at assessing children's misunderstanding of the experimenter's intentions during a number conservation task. In half of the trials they repeated the classical Piagetian experiment with the two rows of items, as in figure 9.9, and asked question (30) twice. In the other half of the trials the experimenter first asked question (30) about the arrangement in figure 9.9a. The transformation from that arrangement to the one in figure 9.9b was performed by a teddy bear, while the experimenter was looking elsewhere. Then the experimenter turned to the experimental workspace, looked with surprise at what had happened, and again asked question (30). The rationale for this procedure was that this time the experimenter did not know which row had more marbles because the teddy bear had mixed everything up; it was therefore sensible to pose the same question twice. Interestingly, when the experimenter manipulated the marbles (the classical Piagetian method), children said that the longer row had more marbles; but when the teddy bear manipulated them, the same children were not hesitant about saying that the two rows had the same number of marbles. This result proves that when the context is suitable for a given question, children can answer correctly. But this is exactly Crain et al.'s point concerning Philip's experiments. In these experiments the yes/no question was not appropriate, likely because only one possible outcome was provided. Children in Brooks and Braine's experiment did not give symmetrical responses because they were not asked yes/no questions, but were invited to choose which of two pictures matched the sentence that they heard.

One may wonder why, when presented with pictures like the one in figure 9.6, children give symmetrical responses while adults tend not to. One reason given by Crain et al. is that in normal circumstances older children and adults are more skilled in accommodating pragmatic infelicities. However, it is worth noticing that even adults may perform poorly in pragmatically infelicitous conditions. Guasti and Chierchia (1999/ 2000) have shown that adults perform significantly worse when the test sentences are presented in pragmatically infelicitous contexts than when they are presented in pragmatically felicitous contexts (that satisfy the condition of plausible dissent).

In the context of number conservation Dehaene (1997) reports that children fail in the classical Piagetian task because of the immaturity of the prefrontal cortex, "a region of the brain that enables us to select a strategy and to hold firm to it despite distraction" (Dehaene 1997, 47). In other words, Piagetian experiments can be interpreted as gauging children's ability to resist distraction. Something of this kind may be responsible for children's symmetrical responses in language experiments, a possibility worth investigating (see Gordon 1996). Be that as it may, the fact that in certain experimental conditions children perform like adults when dealing with universally quantified sentences indicates that they know how these sentences have to be interpreted; they have an adult competence. The fact that in other conditions children give symmetrical responses is interesting; but these trials are likely to assess some aspect of children's cognitive development other than their competence with universally quantified sentences.

9.4 SUMMARY AND CONCLUDING REMARKS

The available evidence shows that children can handle quantified sentences from about 4 years (or a bit earlier). They know that quantified NPs are different from referential NPs and that quantified NPs are interpreted in certain ways; and there is preliminary evidence that they have access to QR. Nevertheless, some investigators have found that children make errors in interpreting universally quantified sentences. This has motivated accounts according to which children's linguistic knowledge is defective. According to one of these, Philip's (1995) symmetrical account, children make errors in interpreting universally quantified sentences because they may assign these sentences a different interpretation than adults do, although they have access to the adult interpretation as well. This approach does not account for all errors children make, encounters conceptual and learnability problems, and runs up against the fact that in certain experimental tasks children do not make mistakes. Why should linguistic competence vary as a function of experimental setting? Is some other competence being affected by the experimental settings and occasionally causing children to fail? Crain et al. (1996) argue that children's errors stem from infelicitous experimental contexts. They point out that it is failure to satisfy pragmatic conditions for the use of sentences that is responsible for children's errors. When the contexts are pragmatically felicitous, children behave like adults, because they share the same syntactic and semantic knowledge.

Summary of Linguistic Development

1. By 4 years children distinguish referential from quantified NPs.
2. By 4 years children know that the restriction of a quantifier is the noun it combines with in the syntax.
3. There is suggestive evidence that children know the mechanism of Quantifier Raising by 4–5 years.

Further Reading

Regarding children's distributive interpretation of plural NPs, see Avrutin and Thornton 1994. Musolino, Crain, and Thornton 2000 discusses the interaction between negation and quantifiers. Experiments on children's interpretation of epistemic modals are reported in Noveck 1996, and experiments on quantification in Chinese in Lee 1991 and Chien 1994. Noveck 2001 and Chierchia et al. 2001 discuss experiments aimed at verifying children's knowledge of some aspects of pragmatics.

Key Words

Adverbs of quantification
Existential wide scope reading
Felicity conditions
Number conservation
Plausible assent/dissent
Quantificational determiners
Symmetrical account

Symmetrical responses
Truth conditions
Universal wide scope reading

Study Questions

1. How have researchers shown that children distinguish between referential and quantified expressions?

2. Discuss the arguments in favor of the view that children's grammar includes Quantifier Raising.

3. Discuss the problems facing the symmetrical account.

4. Discuss Crain et al.'s (1996) explanation of children's symmetrical responses.

5. Design an experiment, to be carried out with adults and children, in which you show them pictures like the ones in figures 9.6 and 9.7 and ask them a question patterned on (22). Compare adults' and children's responses. (This would be a replication of Philip's (1995) experiments.)

6. Design an experiment in which you present children with sentences like (17a) and ask them to choose between two pictures, one displaying three boys building a boat together and the other displaying three boys each building a boat. Comment on the results. (This would be a replication of Brooks and Braine's (1996) experiment discussed in section 9.2.2.)

7. Design an experiment eliciting universally quantified sentences.

Chapter 10
Acquisition of Control

INTRODUCTION

In this chapter we will examine the acquisition of control. *Control theory* is concerned with the principles that determine how the understood subject of a nonfinite clause is interpreted. This is represented as *PRO*, a [+anaphoric, +pronominal] empty category. Simplifying somewhat, PRO is interpreted as anaphorically linked to (or as linguists say, *controlled by*) an argument in the matrix clause, if there is a suitable one. In (1a,c,d,e) PRO is controlled by the subject *Wendy* and in (1b) by the object *Lucy*, as indicated through coindexation. If there is no suitable antecedent, as in (1f), PRO is not controlled by any particular expression and thus can refer to anyone or have arbitrary reference; in this case it is called *arbitrary PRO* or PRO_{arb}.

(1) a. Wendy$_i$ tried PRO$_i$ to get the cake for Lucy.
    b. Ariel told Lucy$_i$ PRO$_i$ to leave early.
    c. Wendy$_i$ promised Lucy PRO$_i$ to leave early.
    d. Wendy$_i$ hit Captain Hook in order PRO$_i$ to run away.
    e. Wendy$_i$ pushes Lucy after PRO$_i$ climbing on the ladder.
    f. PRO to eat fruit is a pleasure.

Since Chomsky's (1969) seminal work, many studies have investigated the acquisition of control under different conditions and using different experimental techniques (elicited-imitation tasks, act-out tasks, truth value judgment tasks). An established result is that children find it hard to interpret PRO and do not attain full competence before school age. However, there is considerable disagreement about the kind of interpretation that children allow and consequently about why children interpret PRO the way they do.

This chapter is organized in four sections. Section 10.1 briefly surveys the theory of control that helps us to state the problem for acquisition. Section 10.2 discusses some errors that children make in interpreting control structures and presents an analysis, the structure-changing hypothesis, according to which children have difficulties in attaching the clause that includes PRO in the structural hierarchy. Section 10.3 presents a second hypothesis about children's errors, couched in maturational terms. According to this view, children do not have access to grammatical objects that are relevant for the adult representation of control structures. Section 10.4 discusses a third hypothesis about children's errors, one that attributes them to a lack of integration between the lexical and syntactic components involved in control.

10.1   ASPECTS OF THE THEORY OF CONTROL

Mastery of control presupposes the availability of different pieces of lexical and structural knowledge (see Haegeman 1994, chap. 5). On the lexical side children must know the argument structure associated with a verb and more specifically which argument is selected for controlling PRO (the **lexical properties of control verbs**). PRO is generally interpreted in relation to a matrix argument, but the specific argument depends on the verb: some verbs, like *try* and *promise*, require PRO to be controlled by the matrix subject (subject control; see (1a,c)); others, like *tell*, require PRO to be controlled by the matrix object (object control; see (1b)). On the syntactic side children must distinguish between finite and nonfinite clauses, something they can do from their earliest multiword productions (see sections 4.2.3, 4.2.4). They must know the structural relation of c-command, as they seem to do by about 3–4 years (see section 8.4). They must also know the properties of pronominal expressions, that is, those expressions that are interpreted by reference to another expression in the linguistic or extralinguistic context: PRO versus (overt) pronouns (reflexive and nonreflexive).

PRO is the subject of nonfinite clauses and is interpreted in relation to another NP in the sentence, called the *controller* of PRO. An NP can control PRO if it c-commands it. Consider sentence (2).

(2) Wendy's brother tried PRO to get a cake for Lucy.

English speakers interpret (2) as meaning that Wendy's brother is the person who both tries and gets; that is, *Wendy's brother* is the subject of both *try* and *get*. We render this interpretation by saying that *Wendy's brother*, which c-commands PRO, also controls it. By contrast, *Wendy* cannot control PRO, because it does not c-command it. When PRO is in a complement clause, it can be controlled by either the matrix subject or the matrix object, as in (1a) and (1b), respectively, because both c-command PRO. When PRO is in an adjunct clause, it is controlled by the matrix subject, as in (1d,e); since the adjunct is attached in the tree in a position higher than object position, PRO is c-commanded by the subject, but not by the object. Finally, in a subject clause like the one in (1f), there is no controller and PRO receives an arbitrary interpretation.

In sum, although the matter is more complex, for our purposes it suffices to keep in mind that the interpretation of PRO depends on whether it occurs in a subject, complement, or adjunct nonfinite clause. These clauses are attached to different sites in the structural representation. This hierarchical arrangement determines how PRO is c-commanded, therefore which argument can control it, and ultimately how it is interpreted.

The various pieces of linguistic knowledge that the child has to master to handle control structures are these:

(3) a. *Lexicon*
    Argument structure and control properties of verbs
   b. *Syntax*
    Structural environments licensing PRO
    Nature of pronominal expressions
    C-command

Failure to master any of this may cause difficulties in interpreting PRO. Children may not know the lexical properties of control verbs or may have difficulties in handling the structural environments including PRO. They may not recognize that different pronominal expressions have different interpretive requirements. Indeed, most studies agree that children do poorly with some control structures and have a hard time figuring out how PRO must be interpreted even up to 5 years of age. However, there is disagreement over what types of errors they make. In some studies like the ones reported in section 10.2, which used the grammaticality judgment task, children aged between 3 and 4 sometimes chose a sentence-internal referent for PRO, and sometimes chose a sentence-external referent for PRO (see McDaniel, Cairns, and Hsu 1991; Cairns et al. 1994; see also Broihier and Wexler 1995). In other studies, which used the act-out task, children never selected a sentence-external referent (see Goodluck 1981; Hsu, Cairns, and Fiengo 1985; Hsu, Eisenberg, and Schlisselberg 1989), but they felt free to choose either the subject or the object as the antecedent of PRO, regardless of the control properties of the matrix verb. In still other studies children frequently chose the object as antecedent of PRO in sentences like (1c,d,e) (see, e.g., Chomsky 1969; Maratsos 1974; Hsu, Cairns, and Fiengo 1985; Hsu, Eisenberg, and Schlisselberg 1989). These data have inspired different analyses of control structures in child grammar, of which we will consider three. One approach claims that children progressively develop different grammars for control charac-terized by different structural analyses of control structures (Cairns et al. 1994). A second approach attributes children's difficulties with control to two factors: first, that PRO is initially unavailable in child grammar; and second, that the empty operators necessary for representing adjunct clauses are lacking (see Broihier and Wexler 1995; see also Wexler 1992). Finally, a third approach holds that acquisition of control is delayed because the lexical and syntactic components have not yet been integrated (Cohen Sherman and Lust 1995).

10.2   THE STRUCTURE-CHANGING HYPOTHESIS

In this section we will review the results of experiments showing that children move through different grammars for control before they achieve adultlike competence. These different grammars arise because children need to acquire knowledge of the lexical properties of verbs and con-junctions and cannot build the relevant syntactic structures in which con-trol principles can apply.

10.2.1   Development of the Interpretation of PRO

McDaniel, Cairns, and Hsu (1991) and Cairns et al. (1994) conducted cross-sectional and longitudinal studies on the acquisition of **control into complements** (both subject and object control verbs were included in the battery of tests) and **control into adjuncts**. They used the act-out task, a grammaticality judgment task, and a task aimed at eliciting a judgment of reference. In the grammaticality judgment task children were asked, "Is it the right way to say it?" In the judgment-of-reference task children heard a sentence like (4a) and were asked, "Who was buying the ice cream?" These authors found that different children in the age range 3;10–4;11 give different patterns of responses to control structures like those in (4).

(4) a. *Object control into complements*
       Ariel told Ernie PRO to buy an ice cream.

   b. *Subject control into complements*
      Ariel wanted PRO to push Peter Pan.
   c. *Subject control into adjuncts*
      Ariel kissed Ernie before PRO buying an ice cream.

These researchers found that children interpret PRO in sentences like (4a–c) differently from adults. They have distinguished the following four response patterns:

(5) a. *Free interpretation of PRO*
       Children take PRO as picking out the individual referred to by the subject of the matrix clause, the individual referred to by the object of the matrix clause, or even an extralinguistic character. Initially this **free interpretation of PRO** happens in both complement and adjunct clauses.
    b. *Free interpretation of PRO only in adjunct clauses*
       Children have converged on the adult grammar insofar as control into complements is concerned. They correctly select the subject or the object depending on whether the matrix verb is a subject control verb (*want, decide, try, like*) or an object control verb (*tell, pick, order, choose*). However, they still allow free interpretation of PRO in adjunct clauses.
    c. *Object control interpretation of PRO in adjunct clauses*
       Children take PRO in an adjunct clause to pick out the individual referred to by the matrix object, rather than the individual referred to by the matrix subject, as the adult grammar requires (see Goodluck 1981; Hsu, Cairns, and Fiengo 1985; Hsu, Eisenberg, and Schlisselberg 1989).
    d. *Mixed subject and object control interpretation of PRO in adjunct clauses*
       Children still make mistakes when they interpret PRO in adjunct clauses. Sometimes they take the matrix subject to control PRO, as adults do; other times they take the matrix object to control PRO. This mixed pattern of responses indicates that children are moving toward the adult grammar.

From this description, it appears that children deviate substantially from the adult target. The question is why.

10.2.2   Development in the Grammar of Control

According to McDaniel, Cairns, and Hsu (1991) and Cairns et al. (1994), children make mistakes in interpreting PRO not because they lack knowledge of the principles governing the distribution and interpretation of PRO, but because they incorrectly represent sentences including sub-ordinate clauses. Children manifest developmental changes in control because in approaching the adult target, they have to learn the lexical properties of verbs and of (subordinating) conjunctions; lacking full knowledge of these properties, they make different hypotheses about the attachment site of subordinate clauses (hence the name for this account, the **structure-changing hypothesis**). In other words, the different patterns of responses outlined in (5) correspond to the following developmentally ordered grammars.

Grammar 1: Free interpretation of PRO Children allow PRO to be interpreted freely because they do not have access to the recursive rule for embedding clauses and thus must analyze control structures as coordinate structures (see section 6.4.3, where a similar claim is advanced to account for children's errors in handling relative clauses). For example, at this stage (4a) would be represented as in (6) and (4c) as in (7) in children's grammar.

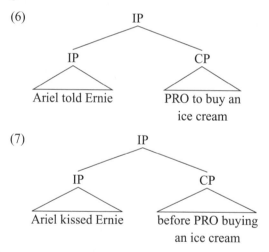

(6)

IP
  IP
    Ariel told Ernie
  CP
    PRO to buy an
    ice cream

(7)

IP
  IP
    Ariel kissed Ernie
  CP
    before PRO buying
    an ice cream

Because children initially analyze control structures in this way, they cannot interpret PRO on the basis of grammatical principles; for one thing, PRO is not c-commanded by the alleged controller (*Ernie* in (6) and *Ariel* in (7)). Instead, they interpret PRO contextually and take it to refer to the individual picked out by the subject, the object, or an extra-linguistic character. Notice that the idea that PRO is interpreted in this way lends support to the claim that the early null subject of nonfinite clauses is PRO (see section 5.2.6).

Grammar 2: Free interpretation of PRO only in adjunct clauses Children's grammar develops to incorporate the recursive rule for embedding clauses. This happens first for complements and only later for adjuncts; that is, children figure out that the structural representation in (6) is not adequate for complements, but still maintain the one in (7) for adjuncts. Therefore, they assign (4a) the representation in (8), where the complement is attached to V'.

(8)

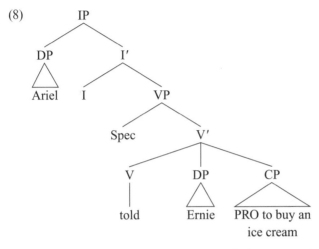

Because children assign the correct analysis to complements of control verbs and know the control principles, they interpret PRO in complements correctly. They still allow the free interpretation of PRO in adjuncts, because they continue to analyze sentences including adjuncts as coordinate clauses (see (7)). The fact that children treat complements as subordinating clauses earlier than adjuncts is attributed to the different relation that complements and adjuncts bear to the verb. Since complements are subcategorized by verbs, children grasp their subordinating status earlier than that of adjuncts as part of acquiring the argument structure of verbs. It is thus through lexical learning that children come to appreciate the subordinating status of verbs' clausal complements.

Grammar 3: Object control of PRO in adjuncts During this stage children come to learn the subordinating status of conjunctions that introduce adjuncts. They thus abandon the coordinate structure analysis for sentences including adjuncts as well; and they no longer treat adjuncts as the second member of a coordinate structure, but treat them like an embedded phrase. However, their first guess is that adjuncts, like complements, must be attached to V', rather than to I' (but see Goodluck and

Behne 1992 for evidence against this conjecture). In other words, they extend to adjuncts the same analysis they have already adopted for complements. At this stage the structure of a child's sentence like (4c) including an adjunct would be (9).

(9)
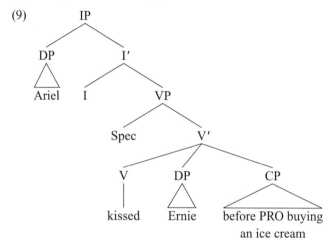

Because children attach adjuncts at the wrong level, they choose the object as the controller of PRO.

Grammar 4: Mixed subject and object interpretation of PRO in adjunct clauses This stage is transitional. Children retain the option of the preceding stage and attach adjuncts in a position where they are c-commanded by the object (as in (9)). However, they feel free to choose another attachment site as well: a higher position where PRO is c-commanded by the subject, but not by the object, as shown in (10).

(10)
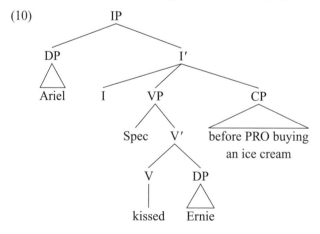

Depending on the attachment site, they take PRO to be controlled either by the object or by the subject.

Notice that children do not necessarily go through each of these grammars; they may skip one grammar. But they cannot move, for example, from grammar 2 to grammar 1; that is, the direction of development is fixed.

The view just presented holds that all along, children know the principles governing the distribution and the interpretation of PRO (e.g., that PRO must be c-commanded by the antecedent and that it must occur in nonfinite clauses). In this respect their grammar for control is like the adult grammar from the start. There is no point during development in which children lack PRO or ignore the rules governing the interpretation of PRO.

It is not knowledge of control that develops, but knowledge of lexical properties of verbs and conjunctions and knowledge of the way clauses are arranged. That lexical knowledge is implicated in mastery of control structures is suggested by the fact that control into adjuncts displays certain lexical effects. For example, Cairns et al. (1994) tested children with four types of adjunct clauses, introduced by *before*, *after*, *while*, and *in order to*. They found that children make more errors with *in order to* adjuncts than with the other types. Lack of knowledge of the lexical properties of *in order to* is responsible for poor performance. Under this view children interpret control sentences in a nonadult way because they do not know the lexical properties of conjunctions and cannot build the relevant structures in which control principles can be applied.

10.2.3   Intermediate Summary

In this section we have discussed the hypothesis that children's nonadult interpretation of control complements and adjuncts is due to failure to properly represent these constructions and not to defective knowledge of control principles. In the course of development children make different hypotheses about the structure of control complements and adjuncts and accordingly they interpret PRO in different ways. Initially children take subordinate clauses to be coordinate clauses and assign them a flat structure. Accordingly they interpret PRO freely, as referring to the subject or object of the main clause or to any extrasentential character. Next they keep the coordinate structure for adjunct clauses, but, since their grammar has incorporated the recursive rule, they treat subordinate complements as embedded clauses. PRO in complements is interpreted in an adultlike way, while PRO in adjuncts is still interpreted freely. Then children extend the embedded-clause analysis to adjuncts, but attach the adjuncts to the wrong node. Therefore, they are obliged to interpret PRO in adjuncts as being controlled by the matrix object rather than by the matrix subject. Finally children start to attach adjuncts to a higher node and can interpret PRO in adjuncts as being controlled by the matrix subject.

10.3   THE MATURATION HYPOTHESIS

Wexler (1992) and Broihier and Wexler (1995) contest the view that children's grammar for control undergoes the developmental changes described in (5). They suggest that a better characterization of children's nonadult responses, the **maturation hypothesis**, includes just two stages:

(11) a. *Stage 1*
Children do not have access to PRO and thus allow free interpretation of PRO in nonfinite complement and adjunct clauses.

b. *Stage 2*
Children have access to PRO. They interpret PRO as adults do when it occurs in nonfinite complement clauses. However, they still allow free interpretation of PRO in nonfinite adjunct clauses.

Essentially, unlike McDaniel, Cairns, and Hsu (1991) and Cairns et al. (1994), Broihier and Wexler (1995) claim that a stage during which children choose the object as antecedent of PRO in adjunct clauses (grammar 3 above) does not exist. They point out that object control responses are often observed even in contexts in which the controller does not c-command PRO (see Goodluck and Behne 1992). For example, children interpret PRO as referring to the individual picked out by the NP *the bear* in (12), even though this NP does not c-command PRO.

(12) The lion pushes on the bear after PRO climbing up the ladder.

Thus, children's choice of the object as the controller of PRO is not guided by the control module, but by a bias to interpret PRO as anaphorically linked to the closest NP. This bias, which must be invoked to explain children's interpretation of PRO in (12), can also be responsible for the interpretation of PRO in sentences like (4c), repeated here.

(4) c. Ariel kissed Ernie before buying an ice cream.

On the basis of these facts, Broihier and Wexler claim that the conclusion that children are behaving in accordance with the grammar of control when they take PRO to be anaphorically linked to the object in (4c) is not warranted. Children may be responding on the basis of some strategy that leads them to interpret PRO as anaphorically linked to the closest NP in sentences like (12). In Broihier and Wexler's view the choice of the object for fixing the interpretation of PRO results from a strong preference and is not the expression of a grammatical option. Thus, for Broihier and Wexler there are two developmental stages in the early grammar of control, one in which children admit a free interpretation of PRO in complement and adjunct clauses and one in which this interpretation is restricted to just adjunct clauses. Let us examine these two stages more closely.

10.3.1   Stage 1: PRO Is Scheduled to Mature

According to Wexler (1992), early in children's linguistic development PRO is not accessible to them; it becomes available upon maturation around 3–4 years (see sections 4.4.4 and 7.2 for other cases in which maturation has been invoked to explain children's nonadult linguistic behavior). Children know how to build complex structures and know the recursive rule for embedding complements and adjuncts. They also know that every clause must have a subject. However, since PRO is not available to them, children must reanalyze subordinate nonfinite clauses and nonfinite adjuncts, as in (13), in a way that avoids the use of PRO.

(13) a. Ariel wants PRO to drink.
     b. Ariel left before PRO finishing the homework.

One way to do so is to analyze the subordinate clause and the adjunct in (13) as nominal structures, with *to* in (13a) taken to be a nominalizing morpheme, an idea suggested by Carlson (1990) and elaborated by Wexler (1992). To see this more clearly, let us focus on (13a). Because children analyze the complement of *want* in (13a) as an NP (or a DP under current assumptions), they do not need to represent PRO. NPs, unlike clauses, do not require a structural subject. Children's representation of (13a) would have to be (14). (The hypothesis that PRO is unavailable is at odds with the claim that PRO is the subject of RIs; see section 5.2.6.)

(14)

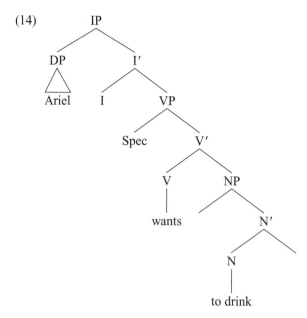

Let us see why by assigning the analysis in (14) to the complement in (13a), children come up with the free interpretation of the understood subject of the embedded clause. Consider the minimal pair in (15), adapted from Wexler 1992, whose structural representation is given in (16).

(15) a. The students enjoyed singing the songs.
     b. The students enjoyed the singing of the songs.

(16) a.

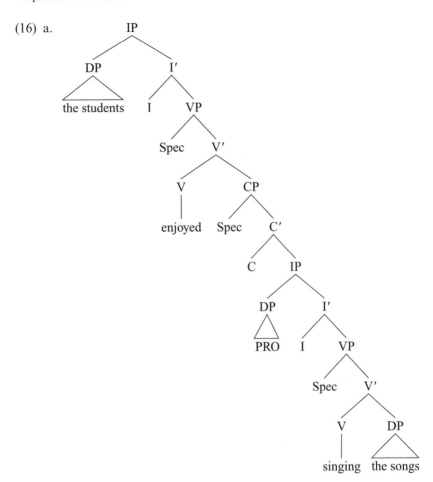

b.

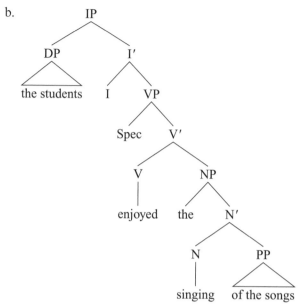

The complement of *enjoy* in (15a) is a nonfinite clause, while the one in (15b) is an NP. (15a) conveys the meaning that the students enjoyed the students' singing (i.e., the singers are the students), something that is captured by saying that the nonfinite complement includes PRO, which is controlled by the matrix subject, the DP *the students.* By contrast, (15b) says that the students enjoyed the singing; the singer can be understood to be anyone who may be relevant in the context. This is rendered by saying that there is no PRO in the NP. Similarly, because children assign to the subordinate clauses in (13) the nominal analysis given in (14), they treat (13) like (15b); in (14) there is no PRO in the complement of *want,* just as there is none in the nominal complement of *enjoy* in (16b). Because of this, children take the drinker to be anyone in the context—either the individual referred to by the subject or an extralinguistic character. In other words, children do not have access to PRO and thus are forced to analyze nonfinite complements and adjuncts as NPs. Accordingly, they take the understood subjects of these reanalyzed NPs to be anyone, as is the case in true NPs in (16b).

10.3.2   Stage 2: Maturation of the Temporal Operator Present in the Representation of Adjunct Clauses

During the second stage maturation makes PRO available in children's grammar. Therefore, children abandon the nominal analysis of control structures in (14). They assign a clausal representation to the complement of verbs like *want* (see (13a)), fill the subject position of this nonfinite clause with PRO, and interpret it correctly. However, they still allow free interpretation of PRO in adjuncts. If PRO is available, why do children still have problems with adjunct clauses? Wexler (1992) and Broihier and Wexler (1995) argue that children have PRO in their grammar and know the relevant principles of control, as proven by the fact that they have no difficulties in handling control in complements. However, they cannot properly represent (temporal) adjuncts. Let us see why.

The structural analysis of temporal adjuncts includes an empty temporal operator, as shown in (17), where *Op* stands for the empty operator.

(17) Big Bird scratched Ernie [before [Op PRO going to the park]].

The role of the temporal operator is to ensure the temporal interpretation of the embedded clause by connecting it to the tense of the main clause expressed on the verb (here, *scratched*). Broihier and Wexler propose that empty operators are not available in children's grammar up to 6 years for maturational reasons (see Goodluck and Behne 1992 for evidence that children have difficulties with temporal adjuncts).[1] Because of this, they are forced to represent (17) in a way that does not require these operators. One solution is to continue to adopt for adjuncts the nominal analysis adopted for both complements and adjuncts in the first stage. The structure of (17) will continue to be (18).

(18)

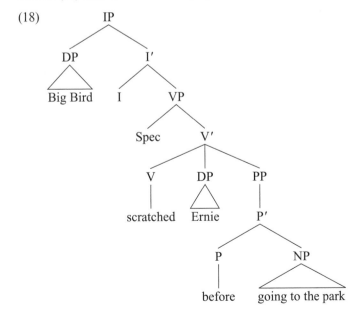

Since, unlike clauses, NPs do not require a subject, PRO will not be present in the representations of adjuncts. By assigning a nominal analysis to the adjunct in (18), children are treating it much like (19).

(19) Big Bird scratched Ernie [PP before [NP the walk to the park]].

In (19) the walker can be anyone; that is, the understood subject of the NP can be interpreted freely. Similarly, the nominal analysis in (18) of the adjunct clause in (17) lends itself to a free interpretation: "the one who goes to the park" can be anyone.

Under this view the free interpretation of adjuncts arises because children cannot avail themselves of empty operators and thus are forced to retain the analysis of adjuncts as nominals. This proposal rests on the assumption that children do not have access to empty operators. Is there independent evidence for this assumption? We turn to this question in the next section.

10.3.3 Empty Operators

Broihier and Wexler's (1995) account holds that empty operators are unavailable to children until age 6. Evidence for this conjecture is provided by children's difficulties with other constructions involving empty operators, such as *tough*-movement constructions (see Chomsky 1969; Cromer 1987) like the one in (20).

(20) The wolf is easy to bite.

The standard analysis holds that *tough*-movement constructions include an empty operator moved from object position to an initial position in the embedded clause. The empty operator in turn is identified by coindexation with a referential NP, here *the wolf*, as in (21) (see Haegeman 1994, chap. 8).

(21)

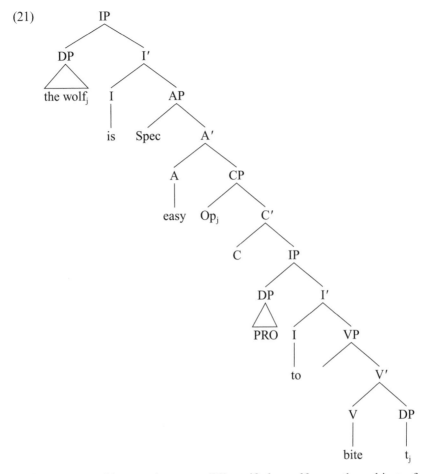

Children up to 10 years interpret (20) as if *the wolf* were the subject of the infinitive complement, rather than the object; that is, children seem to interpret (20) as (22).

(22) The wolf is easy for the wolf to bite.

Similarly, Goodluck and Behne (1992) report poor performance in handling purpose clauses with object gaps by children as old as 10 years. (23) contains this type of purpose clause.

(23) Big Bird chose Cookie Monster to read to.

The representation of purpose clauses also involves empty operators, as (24), the representation of (23), shows.

(24) Big Bird chose Cookie Monster$_i$ [Op$_i$ PRO to read to t$_i$].

As in *tough*-movement constructions, the empty operator in these clauses is moved from object position of the infinitive clause to a suitable position in the subordinate clause, where it is identified by being coindexed with the matrix object.

One way to interpret children's difficulties with *tough*-movement constructions and purpose clauses is to say that the empty operator, which would ensure that *the wolf* in (20) and *Cookie Monster* in (23) are interpreted as the object of the infinitive clause, is not present in the structure that children assign to (20) and (23) (see Wexler 1992 for further evidence).

10.3.4 Intermediate Summary

Studies vary widely regarding children's mastery of control structures. These variations may be due to the experimental setting or to some bias toward one particular interpretation. But what seems to emerge is that children allow a wider range of interpretations for PRO than adults do. According to Wexler (1992) and Broihier and Wexler (1995), the interpretation of PRO goes through two developmental stages:

(25) a. *Stage 1*
          PRO has not matured.
          Nominal analysis of complement and adjunct clauses
          Free interpretation of the understood subject of these clauses
          (reanalyzed as NPs by children)
     b. *Stage 2*
          PRO has matured, but empty temporal operators have not.
          Clausal analysis of nonfinite complements and nominal analysis
          of nonfinite adjuncts
          Free interpretation of the understood subject of adjunct clauses
          (reanalyzed as NPs by children)

The development observed in handling control structures is the result of a biological program that makes different grammatical objects available at different times. Initially PRO is not available to children, and this forces them to analyze nonfinite clauses (complements and adjuncts) as nominals. Upon maturation PRO becomes accessible. This is enough for representing complement clauses in an adultlike way, but not for representing nonfinite adjuncts properly. In the latter case an empty temporal operator is necessary, but this is not available to children. Consequently, children continue to analyze adjunct clauses as nominals, and this explains why they continue to interpret the understood subject of these reanalyzed adjuncts freely when they no longer analyze PRO in nonfinite complement clauses in this way.

10.4   THE LEXICAL-SYNTACTIC INTEGRATION HYPOTHESIS

In a series of experiments Cohen Sherman and Lust (1995) have concentrated on the production and comprehension of control complements. In contrast to what was found in other studies, these authors did not replicate the finding that children allow a free interpretation of PRO in complements. They found that children display knowledge of the various components implicated in control at least by 3 years, both in production and in comprehension. However, like other researchers, they also found that achieving full mastery of control structures takes time. Children tend to interpret PRO in complements after verbs like *promise* as referring to the object, rather than to the subject; that is, they take PRO to refer to *Wendy* in (26), rather than *Ariel*.

(26) Ariel promised Wendy PRO to go to the party.

Cohen Sherman and Lust show that children know the various components involved in control (the distribution of PRO, lexical properties of verbs). They explain the developmental delay in mastery of control structures as a consequence of the need to integrate the independent components—lexical and syntactic—that contribute to mastery of control: the **lexical-syntactic integration hypothesis**. Let us look at these points in more detail.

10.4.1   Production of Control Complements

There are very few studies on the production of control structures. Pinker (1984) (see also references cited there) states that in spontaneous production English-speaking children start to use control complements (see (1a,b)) by the time they are combining 3 and 4 words, that is, when their MLU is around 2.6–3. They first produce subject control structures, as in (1a), and then object control structures, as in (1b). Thus, children use control structures quite early in spontaneous production. However, this fact does not automatically guarantee that children assign control clauses the same structure as adults. To ascertain whether children can handle control structures in an adultlike way, we must establish whether they know the distribution of PRO and the lexical properties of control verbs.

10.4.1.1 Distribution of PRO Using elicited imitation, Cohen Sherman and Lust (1995) showed that, although children's imitation of control structures improves with age, by 3 years they know that PRO is found in infinitive clauses. In this experiment children were required to imitate finite clauses containing lexical pronouns and infinitive clauses (including PRO). Examples with an object control verb (*tell*) and a subject control verb (*promise*) are given in (27).

(27) a. Wendy told Tom that he will leave.
      b. Wendy told Tom PRO to leave.
      c. Ariel promised Wendy that she will go to the party.
      d. Ariel promised Wendy PRO to go to the party.

In repeating these sentences, children sometimes changed the complement type, replacing the finite complement with an infinitive complement or vice versa. Interestingly, the changes involved a corresponding change in the pronominal form of the subject. When children converted the infinitive complement into a finite complement, they also converted the null subject PRO into a lexical pronoun and vice versa. This result indicates that children link PRO with infinitive complements and distinguish between various types of pronouns (PRO vs. lexical pronouns).

10.4.1.2 Lexical Knowledge In the same study Cohen Sherman and Lust (1995) found that children treat subject and object control verbs differently. This fact suggests that they can distinguish the two types of verbs. In their imitations children converted a finite complement into an infinitive one more often when the matrix verb was *tell* (object control) than when it was *promise* (subject control). Conversely, they changed an infinitive complement into a finite one more often when the matrix verb was *promise* than when it was *tell*. Examples of children's conversions are given in (28) (from Cohen Sherman and Lust 1995).

(28) a. Target: Jimmy tells Tom that he will ride the bicycle.
          Response: Jimmy t … tells Tom to ride the bicycle.   (3;0)
      b. Target: Jimmy promises Tom to watch the baseball game.
          Response: Jimmy promises him that he will watch th'ball game.
          (3;9)

While it is not clear why children changed the structures in the way they did, the different response patterns suggest that they know something that distinguishes the two kinds of control verb.

10.4.1.3   Advantage for Object Control Structures   Even though children make some distinction between subject and object control verbs, Cohen Sherman and Lust (1995) found that it was easier for children to imitate sentences including object control verbs than sentences including subject control verbs; that is, (29a) was easier to imitate than (29b).

(29) a. Aladdin told Wendy PRO to leave.
     b. Horace promised Aladdin PRO to leave.

Thus, production data show that by 3 years children know the structural environments in which PRO is found and the lexical properties of control verbs. However, a discrepancy in ease of imitation is observed, favoring object control structures over subject control structures. As we will see in the next section, there is also a discrepancy between production and comprehension of control structures: production is relatively advanced by age 3, while comprehension seems to lag.

10.4.2   Comprehension of Control into Complements
Cohen Sherman and Lust (1995) probed children's comprehension of control structures and found that, as in production, children distinguish between PRO and lexical pronouns. They are sensitive to the lexical properties of verbs; but they do not achieve this until 5 years, and they have marked difficulties in interpreting PRO in complements to *promise*.

10.4.2.1   Lexical Pronouns versus PRO   Do children distinguish between PRO and lexical pronouns? PRO is controlled either by the matrix subject, as in (30a), or by the matrix object, as in (30b).

(30) a. *PRO = Peter*
        Peter promised Ernie PRO to scratch Cookie Monster.
     b. *PRO = Ernie*
        Peter told Ernie PRO to scratch Cookie Monster.

By contrast, the lexical pronoun *he* in the finite complements in (31) can be anaphoric to either *Ernie* or *Peter*; it can also refer to some other character introduced in the discourse.

(31) *he = Peter or Ernie*

    a. Peter told Ernie that he should scratch Cookie Monster.

    b. Peter promised Ernie that he will scratch Cookie Monster.

If children know the properties of PRO, they should not treat it as a lexical pronoun. To test this, Cohen Sherman and Lust (1995) used a pragmatic lead-in, like (32a) or (32b), to introduce either the object or the subject of a following sentence.

(32) a. This is a story about Peter.   (subject)

      b. This is a story about Ernie.   (object)

The pragmatic lead-in was uttered before one of the sentences in (30) or (31) and was meant to modulate the interpretation of lexical pronouns or of PRO. After having heard the pragmatic lead-in and then the sentence, children were asked to act out what the sentence described. It was found that by 3 years of age children's interpretation of lexical pronouns in finite sentences was influenced by the pragmatic lead-in. Specifically, children preferred to take the lexical pronoun as anaphorically linked to the subject or the object depending on whether the pragmatic lead-in introduced the subject or the object, respectively. By contrast, the pragmatic lead-in did not influence children's interpretation of PRO. From this asymmetry in the interpretation of lexical pronouns and PRO, one can infer that lexical pronouns and PRO are two distinct grammatical objects for children; otherwise, they should be interpreted in the same way and should be subject to the same contextual biases. One can also conclude that pragmatic context does not override the grammatical principles of control.

10.4.2.2 Lexical Knowledge   We have seen that one property of control structures is that the choice of the argument that controls PRO depends on the matrix verb. Certain verbs require object control and others require subject control. Are children sensitive to this property of control verbs? Unlike what researchers have found for production, sensitivity to the lexical properties of control verbs is not evident at 3 years. Cohen Sherman and Lust (1995) showed that 3;0- to 3;11-year-old children do not clearly differentiate their responses in comprehension experiments as a function of verb type. When asked to act out the content of sentences like (30a,b), they select the character named by the subject (*Peter*) or the object (*Ernie*) of the main clause and make him scratch Cookie Monster. This is interpreted as evidence showing that children allow either the subject or the object to control PRO, regardless of the verb type.

Therefore, sensitivity to the lexical property of control verbs is evident earlier in production than in comprehension. Children's sensitivity to the lexical properties of control verbs is evident in comprehension by 5 years but still increases between 5 and 7 years. By 5 years English-speaking children choose the object as the controller of PRO more often when the matrix verb is *tell* (see (30b)) than when it is *promise* (see (30a)); conversely, they choose the subject as the controller of PRO more often when the matrix verb is *promise* than when it is *tell*.

10.4.2.3 Problems with the Subject Control Verb *Promise*   Although by 5 years English-speaking children display knowledge of the lexical properties of control verbs, Cohen Sherman and Lust (1995) observe a marked difficulty in handling control structures including the verb *promise*. Children, especially the youngest, frequently treat *promise* as an object control verb, a finding often noted in the literature (e.g., Chomsky 1969; Maratsos 1974). Interestingly, this bias is observed only when the complement contains an infinitive. When the complement contains a finite verb, as in (31b), children prefer to take the lexical pronoun to be anaphorically linked to the subject. If the preference for interpreting PRO as anaphorically linked to the object in (30a) were the result of a performance strategy, as suggested in the literature (see Chomsky 1969), we would expect this strategy to apply across the board, in both finite and infinitive constructions. However, this is not what is found. Cohen Sherman and Lust interpret this result as an indication that object control responses with *promise* arise from a grammatical option: children link object control to infinitive complements; that is, they match the distribution of PRO with an object control interpretation. As noted earlier, Cohen Sherman and Lust observed an advantage in production for object control structures (*tell*) over subject control structures (*promise*). Thus, production and comprehension converge toward recognizing a marked difficulty with *promise* and a significant development in children's comprehension of structures including *promise*.

10.4.2.4 The Source of Children's Difficulties with Control   Cohen Sherman and Lust (1995) have established that children know several components of control. They know that PRO is linked to nonfinite complements. They also know that PRO is obligatorily controlled, and its interpretation cannot be influenced by pragmatic factors, unlike the interpretation of lexical pronouns. In production children show themselves to be sensitive to some lexical properties of control verbs, although they experience difficulties in comprehending these structures. Specifically, they have difficulties in choosing the controller of PRO, and their lexical knowledge takes time to be acquired. Why is this so? Cohen Sherman and Lust account for children's weaknesses by saying that children know the components of control when these are considered independently, but they do not know how to integrate these components, a process that is language specific.

To achieve adult competence with control structures, children must combine their syntactic knowledge about the distribution of PRO and their lexical knowledge about the way PRO is interpreted with specific verbs. We have seen that children tie the distribution of PRO (its occurrence in infinitive clauses) to an object control interpretation. For *promise* this link creates a mismatch. The integration of syntactic properties with lexical properties requires children to override their initial hypothesis about the interpretation of PRO and to modulate it as a function of the lexical properties of the main verb.

This process of integration is language specific, in the sense that languages may vary with respect to the specific components involved in control. For example, crosslinguistic variations exist concerning the syntactic environments licensing PRO. While in English PRO is found in nonfinite clauses, in Greek PRO is found in finite subjunctive clauses (Terzi 1997; Goodluck, Terzi, and Chocano 2001), infinitives being nonexistent in this language. In Indonesian and Korean the verb corresponding to English *promise* takes a finite complement, an infinitival being ungrammatical, as shown in (33a) and (33b), respectively (Indonesian examples from Cohen Sherman and Lust 1995).

(33) a. John$_j$ berjanji kepada Bill$_i$ (bahwa) dia$_{j/*i}$ akan pergi ketoko.
          John promise to   Bill that   he   FUT to go to store
          'John promised Bill that he would go to the store.'
     b. *John berjanji kepada Bill pergi ketoko.
          John promise to   Bill to go to store
          'John promised Bill to go to the store.'

Another variation concerns the way the controllee may be expressed. English *promise* occurs in the double object construction, and the goal may be expressed by an accusative NP, as in (30a), repeated here.

(30) a. Peter promised Ernie PRO to scratch Cookie Monster.

In languages that do not have the double object construction, like Italian or French, the goal is expressed by a PP introduced by a preposition (Italian *a*, French *à*), as the Italian counterpart of (30a) shows.

(34) Peter ha promesso a Ernie di grattare Cookie Monster.

In sum, although children know the individual components involved in control, they have to put them together. The delay observed in mastery of control structures reflects the time children need to integrate the different components.

10.5   SUMMARY AND CONCLUDING REMARKS

In this chapter we have examined how children handle control structures. We have seen that full knowledge of control takes time to manifest itself. Initially children seem to allow free interpretation of PRO, a finding that has been generally observed in certain conditions, but not in others (e.g., Cohen Sherman and Lust 1995). While there is evidence that children master control into complements, they still have difficulties in handling control into adjuncts. By 3 years children know that PRO is distinct from lexical pronouns and also distinguish between subject and object control verbs. This indicates that they have the structural knowledge necessary for handling control and the lexical knowledge that determines which NP in the matrix clause controls PRO. These facts were initially determined in studies on early English, but crosslinguistic evidence from early Greek and Spanish (Goodluck, Terzi, and Chocano 2001) confirms them. Although adultlike behavior is observed earlier with complements than with adjuncts, there is one exception. English learners manifest a marked difficulty in handling control into complements of *promise*. They take the controller to be the object, rather than the subject. According to Cohen Sherman and Lust, in order to properly understand control structures with *promise*, children have to override certain expectations that force them to take *promise* as an object control verb. To do so, they must integrate their lexical and syntactic knowledge.

In sum, various factors must be responsible for the errors that children make in interpreting control structures, factors that may vary cross-linguistically along lexical and morphological dimensions (e.g., structural environments licensing PRO, infinitives vs. subjunctives).

Summary of Linguistic Development

1. Children produce control structures by 3–4 years of age.
2. Children have difficulties with control structures:
   a. they allow free interpretation of PRO, and
   b. they allow PRO to be controlled by the matrix object regardless of the control property of the matrix verb.
3. Children's difficulties with control adjuncts persist longer than their difficulties with control complements.
4. English-speaking children have difficulties with the control verb *promise*.

Further Reading

The papers in Lust 1986b and 1987 discuss whether children treat PRO as distinct from lexical pronouns. For discussion of empty operators in acquisition, see Vainikka and Roeper 1995.

Key Words

Control into adjuncts
Control into complements
Free interpretation of PRO
Lexical properties of control verbs
Lexical-syntactic integration hypothesis
Maturation hypothesis
Structure-changing hypothesis

Study Questions

1. How have researchers accounted for children's free interpretation of PRO? Discuss the pros and cons of one or more analyses.

2. How have researchers proven that children distinguish between PRO and lexical pronouns? Design an experiment that will show that they do.

3. How have researchers explained children's difficulties in handling control complements after the verb *promise*? Consult Larson's (1988) analysis and study question 7 in chapter 7.

4. In section 5.2.6 we evaluated the hypothesis that the subject of root infinitives can be PRO. The reference of the subject is not arbitrary; instead, it is fixed by the context. Comment on this observation in light of the results discussed in this chapter on children's interpretation of PRO.

5. How would you design an experiment to test whether children can interpret PRO arbitrarily?

6. Extracting from coordinate clauses in English is impossible, as proven by the ungrammaticality of (i).

(i) *What did John sell a book and buy t?

If children represent control structures as the second conjunct of a coordinate structure, as the structure-changing hypothesis holds, they should find extraction out of control complements impossible; that is, (ii) should be unacceptable for them.

(ii) Who did Big Bird tell Ernie to scratch t?

How would you design an experiment to test whether this prediction is fulfilled? (For discussion related to this issue, see Thornton 1990; McDaniel, Chiu, and Maxfield 1995; Cairns et al. 1994.)

7. It is possible that children have more difficulties with control into adjuncts because they do not know the meaning of subordinating conjunctions (*before*, *after*, *while*, etc.). How would you design an experiment to test whether children properly understand these conjunctions? (See Gorrell, Crain, and Fodor 1989; see also Cairns et al. 1994 for discussion relevant to this question.)

Chapter 11

Dissociation between Language and Other Cognitive Abilities

INTRODUCTION

Is language independent from other cognitive capacities? In this chapter we will examine this question by looking at two pathological conditions: specific language impairment and Williams syndrome. Specific language impairment is a condition in which language is impaired but other cognitive functions are normal. Williams syndrome is its mirror image: here, language outstrips other cognitive functions. This discussion has two goals. First, by looking at these patterns of skill dissociations, we will gather evidence that language, on the one hand, and other cognitive capacities such as reasoning, memory, action, and perception, on the other, are supported by different representations and mechanisms. If skill A is impaired, while skill B is not, it is likely that they are subserved by different mental and neural systems. Second, we will look at various characterizations of specific language impairment, with special attention to linguistically motivated accounts. Although these descriptions are based on behavioral data, they bear on the question of the biological foundations of language (see Lenneberg 1967). If the language capacity does not develop in the normal way, perhaps something is wrong with the genetic equipment that has caused abnormal neurological development of the brain circuits devoted to language processing. Investigations of language disorders shed new light on the nature of the linguistic capacity and on the process of language acquisition, by offering evidence that might be difficult to pin down in the normal course of development, given its rapid pace (see Rice 1996).

Although the discussion surrounding developmental language disorders is extremely lively and some interesting results have been obtained, linguistically motivated analyses of such disorders are a recent innovation in the psycholinguistic field. So far there are a respectable number of linguistically motivated studies of specific language impairment; similar studies are beginning to appear for Williams syndrome as well. In the future it would be desirable to use the tools of linguistic theory to study the development of language in other conditions (e.g., Down syndrome), to see how language emerges under different exceptional conditions and possibly to prepare the background for linguistically motivated rehabilitation programs.

This chapter is organized in three sections. Section 11.1 introduces the nature of specific language impairment and discusses whether its origin is genetic or environmental. Section 11.2 presents various accounts of this condition that locate the deficit either in a module of the grammar or in other cognitive systems, such as the perceptual system. Section 11.3 profiles the linguistic behavior of individuals with Williams syndrome and their performance in other cognitive domains.

11.1   IMPAIRED LANGUAGE IN OTHERWISE NORMAL CHILDREN: SPECIFIC LANGUAGE IMPAIRMENT

The term **specific language impairment** (SLI) is currently used to refer to a condition in which linguistic disorders are evident despite normal nonlinguistic development and in the absence of any obvious cause.[1] Hence, SLI is an example of **dissociation** between linguistic abilities and other cognitive capacities, the former lagging well behind the latter. SLI is diagnosed if a child scores two standard deviations below age level on a series of language tests (see appendix A for discussion of this point), yet exhibits no perceptual-motor deficits, like hearing loss, neurological dysfunction, or intellectual and socio-emotional deficits (see Bishop 1997 for discussion of these criteria; see Rice 1993 and references cited there for discussion of the social consequences of SLI). See appendix B for a discussion of tests used to assess SLI.

It is evident that these criteria are very loose, for they exclude only populations with mental retardation and populations with sensory deficits. Children with very different language problems may fall into the category of SLI. Although there are resemblances among children with SLI, there are also differences. Common features are the following:

(1) a. Language emerges later.
     b. Language may show unexpected patterns and remains below age expectations.

    c. The affected individual may exhibit problems with inflectional morphology.

Differences concern the extent of the deficit.

(2) a. Not every aspect of inflectional morphology is equally problematic.
    b. Beyond inflectional morphology, other areas of grammatical knowledge may be affected.
    c. The acquisition of words, especially of verbs, is sometimes vulnerable (see Rice et al. 1994; Oetting, Rice, and Swank 1995).
    d. (Mild) phonological deficits can be observed.
    e. The disorders may be receptive and/or expressive.
    f. The disorders may last well into the elementary school years and even persist into adulthood.

This heterogeneity may have various sources. First, the methods for probing children's grammatical knowledge vary; second, the age of the children tested varies from study to study. Given our current state of knowledge, the possibility cannot be excluded that older children have more developed linguistic knowledge, be it because some mechanism has matured or for other reasons. Therefore, *SLI* will be used here as a cover term for possibly a whole range of language disorders (see Bishop 1997 for reviews). Part of the discussion will consist of an attempt to characterize the deficit of some populations with SLI by using linguistically motivated criteria. It is to be hoped that the advent of such linguistic analyses of SLI will help in better characterizing this pathology.

    The etiology of SLI is not known. However, several studies have observed that SLI runs in families: the same linguistic disorder may be observed in different branches of the same family (see Tallal, Ross, and Curtiss 1989; Tomblin 1989), and it is more likely to find individuals with language-related speech disorders (e.g., reading, spelling) in the family of a child with SLI than in the family of a child without SLI. Rice, Haney, and Wexler (1998) report that the incidence of language disorders is about 22% among members of the family (mother, father, brothers, and sisters) of a child with SLI, and only 7% among members of the family of a child without SLI. This **familial aggregation** suggests that SLI has a **genetic basis**, rather than an environmental one, although there is no evidence for a link between a specific gene and linguistic disorders (see Rice 1996 for discussion). This hypothesis is also supported by Hurst et al.'s (1990) linkage study.[2] Additional evidence in the same direction comes from studies of mono- and dizygotic twins with SLI (see Lewis and Thompson 1992; Tomblin and Buckwalter 1994; Bishop, North, and Donlan 1995). Twins share a common environment, but while monozygotic twins also share the same genes (since they originate from the division of a single egg), dizygotic twins do not (and are therefore no more similar than other siblings). Therefore, if genetic endowment is somehow responsible for SLI, the chances that a language-impaired child's twin will also be language-impaired should be higher for monozygotic than for dizygotic twins. On the contrary, if SLI is caused by environmental factors, there should be no difference between mono- and dizygotic twins with respect to incidence of SLI. The evidence to date indicates that the risk for SLI is higher for monozygotic than for dizygotic twins, supporting the hypothesis that genes are implicated in the emergence of SLI. Again, this conclusion in no way implies that a specific gene is the cause of SLI. Genes may cause an abnormal neurological development, and this may be manifested in abnormal language behavior (see Plante 1991 for evidence of neurological anomalies in populations with language impairment). But exactly how these processes occur is a complex topic.

SLI is a natural experiment that offers a special opportunity to explore the contribution of nature and nurture in the acquisition of language.

11.2   APPROACHES TO SPECIFIC LANGUAGE IMPAIRMENT

Systematic comparisons of the linguistic behavior of children with and without SLI have been carried out to reveal patterns of weakness and strength in the linguistic production of children with SLI. Different groups of children display different abnormal language behaviors, and this finding has motivated various hypotheses about the nature of SLI. Linguistically oriented scholars argue that SLI is a modular deficit, that is, a deficit that affects only linguistic abilities (see Fodor 1983 regarding modularity). Some claim that the deficit alters local aspects of the grammar; for example, children with SLI produce sentences in which the feature tense (or finiteness) is absent and consequently the morphemes expressing this feature are not realized (see section 11.2.1.1). Others claim that children with SLI are weak at computing the subject-agreement relation (see section 11.2.1.2), or that SLI is a deficit affecting the ability to compute structure-dependent relations (see section 11.2.1.3), or that children with SLI do not build the same sort of grammar as children without SLI because their grammar lacks the features [±past] and

[±plural] (see section 11.2.1.4). A radically different view attributes the deficit to a weakness of the perceptual system that makes it difficult for children with SLI to perceive phonologically nonsalient morphemes (see section 11.2.2). To summarize:

(3) SLI is a deficit affecting grammatical abilities.
   a. Children with SLI fail to obligatorily express tense.
   b. Children with SLI fail to express agreement.
   c. Children with SLI cannot represent structure-dependent relations.
   d. Children with SLI lack the inflectional features [±past], [±plural].

(4) SLI is a deficit in the auditory processing system.

11.2.1   Modular Accounts of Specific Language Impairment

11.2.1.1   Specific Language Impairment as an Extended Period of Optional Infinitives   A prominent characteristic of the speech of children with SLI is the optional omission of inflectional morphology. Interestingly, careful investigations have shown that for some populations the deficit does not encompass every aspect of the inflectional system. Rice, Wexler, and collaborators (see, e.g., Rice, Wexler, and Cleave 1995; Rice and Wexler 1996) claim that SLI is a linguistic disorder that consists in using optional infinitives (OIs) or root infinitives (RIs) for a protracted period. Recall from section 4.4 that normally developing children between 2 and 3 years of age use infinitives or bare verbs in their main clauses, as shown in (5).

(5) a. Dormir petit bébé.   (Daniel, 1;11)
       sleep-INF little baby
    b. Zähne putzen.   (Simone, 1;10)
       teeth   brush-INF
    c. Papa have it.   (Eve, 1;6)
    d. Cromer wear glasses.   (Eve, 2;0)

While normally developing children cease to use OIs at about age 3, children with SLI still produce OIs at 5 or 6 years or even later; that is, children with SLI have a grammar that allows OIs for an extended period, according to Rice and Wexler. In other respects, the grammar of these children is like that of normally developing children; it includes the same grammatical processes (e.g., head movement) and the same grammatical categories (e.g., I). Thus, like normally developing children, children with SLI employ finite verbs in their main clauses and distinguish between finite and nonfinite verbs in terms of verb raising, the process that raises finite verbs from VP to IP (see section 4.2.4).

In section 4.4 we discussed two accounts of OI/RI. Rice, Wexler, and collaborators endorse Wexler's (1994) analysis of OIs, according to which OIs arise because the tense feature either is underspecified or is omitted from the clausal representation; that is, they adopt the **tense omission model** to explain OIs in the speech of children with SLI (section 4.4.2.1).[3] Unlike adults, children (with and without SLI) optionally leave the tense feature underspecified in main clauses; therefore, they do not use the morphemes that express this feature, they omit auxiliaries, and they produce main clauses including nonfinite verbs or OIs. For example, in French, German, and other languages an OI is an infinitive verb, as in (5a,b). The early English variant of OIs is the bare form. Thus, English learners omit morphemes expressing tense, the third person singular present ending -*s*, the past tense marker -*ed*, and the auxiliaries *be* and *do* and produce bare forms like (5c,d). The claim that SLI consists of an extended period of OIs amounts to making the following predictions:

(6) a. Only the tense feature is optionally missing and thus only tense morphemes are optionally omitted.
   b. Other inflectional morphemes (e.g., the plural marker on nouns) and prepositions are not omitted.
   c. When children do choose the tense feature, they respect all its morphosyntactic properties.

In their study of the spontaneous and elicited production of a group of English and German children with SLI, Rice, Wexler, and collaborators show that the predictions in (6) are borne out.

English-speaking children with SLI between 4;4 and 5;8 years of age display limited proficiency in the use of morphemes marking tense: third person singular present -*s*, past tense -*ed*, and the auxiliaries BE and DO, where *BE* and *DO* are labels for various forms of these verbs (see Rice, Wexler, and Cleave 1995; Rice and Wexler 1996). Figure 11.1 illustrates rate of correct use of these morphemes in obligatory contexts for children with SLI and for two control groups, age-matched (AM) and language-matched (LM).[4]

It is evident from this figure that children with SLI are much less proficient than AM peers on all morphemes tested. They are also weaker

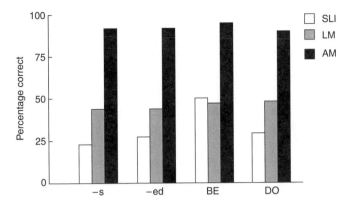

Figure 11.1
Percentage of correct use of the following morphemes in obligatory contexts (linguistic probes): third person singular present *-s*, past tense *-ed*, auxiliary BE, and DO. Data from 37 American English–speaking children with specific language impairment (SLI) (age range 4;4–5;8), from 45 language-matched (LM) controls, and from 40 age-matched (AM) controls. Based on data from Rice and Wexler 1996, table 2.

than LM children on all morphemes tested, except BE. As predicted in (6a), almost all errors illustrated in figure 11.1 are errors of omission. Children with SLI fail to use tense morphemes and say *I good child, He speak*, or *He not come* rather than *I am a good child, He speaks*, or *He does not come*. However, like normally developing children, when they use tense morphemes or auxiliaries, they use them correctly, as anticipated in (6c) (see Rice and Wexler 1996; Hadley and Rice 1996). For example, they use the third person marker with third person subjects, and they inflect auxiliaries. Similarly, German-speaking children with SLI, ranging in age between 4;0 and 4;8, use OIs for a protracted period (see Rice, Noll, and Grimm 1997), but demonstrate a great deal of linguistic knowledge; for example, they know the morphosyntactic correlates of the tense feature. Like normally developing children in the OI stage, German-speaking children with SLI distinguish between finite and nonfinite verbs in terms of verb movement, as proved by their adherence to the form-position correlation revealed in contingency table 11.1 (see also section 4.2.3.2). (Table 11.2 reports data from the LM control group.) Recall that finite verbs in German must move to second position in the clause (i.e., the head of CP), while infinitives remain in clause-final position. As table 11.1 shows, German-speaking children with SLI almost always raise finite

Table 11.1
Finiteness versus verb placement in the speech of 8 German-speaking children
with specific language impairment (age range 4;0–4;8)

	+Finite	−Finite
V2	239	2
V-final	9	72

Source: Data from Rice, Noll, and Grimm 1997
$\chi^2 = 265.59$, $p < .005$

Table 11.2
Finiteness versus verb placement in the speech of 8 language-matched German-
speaking children without specific language impairment (age range 2;1–2;7)

	+Finite	−Finite
V2	604	11
V-final	22	37

Source: Data from Rice, Noll, and Grimm 1997
$\chi^2 = 302.09$, $p < .005$

verbs to C (V2) and leave the nonfinite verb in final position (V-final).
Comparison of tables 11.1 and 11.2 shows that these children in fact perform as well as the LM control group.

The weakness of children with SLI in marking tense contrasts with their
strength in other areas of inflectional morphology, as predicted in (6b).
English-speaking children with SLI are as accurate as AM peers and LM
children in their use of the affix *-ing* (as in *eating*), the prepositions *in/on*,
and the plural marker *-s*, which is homophonous with the third person
singular present marker (see figure 11.2). Their level of accuracy on this
set of morphemes, around 90% or above, is far superior to their level
of accuracy on the morphemes marking tense (cf. figure 11.1; see also
Oetting and Rice 1993). It is evident from figure 11.2 that children with
SLI display the same level of accuracy as LM and AM children. For
plural morphology there is also evidence that children with SLI control
the rule for pluralization, as they regularize irregular plurals; for example,
they say *foots*, *mans* rather than *feet*, *men*. Such productions cannot be the
result of rote learning, for these forms do not exist in the target language,
but arise through overapplication of the internalized rule for forming
plurals (see Oetting and Rice 1993).[5]

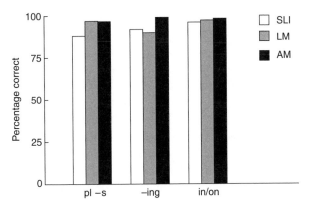

Figure 11.2
Percentage of correct use of the following morphemes in obligatory contexts (linguistic probes): plural -*s*, participle -*ing*, preposition *in/on*. Data from 37 American English–speaking children with specific language impairment (SLI) (age range 4;4–5;8), from 45 language-matched (LM) controls, and from 40 age-matched (AM) controls. Based on data from Rice and Wexler 1996, table 3.

In sum, SLI can be characterized as an extended period of use of OIs, that is, a delay in the acquisition of a specific property: the requirement that tense be obligatorily marked in main clauses. Therefore, children with SLI are poor at using tense morphemes; but whenever they do employ these morphemes, they respect the syntactic processes associated with them (e.g., verb raising, as shown by German-speaking children with SLI; see table 11.1). Furthermore, children with SLI display full control of inflectional morphemes not related to tense, and an intact mechanism for forming rules, witness their command of the rule for forming plural.

Data conflicting with those discussed so far are reported by Leonard et al. (1992). These authors found that English-speaking children with SLI perform less accurately than LM controls on tests involving the plural marker. Thus, the performance of these children is at odds with the predictions in (6b). The conflict may arise because the population studied by Leonard et al. and the one studied by Rice and Wexler (1996) have different deficits. However, an alternative explanation is also possible. Leonard et al. report that the mean for the correct use of the plural marker is 68.6% and the standard deviation (SD) is 34%. These measures (of the central tendency and the dispersion, respectively) do not give much information about the real distribution of the sample. Since the values given by Leonard et al. are percentages, their distribution is likely to be skewed; and given the high value of the SD, a bimodal distribution can be conjectured. In other words, it is possible that there are two groups of children: ones who perform very accurately, like the children studied by Rice and Wexler (1996), and ones who perform very inaccurately.[6]

In section 5.2.2 we saw that when normally developing children produce OIs, they also omit subjects. It would be interesting to know whether this co-occurrence holds for children with SLI as well. If they have the same grammatical competence as normally developing children in the OI stage, we would expect them also to omit subjects, and subject omission and use of OIs should display a similar developmental trend. If children with SLI do not omit subjects (or do not do so in the same manner as normally developing children), we may suspect that the grammatical production of children with SLI is only superficially like that of normally developing 2- to 3-year-olds. These are hypotheses that future research will have to take up.

11.2.1.2 Specific Language Impairment as a Deficit in Establishing Agreement Relations   Clahsen and collaborators claim that SLI is a deficit of the ability to mark agreement in an otherwise intact grammar (see Clahsen 1986, 1991; Rothweiler and Clahsen 1993; Clahsen, Bartke, and Göllner 1997). Agreement markers encode a relation between I, the head carrying the inflectional feature associated with the verb, and a subject in the specifier of I. Thus, a deficit in marking agreement is a deficit in computing the subject **agreement relation** (see section 4.3). This hypothesis predicts that

(7) a. children with SLI have trouble with agreement morphemes, and
   b. children with SLI do not have trouble with other inflectional morphemes.

Indeed, the German-speaking children with SLI studied by Rothweiler and Clahsen (1993) (age range 5;8–7;11) have good control of plural and past participle morphology. They are proficient in using tense morphemes, but not agreement morphemes. Clahsen, Bartke, and Göllner (1997) report (see their table 4) that tense is accurately expressed 99% of the time on lexical verbs and 100% of the time on the verb SEIN (= BE). By contrast, agreement is correctly expressed only 67% of the time on lexical verbs and 93% of the time on the verb SEIN. While the difference between use of tense morphemes and use of agreement morphemes is statistically significant in the case of lexical verbs, it is not in the case of the verb SEIN, however. This discrepancy is surprising and raises the question of why the deficit in computing agreement is not evident with all kinds of verbs. One factor that may be responsible is that SEIN is an irregular verb whose paradigm may be learned by rote.

The error rate in the use of agreement morphemes on lexical verbs may be somewhat inflated, since some of the agreement morphemes are ambiguous. Specifically, -*n* marks the first and third persons plural and the infinitive; the 0 morpheme marks the first person singular and the verbal root. If one discards verbs inflected with these two morphemes, the overall error rate in the use of agreement morphemes decreases, but it is still 26%. While agreement errors are not abundant, the rate of such errors does vary from one morpheme to another: second person singular -*st* is used correctly 87% of the time; third person singular and second person plural -*t* (which are homophonous) together are used correctly 85% of the time; and first person singular -*e* is used correctly just 38% of the time. Thus, certain finite verbs are used incorrectly—and this is at odds with Rice and Wexler's (1996) expectation that when children with SLI use finite verbs, they use them correctly.

In the same study Clahsen, Bartke, and Göllner (1997) show that English-speaking children with SLI use the past tense marker much more accurately than the third person agreement marker (which marks agreement as well as present tense). Recall that on lexical verbs agreement is expressed only in third person contexts in English. The children used tense markers correctly 77% of the time and agreement markers 44% of the time. Similarly, out of 20 third person auxiliaries, only 7 (35%) were correctly inflected for agreement, but out of 154 auxiliaries, 137 (89%) were correctly inflected for past tense, a difference that is statistically significant ($\chi^2 = 36.12$, $p < .005$). Further evidence of a deficit with agreement markers is provided by Tsimpli and Stavrakaki (1999). These researchers studied the production of a 5;5-year-old Greek-speaking child with SLI. (Greek is a language with a rich agreement system and a six-way distinction in person.) This child used agreement markers incorrectly 33% of the time. This error rate is principally due to the second person singular and second person plural agreement markers, which displayed error rates of 78% and 97%, respectively. The other agreement morphemes were used correctly about 90% of the time.

Contrasting findings come from another language with a rich morphological agreement system, Italian. Cipriani, Bottari, and Chilosi (1998) recorded the production of an Italian-speaking child with SLI from age 6;2 to age 13;5. By age 6;2 this child used the first, second, and third person singular and third person plural agreement morphemes correctly. During the whole period of investigation the rate of agreement errors was about 3%. It is not known whether younger Italian-speaking children with SLI are less proficient in the use of verbal agreement. In any event, it is clear that the child studied by Cipriani, Bottari, and Chilosi, who is diagnosed as having SLI, does not have problems with computing the subject agreement relation.

11.2.1.3 Specific Language Impairment as a Representational Deficit for Structure-Dependent Relations Van der Lely and collaborators have carried out extensive investigations of the grammatical knowledge of a group of English learners with SLI (van der Lely and Stollwerck 1997; van der Lely 1997). Unlike the previously mentioned researchers, van der Lely has turned her attention to various aspects of language comprehension by children with SLI. She claims that SLI consists in a deficit with **structure-dependent relations** (van der Lely and Stollwerck 1997, 248). One example is the subject agreement relationship discussed in the previous section. Another is the relation involved in binding (see chapter 8). Recall that the binding principles govern the syntactic relations between reflexives and pronouns and their antecedents. Reflexives must be bound in some local domain, while pronouns must be free in the same local domain (but see chapter 8, note 3).

Van der Lely and Stollwerck show that children with SLI demonstrate a limited ability in applying Principles A and B of the binding theory and attribute this to difficulties in computing the local domain and in finding the proper c-commanding antecedent of a (reflexive) pronoun (see also Franks and Connell 1996).

Children with SLI (age range 9;3–12;10) were tested in comprehension experiments in which they were required to judge whether a sentence that they heard matched (match condition) or did not match (mismatch condition) a displayed picture. These children scored close to 100% when sentences contained a reflexive; that is, they judged the sentence in (8) as an accurate description of a picture in which Mowgli was tickling himself (match condition), but not of a picture in which Mowgli was tickling Baloo Bear (mismatch condition).

(8) Mowgli is tickling himself.

Table 11.3
Summary of experimental conditions used in the test for pronominal reference (reflexive pronouns)

Test sentence	Condition	Picture	Children's response
Mowgli is tickling himself.	Match	Mowgli tickles himself	Correct (yes)
	Mismatch	Mowgli tickles Baloo Bear	Correct (no)
Baloo Bear says Mowgli is tickling himself.	Match	Mowgli tickles himself	Correct (yes)
	Mismatch	Mowgli tickles Baloo Bear	Correct (no)
	Mismatch	Baloo Bear tickles himself	Chance

Source: Data from van der Lely and Stollwerck 1997

However, responses were less accurate when the children were tested with complex sentences, such as (9).

(9) Baloo Bear says Mowgli is tickling himself.

In the match condition they correctly judged the sentence in (9) as an accurate description of a picture in which Mowgli was tickling himself. In the mismatch condition they performed less accurately, but significantly above chance; they rejected (9) as a description of a picture portraying Mowgli tickling Baloo Bear. Interestingly, in another mismatch condition, in which (9) was paired with a picture displaying Baloo Bear tickling himself, children with SLI performed at chance level; that is, they did not obey Principle A. The results for the two sentences in (8) and (9) are summarized in table 11.3.

What is the source of the response to (9) in the second mismatch condition? Van der Lely and Stollwerck argue that children with SLI cannot compute the binding domain and answer by relying not on binding knowledge, but on knowledge of the lexical properties of reflexives. For example, one can conjecture that children with SLI could take the lexical cue expressed by *-self* as an indication that a self-oriented action is to be expected, a strategy discussed in section 8.2.1 (see Grimshaw and Rosen 1990). Then, they could choose the antecedent by looking at the grammatical gender of the pronoun attached to *-self*. This strategy suffices to succeed in pairing a simple sentence like (8) with a picture of Mowgli tickling himself and in rejecting the same sentence as a description of a picture of Mowgli tickling Baloo Bear. It also suffices to succeed in pairing (9) with a picture of Mowgli tickling himself and in rejecting it as a description of a picture of Mowgli tickling Baloo Bear. However, it cannot help children with SLI when lexical cues are not unequivocally interpretable, as when (9) is used in a situation in which Baloo Bear is tickling himself. In this case these children perform at chance level. From the presence of *himself*, they infer that a reflexive action involving a male individual is to be found. However, there are two potential antecedents, *Baloo Bear* and *Mowgli*, and this is likely to confound them.

Reliance on lexical properties might also help children with SLI to interpret sentences including pronouns. These children accept sentence (10) when paired with the picture (match condition) displaying Mowgli tickling Baloo Bear.

(10) Mowgli is tickling him.

However, they perform at chance level (64% rejections) when the same sentence is paired with a picture depicting Mowgli tickling himself (mismatch condition). In so doing, these children take the pronoun to be anaphorically linked to the local antecedent. Table 11.4 summarizes these results.

With complex sentences we observe a similar pattern of responses. Children with SLI correctly accept sentence (11) when it is paired with a picture displaying Mowgli tickling Baloo Bear, but they perform at chance level when the same sentence is paired with a picture displaying Mowgli tickling himself. Table 11.5 summarizes these results.

(11) Baloo Bear says that Mowgli is tickling him.

Table 11.4
Summary of experimental conditions used in the test for pronominal reference (nonreflexive pronouns)

Test sentence	Condition	Picture	Children's response
Mowgli is tickling him.	Match	Mowgli tickles Baloo Bear	Correct (yes)
	Mismatch	Mowgli tickles himself	Chance

Source: Data from van der Lely and Stollwerck 1997

Interestingly, the performance of children with SLI improves when they can use gender or other cues to work out the interpretation of the pronoun. While these children rejected (10) at chance level (64% rejection) when presented with a picture portraying Mowgli tickling himself, they rejected (12) 94% of the time when they were shown the same picture.

(12) Mowgli is tickling her.

This response indicates that children with SLI take *Mowgli*, the name of a boy, as an unsuitable antecedent for the feminine pronoun *her*.

Although it is likely that children with SLI exploit lexical and morphological cues to interpret sentences including reflexive and nonreflexive pronouns, the available data do not warrant the conclusion that such children have no knowledge of binding, as van der Lely and Stollwerck (1997) claim. In all the match conditions children with SLI obtain very high scores; for example, they perform fairly well when the sentences including pronouns, (10) and (11), are presented in the context of a picture depicting Mowgli tickling Baloo Bear. It is not clear what kind of lexical and morphological knowledge guarantees this high performance. It seems that it is knowledge that a pronoun must be free in the local domain that helps children in discarding a local antecedent of the pronoun. One might object that children respond accurately in the match conditions because they take nonreflexive pronouns as an indication that a nonreflexive action is to be expected; their expectations are thus fulfilled when the sentences in (10) and (11) are paired with pictures displaying Mowgli tickling Baloo Bear. If this objection were sound, children with SLI should perform accurately in the mismatch condition, as well. They should reject (10) and (11) as descriptions of a picture displaying Mowgli tickling himself, because a reflexive action is displayed. Similarly, the data

Table 11.5
Summary of experimental conditions used in the test for pronominal reference (nonreflexive pronouns)

Test sentence	Condition	Picture	Children's response
Baloo Bear says that Mowgli is tickling him.	Match	Mowgli tickles Baloo Bear	Correct (yes)
	Mismatch	Mowgli tickles himself	Chance

Source: Data from van der Lely and Stollwerck 1997

gathered in van der Lely and Stollwerck's experiment do not warrant the conclusion that children cannot compute the c-command relation, a structure-dependent relation. One piece of data that would inform us about this is represented by sentences like (13).

(13) Mowgli's brother is tickling himself.

Here the c-commanding antecedent of the reflexive pronoun is *Mowgli's brother*, not *Mowgli* (which is too deeply embedded). If children with SLI accepted (13) as a description of a situation in which Mowgli is tickling himself, then we would be entitled to say that they cannot compute the c-command relation.

Note that 9- to 12-year-old children with SLI manifest a behavior that resembles that of 4- to 5-year-old normally developing children in dealing with nonreflexive pronouns (section 8.3.1). Recall that normally developing children accept an anaphoric reading of the pronoun in (10) and (11), taking *him* to be anaphorically linked to the NP *Mowgli*. But these same children do not accept an anaphoric reading when the possible local antecedent of the pronoun is a quantifier, as in (14).

(14) Every bear washes him.

This asymmetry between referential and quantified NPs was crucial for distinguishing between knowledge of binding and knowledge of coreference and for establishing that children's errors are errors of coreference. While a quantifier and a pronoun can enter an anaphoric relation only via binding, a referential expression and a pronoun can enter an anaphoric relation either via binding or via coreference. Normally developing children reject an anaphoric interpretation of the pronoun in (14), because they tacitly know Principle B. Although Principle B rules out a binding relation in (10), children may still interpret the unbound pronoun *him* as coreferential with *Mowgli*.

If children with SLI have knowledge of the binding principles, they should behave like normally developing children when asked to judge sentences like (14). Van der Lely and Stollwerck included this kind of sentence in their battery of tests, but the results they obtained are difficult to interpret. Children with SLI did not perform very well. Although this might suggest that they do not have knowledge of binding, results on control structures show that children with SLI have difficulty in interpreting quantifiers. Thus, their responses to quantified sentences including pronouns cannot reliably give evidence about their knowledge of binding.

In sum, on the one hand, children with SLI seem to rely heavily on lexical and morphological knowledge to work out the interpretation of pronouns and reflexives. On the other hand, it is not clear that their errors can be attributed to a lack of binding knowledge—specifically, to an inability to compute the local c-command domain.

Van der Lely and Stollwerck (1997) argue that children with SLI have difficulties with structure-dependent representations. Although some findings appear to show that this is correct (recall, e.g., that children with SLI find it hard to perform agreement), this claim might be too strong. Most linguistic knowledge is couched in structure-dependent terms. A deficit in building structure-dependent representations might have much more widespread consequences than those generally observed in studies on SLI. For example, it would prevent individuals with SLI from moving verbs in a hierarchical representation. As a consequence, we would expect finite and nonfinite verbs to have the same distribution in the speech of children with SLI, contrary to the findings discussed in section 11.2.1.1.

11.2.1.4 Specific Language Impairment as a Grammar Lacking Grammatical Inflectional Features   According to yet another account, SLI is a disorder that affects the ability to construct a normal grammar. Gopnik and collaborators (see Gopnik 1990a,b; Gopnik and Crago 1991; Gopnik and Goad 1997) have studied the linguistic behavior of individuals with SLI in the use of inflectional morphology in several languages: Canadian and British English, Greek, Japanese, and Quebec French. They presented various tasks, administered in oral and written form, testing both comprehension and production (spontaneous and elicited). The results show that individuals with SLI display the same difficulties in handling inflectional morphology across all tasks and across all languages investigated. Previously Gopnik and collaborators claimed that the linguistic representations of children with SLI do not include the inflectional features [±past], [±plural]. More recently they have slightly modified this hypothesis and now maintain that children with SLI cannot construct implicit rules governing morphological and phonological processes in grammar (Gopnik et al. 1997). Normally developing children can abstract rules from the language input to build inflectional paradigms and establish agreement relations among elements of a phrase. By contrast, children with SLI do not see the internal structure of inflected words and are not able to build implicit rules for handling inflectional morphology. For them *walks*, *walked*, *houses* are not derived by a rule that assembles stems and inflectional morphemes, but are rote learned as independent lexical items and stored in the lexicon as unanalyzed chunks.

If children with SLI do not have rules for inflecting verbs or nouns, how is it that they sometimes are able to produce correct inflected forms? According to Gopnik, although they do not have rules for inflecting words, they have access to compensatory mechanisms that simulate aspects of the normal language function. They can learn and memorize forms, as they learn and memorize any word, that is, as an unanalyzed chunk; they can learn explicit rules during rehabilitation (e.g., that a plural form is obtained by adding *-s* to a noun) or rely on analogy. This hypothesis predicts that the speech of individuals with SLI should exhibit

(15) a. frequency effects for regular and irregular words,
   b. difficulties with the inflection of novel words,
   c. incorrect segmental and prosodic features of inflected words.

According to the **word-and-rule theory** (see Pinker and Prince 1988; Pinker 1994b; Clahsen et al. 1992 for discussion of a model for learning inflectional morphology; section 1.5.3), there are two processes for producing inflected words depending on whether they are regular or irregular. Regular inflections are based on a productive mental operation that takes members of syntactic categories as input (e.g., verbs) and generates inflected words; for example, regular past tense inflection in English is obtained by an operation of affixation, which adds *-ed* to a verb stem. Regular inflection is extended to novel items. By contrast, inflected forms of irregular verbs cannot be easily predicted from their corresponding base form; they must be learned by rote and stored in long-term memory as unanalyzed wholes together with other lexical items.

In individuals without SLI the retrieval of irregular words is subject to frequency effects, more frequent forms being retrieved more rapidly than less frequent ones. Since individuals with SLI treat all inflected words in the same way (i.e., as irregular words), their speech should exhibit frequency effects not only for irregular forms but also for regular ones (15a). And indeed this is what has been found (see Gopnik et al. 1997). The more frequent a past tense form was, the greater the likelihood that individuals with SLI would use it, whether it was a regular or an irregular form. The fact that regular forms also exhibit frequency effects in the speech of individuals with SLI supports the idea that they are processing

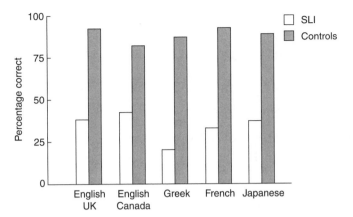

Figure 11.3
Percentage of correct past tense morphemes on novel words in the speech of individuals with specific language impairment (SLI), across languages. Based on data from Gopnik and Goad 1997.

them as irregular forms. For example, *walked* may be stored as an unanalyzed word lacking the grammatical specification of [+past], but including in its meaning the notion of "pastness."

If individuals with SLI do not have access to the morphological rules that introduce inflectional features, then they should be unable to inflect words they have not heard before, as anticipated in (15b). Indeed, Gopnik and Goad (1997) found that individuals with SLI are worse than individuals without SLI at inflecting novel words for past tense or for plural, an indication that their linguistic behavior is not rule-governed. Figures 11.3 and 11.4 show the percentage of correct past tense and plural forms, respectively, in individuals with and without SLI across different languages.

As noted earlier, individuals with SLI produce correctly inflected words (between 30% and 50%), but these are derived by means of compensatory strategies, according to Gopnik (see, e.g., Gopnik and Goad 1997). A closer inspection of the plural forms produced by these individuals reveals that only a small number have the segmental and prosodic shape of plurals of actual English words. In most cases the sound of the plural marker (or of other inflectional markers, when these are being tested) is not correct, as predicted in (15c). When asked to form the plural of [wʌg], individuals with SLI say [wʌgs] rather than [wʌgz], omitting the required voicing assimilation between the stem-final voiced consonant /g/ and the plural marker /s/. In other cases these individuals search their mental lexicon

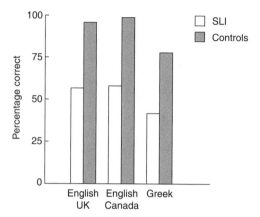

Figure 11.4
Percentage of correct plural morphemes on novel words in the speech of individuals with specific language impairment (SLI), across languages. Based on data from Gopnik and Goad 1997.

for words phonetically close to the target word and ending in a sibilant (/s/-like) sound, regardless of whether this sound encodes plurality. For example, they provide [brɑnz] (*bronze*) as the plural of the novel word [brɑm]. This happens because these individuals have learned, as an explicit rule, that plural is marked by a word-final *s*. Normally developing children unconsciously know that the plural morpheme has three allophonic variations: a voiceless sibilant, [s]; a voiced sibilant, [z]; and an epenthetic vowel plus [z], [ɨz]. These are added to nouns depending on phonological characteristics of their final sound: for example, *cat*[*s*], *dog*[*z*], and *glass*[*ɨz*]. When normally developing children have to pluralize a noun, they choose the correct allophone. By contrast, children with SLI do not, because they have not internalized the rule for forming the plural. Instead, they use a memorized rule or similarity between the target form and a form present in their mental lexicon. Therefore, often the seemingly correct inflected words that they produce are not correct at all.

The frequency effect in the production of regular inflected words, the failure to inflect novel words correctly, and the production of inflected forms that are segmentally and prosodically incorrect indicate that children with SLI do not approach the language-learning task like children without SLI; in particular, they cannot abstract rules for constructing morphological paradigms, instead compensating through other devices. Gopnik and collaborators' results also support the distinction between a rule-based system for learning regular inflection and a lexically based system for learning irregular inflection, as the word-and-rule theory proposes.

The characterization of SLI offered by Gopnik and collaborators may not be valid for all subjects diagnosed as having SLI, a fact that may depend on the previously noted heterogeneity of the SLI population. Clahsen et al. (1992) and Rice and Oetting (1993) have found that some populations with SLI process regular and irregular items in distinct ways.

11.2.2   Specific Language Impairment as a Processing Deficit: The Surface Hypothesis

If children with SLI have problems with functional morphemes, it might be that these morphemes have a special property that makes them especially hard to produce or comprehend. According to the **surface hypothesis** (Leonard et al. 1992), functional morphemes (in English the past tense, third person singular present, and plural markers, etc.) are particularly vulnerable because they are phonologically nonsalient owing to certain acoustic properties. Children with SLI have difficulty processing morphemes that are shorter in duration than adjacent morphemes (see, e.g., Leonard 1998; see also, e.g., Tallal 1976). They have trouble with morphemes that

(16) a. lack stress (e.g., the article *the*, the final inflectional ending in *kisses*),
   b. are nonsyllabic (final *-s* as in *speaks*),
   c. are subject to deletion in production,
   d. do not occur in final position (a position where elements may be subject to lengthening effects).

Why is short duration or lack of salience problematic for children with SLI? According to Leonard (1998), it is not the duration per se of functional morphemes that is at the heart of children's difficulties, but the fact that the perception of nonsalient morphemes exhausts the processing resources available to these children. In so doing, it prevents them from identifying the grammatical function of these morphemes and from placing them in a morphological paradigm. In short, children with SLI have difficulties in handling inflections because they cannot process the inflections' function.

As support for this proposal Leonard et al. (1987), Rom and Leonard (1990), and Leonard et al. (1992) gathered evidence from English-, Italian-, and Hebrew-speaking children with SLI. English learners with SLI omit a range of grammatical morphemes (e.g., the plural marker, the past tense marker, the copula, and articles), because these are nonsalient. By contrast, Italian and Hebrew learners with SLI use grammatical morphemes—the inflections on verbs and nouns—as accurately as their counterparts without SLI, because these are salient (they are final and syllabic). Because of their salience, Italian grammatical morphemes are not difficult to perceive, and thus the processing resources of children with SLI suffice to incorporate these morphemes into a morphological paradigm. Like their English-speaking counterparts, Italian-speaking children with SLI omit articles. According to Leonard and collaborators, this happens because Italian articles are considered nonsalient since they occur in a position where they cannot receive stress.

However, investigation of the speech of Italian- and French-speaking children with SLI reveals an interesting asymmetry. In Italian and French, articles and clitic pronouns are homophonous. Now, if salience were responsible for the accurate use of functional morphemes, we would expect children with SLI to be equally weak in the use of articles and of clitic pronouns. This seems to be the case in Leonard et al.'s (1992) study, although they do report a small advantage for articles over clitics. But this is not confirmed in other studies, in which clitics and articles are differently affected. Jakubowicz et al. (1998) found a significant advantage for articles over clitics in the speech of French learners with SLI. According to Bottari et al. (1998), a dissociation between articles and clitics is manifested in the speech of Italian learners with SLI, but unlike in the French case, the production of articles is more affected than the production of clitics. Why such a discrepancy is found is not clear, but one thing is certain: salience cannot be the relevant factor, since articles and clitics have the same phonological status in both French and Italian. The same point can be made on the basis of data discussed by Rice and collaborators. Recall (section 11.2.1.1) that the children with SLI studied by these researchers have trouble with the -s morpheme when it marks third person on verbs, but not when it marks plural on nouns (see figures 11.1 and 11.2). Salience cannot be responsible for this difference since these morphemes are homophonous. This observation carries over to another troublesome aspect of the production of children with SLI. Besides omitting functional morphemes, English learners with SLI may use accusative pronouns as subjects in place of nominative ones, as illustrated in (17) (examples from Wexler, Schütze, and Rice 1998; for evidence that this phenomenon characterizes normal development as well, see Loeb and Leonard 1991; Rispoli 1994; Schütze 1997).

(17) a. Him stand on chairs.
      b. Her watching TV.

The relative salience of nominative and accusative pronouns can hardly be invoked to explain this kind of error, as their salience does not appear to differ.

A final problem for the surface hypothesis is this. According to this hypothesis, children with SLI differ from normally developing children in that they have a perceptual deficit that makes them weak in the use of functional morphemes. But note that in Leonard et al.'s (1992) study, normally developing English-speaking children (LM controls) perform as badly as children with SLI in the use of articles, but not in the use of other functional morphemes. This is unexpected. How could we explain the poor performance of normally developing children in the use of articles? Is it also due to processing limitations, or does it have another cause? Why do normally developing children in control groups perform better than children with SLI when tested on a range of functional morphemes, but the same as children with SLI when tested on articles?

11.2.3   Intermediate Summary

It is evident that researchers hold diverging views about SLI. For some it is a modular deficit affecting some aspects of the grammatical competence; for others it is a processing limitation. We have evaluated different proposals. Four of these maintain that the impairment affects the organization of the grammar. According to Rice and Wexler and collaborators, SLI is a delay that manifests itself in optional omission of the tense feature from the clausal representation and thus of the morphemes expressing it. Clahsen and collaborators see SLI as the result of an inability to compute subject agreement. Gopnik and collaborators have proposed that SLI arises because children affected by it are not able to build morphological paradigms and abstract symbolic rules from the input. Under this view these children tackle the language acquisition task differently than normally developing children. Van der Lely and collaborators have proposed that subjects with SLI cannot compute structure-dependent relations. Finally, Leonard and collaborators suggest that the grammar of subjects with SLI is intact and that the deficit results instead from an impairment in the processing system. In the next section we will look at another pathological condition: one in which language is relatively good in spite of mental retardation.

11.3   RELATIVELY INTACT LANGUAGE IN AN OTHERWISE IMPAIRED SYSTEM: WILLIAMS SYNDROME

SLI is a case of dissociation in which cognitive abilities are stronger than grammatical abilities and in which language is defective in spite of normal cognitive development. The opposite dissociation is displayed by individuals with **Williams syndrome** (WS): their linguistic ability outstrips their cognitive abilities.

11.3.1   Some Features of Williams Syndrome

Unlike the etiology of SLI, the etiology of WS, also called infantile hypercalcemia, is well understood. It is a rare metabolic disorder, affecting calcium and calcitonin metabolism (see Culler, Jones, and Deftos 1985), whose features include mental retardation, an elfin facial appearance, and several medical anomalies including supravalvular aortic stenosis and renal anomalies (see Williams et al. 1961; Beuren, Apitz, and Harmjanz 1962). Individuals with WS are described as friendly and talkative (see Bennett, La Veck, and Sells 1978). They have intellectual limitations, including difficulties with everyday tasks like tying shoelaces. Moreover, they have trouble with a number of Piagetian cognitive tasks that normally developing children master at the age of 7 or 8. For example, they are unable to put items in order from larger to smaller or higher to lower (seriation task). They do not recognize that certain properties (e.g., the quantity of a liquid) do not change as a result of perceptual transformations (conservation task), and they are weak in problem solving.[7] They are also very poor at drawing (see Bellugi et al. 1993; Bellugi et al. 1999). A striking feature of the drawings of individuals with WS is the lack of integration among the parts of an object, as shown in figure 11.5, free drawings of houses by individuals with WS. The poverty of their drawing is not due to the fact that these individuals had not noticed the parts of the house, since they label them and can explain their role. Nor is it due to a motor deficit. Bellugi and collaborators suggest that instead it results from a visuospatial deficit (see Bihrle et al. 1989).

In contrast with their weakness on nonverbal tasks, the language of individuals with WS is relatively spared, more than that of other populations with similar mental retardation, such as Down syndrome (see Bellugi, Klima, and Wang 1996; Mervis et al. 1999). Despite its late emergence, by adolescence language reaches a level that exceeds the levels reached by other cognitive skills, although it remains below chronological age levels.

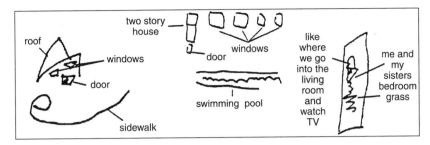

Figure 11.5
Free drawings of houses by individuals with Williams syndrome. The drawings contain many parts of houses but these are not coherently organized. Reprinted from Bellugi et al. 1999. © Dr. Ursula Bellugi, The Salk Institute for Biological Studies, La Jolla, Calif.

This discrepancy, the most outstanding feature of WS, is the source of a lively debate (see, e.g., Thal, Bates, and Bellugi 1989; Capirci, Sabbadini, and Volterra 1996; Volterra et al. 1996; Karmiloff-Smith et al. 1997; Mervis et al. 1999). Some scholars stress that the language of these individuals is not intact, even though they recognize that it is by far better than the language of other populations with mental retardation. Others see the discrepancy as evidence for the autonomy of language from other cognitive functions. They do not claim that language is intact in individuals with WS, only that it is ahead of other cognitive functions. If language were not an independent module, with its own principles of organization, this discrepancy would be unexpected. Language is a complex function, and in principle it is not surprising that individuals with WS may manifest weakness in some area of language. Moreover, as in the case of SLI, individuals with WS may display somewhat different language impairments. As in the case of children with SLI, it is desirable to obtain a precise linguistic profile of individuals with WS, to sort out what is spared and what is not spared and to understand better what kind of linguistic representation these individuals have.

11.3.2   The Language of Individuals with Williams Syndrome

In this section we will examine some aspects of the language of individuals with WS. However, since linguistically motivated investigations like the ones carried out for children with SLI are rare, the discussion of WS will be less detailed than the discussion of SLI.

11.3.2.1   The Acquisition of Words   The lexicon of children with WS is quite unusual for children of their mental age. In a study by Clahsen and Almazan (1998), children with WS (ages 11, 12, 13, 15) obtained scores above their mental age on the British Picture Vocabulary Test (Dunn et al. 1982). However, children with WS enjoy using low-frequency words and know their meaning very well. For example, the children tested by Bellugi et al. (1993) (ages 11, 13, 16) could match the words *canine*, *archaeologist*, and *cornea* with the correct picture by choosing among four pictures (see also Volterra et al. 1996 for similarity between individuals with and without WS in lexical comprehension). They could explain what a word means using long definitions and many examples; they knew how to use the words, for they gave appropriate contexts; however, their definitions were peculiar in that they did not use the most salient feature to explain the word meaning. Examples from Bellugi et al. 1993 are shown in (18) and (19).

(18)   a.   "*Sad* is when someone dies; someone is hurt, like when you cry."

     b.   "[*Sad* is] when you lost somebody that you love and care about. It means something happens to you like your grandmother died . . ."

(19)   a.   "I wish I could *surrender*. That means I give up."

     b.   "I would like to *commentate* it. It means that . . . like all the sportscasters do . . . they tell who's doing what."

11.3.2.2   Inflectional Morphology   Unlike children with SLI, children with WS accurately use a number of inflectional morphemes. Even though they start speaking late, children with WS are more accurate than children with SLI in the use of inflectional morphology, as shown by Clahsen and Almazan (1998) and Rice (1999). As we have seen, English-speaking children with SLI have difficulty marking tense (see section 11.2.2.1). They frequently omit the third person singular marker -*s*, the past tense marker -*ed*, and the copula. By contrast, children with WS do not display such selective difficulty. Table 11.6 compares the performance of children with SLI, children with WS, and two groups of normally developing children. Children with SLI, children with WS, and language-matched (LM) children are at the same MLU level. Intelligence testing shows that the children with SLI and the two control groups are within

Table 11.6
Performance of children with specific language impairment (SLI), children with Williams syndrome (WS), and unaffected children (language matched (LM) and age matched (AM)) in the use of inflectional morphemes in English (-*s*, -*ed*, BE)

	SLI	LM	AM	WS
MLU	3.58	3.57	4.53	3.35
Intelligence testing	96	109	106	60
Age (in months)	58	36	60	91
-*s*	35%	61%	88%	83%
-*ed*	22%	48%	92%	85%
BE	47%	70%	96%	91%

Source: Rice 1999

normal range of cognitive performance, while the children with WS show an intellectual deficit. Children with WS are older than children in the other three groups. Yet their performance on morphemes marking tense is more accurate than that of children with SLI and of LM children; in fact, they achieve adult accuracy, despite their lower cognitive abilities. "The conclusion is that children with Williams syndrome know that tense-marking is obligatory at a time when their language development is comparable to that of children with specific language impairment who do not know that tense marking is obligatory" (Rice 1999, 348). Similar results are reported by Clahsen and Almazan (1998). These researchers elicited past tense forms of regular and irregular verbs from individuals with WS. They showed that these individuals have no trouble with inflecting regular existing and nonce verbs, while matched individuals with SLI (from the study reported in van der Lely and Ullman 1996) achieved lower scores. However, production of irregular past tense forms by individuals with WS was quite poor; moreover, they displayed a marked disposition to overgeneralize -*ed* to irregular verbs. Interestingly, errors of tense affixation by individuals with SLI consist in omitting the tense affix with all verbs, thus producing bare stems, while errors by individuals with WS consist in overgeneralization of the regular inflection.

Therefore, in terms of the word-and-rule theory mentioned in section 11.2.1.4, the dissociation displayed by individuals with WS is the opposite of that displayed by the individuals with SLI studied by Gopnik and collaborators: while regular inflection is spared, irregular inflection is impaired.

Other studies report that children with WS make unusual morpho-syntactic errors, but these are often found when the children are tested in very demanding situations—for example, in describing stories, which requires a logical sequencing of events (see Capirci, Sabbadini, and Volterra 1996). We cannot discard the hypothesis that individuals with WS are less accurate when the task is more difficult and demands the application and coordination of various skills. Obviously, testing individuals with WS in different experimental conditions is of interest and may better highlight their linguistic profile.

11.3.2.3 Syntactic Structures   By recording spontaneous speech samples and administering several linguistic tests, Bellugi et al. (1993) determined that children with WS display good comprehension and production of complex structures, such as reversible passives, conditionals, relative clauses, and comparatives. Some spontaneous sentences produced by three children with WS, from Bellugi et al. 1993, are given in (20).

(20) a. The dog was chased by the bees. (Crystal)
　　 b. Maybe you could ask your son if I could have one of your posters. (Van)
　　 c. After it stopped hurting, I was told I could go to school again and do whatever I feel like doing. (Ben)

Clahsen and Almazan (1998) show that individuals with WS perform at ceiling level on all kinds of passives: reversible verbal passives, as in (21a); short verbal passives, as in (21b); and adjectival passives, as in (21c).

(21) a. The teddy is mended by the girl.
　　 b. The teddy is being mended.
　　 c. The teddy is mended.

By contrast, children with SLI whose chronological age was similar to the mental age of children with WS performed poorly on reversible verbal passives (with and without a *by*-phrase) and at ceiling level on adjectival passives (see section 7.1). Unaffected controls also made some errors (19%) on full verbal passives.

Children with WS performed at ceiling level in another task devised to assess knowledge of Principles A and B of the binding theory (see sections 8.3 and 8.4). They accepted sentence (22a) when it was paired with a picture in which Mowgli was tickling himself and rejected the same sentence when it was paired with a picture in which Mowgli was tickling someone else, say, Baloo Bear. They accepted (22b) as a description of a picture in which Mowgli was tickling Baloo Bear, but rejected it as a description of a picture in which Mowgli was tickling himself. They performed equally well when the potential antecedent was a quantifier, as in (22c,d), rather than a referential expression.

(22) a. Mowgli is tickling himself.
     b. Mowgli is tickling him.
     c. Every boy is tickling himself.
     d. Every boy is tickling him.

By contrast, we have seen (section 11.2.1.3) that children with SLI are poor at rejecting sentence (22b) when shown a picture displaying Mowgli ticking himself. They also obtained low scores with sentences like (22c,d). Thus, children with WS perform better than children with SLI on sentences probing knowledge of binding. Moreover, they obtained higher scores than children without WS matched in mental age.

The evidence examined here indicates that at least some syntactic aspects of the language spoken by children with WS are spared and that their language may even be superior in those respects to the language of populations with linguistic impairments, such as children with SLI. Superior performance with passives shows that children with WS can handle movement operations. High scores on sentences including reflexive and nonreflexive pronouns indicate that these children have some knowledge of the binding principles. More evidence is necessary to establish exactly which pieces of knowledge are available and which are not.

11.4 SUMMARY AND CONCLUDING REMARKS

We have discussed two pathological conditions: specific language impairment (SLI) and Williams syndrome (WS). SLI is a disorder affecting language, but leaving other cognitive capacities intact. Researchers have advanced a wide variety of hypotheses about the nature of SLI. The existence of these widely varying perspectives might have its source, at least in part, in the nonhomogeneity of the population being diagnosed as having SLI. Individuals with SLI are selected for studies on the basis of different language tests; their ages vary considerably (e.g., between 3;1 and 6;0 in Leonard et al. 1992; between 4;4 and 5;8 in the work of Rice, Wexler, and collaborators (see Rice and Wexler 1996); between 5;8 and 7;11 in Clahsen, Bartke, and Göllner 1997; and between 9;3 and 12;10 in van der Lely and

Stollwerck 1997). It would not be surprising that the language of these children grows, as does the language of children without SLI, and that the manifestation of the deficit changes, something that only longitudinal studies can determine. It is also possible that SLI encompasses a range of language pathologies that, it is to be hoped, can be characterized with the tools of linguistic and psycholinguistic theories. Despite all these differences, one point is agreed upon: that children with SLI have normal intellectual development. This fact is evidence for the autonomy of the language module, whose disorders are independent from the functioning of other cognitive capacities.

Children with WS present the opposite dissociation, with language outstripping other cognitive capacities. These children have an unusual cognitive profile: they are mentally retarded, yet their language is relatively well preserved compared with other cognitive functions. Thus, the WS population shows that some aspects of language may develop in spite of weakness in other cognitive domains. There is some evidence that not all aspects of language are equally preserved. While regular inflectional affixation is spared, irregular affixation is not. According to Clahsen and Almazan (1998), this suggests that (contrary to Karmiloff-Smith et al.'s (1997) claims), children with WS are good at "system building." Their problem is with irregular verbs, which are assumed to be learned by rote and stored in memory. Notice that the double dissociation between regular and irregular verbs observed with children with WS and SLI supports the view that the systems that subserve their processing must be distinct, contrary to what connectionist models would hold (see section 1.5.3). Clahsen and Almazan suggest that the computational system that supports syntactic processing is well preserved, while the associative memory system that supports irregular inflections is not.

Children with WS and SLI provide evidence for a dissociation between language and other cognitive functions, indicating that language is not the manifestation of a general cognitive capacity, but the expression of a separate module, with principles of organization not shared by other cognitive functions. Although this claim is much debated, it is undeniable that the speech of individuals with WS is not as damaged as their other cognitive skills, a fact that per se deserves explanation. How intact the language of individuals with WS is may vary from person to person; some researchers point out within-domain dissociations (e.g., Karmiloff-Smith et al. (1997) show that French-speaking individuals with WS have trouble with gender). It is certainly desirable to obtain more evidence about these dissociations and understand which process subserves a given linguistic phenomenon, as Clahsen and Almazan's study shows. It is also desirable to carefully investigate the weaknesses and strengths of the speech of children with WS and to compare their linguistic production with that of children with SLI or with other kinds of mental retardation, such as Down syndrome (see Fowler 1988; Randall 1993). Then we would better understand the course of language development in atypical conditions and possibly gain information about normal development and more generally about the nature of language.

A final point deserves to be mentioned. Individuals are diagnosed as having SLI if they do not have other cognitive deficits. This criterion is the basis for excluding the hypothesis that some cognitive deficit is the cause for the language impairment. Notice, however, that there is no a priori reason to exclude the possibility that an individual with mental retardation also has SLI, although for this case defenders of the non-autonomy of language can claim that the mental retardation is sufficient to account for the language disorder. But logically, this is not the only explanation. Assuming that language is an autonomous module, the different linguistic performances of individuals with mental retardation plus SLI and of individuals with only SLI may be explained as follows:

If impaired subjects cannot use their normal instinct for acquiring rules of inflectional morphology and, therefore, have to resort to other cognitive skills to simulate these aspects of language, then those individuals who have better general cognitive skills should be better at, for example, applying compensatory strategies which simulate unimpaired linguistic forms. Thus, while an impairment in intelligence may not cause the language disorder, it may affect the ability of speakers to use various strategies to compensate for the deficit. (Gopnik and Goad 1997, 122–123)

Appendix A: Normal or Gaussian Distribution

The tests used to assess verbal and nonverbal skills are standardized by administering them to a sufficiently large population representative of the subjects for which the tests are prepared. As with many biological measures, the scores obtained in this kind of test form a bell-shaped curve, called the Gaussian or normal distribution. A typical curve of this type is shown in figure 11.6. This distribution can be characterized by, among other things, a central tendency and a measure of dispersion from the central tendency. A measure of the central tendency is the mean (μ), transformed into z-scores; a measure of the dispersion is the standard deviation (σ). The area under the curve between -1σ and $+1\sigma$ from the mean has a probability of 67%; that is, 67% of the population obtains a score

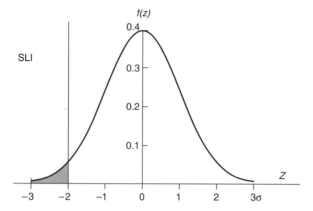

Figure 11.6
Normal or Gaussian distribution

included in the boundaries between -1σ and $+1\sigma$. The area included between -2σ and $+2\sigma$ has a probability of 97%. Thus, beyond 2σ from the mean, the probabilities are very low. The scores that are very far from the mean have a low probability. One criterion for diagnosing SLI is that the scores obtained in various language tests be lower than 22σ (or -1.5σ) from the mean (Bishop, 1977). In other words, the scores obtained must be located in the shaded area in figure 11.6.

Appendix B: Tests to Assess Specific Language Impairment

To establish whether a child has specific language impairment, one must know the average level of verbal and nonverbal performance at different ages. This information is obtained from standardized tests, which may vary from one study to the next. The nonverbal tests assess children's abilities in various tasks: for example, in completing pictures, assembling blocks, arranging pictures into a sequence to tell a story (*Wechsler Intelligence Scale for Children-Revised*, WISC-R; Wechsler 1992); in singling out an item unrelated to the others from an array of three to five, which requires the ability to formulate a rule for organizing the items (*Columbia Mental Maturity Scale*; Burgemeister, Blum, and Lorge 1972). The verbal tests assess children's speech discrimination abilities: for example, in selecting an object matching a spoken word from an array including objects whose names sound similar to the name of the target (*Goldman-Fristoe-Woodcock Test of Auditory Discrimination*; Goldman, Fristoe, and Woodcock 1970); in comprehending single words, for example by selecting a picture matching a spoken word from an array of four pictures (*Peabody Picture Vocabulary Test-Revised*, PPVT-R (US); Dunn and Dunn 1981; *British Picture Vocabulary Scale* (UK); Dunn et al. 1982); in selecting a picture from an array of four that matches a spoken sentence, a test of grammatical competence (*Test for Reception of Grammar*, TROG; Bishop 1989).

Further Reading

Bishop 1997 extensively surveys SLI and the accounts offered in the literature. Other books and collections devoted to SLI are Leonard 1998, Gopnik 1997, issue 7 of *Language Acquisition* (1998), and issue 2/3 of *Journal of Neurolinguistics* (1997).

The language of children with SLI and WS develops in unusual circumstances since the biological equipment is impaired. Regarding other unusual circumstances in which language does or does not develop normally, see Bishop and Mogford 1993.

Key Words

Agreement relation
Dissociation
Familial aggregation
Genetic basis
Specific language impairment (SLI)
Structure-dependent relations
Surface hypothesis
Tense omission model
Williams syndrome (WS)
Word-and-rule theory

Study Questions

1. What factors indicate that SLI has a genetic origin?

2. How do twin studies bear on the question of the nature of SLI?

3. What are the most salient characteristics of SLI?

4. What are the sources of differences among SLI populations?

5. Discuss the evidence in favor of and against the idea that SLI is an extension of the OI stage.

6. Discuss the idea that SLI is an impairment in computing agreement relations. Consider also the discussion in section 4.3.

7. Discuss the idea that SLI is an impairment in establishing structure-dependent relations.

8. Discuss the hypothesis that the grammar of individuals with SLI does not include grammatical features. What would the structural implications of this hypothesis be? (What kind of structural representation could an individual lacking the feature [past] have?)

9. What is the evidence for and against the surface hypothesis?

10. Why is it relevant to contrast SLI and WS?

11. Describe some salient features of WS.

Notes

Chapter 1

1. Here and throughout the book the expression *the linguistic data that children hear* refers also to the linguistic data that deaf children see.

2. Here and throughout, statements that "all children acquire language" or "all children achieve adult linguistic competence" mean that all children with normal brain function do so.

3. To say that adults or children know a given linguistic property or process means that they know it implicitly; in other words, speakers possess unconscious knowledge of grammatical properties and processes.

Chapter 2

1. Bosch and Sebastián-Gallés (1997), who tested 4-month-old babies, did not use the HAS, but a visual orientation procedure (see Dehaene-Lambertz and Houston 1998). In this procedure stimuli are randomly presented through one of two loudspeakers placed to the right and the left of the baby. Discrimination is inferred from infants' orienting behavior (i.e., their turning their gaze toward one of the loudspeakers). This technique exploits the fact that infants react faster to familiar stimuli than to unfamiliar ones. If babies hear sentences from two languages, the native language and a foreign one, they are expected to show shorter orientation latencies to the native language (a familiar language) than to the foreign language. In other words, the time difference between the delivery of the stimulus (calculated from the beginning of the utterance) and the orientation response toward one of the loudspeakers should be shorter when the stimulus is from the native language than when it is from the foreign language.

2. It is possible that newborns benefit from some prenatal experience with speech sounds. The mother's speech can reach the fetus through the uterine wall (see Querleu et al. 1988), although as a sort of filtered speech. High frequencies are greatly attenuated by the uterus, amniotic fluid, and abdominal muscles, but low frequencies, which carry most of the prosodic information, are preserved (see Armitage, Baldwin, and Vince 1980). Moreover, at around 35 weeks of gestation, the auditory system of the human fetus is mature enough to process sounds (see Busnel and Granier-Deferre 1983; Lecanuet et al. 1992; DeCasper et al. 1994).

Dehaene-Lambertz (1998) found that premature healthy babies (35–36 weeks of gestation) can discriminate two different syllables. Obviously, the facts that the fetus's auditory system is mature and that speech sounds can reach it do not guarantee that the fetus indeed processes speech, since to date the relation between the maturity of the auditory system and the ability to process speech is unclear.

3. To get an idea of what filtered speech sounds like, imagine yourself immersed in a swimming pool, hearing an unknown speaker outside. You might hear something that would allow you to recognize the language, but you would not understand what this speaker was saying.

4. (2) is a coarse representation of rhythm in that it does not include information about different levels of prominence. Not all syllables are equally prominent. Some are more prominent than others—for example, because they bear the accent of a word.

5. The voicing contrast (e.g., between [pa] and [ba]) depends on the voice onset time (VOT). When the VOT is longer than 25 ms, listeners perceive the syllable [pa], in which the consonant is voiceless; when it is shorter, they perceive the syllable [ba], in which the consonant is voiced (see Lisker and Abramson 1964).

6. Although in a natural setting adults have difficulties in discriminating nonnative sounds, with training they can learn to do it. For example, Japanese adults, who cannot discriminate /l/ and /r/ spontaneously, can be trained to do so in the laboratory (see Lively et al. 1994).

7. It has been shown that the ability to discriminate foreign contrasts does not decline for all kinds of contrasts. English-speaking adults can discriminate certain nonnative contrasts quite easily, for example, Zulu click contrasts (see Best, McRoberts, and Sithole 1988). This fact suggests that sounds that can be assimilated to the phonemic categories of the native language (i.e., sounds that are phonetically similar to native sounds) fail to be discriminated, whereas sounds that cannot be assimilated to any native sound (e.g., Zulu clicks for English speakers) can still be discriminated, like any other nonlinguistic sound.

8. Pallier, Bosch, and Sebastián-Gallés (1997) point out that their results hold for groups of subjects. It is not impossible that an individual native speaker of Spanish can also achieve native proficiency in Catalan; but most do not.

Chapter 3

1. In the literature the term *prosodic bootstrapping* is often employed. But this term conveys the idea that infants avail themselves only of suprasegmental cues (e.g., stress), whereas in fact segmental cues contribute useful information as well (see Morgan and Demuth 1996b). The term *phonological bootstrapping* is therefore more accurate.

2. The generalization seems to be that negative polarity items are licensed by expressions whose meaning is downward entailing, that is, that legitimate an inference from a set to a subset. Consider (i) and (ii).

(i) Every student is blond.

(ii) Every Italian student is blond.

Assume that the restriction or modifier of *every* in (i) (i.e., *student*) denotes a set of students. *Italian student* in (ii) denotes a subset of the set of students. From (i) we can infer or deduce (ii); that is, if we know that (i) is true, we also know that (ii) is true. Truthfulness is preserved when we go from a set to a subset.

Assume now that the predicate *reads a novel* in (iii) denotes the set of individuals who read a novel.

(iii) Every student reads a novel.

Then the predicate *reads a German novel* in (iv) denotes a subset of the set of individuals who read a novel.

(iv) Every student reads a German novel.

In contrast to what we have established for (i) and (ii), the inference from (iii) to (iv) is not legitimate; that is, if we know that *Every student reads a novel* is true, we do not also know that *Every student reads a German novel* is true; there might be students who read an Italian or an English novel. Thus, (iii) does not entail (iv). *Every* is downward entailing with respect to its restriction (*student* in (i)), but not with respect to its predicate.

3. Names for basic-level object categories (like *cat*, *dish*) represent the first words children acquire (Macnamara 1982; Pinker 1984). Nevertheless, at about 21 months half of children's nouns do not refer exclusively to such categories. The other half refer to things we cannot perceive—for example, children use abstract nouns such as *morning* or *day* and names for social roles, such as *doctor* (see Nelson, Hampson, and Shaw 1993; Bates, Bretherton, and Snyder 1988). Thus, at this age children are able to learn nouns that do not refer to perceivable entities.

4. Children between 1 and 2 years may make errors in the use of words. For example, Clark (1993) reports that children may overextend a word, that is, use it to name members of the adult category and members of other perceptually similar categories. They may use *ball* not only for balls but also for the moon, or *apples* for both apples and oranges. This overextension typically occurs in production, but rarely in comprehension. For example, while children may *use* the word *doggie* for dogs, bears, horsies, and so on, they *understand* that the word *doggie* stands for dogs. This is a hint that they have not assigned words the wrong meaning. Regarding why such a discrepancy exists between word comprehension and production, Clark (1993, 35) suggests that "over-extension [is] a communicative strategy: use the nearest word that seems appropriate" when it is difficult to retrieve the right word.

5. In the literature about acquisition of word meaning the term *constraint* rather than *bias* is used. I prefer to reserve the term *constraint* for linguistic principles regarding the form of sentences or the meaning that can be assigned to sentences (see section 1.4) and to speak of the whole object, mutual exclusivity, and taxonomic *bias*, because these represent tendencies and not absolute prohibitions.

6. This procedure is also called *syntactic bootstrapping*. However, this term is a misnomer; Pinker (1994a) suggests that a more appropriate term is *syntactic cueing of verb meaning*, and that term is used here.

7. Children did not look longer at the contact action, as might have been expected. For an explanation of this fact, see Naigles 1996.

8. In section 3.1.2.2 we saw that infants view speech in which pauses do not co-occur with the other cues signaling prosodic boundaries as aberrant, preferring to listen to speech in which the prosodic integrity of constituents is preserved. It is often noted in the literature that children do not always hear syntactically well formed sentences. Because speakers hesitate and interrupt themselves, children also hear fragments of speech that are syntactically ill formed and whose prosody is disrupted. If infants perceive these fragments the same way they perceive experimental speech samples with aberrant prosody, then one might conclude that they disregard them. Infants will be advised that these fragments cannot form the basis for discovering the properties of their ambient language, as suggested by Jusczyk (1997).

9. Two remarks are in order here.

First, a challenge for the phonological bootstrapping hypothesis comes from the fact that prosodic representation does not faithfully reflect syntactic representation; therefore, one cannot always rely on the former to infer the latter. Moreover, there is evidence that when a mismatch occurs between prosodic and syntactic constituency, infants are sensitive to the former and not to the latter (see Gerken, Jusczyk, and Mandel 1994). If children deduce aspects of syntactic organization from prosody, the existence of mismatches should lead them to err. Another question is what prevents children from hypothesizing the wrong syntactic structure. Gerken (1996a) suggests that learners deduce some aspects of syntactic structure not from a single prosodic representation, but from comparing the prosodic representations associated with multiple sentences (see section 3.3.3 for evidence that children make cross-sentential comparisons).

Second, prosodic representation is likely not immediately translatable into hierarchical geometry. Little is known about whether different levels of embedding are prosodically marked in distinct ways. However, it has been proposed that some configurational parameters, such as the parameter governing the relative order of heads and complements, can be set through prosodic cues (see Mazuka 1996; Guasti et al. 2001). If this hypothesis holds true, then prosody may provide more than segmentation and bracketing. It may offer information that has a direct bearing on the acquisition of specific syntactic parameters.

10. Semantically transparent notions cannot be found in all kinds of sentences. For example, in passive sentences the grammatical subject is not an agent.

(i) The car was repaired by John.

Initially, children must disregard this kind of sentence (see Pinker 1984 for discussion).

Chapter 4

1. The traditional view, adopted here, is that the different orders of words are a primitive property. Kayne (1994) challenges this view by claiming that all languages have an underlying SVO order and that the different surface orders are

derived by movement. This new perspective does not necessarily alleviate the learner's problem; it surely switches the burden to another system that is responsible for how the surface order is obtained. For example, the SOV order may be derived from the underlying SVO order by moving the object in front of the verb.

2. Children attain linguistic milestones at different ages. Some children start to combine words before age 2. This is the case with Eve. As shown in Brown 1973, Eve is more advanced than other children. However, her *pattern* of linguistic development is like that of other children.

3. Notice that in French negation is expressed by two discontinuous elements, *ne* and *pas*. *Ne* is a clitic that is often omitted in spoken adult language and in child speech. *Pas* is generally considered the equivalent of English *not* (see Pollock 1989).

4. The negative element *ne* is a clitic generated in Neg that, like all clitics, moves to I^0 (see Belletti 1990), where it appears in the representations in (21) and (22).

5. Friedemann (1993) in part contests the validity of this result for early French. First, he notes that Nathalie produced many instances of the negation with infinitives in the first session when she was interviewed. Second, he claims that the negation in infinitive clauses is an instance of constituent negation and as such does not project a NegP. He concludes that, in early French, clausal negation is not possible in infinitive clauses. If Friedemann is right, we cannot use the distribution of verbs with respect to the negation as a criterion for deciding whether French learners distinguish between finite and nonfinite verbs. The test remains valid for early Germanic languages, however. See Haegeman 1995b for discussion of the discrepancy between early French and early Dutch concerning the negation in infinitives.

6. Clahsen, Penke, and Parodi (1993/1994) claim that initially there is just one functional category to which verbs raise in early V2 languages, most likely IP. Essentially this claim is based on the absence of unambiguous evidence for CP. In the child language data they examine, these authors find sentences with the order V_{fin} S, which they account for by assuming that the verb has raised to I and the subject is in VP. This hypothesis is only compatible with the view that I is head initial in German, however.

7. Poeppel and Wexler's conclusions seem to be at odds with findings reported by Clahsen and Smolka (1985) and by Clahsen and Penke (1992), who argue that German-speaking children initially make agreement errors. The discrepancy may arise from the fact that Clahsen and coauthors included infinitives used as main verbs in their counts, while Poeppel and Wexler did not.

8. (39b) illustrates a case of agreement with a postverbal subject, here *i bambini* 'the kids'. It is generally assumed that a null expletive pro in Spec IP is coindexed with the postverbal subject and that specifier-head agreement is structurally realized between pro and the inflected verb in I (see Rizzi 1982).

9. A third approach, proposed to account for RIs in V2 languages, holds that these infinitives are selected by a null auxiliary located in C. For discussion of this

approach, see Boser et al. 1992, Whitman 1994, and Ingram and Thompson 1996; for criticism, see Poeppel and Wexler 1993 and Haegeman 1995b.

10. An uninterpretable feature is one that plays no role at LF. According to Chomsky (1995), features that trigger movement, usually features of functional categories, are uninterpretable; movement of an element with a corresponding feature is thus required to eliminate the uninterpretable feature.

11. The subject may appear preverbally in a pro-drop language such as Italian.

(i) Lia corre.
     Lia runs

According to Wexler, the order in (i) is obtained by moving the subject not to Spec Agr (or IP), but to some kind of dislocated position.

12. Negated RIs in early French have the structure in (i), with a NegP taking the VP as complement.

(i) [$_{NegP}$ Pas [$_{VP}$ la   poupée dormir]].   (Nathalie, 1;9)
         not   the doll   sleep-INF

This representation is compatible only with the view that the hierarchy of functional projections is AgrP > TP > NegP > VP, with truncation applying below TP. If the hierarchy were AgrP > NegP > TP > VP, as in Belletti 1990, then truncation below NegP would result in a structure containing TP. The anaphoric tense would need to be identified sentence-internally, but there would not be any identifier. Which hierarchy is correct is a matter of debate, as is the status of French negated RIs. (For discussion of these issues, see Friedemann 1993; Rizzi 1993/1994; Haegeman 1995b; and for discussion of the position of NegP in the clause, see also Zanuttini 1997.)

Chapter 5

1. Null subjects in Chinese are variables (R-expressions) bound by a null operator, unless they occupy the subject position of an embedded clause, in which case they are null pronouns (pro) identified by the matrix subject. Strong crossover effects or lack thereof support this view. For some speakers of Chinese, the embedded null subject in a sentence like (i) can be anaphorically linked to the matrix subject, while the embedded null object in a sentence like (ii) cannot (examples from Huang 1984).

(i) Zhangsan$_i$ shuo [t$_i$ bu renshi Lisi].
     Zhangsan say   (he) not know Lisi
     'Zhangsan said that (he) does not know Lisi.'

(ii) *Zhangsan$_i$ shuo [Lisi bu renshi t$_i$].
      Zhangsan say   Lisi not know (him)
      'Zhangsan said that Lisi does not know (him).'

This subject/object asymmetry follows from binding principles (see section 8.1), if we assume that the embedded object is a variable, while the embedded subject is a pronoun (see Huang 1984). As a variable, the embedded object must be A-free in any domain (and thus cannot be anaphorically linked to the matrix subject); as a pronoun, the embedded subject needs to be A-free only in the local domain (the embedded clause) and can be anaphorically linked to an NP outside the local domain. The matter is very complex, and the judgments on (i) and (ii) are controversial. For present purposes it suffices to note that the possible presence of null pronominal subjects in Chinese does not cancel the fundamental distinction between null subjects in Chinese and Italian that is captured by the two parameters presented in the text (see also Lillo-Martin 1991).

2. The different rates of subject and object omission are not unique to early Chinese, but are found in adult Chinese as well (see Wang et al. 1992).

3. Early English seems to be an exception to the generalization in (11a), since some null subjects do occur in *wh*-questions in this early language, as originally pointed out by Roeper and Rohrbacher (2000).

4. Empty operators are available in English, but unlike in Chinese, they are not discourse bound. They must be identified sentence-internally and not through a topic present in the preceding discourse. For example, in topicalization structures the empty operator binding the NC is identified through its connection with the overt topic, as indicated through coindexation in (i).

(i) This book$_i$, Op$_i$ I really like NC$_i$.

5. Under the development introduced in section 5.2.3.1 the null object (and the null subject, with the exception discussed in note 1) in Chinese is better analyzed as being an NC. Its Ā-bound status was ascertained in note 1, where we saw that this empty category is subject to SCO effects. Unlike a true variable, however, it is not subject to WCO (see also Lillo-Martin 1991). Sentence (ii) is an appropriate answer to question (i); it may mean that Zhangsan is the person x such that x's mother most likes x. This meaning is captured by saying that the empty category, an NC, can refer to the discourse topic, which can happen to be Zhangsan. (Thanks to Jim Huang for these examples.)

(i) Shei zui   xihuan Zhangsan?
   who most likes   Zhangsan

(ii) Ta de mama zui   xihuan NC.
    his   mother most likes   NC

Similarly, the null subject and the null object in Germanic languages (see (31a,b) in the text) are NCs.

6. Although subjectless sentences in early languages include the same empty category that is found in Chinese—an NC, according to the revision in note 5—early null subjects and Chinese null subjects are two distinct grammatical objects. First, in Chinese the NC is identified sentence-internally by the null operator and topic drop is contingent on the availability in the language of this discourse-bound empty operator. Second, the NC originates from movement of the empty operator in Chinese, while it is base-generated in early languages.

7. If clausal truncation is available in the diary style, one might expect to find RIs in this register, along with null subjects. But this does not happen. This difference

might be traced to the following observation: the truncation site is lower in RIs than in finite subjectless clauses, and in diaries only the option of truncation at higher functional levels is exploited. For a development along these lines, see Haegeman 1995a.

8. Although the restriction to clause-initial position may lead to the conjecture that null subjects in Germanic languages are like null subjects in the diary style, an analysis indeed proposed by Rizzi (1993/1994), empirical evidence from the acquisition of Dutch does not warrant this conjecture.

9. In adult Dutch null subjects are NCs bound by a null discourse-bound operator. The nature of this operator makes it compatible with argumental empty categories, but not with expletives or quasi arguments. For this reason, these expletives and quasi arguments cannot be dropped in the adult language.

Chapter 6

1. Unlike in English, in Italian the configuration Wh Aux S V is not acceptable; that is, (i) is ungrammatical.

(i) *Cosa ha Gianni fatto?
    what has Gianni made

In Rizzi's (1996) view, this follows from a language-specific property: in Italian the verb in C does not have the option of assigning case under government to the subject in Spec IP.

2. Adjacency between the *wh*-operator and the verb is not the only way to satisfy the *Wh*-Criterion. Languages such as Brazilian Portuguese and Hebrew display the order Wh S V, as the Hebrew example (i) illustrates.

(i) Ma   Jean 'axal?
    what Jean ate
    'What did Jean eat?'

Here the *wh*-operator has been fronted, but the verb has not moved from the position it occupies in a declarative clause. Rizzi (1996) accounts for this pattern by assuming that the *wh*-operator endows the C head with the relevant *wh*-feature through a mechanism of dynamic agreement.

3. One may wonder how the *Wh*-Criterion is satisfied in the noninverted structures. A hypothesis is that these structures include a null auxiliary (the null counterpart of *do* in (16b)) that carries the *wh*-feature to C. The conjecture that there is a null auxiliary in early English is needed to account for another kind of early question, the auxless question, discussed in section 6.2.

4. Another structure, which will not be discussed here, has the lexical verb inflected with the third person marker, as in (i) (see Stromswold 1990; Guasti 2000).

(i) What it carries?   (Adam, 3;0)

5. The total number of questions includes adultlike questions featuring SAI, questions failing to display SAI, the two types of auxless questions shown in (21), and another type of auxless question in which the lexical verb is inflected for tense or agreement (see also note 4).

6. Radford (1990) proposes that in auxless questions the *wh*-operator has not moved to Spec CP, but is adjoined to VP, with the subject located in Spec VP. If adjunction to a projection is a viable mechanism for deriving questions in early systems, we should expect to find interrogative constructions like (i) in early Italian.

(i) Cosa Gianni mangia?
     what Gianni eats

The representation of (i) would be (ii), where the *wh*-operator *cosa* is adjoined to IP and the subject is located in Spec IP (remember that finite verbs raise to I in Italian).

(ii) [$_{IP}$ Cosa [$_{IP}$ Gianni mangia]]?
      what   Gianni eats

However, such questions do not occur in early Italian. Their absence makes the hypothesis that adjunction is responsible for question formation in early English highly suspect. Why would English learners be forced to use such an option, when Italian learners are not?

7. Root null subjects disappear from children's speech at around 3 years, while null auxiliaries seem to last longer; auxless questions are still found at $4\frac{1}{2}$ years. If the source of the two phenomena is the same—namely, truncation—a developmental discrepancy is not expected. Guasti and Rizzi (1996) propose that the discrepancy might ensue from the differing natures of the IP and CP systems. Principles governing the IP architecture preclude truncation at this level earlier than principles governing the CP architecture (see Haegeman 1996b for a somewhat analogous discrepancy; also see chapter 5, note 7).

8. The absence of *do* in subject questions, (26a), is presumably due to the Empty Category Principle (ECP), which states that a nonpronominal empty category must be properly governed. If I-to-C movement occurred in subject questions, the trace of the subject in Spec IP would not be properly governed in Rizzi's (1990) sense, that is, governed by a head X^0 within its immediate projection (see Haegeman 1994, secs. 7.5.2 and 12.2, for an introduction to the ECP).

9. The proposal that auxless questions include an auxiliary in the specifier of the root also predicts that children should not produce subject questions like (i).

(i) Who laugh?

A null auxiliary (the counterpart of *do*) selecting the bare verb could not be licensed in (i) for the same reason that the null auxiliary *be* is not licensed in (27b). Contrary to expectations, however, questions like (i) represent 41% of the subject questions produced by the three children (Adam, Eve, Sarah) whose speech was investigated by Guasti and Rizzi (1996). This high percentage contrasts sharply with the children's very low rate (2%) of subject questions like (27b).

   A plausible analysis of (i) is that the verb is not a bare form selected by a null auxiliary, but a finite form missing the overt third person specification. Evidence for the hypothesis that children produce finite verbs missing some tense/agreement specification is the omission of the third person singular specification with negative *do*, illustrated in (ii) (see Guasti and Rizzi 2002).

(ii) He don't hear me.   (Sarah, 3;5)

In sentences like this *does* rather than *do* should be used. Since *do* is intrinsically finite (it cannot be used in nonfinite clauses), it unequivocally lacks the morphological specification for third person (-*s*) in (ii). But if children make a morphological error with *do*, they can make the same error with lexical verbs. This makes the hypothesis that the lexical verb in subject questions like (i) is a finite verb lacking the morphological third person specification highly plausible.

This conjecture is compatible with the idea discussed in section 4.4 that bare verbs in early English are the counterparts of root infinitives in other early languages, but it requires further specification. Only a subset of the early English bare forms are genuine root infinitives; some of the other bare forms are likely finite forms with a morphological error, as suggested by Guasti and Rizzi (2002) (see section 4.4.3 for a similar conclusion).

10. This subject/object asymmetry is generally traced to the ECP (see note 8). In (30a) the verb *eat* properly governs the object trace, but in (30b), a *that*-t(race) violation, the complementizer *that* in C does not properly govern the subject trace.

11. Children also produced the partial movement structure shown in (i), where the *wh*-element remains in the intermediate CP and an element marking the structure as a question fills the initial position. This structure will not be discussed here.

(i) What do you think which Smurf really has roller skates?   (Tiffany, 4;9)

12. Resumptive NPs are present in early relatives, although they are less frequent than resumptive pronouns. An example is reported in (i) (from Labelle 1990).

(i) sur la balle qu'i(l) lance   la balle
    on the ball that he throws the ball

One can regard resumptive NPs as a variant of resumptive pronouns (but see Guasti and Shlonsky 1995 for an alternative analysis).

13. Adult Serbo-Croatian allows resumptive pronouns in some structures, but children's use of resumptive pronouns does not always fit the adult pattern.

14. This is a simplification, since there are different types of resumptive pronouns, one of which is likely compatible with *wh*-movement (see, e.g., Georgopoulos 1991). Hence, the occurrence of resumptive relatives is not necessarily a decisive argument in favor of a nonmovement analysis for relative clauses, according to Goodluck and Stojanovic (1996) and Pérez-Leroux (1995).

15. Along with sentences like (43c), Canadian French learners produce sentences like (i) (from Labelle 1990), a subject resumptive relative introduced by the complementizer *que* 'that' (*a* is the subject pronoun).

(i) C'est celle-là   qu'a   dessine. (3;4)
    it's   that one there that she draws
    'It's that one there that she's drawing.'

Interestingly, children never use *qui* with resumptive pronouns; that is, they never say phrases like (ii).

(ii) *la fille qui a   court
     the girl that she runs

This suggests that they tie *qui* to the presence of a subject trace left by movement of a *wh*-operator to Spec CP and *que* to the presence of a resumptive pronoun and likely to the absence of *wh*-movement.

Chapter 7

1. The diagnostics for adjectival and verbal passives are discussed in Wasow 1977 for English and in Burzio 1986 and Belletti and Rizzi 1988 for Italian. For English they include the ability of adjectival passives to appear in prenominal position (*a closed door*), as complements to verbs such as *seem* (*The door seems closed*), and following *very*.

2. As Fox and Grodzinsky (1998) note, it is not clear why the first landing site of NP-movement in passive sentences must be Spec VP; that is, it is not clear why the object cannot move directly to Spec IP. However, if we want to implement the idea that children have trouble with A-chains connecting two potential theta positions, we cannot dispense with this assumption.

Chapter 8

1. In general, the local domain is the sentence including the reflexive, but an NP also may serve as the local domain—for example, in (i), where the legitimate antecedent of *himself* can only be *John* (see Chomsky 1986).

(i) Paul$_j$ likes [$_{NP}$ John's$_i$ picture of himself$_{i/*j}$].

2. By the definition of semantic binding adopted here, the pronoun *him* in (i) is syntactically, but not semantically, bound by the pronoun *he*.

(i) He$_i$ said that John admires him$_i$.

3. This complementarity holds in many environments, but in certain contexts it breaks down, for instance, with adjuncts and with NPs (examples from Reinhart and Reuland 1993, 661; see also Reinhart 1983).

(i) Max saw a gun near himself/him.

(ii) Lucie saw a picture of herself/her.

4. The choice of an indefinite, rather than another quantifier, was motivated by the fact that indefinites, but not universal quantifiers, can be extracted from the temporal clause, which is an island for extraction.

5. The use of null pronouns is the most natural option in these examples.

Chapter 9

1. This coarse definition excludes, for example, *only* because it can modify pronouns, as in *only him*.

2. There is a debate about whether the quantificational determiner *many* always respects the property of conservativity. *Many* has both a proportional and a non-proportional reading. Consider sentence (i).

(i) Many Italians drink coffee.

In the nonproportional reading a sentence like (i) means that the proportion of Italians who drink coffee is more than an expected number—say, much more than half of the Italian citizens. On this reading the numerical value of *many* is established on the basis of the denotation of the noun *Italian* and therefore *many* is conservative. The sentence is equivalent in meaning to *Many Italians are coffee-drinkers*. However, *many* has also a proportional reading that requires us to take coffee-drinkers into account. On this reading sentence (i) means that the number of Italian coffee-drinkers is larger than one might expect to find in a single country; it is equivalent in meaning to *Many coffee-drinkers are Italians*. If there are 50 million coffee-drinkers in the world and 40 million of them are Italian, then 40 million constitutes many of the total number of coffee-drinkers (see Westerståhl 1985 for a discussion of the two readings). The fact that *many* has a proportional reading is problematic for the hypothesis that quantificational determiners are conservative. However, Partee (1989) has challenged the hypothesis that *many* is not always conservative. If she is right, then even *many* is always conservative.

3. It is generally assumed that the structure of a quantificational determiner like *all of the men* includes an empty nominal head following *all*, as in (i).

(i) [$_{NP}$ all [$_N$ $\emptyset$] [$_{PP}$ of the men]]

4. Gordon (1996) does not deny children's competence in the interpretation of quantified sentences, as demonstrated by Crain et al. (1996); however, he raises doubts about the view that children's superior performance in Crain et al.'s experiment is due to satisfaction of the condition of plausible dissent/assent. He suggests that what matters is the notion of foreground and background. Gordon conjectures that in the story about skiers, children ignore the extra cups because these are backgrounded and are not prominent in the story. By contrast, the extra farmer in figure 9.7 is foregrounded and likely to bias children into thinking that he is relevant. Crain et al. counter this objection by pointing out that the cups do figure prominently in the trial.

Chapter 10

1. The idea that empty operators are not present in the early grammar up to a certain age is at odds with two facts discussed in previous chapters. An empty operator that is discourse bound is available to Chinese learners for representing subjectless and objectless sentences (see section 5.1.4). Empty operators may be available in child grammar for the formation of relative clauses, as suggested in section 6.4.7.

Chapter 11

1. The terms *developmental aphasia* and *developmental dysphasia* are also used to refer to this condition (see Bishop 1997, chap. 2, for discussion of these terms).

2. Linkage studies look directly at DNA and can reveal whether the sequence of bases of a given chromosome is different in affected and unaffected individuals. But they cannot identify a precise gene that causes the disorder.

3. As noted in section 4.4.2.1, the tense omission model has been revised by Schütze (1997) and Wexler (1999); under this revision the agreement feature may also remain underspecified. Since this revision does not affect the presentation, we will stay with the original model here.

4. The performance of children with SLI is generally compared with the performance of two other groups of children. One group, the *language-matched* (LM) or *MLU-matched* group, includes normally developing children matched on language development, as established through a battery of linguistic tests and through the MLU. The second, the *age-matched* (AM) group, consists of normally developing children matched in age.

5. Overregularization errors are common among normally developing children and are taken as an indication that they have mastered the rules for forming plural, past tense, and so on.

6. To know the real form of the distribution, Leonard et al. should have given another measure of the central tendency—specifically, the median and the first and third quartiles—as Rice and Wexler (1996) did. The median is the middle value that splits a distribution in two equal parts. For example, given the percentages 0%, 5%, 9%, 10%, 10%, 12%, 100%, the median is 10% (the mean, instead, is 20.8%). The first quartile is a value lower than the median below which 25% of the scores fall and above which 75% fall. The third quartile is a value higher than the median below which 75% of the scores fall and above which 25% fall.

7. In a typical Piagetian conservation task, the child is shown two identical bottles (A and B) each containing the same quantity of water. The child acknowledges that it is the same quantity. Next, the water in bottle A is poured into a bigger bottle (C). This time a child younger than 8 years does not recognize that the quantity of water in the new bottle C is the same as the quantity of water in bottle B.

Glossary

adjunct (1) An optional phrasal constituent, typically used to indicate time, location, or manner. (2) A constituent adjoined to another constituent (e.g., quantified expressions are adjoined to IP and are thus adjuncts).

adjunction A movement operation by which a constituent (or a head) is attached to another constituent, thus enlarging it.

A-movement An operation that moves an NP/DP constituent from an A-position to another A-position (e.g., NP-/DP-movement in passives).

Ā-movement An operation that moves a constituent in some Ā-position (e.g., *wh*-movement, quantifier movement).

anaphor An expression that is interpreted in relation to some other expression in the clause (antecedent). Reflexive pronouns are always anaphors. Nonreflexive pronouns may be anaphors.

antecedent An expression to which pronouns may refer back. For example, in *Ariel admires herself* the noun *Ariel* is the antecedent of the anaphor *herself*.

A-position (argument position) A thematic position or specifier of Agr.

Ā-position (nonargument position) A position typically occupied by an operator.

argument A term used in describing the semantic structure of sentences. It refers to particular expressions in the sentence that serve to pick out individuals and things. In a sentence like *Ariel kisses Peter Pan*, the verb *kiss* is the predicate and describes some event of kissing. It takes two arguments, *Ariel* and *Peter Pan*, that represent the two participants in that event.

argument structure A description of the set of arguments occurring with a predicate (e.g., a verb). Complements are internal to V′ and are called internal arguments. The subject is external to V′ and is called the external argument.

categorical perception A term referring to the ability to discriminate among stimuli in a certain way. Perception is categorical when discrimination between two members of the same category is more difficult than discrimination between members of different categories. For example, humans are better able to discriminate between /p/ and /b/ than between two different instances of /p/.

causative meaning An expression conveying the idea that someone or something has acted in such a way as to cause someone else to do something is said to have a causative meaning. For example, in *Mary made John work hard*, John's working hard has been caused by Mary.

c-command   A structural relation between two elements. If A c-commands B, A is higher in the structural hierarchy than B. More formally, A c-commands B iff A does not include/dominate B and the first node that dominates A also dominates B.

conditioned head turn procedure   An experimental method used with 6- to 12-month-old infants in order to test discrimination between stimuli. It consists of two phases: a conditioning phase and an experimental phase. During the conditioning phase infants are conditioned to turn their head when they hear a sound change, by associating the sound change with the activation of a visual reinforcer. Seated on a parent's lap facing an experimenter, infants hear exemplars of the same stimulus. At a certain point the stimulus changes and infants hear a new stimulus; this is called a change trial. If infants turn their head toward a transparent box (or toward the experimenter) when they hear the change, they are reinforced with a flashing light and the activation of a toy animal inside the transparent box (or manipulated by the experimenter). In addition to change trials, the conditioning phase includes no-change trials, in which infants continue to hear the same stimulus. In this case head turns toward the transparent box (or the experimenter) are coded as incorrect and are not reinforced. In the experimental phase infants hear change and no-change stimuli; every time infants turn their head, the experimenter presses a button. Discrimination is inferred from the number of correct responses (head turn) to the change trials. Werker and Tees (1984) set 8 out of 10 correct responses to the change trials as a criterion for discrimination.

Empty Category Principle (ECP)   A principle stating that every nonpronominal empty category must be properly governed.

exceptional case marking (ECM)   The phenomenon whereby verbs like *believe* assign objective case to the embedded subject of their infinitival complement clause: for example, *Mary believed him to have left earlier.*

filtered speech   A speech sequence from which bands of frequencies have selectively been removed.

foot   A prosodic unit that contains a strong syllable and optionally some adjacent weak syllables.

formant   A peak of acoustic energy, caused by the resonance of the vocal tract, that appears in a spectrogram. Formant F_1 is the lowest in frequency; F_2 is higher than F_1; and so on. Formants F_1–F_3 are relevant for the identification of vowels.

frequency (acoustic)   Number of vibrations per second measured in hertz (Hz; 1 Hz = 1 cycle per second).

fundamental frequency (F_0)   The frequency (number of times per second) of vibrations of the vocal folds measured in hertz. Its perceptual correlate is called pitch.

geminate   A consonant that is lengthened. In Italian, for example, some consonants are short (e.g., the sound written as *t* in *note* 'notes') and others are long (e.g., the sound written as *tt* in *notte* 'night').

head turn preference procedure An experimental procedure used with infants between 4 and 11 months that, unlike the conditioned head turn procedure, allows one to investigate properties extending over long stretches of speech (used with samples lasting up to 30 seconds). The infant sits on a parent's lap. Two loudspeakers, mounted to the left and the right of the infant, deliver speech samples. During the test phase the infant receives speech stimuli of different kinds contingent upon a 30° head turn. Preference for one speech sample over another is inferred from the direction of infants' headturns and from the amount of time that they orient their head toward the loudspeakers delivering one of the two samples.

intonation A rising and falling or other characteristic inflection of the voice (pitch modulation). Intonation in English distinguishes between declarative and interrogative sentences. For example, in English yes/no questions the pitch rises on the final accented syllable.

Logical Form (LF) The level of representation of language where properties or operations relevant for the interpretation of sentences are computed. Quantifier Raising (QR) is a typical operation that occurs at Logical Form.

mean length of utterance (MLU) A measure originally used by Brown (1973) to indicate the length of utterances produced by children, where an utterance is a sequence of words preceded and followed by silence or followed by change of turn in a conversation. It is calculated in morphemes or in words by dividing the number of morphemes or words by the total number of utterances. Originally it was calculated in morphemes; currently it is often calculated in words. One reason for that choice is the fact that some morphemes, in languages like Italian or Spanish, encode more than one function. For example, the -*a* in Italian *bambina* 'girl' encodes gender (feminine) and number (singular). In this case the question is whether -*a* should be counted as one or two morphemes. If it is counted as two, the MLU of a child learning Italian may become inflated. This problem does not arise if the MLU is calculated in words. The MLU gives a global measure of grammatical development that is reliable for children up to age 3 (Bowerman 1973).

mora The rhythmic unit of, for example, Japanese. A syllable can be mono- or bimoraic. An open syllable with a short vowel (V or CV) is monomoraic; a closed syllable or a syllable with a long vowel (CVC, CVV) is bimoraic. Since the final consonant of a CVC syllable can only be a nasal or a geminate, only these consonants can count as morae. For example, *kango* has two syllables, *kan-go*, and three morae, *ka-n-go*.

phonemes An abstract representation of speech sounds that have a distinctive function in a given language; that is, they serve to distinguish meanings. A given sound may be phonemic in one language but not in others. For example, /l/ and /r/ are phonemes in English, because they distinguish minimal pairs (e.g., *lace* vs. *race*), but they are not phonemes in Japanese.

phonetic boundary A point at which humans hear a categorical change in a sound when acoustic variables are varied incrementally. For example, when the voice onset time is greater than 25 ms, listeners perceive the syllable [pa], in which the consonant is voiceless; when it is less than 25 ms, they perceive the syllable [ba], in which the consonant is voiced.

pied-piping   A process by which some constituent is moved along with some other relevant element (having a certain feature). For example, in relative clauses the relative pronoun may take the preposition with it when it moves (e.g., *the man to whom John spoke*).

pitch   The perceived correlate of fundamental frequency. In adult males the rate of vocal cord vibration is lower than in females and children. Accordingly, the pitch of adult males' voices is perceived as lower than that of females' and children's voices. Pitch determines the prominence of a syllable.

prosody   A level of organization of speech concerned with stress and intonation; also known as the *suprasegmental organization of speech*.

Quantifier Raising   The operation that moves quantifiers into a position where they can be interpreted.

scope   The c-command domain of a quantifier or more generally of an operator.

segment   In phonology, a discrete entity of speech. Phones and phonemes are segments. The word *dog* includes three segments: /d/, /ɑ/, /g/.

spectrogram   A three-dimensional graphic display of the physical parameters of an acoustic signal (intensity, frequency, duration). Duration is represented on the horizontal axis; frequency is represented on the vertical axis; and the magnitude of acoustic energy is represented by the darkness or brightness of the display. (For an example, see figure 3.1.)

stress   A phonological category of prominence that has no uniform phonetic correlate. Its perception is determined by a range of features such as increased duration and heightened pitch.

suprasegmentals   Features extending over stretches of speech (e.g., stress, pitch). The term implies an opposition with segments.

syllable   A phonological constituent including at least one syllabic element, generally a vowel, and optionally some consonants preceding or following it.

thematic grid   A representation specifying the thematic roles that the arguments of a verb receive. Thematic roles encode the roles (e.g., agent, patient) played by individuals and objects in the event described by the verb.

***tough*-movement**   Movement of an empty operator that occurs in the complement of an adjective like *tough* or *stubborn*. The empty operator moves from the base position to an initial position inside the complement. From that position it is coindexed with the matrix subject, as illustrated in *John$_i$ is too stubborn [Op$_i$ to talk to t$_i$]*.

transitional probability   The likelihood that two adjacent events co-occur. It is computed by calculating the frequency of co-occurrence of the two events.

verb second (V2)   A property of a language whereby the verb occupies the second position of the clause, the first being occupied by a constituent of various kinds. In some languages (e.g., German, Dutch, Swedish) this property holds only for main clauses; in others (e.g., Icelandic) it holds for subordinate clauses as well.

voice onset time (VOT)   The short interval between the release of air occurring when the lips open and the onset of voiced phonation. VOT is briefer for sounds like /b/ than for sounds like /p/.

voicing feature   The voicing feature encodes the fact that the vocal cords do or do not vibrate while a consonant is produced.

X-bar schema, X-bar structure   Phrase structure rules establishing that phrases take the same structure in all languages (modulo word order variation). X is a variable standing for lexical categories (Verb, Noun, Adjective) or functional categories (Preposition, Inflection, Tense, Agreement, Complementizer, Determiner). The nucleus of the phrase is a single element, the head, that determines the properties of the whole phrase. For example, a phrase whose head is a Verb is a Verb Phrase (VP).

References

Abercrombie, D. 1967. *Elements of general phonetics*. Edinburgh: Edinburgh University Press.

Akmajian, A., R. A. Demers, A. K. Farmer, and R. M. Harnish. 2001. *Linguistics*. 5th ed. Cambridge, Mass.: MIT Press.

Archangeli, D., and D. T. Langendoen. 1997. *Optimality Theory: An overview*. Oxford: Blackwell.

Armitage, S. E., B. A. Baldwin, and M. A. Vince. 1980. The fetal sound environment of sheep. *Science* 208, 1173–1174.

Aslin, R., and D. Pisoni. 1980. Some developmental processes in speech perception. In G. H. Yeni-Komshian, J. F. Kavanagh, and C. A. Ferguson, eds., *Child phonology*. Vol. 2, *Perception*. New York: Academic Press.

Aslin, R. N., J. Z. Woodward, N. P. LaMendola, and T. G. Bever. 1996. Models of word segmentation in fluent maternal speech to infants. In J. L. Morgan and K. Demuth, eds., *Signal to syntax*. Mahwah, N.J.: Lawrence Erlbaum.

Atkinson, M. 1982. *Explanations in the study of child language development*. Cambridge: Cambridge University Press.

Avrutin, S., and R. Thornton. 1994. Distributivity and binding in child grammar. *Linguistic Inquiry* 25, 165–170.

Avrutin, S., and K. Wexler. 1992. Development of Principle B in Russian: Coindexation at LF and coreference. *Language Acquisition* 2, 259–306.

Babyonyshev, M., J. Ganger, D. Pesetsky, and K. Wexler. 2001. The maturation of grammatical principles: Evidence from Russian unaccusatives. *Linguistic Inquiry* 32, 1–44.

Bailyn, J. F. 1992. LF movement of anaphors and the acquisition of embedded clauses in Russian. *Language Acquisition* 2, 307–335.

Baker, C. L., and J. J. McCarthy, eds. 1981. *The logical problem of language acquisition*. Cambridge, Mass.: MIT Press.

Baker, M. 1988. *Incorporation: A theory of grammatical function changing*. Chicago: University of Chicago Press.

Baker, M., K. Johnson, and I. Roberts. 1989. Passive arguments raised. *Linguistic Inquiry* 20, 219–251.

Baldwin, D. A. 1991. Infant contributions to the achievement of joint reference. *Child Development* 62, 875–890. [Reprinted in P. Bloom, ed., *Language acquisition*. Cambridge, Mass.: MIT Press, 1994.]

Barbosa, P., D. Fox, P. Hagstrom, M. McGinnis, and D. Pesetsky, eds. 1998. *Is the best good enough? Optimality and competition in syntax*. Cambridge, Mass.: MIT Press.

Bates, E., I. Bretherton, and L. Snyder. 1988. *From first words to grammar: Individual differences and dissociable mechanisms*. Cambridge: Cambridge University Press.

Bates, E., P. S. Dale, and D. Thal. 1995. Individual differences and their implications for theories of language development. In P. Fletcher and B. MacWhinney, eds., *Handbook of child language*. Oxford: Blackwell.

Beherens, H. 1993. Temporal reference in German child language. Doctoral dissertation, University of Amsterdam.

Belletti, A. 1990. *Generalized verb movement*. Turin: Rosenberg and Sellier.

Belletti, A., and L. Rizzi. 1988. Psych-verbs and theta-theory. *Natural Language & Linguistic Theory* 6, 291–352.

Bellugi, U. 1971. Simplification in children's language. In R. Huxley and D. Ingram, eds., *Language acquisition: Models and methods*. New York: Academic Press.

Bellugi, U., A. Bihrle, T. Jernigan, D. Trauner, and S. Doherty. 1990. Neuropsychological, neurological and neuroanatomic profile of Williams syndrome. *American Journal of Medical Genetics* 6, 115–125.

Bellugi, U., E. S. Klima, and P. P. Wang. 1996. Cognitive and neural development: Clues from genetically-based syndromes. In D. Magnusson, ed., *The life-span development of individuals: Behavioral, neurobiological, and psychosocial perspectives*. New York: Cambridge University Press.

Bellugi, U., S. Marks, A. Bihrle, and H. Sabo. 1993. Dissociation between language and cognitive functions in Williams syndrome. In D. Bishop and K. Mogford, eds., *Language development in exceptional circumstances*. Hillsdale, N.J.: Lawrence Erlbaum.

Bellugi, U., D. Mills, T. Jernigan, G. Hickok, and A. Galaburda. 1999. Linking cognition, brain structure, and brain function in Williams syndrome. In H. Tager-Flusberg, ed., *Neurodevelopmental disorders*. Cambridge, Mass.: MIT Press.

Benedict, H. 1979. Early lexical development: Comprehension and production. *Journal of Child Language* 6, 183–201.

Bennett, F., B. La Veck, and C. Sells. 1978. The Williams elfin facies syndrome: The psychological profile as an aid in syndrome identification. *Pediatrics* 61, 303–306.

Bergeijk, W. A., J. R. van Pierce, and E. E. David, Jr. 1960. *Waves and the ear*. Garden City, N.Y.: Anchor Books/Doubleday.

Berman, R., and I. Sagi. 1981. On word formation and word innovations in early age. *Balshanut Ivrit Xofshit* 18.

Bertinetto, P. M. 1989. Reflections on the dichotomy "stress" vs. "syllable-timing." *Revue de Phonétique Appliquée* 91–93, 99–130.

Bertoncini, J., R. Bijeljac-Babic, P. W. Jusczyk, L. Kennedy, and J. Mehler. 1988. An investigation of young infants' perceptual representations of speech sounds. *Journal of Experimental Psychology: General* 117, 21–33.

Bertoncini, J., C. Floccia, T. Nazzi, and J. Mehler. 1995. Morae and syllables: Rhythmical basis of speech representations in neonates. *Language and Speech* 38, 311–329.

Bertoncini, J., and J. Mehler. 1981. Syllables as units in infant speech perception. *Infant Behavior and Development* 4, 247–260.

Best, C. T. 1995. Learning to perceive the sound patterns of English. In C. Rovee-Collier and L. P. Lipsitt, eds., *Advances in infancy research*. Norwood, N.J.: Ablex.

Best, C. T., G. W. McRoberts, and N. M. Sithole. 1988. Examination of perceptual re-organization for speech contrasts: Zulu click discrimination by English-speaking adults and infants. *Journal of Experimental Psychology: Human Perception and Performance* 14, 345–360.

Beuren, A. J., J. Apitz, and D. Harmjanz. 1962. Supravalvular aortic stenosis in association with mental retardation and a certain facial appearance. *Circulation* 26, 1235–1240.

Bickerton, D. 1988. Creole languages and the bioprogram. In F. Newmeyer, ed., *Linguistics: The Cambridge survey*. Vol. 2, *Linguistic theory: Extensions and implications*. Cambridge: Cambridge University Press.

Bickerton, D. 1996. An innate language faculty needs neither modularity nor localization. Open peer commentary to R.-A. Müller. Innateness, autonomy, universality? Neurobiological approaches to language. *Behavioral and Brain Sciences* 19, 631–632.

Bihrle, A. M., U. Bellugi, D. Delis, and S. Marks. 1989. Seeing either the forest or the trees: Dissociation in visuospatial processing. *Brain and Cognition* 11, 37–49.

Bijeljac-Babic, R., J. Bertoncini, and J. Mehler. 1993. How do four-day-old infants categorize multisyllabic utterances? *Developmental Psychology* 29, 711–721.

Bishop, D. V. M. 1989. *Test for Reception of Grammar*. 2nd ed. Manchester: University of Manchester.

Bishop, D. V. M. 1997. *Uncommon understanding: Development and disorders of language comprehension in children*. Hove: Psychology Press Limited.

Bishop, D. V. M., and K. Mogford, eds. 1993. *Language development in exceptional circumstances*. Hillsdale, N.J.: Lawrence Erlbaum.

Bishop, D. V. M., T. North, and C. Donlan. 1995. Genetic basis of specific language impairment: Evidence from a twin study. *Developmental Medicine and Child Neurology* 37, 56–71.

Blackmore, C., and C. F. Cooper. 1970. Development of the brain depends on the visual environment. *Nature* 228, 477–478.

Bloom, L. 1970. *Language development: Form and function in emerging grammars.* Cambridge, Mass.: MIT Press.

Bloom, P. 1990. Subjectless sentences in child language. *Linguistic Inquiry* 21, 491–504.

Bloom, P. 1994a. Language development. In M. A. Gernsbacher, ed., *Handbook of psycholinguistics.* San Diego, Calif.: Academic Press. [Reprinted in P. Bloom, ed., *Language acquisition.* Cambridge, Mass.: MIT Press, 1994.]

Bloom, P. 1994b. Possible names: The role of syntax-semantics mapping in the acquisition of names. *Lingua* 92, 297–329. [Reprinted in L. R. Gleitman and B. Landau, eds., *The acquisition of the lexicon.* Cambridge, Mass.: MIT Press, 1994.]

Bloom, P. 1994c. Semantic competence as an explanation for some transitions in language development. In Y. Levy, ed., *Other children, other languages: Theoretical issues in language development.* Hillsdale, N.J.: Lawrence Erlbaum.

Bloom, P. 1997. Intentionality and word learning. *Trends in Cognitive Sciences* 1, 9–11.

Bloom, P. 1999. Theories of word learning: Rationalist alternatives to associationism. In T. K. Bhatia and W. C. Ritchie, eds., *Handbook of child language acquisition.* San Diego, Calif.: Academic Press.

Bloom, P., A. Barss, J. Nicol, and L. Conway. 1994. Children's knowledge of binding and coreference: Evidence from spontaneous speech. *Language* 70, 53–71.

Bloom, P., and D. Kelemen. 1995. Syntactic cues in the acquisition of collective nouns. *Cognition* 56, 1–30.

Bohannon, J. N., and L. Stanowicz. 1988. The issue of negative evidence: Adult responses to children's language errors. *Developmental Psychology* 24, 684–689.

Bohnacker, U. 1997. Determiner phrases and the debate on functional categories in early child language. *Language Acquisition* 6, 49–90.

Borer, H., and K. Wexler. 1987. The maturation of syntax. In T. Roeper and E. Williams, eds., *Parameter setting.* Dordrecht: Reidel.

Borer, H., and K. Wexler. 1992. Bi-unique relations and the maturation of grammatical principles. *Natural Language & Linguistic Theory* 10, 147–189.

Bosch, L., and N. Sebastián-Gallés. 1997. Native-language recognition abilities in four-month-old infants from monolingual and bilingual environments. *Cognition* 65, 33–69.

Boser, K., B. Lust, L. Santelmann, and J. Whitman. 1992. The syntax of CP and V-2 in early child German: The strong continuity hypothesis. In K. Broderick, ed., *NELS 23.* Amherst: University of Massachusetts, GLSA.

Bottari, P., P. Cipriani, A. M. Chilosi, and L. Pfanner. 1998. The determiner system in a group of Italian children with SLI. *Language Acquisition* 7, 285–315.

Bowerman, M. 1973. *Early syntactic development: A cross-linguistic study with special reference to Finnish.* Cambridge: Cambridge University Press.

Bowerman, M. 1988. The "no negative evidence" problem: How do children avoid an overly general grammar? In J. Hawkins, ed., *Explaining language universals.* Oxford: Blackwell.

Boysson-Bardies, B. de. 1993. Ontogeny of language-specific syllabic productions. In B. de Boysson-Bardies, S. de Schonen, P. W. Jusczyk, P. MacNeilage, and J. Morton, eds., *Developmental neurocognition: Speech and face processing in the first year of life.* Dordrecht: Kluwer.

Boysson-Bardies, B. de. 1999. *How language comes to children.* Cambridge, Mass.: MIT Press.

Boysson-Bardies, B. de, P. Hallé, L. Sagart, and C. Durand. 1989. A cross-linguistic investigation of vowel formants in babbling. *Journal of Child Language* 16, 1–17.

Boysson-Bardies, B. de, and M. M. Vihman. 1991. Adaptation to language: Evidence from babbling and first words in four languages. *Language* 67, 297–319.

Braine, M., and B. Rumain. 1983. Logical reasoning. In P. Mussen, ed., *Handbook of child psychology.* Vol. 3, *Cognitive development.* New York: Wiley.

Brent, M., and T. A. Cartwright. 1996. Distributional regularity and phonotactic constraints are useful for segmentation. *Cognition* 61, 93–125.

Broihier, K., and K. Wexler. 1995. Children's acquisition of control in temporal adjuncts. In C. T. Schütze, J. B. Ganger, and K. Broihier, eds., *Papers on language processing and acquisition.* MIT Working Papers in Linguistics 26. Cambridge, Mass.: MIT, MITWPL.

Bromberg, H. S., and K. Wexler. 1995. Null subjects in *wh*-questions. In C. T. Schütze, J. B. Ganger, and K. Broihier, eds., *Papers on language processing and acquisition.* MIT Working Papers in Linguistics 26. Cambridge, Mass.: MIT, MITWPL.

Brooks, P. J., and M. D. S. Braine. 1996. What do children know about the universal quantifiers *all* and *each*? *Cognition* 60, 235–268.

Brown, R. 1957. Linguistic determinism and part of speech. *Journal of Abnormal and Social Psychology* 49, 454–462.

Brown, R. 1968. The development of *wh*-questions in child speech. *Journal of Verbal Learning and Verbal Behavior* 7, 277–290.

Brown, R. 1973. *A first language.* Cambridge, Mass.: Harvard University Press.

Brown, R., and C. Hanlon. 1970. Derivational complexity and the order of acquisition in child speech. In J. R. Hayes, ed., *Cognition and the development of language.* New York: Wiley.

Bruner, J. S. 1978. From communication to language: A psychological perspective. In I. Markova, ed., *The social context of language.* New York: Wiley.

Bruner, J. S., R. Olver, and P. M. Greenfield, eds. 1966. *Studies in cognitive growth.* New York: Wiley.

Bucci, W. 1978. The interpretation of universal affirmative propositions. *Cognition* 60, 55–77.

Burgemeister, B., H. Blum, and I. Lorge. 1972. *The Columbia Mental Maturity Scale*. New York: Harcourt Brace Jovanovich.

Burzio, L. 1986. *Italian syntax: A government and binding approach*. Dordrecht: Reidel.

Busnel, M. C., and C. Granier-Deferre. 1983. And what of fetal audition? In A. Oliverio and M. Zapelle, eds., *The behavior of human infants*. New York: Plenum.

Cairns, H. S., D. McDaniel, J. R. Hsu, and M. Rapp. 1994. A longitudinal study of principles of control and pronominal reference in child English. *Language* 70, 260–288.

Capirci, O., L. Sabbadini, and V. Volterra. 1996. Language development in Williams syndrome: A case study. *Cognitive Neuropsychology* 13, 1017–1039.

Carden, G. 1986. Blocked forward coreference. In B. Lust, ed., *Studies in the acquisition of anaphora*. Vol. 1, *Defining the constraints*. Dordrecht: Reidel.

Cardinaletti, A., and M. T. Guasti. 1995. Small clauses: Some controversies and issues of acquisition. In A. Cardinaletti and M. T. Guasti, eds., *Small clauses*. Syntax and Semantics 28. San Diego, Calif.: Academic Press.

Cardinaletti, A., and M. Starke. 1999. The typology of structural deficiency: A case study of three classes of pronouns. In H. van Riemsdijk, ed., *Clitics in the languages of Europe*. Berlin: Mouton de Gruyter.

Carey, S. 1978. The child as word learner. In M. Halle, J. Bresnan, and G. A. Miller, eds., *Linguistic theory and psychological reality*. Cambridge, Mass.: MIT Press.

Carlson, G. N. 1990. Intuitions, category and structure: Comments on McDaniel and Cairns. In L. Frazier and J. de Villiers, eds., *Language processing and language acquisition*. Dordrecht: Kluwer.

Caselli, M. C., E. Bates, P. Casadio, J. Fenson, L. Fenson, L. Sanderl, and J. Weir. 1995. A cross-linguistic study of early lexical development. *Cognitive Development* 10, 159–199.

Chien, Y.-C. 1994. Structural determinants of quantifier scope: An experimental study of Chinese first language acquisition. In B. Lust, G. Hermon, and J. Kornfilt, eds., *Syntactic theory and first language acquisition: Cross-linguistic perspectives*. Vol. 2, *Binding, dependencies and learnability*. Hillsdale, N.J.: Lawrence Erlbaum.

Chien, Y.-C., and K. Wexler. 1990. Children's knowledge of locality conditions in binding as evidence for the modularity of syntax and pragmatics. *Language Acquisition* 1, 225–295.

Chien, Y.-C., K. Wexler, and H.-W. Chang. 1993. Children's development of long distance binding in Chinese. *Journal of East Asian Linguistics* 2, 229–259.

Chierchia, G. 1995. *Dynamics of meaning: Anaphora, presupposition and syntactic theory*. Chicago: University of Chicago Press.

Chierchia, G., S. Crain, M. T. Guasti, A. Gualmini, and L. Meroni. 2001. The acquisition of disjunction: Evidence for a grammatical view of scalar implicatures. In *Proceedings of the 25th Annual Boston University Conference on Language Development*. Somerville, Mass.: Cascadilla Press.

Chierchia, G., and S. McConnell-Ginet. 2000. *Meaning and grammar: An introduction to semantics*. 2nd ed. Cambridge, Mass.: MIT Press.

Chomsky, C. 1969. *The acquisition of syntax in children from 5 to 10*. Cambridge, Mass.: MIT Press.

Chomsky, N. 1959. A review of B. F. Skinner, *Verbal behavior*. *Language* 35, 26–58.

Chomsky, N. 1975. *The logical structure of linguistic theory*. New York: Plenum.

Chomsky, N. 1981. *Lectures on government and binding*. Dordrecht: Foris.

Chomsky, N. 1982. *Some concepts and consequences of the theory of government and binding*. Cambridge, Mass.: MIT Press.

Chomsky, N. 1986. *Knowledge of language: Its nature, origin, and use*. New York: Praeger.

Chomsky, N. 1995. *The Minimalist Program*. Cambridge, Mass.: MIT Press.

Christophe, A., and E. Dupoux. 1996. Bootstrapping lexical acquisition: The role of prosodic structure. *The Linguistic Review* 13, 383–412.

Christophe, A., E. Dupoux, J. Bertoncini, and J. Mehler. 1994. Do infants perceive word boundaries? An empirical approach to the bootstrapping problem for lexical acquisition. *Journal of the Acoustical Society of America* 95, 1570–1580.

Christophe, A., and J. Morton. 1998. Is Dutch native English? Linguistic analysis by 2-month-olds. *Developmental Science* 1, 215–219.

Christophe, A., M. Nespor, M. T. Guasti, and B. van Ooyen. 1997. Reflections on phonological bootstrapping: Its role in lexical and syntactic acquisition. In G. T. M. Altmann, ed., *Cognitive models of speech processing: A special issue of Language and Cognitive Processes*. Mahwah, N.J.: Lawrence Erlbaum.

Cinque, G. 1998. *Adverbs and functional heads: A cross-linguistic perspective*. Oxford: Oxford University Press.

Cipriani, P., P. Bottari, and A. M. Chilosi. 1998. The longitudinal perspective in the study of specific language impairment: The case of a long-term follow-up of an Italian child. *International Journal of Language and Communication Disorders* 33, 245–280.

Cipriani, P., P. Pfanner, A. M. Chilosi, L. Cittadoni, A. Ciuti, A. Maccari, N. Pantano, L. Pfanner, P. Poli, S. Sarno, P. Bottari, G. Cappelli, C. Colombo, and E. Veneziano. 1989. *Protocolli diagnostici e terapeutici nello sviluppo e nella patologia del linguaggio* (Therapeutic and diagnostic protocols in language development and language pathology). (1/84 Italian Ministry of Health): Stella Maris Foundation.

Clahsen, H. 1986. Verb inflections in German child language: Acquisition of agreement markings and the function they encode. *Linguistics* 26, 79–121.

Clahsen, H. 1991. *Child language and developmental dysphasia.* Amsterdam: John Benjamins.

Clahsen, H., and M. Almazan. 1998. Syntax and morphology in Williams syndrome. *Cognition* 68, 167–198.

Clahsen, H., S. Bartke, and S. Göllner. 1997. Formal features in impaired grammars: A comparison of English and German SLI children. *Journal of Neurolinguistics* 10, 151–171.

Clahsen, H., C. Kursawe, and M. Penke. 1995. Introducing CP: *Wh*-questions and subordinate clauses in German child language. In *Essex Research Reports in Linguistics 7*, 1–28. Essex, England: University of Essex, Department of Linguistics.

Clahsen, H., and M. Penke. 1992. The acquisition of agreement morphology and its syntactic consequences. In J. Meisel, ed., *The acquisition of verb placement.* Dordrecht: Kluwer.

Clahsen, H., M. Penke, and T. Parodi. 1993/1994. Functional categories in early child German. *Language Acquisition* 3, 395–429.

Clahsen, H., M. Rothweiler, A. Woest, and G. F. Marcus. 1992. Regular and irregular inflections in the acquisition of German noun plurals. *Cognition* 45, 225–255.

Clahsen, H., and K. Smolka. 1985. Psycholinguistic evidence and the description of V2 phenomena in German. In H. Haider and M. Prinzhorn, eds., *Verb second phenomena in Germanic languages.* Dordrecht: Foris.

Clark, E. 1993. *The lexicon in acquisition.* Cambridge: Cambridge University Press.

Cohen Sherman, J., and B. Lust. 1995. Children are in control. *Cognition* 46, 1–51.

Cooper, W., and J. Paccia-Cooper. 1980. *Syntax and speech.* Cambridge, Mass.: Harvard University Press.

Cooper, W. E., and J. M. Sorensen. 1981. *Fundamental frequency in sentence production.* New York: Springer-Verlag.

Crain, S., and J. D. Fodor. 1993. Competence and performance. In E. Dromi, ed., *Language and cognition: A developmental perspective.* Norwood, N.J.: Ablex.

Crain, S., and C. McKee. 1985. Acquisition of structural restrictions on anaphora. In S. Berman, J. Choe, and J. McDonough, eds., *Proceedings of NELS 15.* Amherst: University of Massachusetts, GLSA.

Crain, S., C. McKee, and M. Emiliani. 1990. Visiting relatives in Italy. In L. Frazier and J. de Villiers, eds., *Language processing and language acquisition.* Dordrecht: Kluwer.

Crain, S., and M. Nakayama. 1987. Structure dependence in grammar formation. *Language* 63, 522–543.

Crain, S., and R. Thornton. 1998. *Investigations in Universal Grammar.* Cambridge, Mass.: MIT Press.

Crain, S., R. Thornton, C. Boster, L. Conway, D. Lillo-Martin, and E. Woodams. 1996. Quantification without qualification. *Language Acquisition* 5, 83–153.

Crisma, P. 1992. On the acquisition of *wh*-questions in French. In *GenGenP 0*, 115–122. Geneva: University of Geneva, Department of General Linguistics.

Cromer, R. 1987. Language growth with experience without feedback. *Journal of Psycholinguistic Research* 16, 223–231.

Crystal, T. H., and A. S. House. 1988. Segmental duration in connected speech signals: Current results. *Journal of the Acoustical Society of America* 83, 1553–1573.

Culler, F. L., K. L. Jones, and L. J. Deftos. 1985. Impaired calcitonin secretion in patients with Williams syndrome. *Journal of Paediatrics* 107, 720–723.

Curtiss, S. 1977. *Genie: A psycholinguistic study of a modern-day "wild child."* New York: Academic Press.

Cutler, A., and D. M. Carter. 1987. The predominance of strong initial syllables in the English vocabulary. *Computer Speech and Language* 2, 133–142.

Cutler, A., J. Mehler, D. Norris, and J. Segui. 1986. The syllable's differing role in the segmentation of French and English. *Journal of Memory and Language* 25, 385–400.

Cutler, A., J. Mehler, D. Norris, and J. Segui. 1992. The monolingual nature of speech segmentation by bilinguals. *Cognitive Psychology* 24, 381–410.

Cutler, A., and D. A. Swinney. 1987. Prosody and the development of comprehension. *Journal of Child Language* 14, 145–167.

Dasher, R., and D. Bolinger. 1982. On pre-accentual lengthening. *Journal of the International Phonetic Association* 12, 58–69.

Dauer, R. M. 1983. Stress-timing and syllable-timing reanalyzed. *Journal of Phonetics* 11, 51–62.

DeCasper, A. J., J. P. Lecanuet, M. C. Busnel, C. Granier-Deferre, and R. Maugeais. 1994. Fetal reaction to recurrent maternal speech. *Infant Behavior and Development* 17, 159–164.

De Haan, G. J., and K. Tuijnman. 1988. Missing subjects and objects in child grammar. In P. Jordens and J. Lallemans, eds., *Language development*. Dordrecht: Foris.

Dehaene, S. 1997. *The number sense*. London: Penguin.

Dehaene-Lambertz, G. 1998. Syllable discrimination by premature neonates with or without subcortical lesion. *Developmental Neuropsychology* 14, 579–597.

Dehaene-Lambertz, G., and D. Houston. 1998. Faster orientation latency toward native language in two-month-old infants. *Language and Speech* 41, 21–43.

Demetras, M. J., K. N. Post, and C. E. Snow. 1986. Feedback to first language learners: The role of repetitions and clarification questions. *Journal of Child Language* 13, 275–292.

Demuth, K. 1989. Maturation and the acquisition of the Sesotho passive. *Language* 65, 56–80.

Demuth, K. 1996. The prosodic structure of early words. In J. L. Morgan and K. Demuth, eds., *Signal to syntax*. Mahwah, N.J.: Lawrence Erlbaum.

Déprez, V., and A. Pierce. 1993. Negation and functional projections in early grammar. *Linguistic Inquiry* 24, 25–67.

Deutsch, W., C. Koster, and J. Koster. 1986. Children's errors in understanding anaphora. *Linguistics* 24, 203–225.

de Villiers, J., and T. Roeper. 1995. Relative clauses are barriers to *wh*-movement for young children. *Journal of Child Language* 22, 389–404.

de Villiers, J., T. Roeper, and A. Vainikka. 1990. The acquisition of long-distance rules. In L. Frazier and J. de Villiers, eds., *Language processing and language acquisition*. Dordrecht: Kluwer.

de Villiers, J., H. Tager-Flusberg, K. Hakuta, and M. Cohen. 1979. Children's comprehension of relative clauses. *Journal of Psycholinguistic Research* 8, 499–518.

Donaldson, M., and J. McGarrigle. 1973. Some clues to the nature of semantic development. *Journal of Child Language* 1, 185–194.

Donati, C., and A. Tomaselli. 1997. Language types and generative grammar: A review of some consequences of the universal VO hypothesis. In D. Beerman, D. LeBlanc, and H. van Riemsdijk, eds., *Rightward movement*. Amsterdam: John Benjamins.

Drozd, K. F. 1995. Child English pre-sentential negation as metalinguistic exclamatory sentence negation. *Journal of Child Language* 22, 583–610.

Dunn, L. M., and L. M. Dunn. 1981. *Peabody Picture Vocabulary Test-Revised*. Circle Pines, Minn.: American Guidance Service.

Dunn, L. M., L. M. Dunn, C. Whetton, and D. Pintilie. 1982. *British Picture Vocabulary Scale*. Windsor: NFER-Nelson Publishing Co.

Eimas, P. 1974. Auditory and linguistic processing of cues for place of articulation by infants. *Perception and Psychophysics* 16, 513–521.

Eimas, P., and J. D. Miller. 1980. Discrimination of the information for manner of articulation. *Infant Behavior and Development* 3, 367–375.

Eimas, P., and J. D. Miller. 1991. A constraint on the discrimination of speech by infants. *Language and Speech* 34, 251–263.

Eimas, P., E. R. Siqueland, P. W. Jusczyk, and J. Vigorito. 1971. Speech perception in infants. *Science* 17, 303–306.

Eisenbeiss, S. 2000. The acquisition of the determiner phrase in German child language. In M.-A. Friedemann and L. Rizzi, eds., *The acquisition of syntax*. Harlow, England: Longman.

Elbers, L. 1982. Operating principles in repetitive babbling: A cognitive continuity approach. *Cognition* 12, 45–64.

Elman, J. L. 1993. Learning and development in neural networks: The importance of starting small. *Cognition* 48, 71–99.

Elman, J. L., E. A. Bates, M. H. Johnson, A. Karmiloff-Smith, D. Parisi, and K. Plunkett. 1996. *Rethinking innateness*. Cambridge, Mass.: MIT Press.

Erreich, A. 1984. Learning how to ask: Patterns of inversion in yes/no and *wh*-questions. *Journal of Child Language* 11, 502–579.

Evans, G. 1980. Pronouns. *Linguistic Inquiry* 11, 337–362.

Feldman, H., S. Goldin-Meadow, and L. R. Gleitman. 1978. Beyond Herodotus: The creation of language by linguistically deprived deaf children. In A. Lock, ed., *Action, symbol, and gesture: The emergence of language*. New York: Academic Press.

Felix, S. 1987. *Cognition and language growth*. Dordrecht: Foris.

Felix, S. 1992. Language acquisition as a maturational hypothesis. In J. Weissenborn, H. Goodluck, and T. Roeper, eds., *Theoretical issues in language acquisition*. Hillsdale, N.J.: Lawrence Erlbaum.

Ferreiro, E., C. Othenin-Girard, H. Chipman, and H. Sinclair. 1976. How do children handle relative clauses? *Archives de Psychologie* 44, 229–266.

Fisher, C., D. G. Hall, S. Rakowitz, and L. R. Gleitman. 1994. When it is better to receive than to give: Syntactic and conceptual constraints on vocabulary growth. *Lingua* 92, 333–375. [Reprinted in L. R. Gleitman and B. Landau, eds., *The acquisition of the lexicon*. Cambridge, Mass.: MIT Press, 1994.]

Flege, J. E. 1993. Production and perception of a novel second language phonetic contrast. *Journal of the Acoustical Society of America* 93, 1589–1608.

Flege, J. E., M. J. Munro, and I. R. A. MacKay. 1995. The effect of age of second-language learning on the production of English consonants. *Speech Communication* 16, 1–26.

Flege, J. E., G. H. Yeni-Komshian, and S. Liu. 1999. Age constraints on second-language acquisition. *Journal of Memory and Language* 41, 78–104.

Fletcher, H. 1952. *Speech and hearing*. Rev. ed. New York: D. Van Nostrand.

Fodor, J. A. 1966. How to learn to talk: Some simple ways. In F. Smith and G. A. Miller, eds., *The genesis of language*. Cambridge, Mass.: MIT Press.

Fodor, J. A. 1983. *The modularity of mind*. Cambridge, Mass.: MIT Press.

Foster-Cohen, S. H. 1994. Exploring the boundary between syntax and pragmatics: Relevance and the binding of pronouns. *Journal of Child Language* 21, 237–255.

Fowler, A. E. 1988. Determinants of rate of language growth in children with Down syndrome. In L. Nadel, ed., *The psychobiology of Down syndrome*. Cambridge, Mass.: MIT Press.

Fox, D., and Y. Grodzinsky. 1998. Children's passive: A view from the *by*-phrase. *Linguistic Inquiry* 29, 311–332.

Franks, S. L., and P. J. Connell. 1996. Knowledge of binding in normal and SLI children. *Journal of Child Language* 23, 431–464.

Freeman, N. H. 1985. Reasonable errors in basic reasoning. *Educational Psychology* 5, 239–249.

Friedemann, M.-A. 1993. The underlying position of external arguments in French: A study of adult and child grammar. *Language Acquisition* 3, 209–255.

Friedemann, M.-A. 2000. Early French postverbal subjects. In M.-A. Friedemann and L. Rizzi, eds., *The acquisition of syntax*. Harlow, England: Longman.

Friederici, A., and J. M. I. Wessels. 1993. Phonotactic knowledge and its use in infant speech perception. *Perception and Psychophysics* 54, 287–295.

Gentner, D. 1982. Why nouns are learned before verbs: Linguistic relativity versus natural partitioning. In S. A. Kuczaj, ed., *Language, thought, and culture*. Vol. II, *Language development*. Hillsdale, N.J.: Lawrence Erlbaum.

Georgopoulos, C. 1991. *Resumptive pronouns and A' binding in Palauan*. Dordrecht: Kluwer.

Gerken, L. A. 1991. The metrical basis of children's subjectless sentences. *Journal of Memory and Language* 30, 431–451.

Gerken, L. A. 1994a. Child phonology: Past research, present questions, future directions. In M. A. Gernsbacher, ed., *Handbook of psycholinguistics*. San Diego, Calif.: Academic Press.

Gerken, L. A. 1994b. A metrical template account of children's weak syllable omissions from multisyllabic words. *Journal of Child Language* 21, 565–584.

Gerken, L. A. 1994c. Young children's representation of prosodic phonology: Evidence from English speakers' weak syllable production. *Journal of Memory and Language* 33, 19–38.

Gerken, L. A. 1996a. Phonological and distributional information in syntax acquisition. In J. L. Morgan and K. Demuth, eds., *Signal to syntax*. Mahwah, N.J.: Lawrence Erlbaum.

Gerken, L. A. 1996b. Prosodic structure in young children's language production. *Language* 72, 683–712.

Gerken, L. A., P. W. Jusczyk, and D. R. Mandel. 1994. When prosody fails to cue syntactic structure: Nine-month-olds' sensitivity to phonological versus syntactic phrases. *Cognition* 51, 237–265.

Gillette, J., H. Gleitman, L. R. Gleitman, and A. Lederer. 1999. Human simulation of vocabulary learning. *Cognition* 73, 135–176.

Gleitman, L. R. 1990. The structural sources of verb meaning. *Language Acquisition* 1, 3–55. [Reprinted in P. Bloom, ed., *Language acquisition*. Cambridge, Mass.: MIT Press, 1994.]

Gleitman, L. R., and J. Gillette. 1995. The role of syntax in verb learning. In P. Fletcher and B. MacWhinney, eds., *Handbook of child language*. Oxford: Blackwell.

Gleitman, L. R., H. Gleitman, B. Landau, and E. Wanner. 1988. Where learning begins: Initial representation for language learning. In F. Newmeyer, ed., *Linguistics: The Cambridge survey*. Vol. 3, *Language: Psychological and biological aspects*. Cambridge: Cambridge University Press.

Gleitman, L. R., and B. Landau, eds. 1994. *The acquisition of the lexicon*. Cambridge, Mass.: MIT Press.

Gleitman, L. R., and M. Lieberman. 1995. The cognitive science of language: Introduction. In L. R. Gleitman and M. Liberman, eds., *An invitation to cognitive science*. Vol. 1, *Language*. 2nd ed. Cambridge, Mass.: MIT Press.

Gleitman, L. R., and E. Wanner. 1982. Language acquisition: The state of the art. In E. Wanner and L. R. Gleitman, eds., *Language acquisition: The state of the art*. Cambridge: Cambridge University Press.

Goldin-Meadow, S., and C. Mylander. 1984. Gestural communication in deaf children: The effects and noneffects of parental input in early language development. *Monographs of the Society for Research in Child Development* 49, 1–121.

Goldin-Meadow, S., and C. Mylander. 1998. Spontaneous sign systems created by deaf children in two cultures. *Nature* 391, 279–281.

Goldman, R. W., M. Fristoe, and R. W. Woodcock. 1970. *Goldman-Fristoe-Woodcock Test of Auditory Discrimination*. Circle Pines, Minn.: American Guidance Service.

Goodluck, H. 1981. Children's grammar of complement subject interpretation. In S. Tavakolian, ed., *Language acquisition and linguistic theory*. Cambridge, Mass.: MIT Press.

Goodluck, H., and D. Behne. 1992. Development in control and extraction. In J. Weissenborn, H. Goodluck, and T. Roeper, eds., *Theoretical studies in language acquisition*. Hillsdale, N.J.: Lawrence Erlbaum.

Goodluck, H., M. Foley, and J. Sedivy. 1992. Adjunct islands and acquisition. In H. Goodluck and M. Rochemont, eds., *Island constraints*. Dordrecht: Kluwer.

Goodluck, H., and D. Stojanovic. 1996. The structure and acquisition of relative clauses in Serbo-Croatian. *Language Acquisition* 5, 285–314.

Goodluck, H., and S. Tavakolian. 1982. Competence and processing in children's grammar of relative clauses. *Cognition* 11, 1–27.

Goodluck, H., A. Terzi, and D. G. Chocano. 2001. The acquisition of control crosslinguistically: Structural and lexical factors in learning to license PRO. *Journal of Child Language* 28, 153–157.

Goodman, J., and H. C. Nusbaum, eds. 1994. *The development of speech perception: The transition from speech sounds to spoken words*. Cambridge, Mass.: MIT Press.

Goodsitt, J. V., J. L. Morgan, and P. Kuhl. 1993. Perceptual strategies in prelingual speech segmentation. *Journal of Child Language* 20, 229–252.

Gopnik, M. 1990a. Feature-blind grammar and dysphasia. *Nature* 344, 715.

Gopnik, M. 1990b. Feature blindness: A case study. *Language Acquisition* 1, 139–164.

Gopnik, M., ed. 1997. *The inheritance and innateness of grammars*. Oxford: Oxford University Press.

Gopnik, M., and M. B. Crago. 1991. Familial aggregation of a developmental language disorder. *Cognition* 39, 1–50.

Gopnik, M., J. Dalalakis, S. E. Fukuda, and S. Fukuda. 1997. The biological basis of language: Familial language impairment. In M. Gopnik, ed., *The inheritance and innateness of grammars*. Oxford: Oxford University Press.

Gopnik, M., and H. Goad. 1997. What underlies inflectional error patterns in genetic dysphasia? *Journal of Neurolinguistics* 10, 109–137.

Gordon, P. 1985. Evaluating the semantic categories hypothesis: The case of the count/mass distinction. *Cognition* 20, 209–242.

Gordon, P. 1996. The truth value judgment task. In D. McDaniel, C. McKee, and H. S. Cairns, eds., *Methods for assessing children's syntax*. Cambridge, Mass.: MIT Press.

Gordon, P., and J. Chafetz. 1990. Verb-based versus class-based accounts of actionality effects in children's comprehension of passives. *Cognition* 36, 227–254.

Gorrell, P., S. Crain, and J. D. Fodor. 1989. Contextual information and temporal terms. *Journal of Child Language* 16, 623–632.

Goto, H. 1977. Auditory perception by normal Japanese adults of the sounds 'R' and 'L'. *Neuropsychologia* 9, 317–323.

Grice, H. P. 1989. *Studies in the way of words*. Cambridge, Mass.: Harvard University Press.

Grimshaw, J. 1979. Complement selection and the lexicon. *Linguistic Inquiry* 10, 279–326.

Grimshaw, J. 1981. Form, function, and the language acquisition device. In C. L. Baker and J. J. McCarthy, eds., *The logical problem of language acquisition*. Cambridge, Mass.: MIT Press.

Grimshaw, J. 1990. *Argument structure*. Cambridge, Mass.: MIT Press.

Grimshaw, J., and S. T. Rosen. 1990. Knowledge and obedience: The developmental status of the binding theory. *Linguistic Inquiry* 21, 187–222.

Grodzinsky, Y., and G. Kave. 1993. Do children really know Condition A? *Language Acquisition* 3, 41–54.

Grodzinsky, Y., and T. Reinhart. 1993. The innateness of binding and coreference. *Linguistic Inquiry* 24, 69–101.

Groepen, J., S. Pinker, M. Hollander, R. Goldberg, and R. Wilson. 1989. The learnability and acquisition of the dative alternation in English. *Language* 65, 203–255.

Guasti, M. T. 1993. *Causative and perception verbs*. Turin: Rosenberg and Sellier.

Guasti, M. T. 1993/1994. Verb syntax in Italian child grammar: Finite and nonfinite verbs. *Language Acquisition* 3, 1–40.

Guasti, M. T. 1996. The acquisition of Italian interrogatives. In H. Clahsen, ed., *Generative perspectives on language acquisition*. Amsterdam: John Benjamins.

Guasti, M. T. 2000. An excursion into interrogatives in early English and Italian. In M.-A. Friedemann and L. Rizzi, eds., *The acquisition of syntax*. Harlow, England: Longman.

Guasti, M. T., and G. Chierchia. 1999/2000. Reconstruction in child grammar. *Language Acquisition* 8, 129–170.

Guasti, M. T., C. Dubugnon, S. Hasan-Shlonsky, and M. Schnitter. 1996. Les relatives que nous apprenons (Relatives we learn). *Rivista di Grammatica Generativa* 21, 107–128.

Guasti, M. T., M. Nespor, A. Christophe, and B. van Ooyen. 2001. Pre-lexical setting of the head-complement parameter through prosody. In B. Höhle and J. Weissenborn, eds., *Approaches to bootstrapping* Vol. 1. Amsterdam: John Benjamins.

Guasti, M. T., and L. Rizzi. 1996. Null Aux and the acquisition of residual V2. In A. Stringfellow, D. Cahana-Amitay, E. Hughes, and A. Zukowski, eds., *BUCLD 20: Proceedings of the 20th annual Boston University Conference on Language Development*. Somerville, Mass.: Cascadilla Press.

Guasti, M. T., and L. Rizzi. 2002. Agr and Tense as distinctive syntactic projections: Evidence from acquisition. In G. Cinque, ed., *The cartography of syntactic structures*. New York: Oxford University Press.

Guasti, M. T., and U. Shlonsky. 1995. The acquisition of French relative clauses reconsidered. *Language Acquisition* 4, 257–276.

Guasti, M. T., R. Thornton, and K. Wexler. 1995. Negation in children's questions: The case of English. In D. MacLaughlin and S. McEwen, eds., *BUCLD 19: Proceedings of the 19th annual Boston University Conference on Language Development*. Somerville, Mass.: Cascadilla Press.

Hadley, P. A., and M. L. Rice. 1996. Emergent uses of BE and DO: Evidence from children with specific language impairment. *Language Acquisition* 5, 155–208.

Haegeman, L. 1994. *Introduction to government and binding*. Oxford: Blackwell.

Haegeman, L. 1995a. Root infinitives and initial root null subjects in early Dutch. In C. Koster and F. Wijnen, eds., *Proceedings of Groningen Assembly on Language Acquisition*. Groningen University.

Haegeman, L. 1995b. Root infinitives, tense and truncated structures in Dutch. *Language Acquisition* 4, 205–255.

Haegeman, L. 1996a. Root infinitives, clitics and truncated structures. In H. Clahsen, ed., *Generative perspectives on language acquisition*. Amsterdam: John Benjamins.

Haegeman, L. 1996b. Verb second, the split CP and early null subjects in Dutch finite clauses. In *GenGenP 4*, 133–175. Geneva: Department of General Linguistics, University of Geneva.

Haegeman, L. 2000. Adult null subjects in non pro-drop languages. In M.-A. Friedemann and L. Rizzi, eds., *The acquisition of syntax*. Harlow, England: Longman.

Hamann, C. 1996. Null arguments in German child language. *Language Acquisition* 5, 155–208.

Hamann, C. 2000. The acquisition of constituent questions and the requirement of interpretation. In M.-A. Friedemann and L. Rizzi, eds., *The acquisition of syntax*. Harlow, England: Longman.

Hamann, C., and K. Plunkett. 1998. Subjectless sentences in child Danish. *Cognition* 69, 35–72.

Hamann, C., L. Rizzi, and U. Frauenfelder. 1996. On the acquisition of the pronominal system in French. *Recherches Linguistiques* 24, 83–101.

Hamburger, H., and S. Crain. 1982. Relative acquisition. In S. Kuczaj, ed., *Language development: Syntax and semantics*. Hillsdale, N.J.: Lawrence Erlbaum.

Harbert, W. 1995. Binding theory, control, and pro. In G. Webelhuth, ed., *Government and Binding Theory and the Minimalist Program*. Oxford: Blackwell.

Harris, T., and K. Wexler. 1996. The optional infinitive stage in child English: Evidence from negation. In H. Clahsen, ed., *Generative perspectives on language acquisition*. Amsterdam: John Benjamins.

Harris, Z. 1954. Distributional structure. *Word* 10, 146–162.

Haugen, E., and M. Joos. 1972. Tone and intonation in East Norwegian. In D. Bolinger, ed., *Intonation*. Harmondsworth, England: Penguin.

Heim, I. 1982. The semantics of definite and indefinite NPs. Doctoral dissertation, University of Massachusetts, Amherst. [Published, New York: Garland, 1989.]

Heim, I., and A. Kratzer. 1998. *Semantics in generative grammar*. Oxford: Blackwell.

Hermon, G. 1994. Long-distance reflexives in UG: Theoretical approaches and predictions for acquisition. In B. Lust, G. Hermon, and J. Kornfilt, eds., *Syntactic theory and first language acquisition: Cross-linguistic perspectives*. Vol. 2, *Binding, dependencies, and learnability*. Hillsdale, N.J.: Lawrence Erlbaum.

Hess, E. H. 1972. "Imprinting" in a natural laboratory. *Scientific American* 227, 24–31.

Higginbotham, J. 1983. Logical form, binding, and nominals. *Linguistic Inquiry* 14, 547–593.

Hirsh-Pasek, K., and R. M. Golinkoff. 1996. *The origins of grammar*. Cambridge, Mass.: MIT Press.

Hirsh-Pasek, K., D. G. Kemler Nelson, P. W. Jusczyk, K. Wright Cassidy, B. Druss, and L. Kennedy. 1987. Clauses are perceptual units for young infants. *Cognition* 26, 269–286.

Hirsh-Pasek, K., R. Treiman, and M. Schneiderman. 1984. Brown and Hanlon revisited: Mother's sensitivity to ungrammatical forms. *Journal of Child Language* 11, 81–88.

Hoekstra, T., and N. Hyams. 1995. The syntax and interpretation of dropped categories in child language: A unified account. In *Proceedings of the 14th West Coast Conference on Formal Linguistics*. Stanford, Calif.: CSLI Publications.

Hoekstra, T., and N. Hyams. 1998. Agreement and finiteness of V2: Evidence from child language. In A. Greenhill, M. Hughes, H. Littlefield, and H. Walsh, eds., *BUCLD 22: Proceedings of the 22nd annual Boston University Conference on Language Development*. Somerville, Mass.: Cascadilla Press.

Hoekstra, T., and N. Hyams. 1999. Aspects of root infinitives. In A. Sorace, C. Heycock, and R. Shillock, eds., *Language acquisition: Knowledge representation and processing*. Amsterdam: North-Holland.

Höhle, B., and J. Weissenborn, eds. 2001. *Approaches to bootstrapping*. Amsterdam: John Benjamins.

Horgan, D. M. 1978. The development of the full passive. *Journal of Child Language* 5, 65–80.

Hornstein, N., and A. Weinberg. 1995. The Empty Category Principle. In G. Webelhuth, ed., *Government and Binding Theory and the Minimalist Program*. Oxford: Blackwell.

Hsu, J. R., H. S. Cairns, and R. Fiengo. 1985. The development of grammars underlying children's interpretation of complex sentences. *Cognition* 20, 25–48.

Hsu, J. R., S. Eisenberg, and G. Schlisselberg. 1989. Control and coreference in early child language. *Journal of Child Language* 16, 599–622.

Huang, C.-T. J. 1984. On the distribution and reference of empty pronouns. *Linguistic Inquiry* 15, 531–574.

Hurst, J. A., M. Baraitser, E. Auger, F. Graham, and S. Norell. 1990. An extended family with a dominantly inherited speech disorder. *Developmental Medicine and Child Neurology* 32, 352–355.

Huttenlocher, J. 1974. The origins of language comprehension. In R. L. Solso, ed., *Theories in cognitive psychology*. New York: Wiley.

Hyams, N. 1986. *Language acquisition and the theory of parameters*. Dordrecht: Reidel.

Hyams, N. 1992. A reanalysis of null subjects in child language. In J. Weissenborn, H. Goodluck, and T. Roeper, eds., *Theoretical issues in language acquisition*. Hillsdale, N.J.: Lawrence Erlbaum.

Hyams, N. 1996. The underspecification of functional categories in early grammar. In H. Clahsen, ed., *Generative perspectives on language acquisition*. Amsterdam: John Benjamins.

Hyams, N., and S. Sigurjónsdóttir. 1990. The development of "long distance anaphora": A cross-linguistic comparison with special reference to Icelandic. *Language Acquisition* 1, 57–93.

Hyams, N., and K. Wexler. 1993. On the grammatical basis of null subjects in child language. *Linguistic Inquiry* 24, 421–459.

Ingham, R. 1992. The optional subject phenomenon in young children's English: A case study. *Journal of Child Language* 19, 133–151.

Ingham, R. 1998. Tense without agreement in early clause structure. *Language Acquisition* 7, 51–81.

Ingram, D., and W. Thompson. 1996. Early syntactic acquisition in German: Evidence for the modal hypothesis. *Language* 72, 97–120.

Inhelder, B., and J. Piaget. 1964. *The early growth of logic in the child.* London: Routledge and Kegan Paul.

Jaeggli, O. 1986. Passive. *Linguistic Inquiry* 17, 587–622.

Jaeggli, O., and K. Safir. 1989. The null subject parameter and parametric theory. In O. Jaeggli and K. Safir, eds., *The null subject parameter.* Dordrecht: Kluwer.

Jakobson, R. 1968. *Child language, aphasia and phonological universals.* The Hague: Mouton.

Jakubowicz, C. 1994. Reflexives in French and Danish: Morphology, syntax and acquisition. In B. Lust, G. Hermon, and J. Kornfilt, eds., *Syntactic theory and first language acquisition: Cross-linguistic perspectives.* Vol. 2, *Binding, dependencies, and learnability.* Hillsdale, N.J.: Lawrence Erlbaum.

Jakubowicz, C., L. Nash, C. Rigaut, and C.-L. Gérard. 1998. Determiners and clitic pronouns in French-speaking children with SLI. *Language Acquisition* 7, 113–160.

Jerne, N. K. 1967. Antibodies and learning: Selection versus instruction. In G. C. Quarton, T. Melnechuck, and F. O. Schmitt, eds., *The neurosciences: A study program.* New York: Rockefeller University Press.

Jerne, N. K. 1985. The generative grammar of the immune system. *Science* 229, 1057–1059.

Johnson, J., and E. L. Newport. 1989. Critical period effects in second language learning: The status of subjacency in the acquisition of a second language. *Cognitive Psychology* 21, 60–99.

Jordens, P. 1990. The acquisition of verb placement in Dutch and German. *Linguistics* 28, 1407–1448.

Jusczyk, P. W. 1997. *The discovery of spoken language.* Cambridge, Mass.: MIT Press.

Jusczyk, P. W., A. Cutler, and N. Redanz. 1993. Preference for the predominant stress patterns in English words. *Child Development* 64, 675–687.

Jusczyk, P. W., A. D. Friederici, J. Wessels, V. Y. Svenkerund, and A. M. Jusczyk. 1993. Infants' sensitivity to the sound patterns of native language words. *Journal of Memory and Language* 32, 402–420.

Jusczyk, P. W., K. Hirsh-Pasek, D. G. Kemler Nelson, L. J. Kennedy, A. Woodward, and J. Piwoz. 1992. Perception of acoustic correlates of major phrasal units by young infants. *Cognitive Psychology* 24, 252–293.

Jusczyk, P. W., and E. A. Hohne. 1997. Infants' memory for spoken words. *Science* 277, 1984–1986.

Jusczyk, P. W., D. B. Pisoni, A. C. Walley, and J. Murray. 1980. Discrimination of the relative onset of two-component tones by infants. *Journal of the Acoustical Society of America* 67, 262–270.

Kamp, H. 1981. A theory of truth and discourse representation. In J. Groenendijk, T. Janssen, and M. Stokhof, eds., *Formal methods in the study of language*. Amsterdam: Mathematisch Centrum.

Karmiloff-Smith, A., J. Grant, I. Berthoud, M. Davies, P. Howlin, and O. Udwin. 1997. Language and Williams syndrome: How intact is "intact"? *Child Development* 68, 246–262.

Katz, N., E. Baker, and J. Macnamara. 1974. What's in a name? A study of how children learn common and proper names. *Child Development* 45, 469–473.

Kayne, R. 1994. *The antisymmetry of syntax*. Cambridge, Mass.: MIT Press.

Kegl, J. 1994. The Nicaraguan Sign Language project: An overview. *Signpost* 7, 24–31.

Kempen, J. van. 1997. First steps in *wh*-movement. Doctoral dissertation, Utrecht University.

Kim, J., G. F. Marcus, S. Pinker, and M. Hollander. 1994. Sensitivity of children's inflection to grammatical structure. *Journal of Child Language* 21, 173–209.

Kim, Y.-J. 1997. The acquisition of Korean. In D. I. Slobin, ed., *The cross-linguistic study of language acquisition, vol. 4*. Hillsdale, N.J.: Lawrence Erlbaum.

Klatt, D. H. 1975. Vowel lengthening is syntactically determined in connected discourse. *Journal of Phonetics* 3, 129–140.

Klatt, D. H. 1976. Linguistic uses of segment duration in English: Acoustic and perceptual evidence. *Journal of the Acoustical Society of America* 59, 1208–1221.

Kluender, K. R., R. L. Diehl, and P. R. Killeen. 1987. Japanese quail can learn phonetic categories. *Science* 237, 1195–1197.

Koopman, H., and D. Sportiche. 1991. The position of subjects. *Lingua* 85, 211–258.

Koster, C. 1993. *Errors in anaphora acquisition*. Utrecht: OTS.

Koster, C. 1994. Problems with pronoun acquisition. In B. Lust, G. Hermon, and J. Kornfilt, eds., *Syntactic theory and first language acquisition: Cross-linguistic perspectives*. Vol. 2, *Binding, dependencies, and learnability*. Hillsdale, N.J.: Lawrence Erlbaum.

Krämer, I. 1993. The licensing of subjects in early child language. In C. Phillips, ed., *Papers on case and agreement II*. MIT Working Papers in Linguistics 19. Cambridge, Mass.: MIT, MITWPL.

Kratzer, A. 1995. Stage-level and individual-level predicates. In G. N. Carlson and F. G. Pelletier, eds., *The generic book*. Chicago: University of Chicago Press.

Kuczaj, S., and M. Maratsos. 1975. What children can say before they will. *Merrill-Palmer Quarterly* 21, 89–111.

Kuhl, P. K. 1991. Human adults and human infants show a "perceptual magnet effect" for prototypes of speech categories, monkeys do not. *Perception and Psychophysics* 50, 93–107.

Kuhl, P. K., and J. D. Miller. 1975. Speech perception by the chinchilla: Voiced-voiceless distinction in alveolar plosive consonants. *Science* 190, 69–72.

Kuhl, P. K., and D. M. Padden. 1982. Enhanced discriminability at the phonetic boundaries for the voicing feature in macaques. *Perception and Psychophysics* 32, 542–550.

Kuhl, P. K., K. A. Williams, F. Lacerda, K. N. Stevens, and B. Lindblom. 1992. Linguistic experiences alter phonetic perception in infants by 6 months of age. *Science* 255, 606–608.

Labelle, M. 1990. Predication, *wh*-movement and the development of relative clauses. *Language Acquisition* 1, 95–119.

Labelle, M. 1996. The acquisition of relative clauses: Movement or no movement? *Language Acquisition* 5, 65–82.

Labelle, M., and D. Valois. 1996. The status of post-verbal subjects in French child language. *Probus* 8, 53–80.

Labov, W. 1995. The case of the missing copula: The interpretation of zeroes in African-American English. In L. R. Gleitman and M. Liberman, eds., *An invitation to cognitive science*. Vol. 1, *Language*. 2nd ed. Cambridge, Mass.: MIT Press.

Labov, W., and T. Labov. 1978. Learning the syntax of questions. In R. Campbell and P. Smith, eds., *Recent advances in the psychology of language: Formal and experimental approaches*. New York: Plenum.

Ladefoged, P. 1975. *A course in phonetics*. New York: Harcourt Brace Jovanovich.

Landau, B., and L. R. Gleitman. 1985. *Language and experience: Evidence from the blind child*. Cambridge, Mass.: Harvard University Press.

Larson, R. 1988. On the double object construction. *Linguistic Inquiry* 19, 335–391.

Lasnik, H., and T. Stowell. 1991. Weakest crossover. *Linguistic Inquiry* 22, 687–720.

Léautaud, P. 1989. *Le Fléau. Journal particulier. 1917–1939*. Paris: Mercure de France.

Lebeaux, D. 1988. The feature +affected and the formation of the passive. In W. Wilkins, ed., *Thematic relations*. Syntax and Semantics 19. New York: Academic Press.

Lebeaux, D. 1990. The grammatical nature of the acquisition sequence: Adjoin-α and the formation of relative clauses. In L. Frazier and J. de Villiers, eds., *Language processing and language development*. Dordrecht: Kluwer.

Lecanuet, J. P., C. Granier-Deferre, A. Y. Jacques, and M. C. Busnel. 1992. Decelerative cardiac responsiveness to acoustical stimulation in the near term fetus. *The Quarterly Journal of Experimental Psychology* 44, 279–303.

Lee, T. H.-T. 1991. Linearity as a scope principle for Chinese: The evidence from first language acquisition. In D. Napoli and J. Kegl, eds., *Bridges between psychology and linguistics*. Hillsdale, N.J.: Lawrence Erlbaum.

Lee, T. H.-T. 1992. The inadequacy of processing heuristics: Evidence from relative clause acquisition in Mandarin Chinese. In T. H.-T. Lee, ed., *Research on Chinese linguistics in Hong Kong*. Hong Kong: The Linguistic Society of Hong Kong.

Lee, T. H.-T. 1996. Theoretical issues in language development and Chinese child language. In C.-T. J. Huang and Y.-H. A. Li, eds., *New horizons in Chinese linguistics*. Dordrecht: Kluwer.

Lehiste, I. 1970. *Suprasegmentals*. Cambridge, Mass.: MIT Press.

Lehiste, I. 1977. Isochrony reconsidered. *Journal of Phonetics* 5, 253–263.

Lenneberg, E. H. 1967. *Biological foundations of language*. New York: Wiley.

Leonard, L. B. 1998. *Children with specific language impairment*. Cambridge, Mass.: MIT Press.

Leonard, L. B., U. Bortolini, M. C. Caselli, K. K. McGregor, and L. Sabbadini. 1992. Morphological deficits in children with specific language impairment: The status of features in the underlying grammar. *Language Acquisition* 2, 151–179.

Leonard, L. B., L. Sabbadini, J. Leonard, and V. Volterra. 1987. Specific language impairment in children: A crosslinguistic study. *Brain and Language* 32, 233–252.

Levin, B., and M. Rappaport Hovav. 1996. *Unaccusativity: At the syntax–lexical semantics interface*. Cambridge, Mass.: MIT Press.

Lewis, B. A., and L. A. Thompson. 1992. A study of developmental speech and language disorders in twins. *Journal of Speech and Hearing Research* 35, 1086–1094.

Lewis, D. 1975. Adverbs of quantification. In E. Keenan, ed., *Formal semantics and natural language*. Cambridge: Cambridge University Press.

Lieberman, P. 1984. *The biology and evolution of language*. Cambridge, Mass.: Harvard University Press.

Lieberman, P. 1988. Some biological constraints on Universal Grammar and learnability. In M. L. Rice and R. L. Schiefelbusch, eds., *The teachability of language*. Baltimore, Md.: Paul H. Brookes.

Lieberman, P., E. S. Crelin, and D. H. Klatt. 1972. Phonetic ability and related anatomy of the newborn and adult human, Neanderthal man and chimpanzee. *American Anthropologist* 84, 287–307.

Lightbown, P. 1977. Consistency and variation in the acquisition of French. Doctoral dissertation, Columbia University.

Lightfoot, D. 1982. *The language lottery*. Cambridge, Mass.: MIT Press.

Lightfoot, D. 1991. *How to set parameters*. Cambridge, Mass.: MIT Press.

Lillo-Martin, D. 1986. Two kinds of null arguments in American Sign Language. *Natural Language & Linguistic Theory* 86, 415–444.

Lillo-Martin, D. 1991. *Universal Grammar and American Sign Language: Setting the null argument parameters*. Dordrecht: Kluwer.

Lillo-Martin, D. 1994. Setting the null argument parameters: Evidence from American Sign Language. In B. Lust, G. Hermon, and J. Kornfilt, eds., *Syntactic theory and first language acquisition: Cross-linguistic perspectives*. Vol. 2, *Binding, dependencies, and learnability*. Hillsdale, N.J.: Lawrence Erlbaum.

Lisker, L., and A. S. Abramson. 1964. A cross language study of voicing in initial stops: Acoustical measurements. *Word* 20, 384–422.

Lively, S. E., D. B. Pisoni, R. A. Yamada, Y. I. Tohkura, and T. Yamada. 1994. Training Japanese listeners to identify English /r/ and /l/: Long term retention of new phonetic categories. *Journal of the Acoustical Society of America* 96, 2076–2087.

Lloyd James, A. 1940. *Speech signals in telephony*. London.

Locke, J. 1983. *Phonological acquisition and change*. New York: Academic Press.

Locke, J. 1995. Development of the capacity for spoken language. In P. Fletcher and B. MacWhinney, eds., *Handbook of child language*. Oxford: Blackwell.

Loeb, D., and L. B. Leonard. 1991. Subject case marking and verb morphology in normally-developing and specifically-language-impaired children. *Journal of Speech and Hearing Research* 34, 340–346.

Lust, B. 1986a. Introduction. In B. Lust, ed., *Studies in the acquisition of anaphora*. Vol. 1, *Defining the constraints*. Dordrecht: Kluwer.

Lust, B., ed. 1986b. *Studies in the acquisition of anaphora*. Vol. 1, *Defining the constraints*. Dordrecht: Kluwer.

Lust, B., ed. 1987. *Studies in the acquisition of anaphora*. Vol. 2, *Applying the constraints*. Dordrecht: Kluwer.

Lust, B., Y.-C. Chien, C.-P. Chiang, and J. Eisele. 1996. Chinese pronominals in Universal Grammar: A study of linear precedence and command in Chinese and English children's first language acquisition. *Journal of East Asian Linguistics* 5, 1–47.

Lust, B., and T. Clifford. 1986. The 3-D study: Effects of depth, distance and directionality on children's acquisition of anaphora. In B. Lust, ed., *Studies in the acquisition of anaphora*. Vol. 1, *Defining the constraints*. Dordrecht: Kluwer.

Lust, B., J. Eisele, and R. Mazuka. 1992. The binding theory module: Evidence from first language acquisition for Principle C. *Language* 68, 333–358.

Lust, B., K. Loveland, and R. Kornet. 1980. The development of anaphora in first language: Syntactic and pragmatic constraints. *Linguistic Analysis* 6, 359–391.

Lust, B., and R. Mazuka. 1989. Cross-linguistic studies of directionality in first language acquisition: The Japanese data. *Journal of Child Language* 16, 665–684.

Macnamara, J. 1982. *Names for things: A study of child language*. Cambridge, Mass.: MIT Press.

MacNeilage, P. F. 1980. The control of speech production. In G. Yeni-Komshian, C. Kavanagh, and C. Ferguson, eds., *Child phonology*. Vol. 1, *Production*. New York: Academic Press.

MacWhinney, B., and C. Snow. 1985. The Child Language Data Exchange System. *Journal of Child Language* 12, 271–296.

Marantz, A. 1984. *On the nature of grammatical relations*. Cambridge, Mass.: MIT Press.

Maratsos, M. 1974. How preschool children understand missing complement sentences. *Child Development* 45, 700–706.

Maratsos, M., D. Fox, J. Becker, and M. A. Chalkley. 1985. Semantic restrictions on children's passives. *Cognition* 19, 167–191.

Marcus, G. F. 1993. Negative evidence in language acquisition. *Cognition* 46, 53–85.

Marcus, G. F. 1995. The acquisition of English past tense in children and multi-layered connectionist networks. *Cognition* 56, 271–279.

Marcus, G. F. 1998. Can connectionism save constructivism? *Cognition* 66, 153–182.

Marcus, G. F. 1999. Connectionism: With or without rules? *Trends in Cognitive Sciences* 3, 168–170.

Marcus, G. F. 2001. *The algebraic mind: Integrating connectionism and cognitive science*. Cambridge, Mass.: MIT Press.

Markman, E. M. 1994. Constraints children place on word meanings. In P. Bloom, ed., *Language acquisition*. Cambridge, Mass.: MIT Press. [Reprinted from *Cognitive Science* 14, 57–77, 1990.]

Markman, E. M., and J. E. Hutchinson. 1984. Children's sensitivity to constraints on word meaning: Taxonomic vs. thematic relations. *Cognitive Psychology* 16, 1–27.

Marler, P. 1970. A comparative approach to vocal learning: Song development in white crowned sparrows. *Journal of Comparative and Physiological Psychology*, monograph 7, 1–25.

May, R. 1985. *Logical Form: Its structure and derivation*. Cambridge, Mass.: MIT Press.

Mazuka, R. 1996. Can a grammatical parameter be set before the first word? Prosodic contributions to early setting of a grammatical parameter. In J. L. Morgan and K. Demuth, eds., *Signal to syntax*. Mahwah, N.J.: Lawrence Erlbaum.

Mazuka, R., B. Lust, T. Wakayama, and W. Snyder. 1986. Distinguishing effects of parameters in early syntax acquisition: A cross-linguistic study of Japanese and English. *Papers and Reports in Child Language Development* 25, 73–82.

McCloskey, J. 1979. *Transformational syntax and model theoretic semantics*. Dordrecht: Reidel.

McCloskey, J. 1990. Resumptive pronouns, A′-binding and levels of representation in Irish. In R. Hendrick, ed., *The syntax and semantics of modern Celtic languages*. Syntax and Semantics 23. New York: Academic Press.

McDaniel, D., H. S. Cairns, and J. R. Hsu. 1990. Binding principles in the grammars of young children. *Language Acquisition* 1, 121–138.

McDaniel, D., H. S. Cairns, and J. R. Hsu. 1991. Control principles in the grammars of young children. *Language Acquisition* 1, 297–335.

McDaniel, D., B. Chiu, and T. L. Maxfield. 1995. Parameters for *wh*-movement types: Evidence from child English. *Natural Language & Linguistic Theory* 13, 709–753.

McDaniel, D., and T. L. Maxfield. 1992. Principle B and contrastive stress. *Language Acquisition* 2, 337–358.

McDaniel, D., and C. McKee. 1992. Which children did they show obey strong crossover? In H. Goodluck and M. Rochemont, eds., *Island constraints*. Dordrecht: Kluwer.

McDaniel, D., C. McKee, and J. Berstein. 1998. How children's relatives solve a problem for minimalism. *Language* 74, 308–364.

McGarrigle, J., and M. Donaldson. 1974. Conservation accidents. *Cognition* 3, 341–350.

McKee, C. 1992. A comparison of pronouns and anaphors in Italian and English acquisition. *Language Acquisition* 1, 21–55.

McKee, C., D. McDaniel, and J. Snedeker. 1998. Relatives children say. *Journal of Psycholinguistic Research* 27, 573–596.

McNeill, D. 1966. Developmental psycholinguistics. In F. Smith and G. A. Miller, eds., *The genesis of language*. Cambridge, Mass.: MIT Press.

Mehler, J., and T. G. Bever. 1967. Cognitive capacity in very young children. *Science* 158, 141–142.

Mehler, J., and A. Christophe. 1995. Maturation and learning of language in the first year of life. In M. Gazzaniga, ed., *The cognitive neurosciences*. Cambridge, Mass.: MIT Press.

Mehler, J., E. Dupoux, T. Nazzi, and G. Dehaene-Lambertz. 1996. Coping with linguistic diversity: The infant's viewpoint. In J. L. Morgan and K. Demuth, eds., *Signal to syntax*. Mahwah, N.J.: Lawrence Erlbaum.

Mehler, J., P. Jusczyk, G. Lambertz, N. Halsted, J. Bertoncini, and C. Amiel-Tison. 1988. A precursor of language acquisition in young infants. *Cognition* 29, 144–178.

Meier, R. O., and E. L. Newport. 1990. Out of the hands of babies: On a possible sign advantage in language acquisition. *Language* 66, 1–23.

Menn, L., and C. Stoel-Gammon. 1995. Phonological development. In P. Fletcher and B. MacWhinney, eds., *Handbook of child language*. Oxford: Blackwell.

Mervis, C. B., C. A. Morris, J. Bertrand, and B. F. Robinson. 1999. Williams syndrome: Findings from an integrated program of research. In H. Tager-Flusberg, ed., *Neurodevelopmental disorders*. Cambridge, Mass.: MIT Press.

Miller, M. 1976. *Zur Logik der frühkindlichen Sprachentwicklung* (On the logic of early child language development). Stuttgart: Klatt.

Mills, A. E. 1985. The acquisition of German. In D. I. Slobin, ed., *The cross-linguistic study of language acquisition*. Vol. 1, *The data*. Hillsdale, N.J.: Lawrence Erlbaum.

Moon, C., R. Cooper, and W. Fifer. 1993. Two-day-olds prefer their native language. *Infant Behavior and Development* 16, 495–500.

Morgan, J. L. 1986. *From simple input to complex grammar*. Cambridge, Mass.: MIT Press.

Morgan, J. L., and K. Demuth, eds. 1996a. *Signal to syntax*. Mahwah, N.J.: Lawrence Erlbaum.

Morgan, J. L., and K. Demuth. 1996b. Signal to syntax: An overview. In J. L. Morgan and K. Demuth, eds., *Signal to syntax*. Mahwah, N.J.: Lawrence Erlbaum.

Morgan, J. L., R. P. Meier, and E. L. Newport. 1987. Structural packaging in the input to language learning: Contributions of prosodic and morphological marking of phrases to the acquisition of language. *Cognitive Psychology* 19, 498–550.

Morgan, J. L., and L. Travis. 1989. Limits on negative information in language input. *Journal of Child Language* 16, 531–552.

Moro, A. 1995. Small clauses with predicative nominals. In A. Cardinaletti and M. T. Guasti, eds., *Small clauses*. Syntax and Semantics 28. San Diego, Calif.: Academic Press.

Moro, A. 1997. *The raising of predicates: Predicative noun phrases and the theory of clause structures*. Cambridge: Cambridge University Press.

Morse, P. A. 1972. The discrimination of speech and nonspeech stimuli in early infancy. *Journal of Experimental Child Psychology* 13, 477–492.

Müller, N., B. Crysmann, and G. A. Kaiser. 1996. Interactions between the acquisition of French object drop and the development of the C-system. *Language Acquisition* 5, 35–63.

Murray, J. 1980. Discrimination of relative onset time of two component tones by infants. *Journal of the Acoustical Society of America* 67, 262–270.

Musolino, J., S. Crain, and R. Thornton. 2000. Navigating negative quantificational space. *Linguistics* 38, 1–32.

Naigles, L. 1990. Children use syntax to learn verb meaning. *Journal of Child Language* 17, 357–374.

Naigles, L. 1996. The use of multiple frames in verb learning via syntactic bootstrapping. *Cognition* 58, 221–251.

Naigles, L., and E. Hoff-Ginsberg. 1995. Input to verb learning: Evidence for the plausibility of syntactic bootstrapping. *Developmental Psychology* 31, 827–837.

Naigles, L. G., and E. T. Kako. 1993. First contact in verb acquisition: Defining a role for syntax. *Child Development* 64, 1665–1687.

Nazzi, T., J. Bertoncini, and J. Mehler. 1998. Language discrimination by newborns: Towards an understanding of the role of rhythm. *Journal of Experimental Psychology: Human Perception and Performance* 24, 756–766.

Nazzi, T., P. W. Jusczyk, and E. K. Johnson. 2000. Language discrimination by English-learning 5-month-olds: Effects of rhythm and familiarity. *Journal of Memory and Language* 43, 1–19.

Nelson, K. 1988. Constraints on word learning? *Cognitive Development* 3, 221–246.

Nelson, K., J. Hampson, and L. K. Shaw. 1993. Nouns in early lexicons: Evidence, explanations and implications. *Journal of Child Language* 20, 61–84.

Nespor, M. 1990. On the rhythm parameter in phonology. In I. Roca, ed., *The logical issue of language acquisition*. Dordrecht: Foris.

Nespor, M., and I. Vogel. 1986. *Prosodic phonology*. Dordrecht: Foris.

Newport, E. L. 1988. Constraints on learning and their role in language acquisition: Studies of the acquisition of American Sign Language. *Language Science* 10, 147–172.

Newport, E. L. 1990. Maturational constraints on language learning. *Cognitive Science* 14, 11–28.

Newport, E. L., H. Gleitman, and L. R. Gleitman. 1977. Mother, I'd rather do it myself: Some effects of maternal speech style. In C. E. Snow and C. A. Ferguson, eds., *Talking to children*. Cambridge: Cambridge University Press.

Noveck, I. A. 1996. Children's understanding of epistemic modals. *Journal of Child Language* 23, 621–643.

Noveck, I. A. 2001. When children are more logical than adults: Experimental investigation of scalar implicatures. *Cognition* 78, 165–188.

Oetting, J. B., and M. L. Rice. 1993. Plural acquisition in children with specific language impairment. *Journal of Speech and Hearing Research* 36, 1236–1248.

Oetting, J. B., M. L. Rice, and L. K. Swank. 1995. Quick incidental learning (QUIL) of words by school-age children with and without SLI. *Journal of Speech and Hearing Research* 38, 434–445.

O'Grady, W., A. M. Peters, and O. Masterson. 1989. The transition from optional to required subjects. *Journal of Child Language* 16, 513–529.

O'Grady, W., Y. Suzuki-Wei, and S. W. Cho. 1986. Directionality preferences in the interpretation of anaphora: Data from Korean and Japanese. *Journal of Child Language* 13, 409–420.

Oller, D. K. 1980. The emergence of the sounds of speech in infancy. In G. H. Yeni-Komshian, J. F. Kavanagh, and C. A. Ferguson, eds., *Child phonology*. Vol. 1, *Production*. New York: Academic Press.

Oller, D. K., and E. Eilers. 1988. The role of audition in infant babbling. *Child Development* 59, 441–449.

Oviatt, S. L. 1980. The emerging ability to comprehend language: An experimental approach. *Child Development* 51, 97–106.

Padilla, J. A. 1990. *On the definition of binding domains in Spanish*. Dordrecht: Kluwer.

Pallier, C., L. Bosch, and N. Sebastián-Gallés. 1997. A limit on behavioral plasticity in speech perception. *Cognition* 64, B9–B17.

Paradis, J., and F. Genesee. 1997. On the continuity and the emergence of functional categories in bilingual first-language acquisition. *Language Acquisition* 6, 91–124.

Partee, B. 1989. Many quantifiers. In *Proceedings of ESCOL '88*. Columbus: Ohio State University, Department of Linguistics.

Pastore, R. E., W. A. Ahroon, K. A. Buffuto, C. J. Friedman, J. S. Puleo, and E. A. Fink. 1977. Common factor model of categorical perception. *Journal of Experimental Psychology: Human Perception and Performance* 4, 686–696.

Penner, Z., and J. Weissenborn. 1996. Strong continuity, parameter setting and the trigger hierarchy: On the acquisition of the DP in Bernese Swiss German and High German. In H. Clahsen, ed., *Generative perspectives on language acquisition*. Amsterdam: John Benjamins.

Pérez-Leroux, A. T. 1995. Resumptives in the acquisition of relative clauses. *Language Acquisition* 4, 105–138.

Peters, A. M. 1983. *The units of language acquisition*. Cambridge: Cambridge University Press.

Petitto, L. A. 1992. Modularity and constraints in early acquisition: Evidence from children's early language and gesture. In M. R. Gunnar and M. Maratsos, eds., *Modularity and constraints in language and cognition*. Hillsdale, N.J.: Lawrence Erlbaum.

Petitto, L. A. 1997. In the beginning: On the genetic and environmental factors that make early language acquisition possible. In M. Gopnik, ed., *The inheritance and innateness of grammars*. Oxford: Oxford University Press.

Petitto, L. A. 1999. On the biological foundation of human language. In K. Emmorey and H. Lane, eds., *The signs of language revisited: An anthology in honor of Ursula Bellugi and Edward Klima*. Mahwah, N.J.: Lawrence Erlbaum.

Petitto, L. A., and P. Marentette. 1991. Babbling in the manual mode: Evidence for the ontogeny of language. *Science* 251, 1483–1496.

Philip, W. 1995. Event quantification in the acquisition of universal quantification. Doctoral dissertation, University of Massachusetts, Amherst.

Phillips, C. 1995. Syntax at age two: Cross-linguistic differences. In C. T. Schütze, J. B. Ganger, and K. Broihier, eds., *Papers on language processing and acquisition.* MIT Working Papers in Linguistics 26. Cambridge, Mass.: MIT, MITWPL.

Piattelli-Palmarini, M. 1986. The rise of selective theories: A case study and some lessons from immunology. In W. Demopoulos and A. Marras, eds., *Language learning and concept acquisition.* Norwood, N.J.: Ablex.

Pierce, A. 1992a. The acquisition of passive in Spanish and the question of A-chain maturation. *Language Acquisition* 2, 55–81.

Pierce, A. 1992b. *Language acquisition and syntactic theory: A comparative analysis of French and English child grammar.* Dordrecht: Kluwer.

Pike, K. L. 1945. *The intonation of American English.* Ann Arbor: University of Michigan Press.

Pinker, S. 1984. *Language learnability and language development.* Cambridge, Mass.: Harvard University Press.

Pinker, S. 1987. The bootstrapping problem in language acquisition. In B. Mac-Whinney, ed., *Mechanisms of language acquisition.* Hillsdale, N.J.: Lawrence Erlbaum.

Pinker, S. 1989. *Learnability and cognition.* Cambridge, Mass.: MIT Press.

Pinker, S. 1994a. How could a child use verb syntax to learn verb semantics? *Lingua* 92, 377–410. [Reprinted in L. R. Gleitman and B. Landau, eds., *The acquisition of the lexicon.* Cambridge, Mass.: MIT Press, 1994.]

Pinker, S. 1994b. Rules of language. In P. Bloom, ed., *Language acquisition.* Cambridge, Mass.: MIT Press. [Reprinted from *Science* 253, 530–535, 1991.]

Pinker, S. 1997. Words and rules in the human brain. *Nature* 387, 547–548.

Pinker, S. 1999. *Words and rules.* New York: Basic Books.

Pinker, S., D. S. Lebeaux, and L. A. Frost. 1987. Productivity and constraints in the acquisition of the passive. *Cognition* 26, 195–267.

Pinker, S., and A. Prince. 1988. On language and connectionism: Analysis of a parallel distributed processing model of language acquisition. *Cognition* 28, 73–193. [Reprinted in S. Pinker and J. Mehler, eds., *Connections and symbols.* Cambridge, Mass.: MIT Press, 1988.]

Pisoni, D. B., T. D. Carrell, and S. J. Gans. 1983. Perception of the duration of rapid spectrum changes in speech and nonspeech signals. *Perception and Psychophysics* 34, 314–322.

Pizzuto, E., and M. C. Caselli. 1992. The acquisition of Italian morphology: Implications for models of language development. *Journal of Child Language* 19, 491–557.

Plante, E. 1991. MRI findings in the parents and siblings of specifically language-impaired boys. *Brain and Language* 41, 67–80.

Plath, S. 1983. *The journal of Sylvia Plath.* Ed. by T. Hughes and F. McCollough. New York: Ballantine Books.

Platzack, C. 1992. Functional categories in early Swedish. In J. Meisel, ed., *The acquisition of verb placement*. Dordrecht: Kluwer.

Plunkett, K., and V. Marchman. 1993. From rote learning to system building: Acquiring verb morphology in children and connectionist nets. *Cognition* 48, 21–69.

Poeppel, D., and K. Wexler. 1993. The full competence hypothesis of clause structure in early German. *Language* 69, 365–424.

Poletto, C. 1993. Subject clitic-verb inversion in North Eastern Italian dialects. In A. Belletti, ed., *Syntactic theory and the dialects of Italy*. Turin: Rosenberg and Sellier.

Polka, L., and J. F. Werker. 1994. Developmental changes in perception of nonnative vowel contrasts. *Journal of Experimental Psychology: Human Perception and Psychophysics* 20, 421–435.

Pollock, J.-Y. 1989. Verb movement, Universal Grammar, and the structure of IP. *Linguistic Inquiry* 20, 365–424.

Prasada, S., and S. Pinker. 1993. Generalization of regular and irregular morphological patterns. *Language and Cognitive Processes* 8, 1–56.

Prévost, P., and L. White. 2000. Accounting for morphological variation in second language acquisition: Truncation or missing inflection? In M.-A. Friedemann and L. Rizzi, eds., *The acquisition of syntax*. Harlow, England: Longman.

Prince, E. 1990. Syntax and discourse: A look at resumptive pronouns. In K. Hall, J.-P. Koenig, M. Meacham, S. Reinman, and L. A. Sutton, eds., *Proceedings of the Sixteenth Annual Meeting of the Berkeley Linguistics Society*. Berkeley, Calif.: University of California at Berkeley, Berkeley Linguistics Society.

Querleu, D., X. Renard, F. Versyp, L. Paris-Delrue, and G. Crépin. 1988. Fetal hearing. *European Journal of Obstetrics, Gynecology and Reproductive Biology* 29, 191–212.

Radford, A. 1990. *Syntactic theory and the acquisition of English syntax: The nature of early child grammar of English*. Oxford: Blackwell.

Radford, A. 1994. The syntax of questions in child English. *Journal of Child Language* 21, 211–236.

Radford, A. 1996. Toward a structure-building model of language acquisition. In H. Clahsen, ed., *Generative perspectives on language acquisition*. Amsterdam: John Benjamins.

Radford, A. 1997. *Syntactic theory and the structure of English*. Cambridge: Cambridge University Press.

Ramus, F., M. D. Hauser, C. Miller, D. Morris, and J. Mehler. 2000. Language discrimination by human newborns and by cotton-top tamarin monkeys. *Science* 288, 349–351.

Ramus, F., and J. Mehler. 1999. Language identification with suprasegmental cues: A study based on speech resynthesis. *Journal of the Acoustical Society of America* 105, 1–10.

Ramus, F., M. Nespor, and J. Mehler. 1999. Correlates of linguistic rhythm in the speech signal. *Cognition* 73, 265–292.

Randall, J. A. 1993. Down syndrome. In D. V. M. Bishop and K. Mogford, eds., *Language development in exceptional circumstances.* Hillsdale, N.J.: Lawrence Erlbaum.

Rasetti, L. 2000. Null subjects and root infinitives in child grammar of French. In M.-A. Friedemann and L. Rizzi, eds., *The acquisition of syntax.* Harlow, England: Longman.

Reinhart, T. 1983. Coreference and bound anaphora: A restatement of the anaphora questions. *Linguistics and Philosophy* 6, 47–88.

Reinhart, T. 1986. Center and periphery in the grammar of anaphora. In B. Lust, ed., *Studies in the acquisition of anaphora.* Vol. 1, *Defining the constraints.* Dordrecht: Reidel.

Reinhart, T., and E. Reuland. 1993. Reflexivity. *Linguistic Inquiry* 24, 657–720.

Reitveld, A. C. M., and F. J. Koopmans-van Beinum. 1987. Vowel reduction and stress. *Speech and Communication* 6, 217–229.

Rice, M. L. 1993. Social consequences of specific language impairment. In H. Grimm and H. Skowronek, eds., *Language acquisition problems and reading disorders: Aspects of diagnosis and intervention.* New York: Walter de Gruyter.

Rice, M. L., ed. 1996. *Towards a genetics of language.* Mahwah, N.J.: Lawrence Erlbaum.

Rice, M. L. 1999. Specific grammatical limitations in children with specific language impairment. In H. Tager-Flusberg, ed., *Neurodevelopmental disorders.* Cambridge, Mass.: MIT Press.

Rice, M. L., K. R. Haney, and K. Wexler. 1998. Family histories of children with SLI who show extended optional infinitives. *Journal of Speech and Hearing Research* 41, 419–432.

Rice, M. L., K. R. Noll, and H. Grimm. 1997. An extended optional infinitive stage in German-speaking children with specific language impairment. *Language Acquisition* 6, 255–295.

Rice, M. L., and J. B. Oetting. 1993. Morphological deficits of children with SLI: Evaluation of number marking and agreement. *Journal of Speech and Hearing Research* 36, 1249–1257.

Rice, M. L., J. B. Oetting, J. Marquis, J. Bode, and S. Pae. 1994. Frequency of input effects on word comprehension of children with specific language impairment. *Journal of Speech and Hearing Research* 37, 106–122.

Rice, M. L., and K. Wexler. 1996. Toward Tense as a clinical marker of specific language impairment in English-speaking children. *Journal of Speech and Hearing Research* 39, 1239–1257.

Rice, M. L., K. Wexler, and P. L. Cleave. 1995. Specific language impairment as a period of extended optional infinitive. *Journal of Speech and Hearing Research* 38, 850–863.

Rispoli, M. 1994. Pronoun case overextensions and paradigm building. *Journal of Child Language* 21, 157–172.

Rizzi, L. 1982. *Issues in Italian syntax*. Dordrecht: Foris.

Rizzi, L. 1986. Null objects in Italian and the theory of pro. *Linguistic Inquiry* 17, 501–557.

Rizzi, L. 1990. *Relativized Minimality*. Cambridge, Mass.: MIT Press.

Rizzi, L. 1993/1994. Some notes on linguistic theory and language development: The case of root infinitives. *Language Acquisition* 3, 371–393.

Rizzi, L. 1994. Early null subjects and root null subjects. In T. Hoekstra and B. D. Schwartz, eds., *Language acquisition studies in generative grammar*. Amsterdam: John Benjamins.

Rizzi, L. 1996. Residual verb second and the *Wh* Criterion. In A. Belletti and L. Rizzi, eds., *Parameters and functional heads*. Oxford: Oxford University Press.

Rizzi, L. 1997. The fine structure of the left periphery. In L. Haegeman, ed., *Elements of grammar*. Dordrecht: Kluwer.

Rizzi, L. 2000. Remarks on early null subjects. In M.-A. Friedemann and L. Rizzi, eds., *The acquisition of syntax*. Harlow, England: Longman.

Roberts, I. 1998. *Comparative syntax*. London: Arnold.

Roeper, T., and J. de Villiers. 1991. The emergence of bound variable structures. In T. Maxfield and B. Plunkett, eds., *Papers in the acquisition of WH*. Amherst: University of Massachusetts, GLSA.

Roeper, T., and J. de Villiers. 1992. Ordered decision in the acquisition of *wh*-questions. In J. Weissenborn, H. Goodluck, and T. Roeper, eds., *Theoretical issues in language acquisition*. Hillsdale, N.J.: Lawrence Erlbaum.

Roeper, T., and J. de Villiers. 1994. Lexical links in the *wh*-chain. In B. Lust, G. Hermon, and J. Kornfilt, eds., *Syntactic theory and first language acquisition: Cross-linguistic perspectives*. Vol. 2, *Binding, dependencies, and learnability*. Hillsdale, N.J.: Lawrence Erlbaum.

Roeper, T., and B. Rohrbacher. 2000. True pro-drop in child English and the principle of economy of projection. In C. Hamann and S. Powers, eds., *The acquisition of scrambling and cliticization*. Dordrecht: Kluwer.

Rohde, D. L. T., and D. Plaut. 1999. Language acquisition in the absence of explicit negative evidence: How important is starting small? *Cognition* 72, 67–109.

Rom, A., and L. Leonard. 1990. Interpreting deficits in grammatical morphology in specifically language-impaired children: Preliminary evidence from Hebrew. *Clinical Linguistics and Phonetics* 4, 93–105.

Rooth, M. 1985. Association with focus. Doctoral dissertation, University of Massachusetts, Amherst.

Rothweiler, M., and H. Clahsen. 1993. Dissociation in SLI children's inflectional systems: A study of participle inflection and subject-verb agreement. *Journal of Logopedics and Phoniatrics* 18, 169–179.

Rumelhart, D. E., and J. L. McClelland. 1986. On learning the past tense of English verbs. In D. E. Rumelhart and J. L. McClelland, *Parallel distributed processing*. Vol. 2, *Psychological and biological models*. Cambridge, Mass.: MIT Press. [Reprinted in P. Bloom, ed., *Language acquisition*. Cambridge, Mass.: MIT Press, 1994.]

Saffran, J. R., R. N. Aslin, and E. L. Newport. 1996. Statistical learning by 8-month-old infants. *Science* 274, 1926–1928.

Saffran, J. R., R. N. Aslin, E. L. Newport, and E. K. Johnson. 1999. Statistical learning of tone sequences by human infants and adults. *Cognition* 70, 27–52.

Sansavini, A., J. Bertoncini, and G. Giovanelli. 1997. Newborns discriminate the rhythm of multisyllabic stressed words. *Developmental Psychology* 33, 3–11.

Santelmann, L. 1998. The acquisition of verb movement and spec-head relationships in child Swedish. In D. Adger, S. Pintzuk, B. Plunkett, and G. Tsoulas, eds., *Specifiers: Minimalist approaches*. Oxford: Oxford University Press.

Schaerlaekens, A., and S. Gillis. 1987. *De taalverwerving van het kind: Een hernieuwde orientatie in het Nederlandstalig onderzoeks*. Groningen: Wolters-Noordhoff.

Schütze, C. T. 1997. INFL in child and adult language: Agreement, case and licensing. Doctoral dissertation, MIT.

Scott, D. R. 1982. Duration as a cue to the duration of phrase boundary. *Journal of the Acoustical Society of America* 71, 996–1007.

Sebastián-Gallés, N., and S. Soto-Faraco. 1999. Online processing of native and non-native phonemic contrasts in early bilinguals. *Cognition* 72, 111–123.

Selkirk, E. 1984. *Phonology and syntax: The relation between sound and structure*. Cambridge, Mass.: MIT Press.

Shastri, L., and V. Ajjanagadde. 1993. From simple associations to systematic reasoning: A connectionist representation of rules, variables, and dynamic bindings using temporal synchrony. *Behavioral and Brain Sciences* 16, 417–494.

Sheldon, A. 1974. The role of parallel functions in the acquisition of relative clauses in English. *Journal of Verbal Learning and Verbal Behavior* 13, 272–281.

Shiffman, H. R. 1990. *Sensation and perception: An integrated approach*. New York: Wiley.

Shlonsky, U. 1992. Resumptive pronouns as a last resort. *Linguistic Inquiry* 23, 443–468.

Sigurjónsdóttir, S., and N. Hyams. 1992. Reflexivization and logophoricity: Evidence from the acquisition of Icelandic. *Language Acquisition* 2, 359–413.

Singleton, J., and E. L. Newport. 1994. When learners surpass their model: The acquisition of American Sign Language from impoverished input. Ms., University of Rochester.

Sivian, L. J., and S. D. White. 1933. On minimum audible sound fields. *Journal of the Acoustical Society of America* 4, 288–321.

Skinner, B. F. 1957. *Verbal behavior*. New York: Appleton-Century-Crofts.

Smolensky, P. 1996. On the comprehension/production dilemma in child language. *Linguistic Inquiry* 27, 720–731.

Snyder, W., N. Hyams, and P. Crisma. 1995. Romance auxiliary selection with reflexive clitics: Evidence for early knowledge of unaccusativity. In E. Clark, ed., *Proceedings of the 26th annual Child Language Research Forum*. Stanford, Calif.: CSLI Publications.

Snyder, W., and K. Stromswold. 1997. The structure and acquisition of English dative constructions. *Linguistic Inquiry* 28, 281–317.

Soja, N. N., S. Carey, and E. S. Spelke. 1991. Ontological categories guide young children's indications of word meaning: Object terms and substance terms. *Cognition* 38, 179–211.

Solan, L. 1983. *Pronominal reference: Child language and the theory of grammar*. Dordrecht: Reidel.

Sperber, D., and D. Wilson. 1986. *Relevance: Communication and cognition*. Cambridge, Mass.: Harvard University Press.

Stager, C. L., and J. F. Werker. 1997. Infants listen for more phonetic detail in speech perception than in word-learning tasks. *Nature* 388, 381–382.

Stowell, T. 1983. Subjects across categories. *The Linguistic Review* 2, 285–312.

Strange, W., and J. J. Jenkins. 1978. Role of the linguistic experience in the perception of speech. In R. D. Walk and H. L. Pick, eds., *Perception and experience*. New York: Plenum.

Stromswold, K. 1990. Learnability and the acquisition of auxiliaries. Doctoral dissertation, MIT.

Stromswold, K. 1995. The acquisition of subject and object *wh*-questions. *Language Acquisition* 4, 5–48.

Stromswold, K., and K. Zimmermann. 1999/2000. Acquisition of *nein* and *nicht* and the V-internal subject stage in German. *Language Acquisition* 8, 101–127.

Studdert-Kennedy, M. G. 1991. Language development from an evolutionary perspective. In N. Krasnegor, D. Rumbaugh, R. Schiefelbusch, and M. Studdert-Kennedy, eds., *Biobehavioral foundations of language development*. Hillsdale, N.J.: Lawrence Erlbaum.

Stump, G. T. 1985. *The semantic variability of absolute constructions*. Dordrecht: Reidel.

Sudhalter, V., and M. Braine. 1985. How does comprehension of passives develop? A comparison of actional and experiential verbs. *Journal of Child Language* 12, 455–470.

Suñer, M. 1998. Resumptive restrictive relatives: A crosslinguistic perspective. *Language* 74, 335–364.

Suppes, P. 1974. The semantics of children's language. *American Psychologist* 29, 103–114.

Suppes, P., R. Smith, and M. Leveillé. 1973. The French syntax of a child's noun phrases. *Archives de Psychologie* 42, 207–269.

Tallal, P. 1976. Rapid auditory processing in normal and disordered language development. *Journal of Speech and Hearing Research* 19, 561–571.

Tallal, P., R. Ross, and S. Curtiss. 1989. Familial aggregation in specific language impairment. *Journal of Speech and Hearing Research* 54, 167–173.

Tavakolian, S. 1978. Children's comprehension of pronominal subjects and missing subjects in complicated sentences. In H. Goodluck and L. Solan, eds., *Papers in the structure and development of child language.* Amherst: University of Massachusetts, GLSA.

Tavakolian, S. 1981. The conjoined-clause analysis of relative clauses and other structures. In S. Tavakolian, ed., *Language acquisition and linguistic theory.* Cambridge, Mass.: MIT Press.

Taylor, M., and S. A. Gelman. 1989. Incorporating new words into the lexicon: Preliminary evidence for language hierarchies in two-year-old children. *Child Development* 59, 411–419.

Terzi, A. 1997. PRO and null case in finite clauses. *The Linguistic Review* 14, 335–360.

Thal, D., E. Bates, and U. Bellugi. 1989. Language and cognition in two children with Williams syndrome. *Journal of Speech and Hearing Research* 32, 489–500.

Thelen, E. 1991. Motor aspects of emergent speech: A dynamic approach. In N. A. Krasnegor, D. M. Rumbaugh, R. L. Schiefelbusch, and M. Studdert-Kennedy, eds., *Biological and behavioral determinants of language development.* Hillsdale, N.J.: Lawrence Erlbaum.

Thornton, R. 1990. Adventures in long-distance moving: The acquisition of complex *wh*-questions. Doctoral dissertation, University of Connecticut, Storrs.

Thornton, R., and S. Crain. 1994. Successful cyclic movement. In T. Hoekstra and B. Schwartz, eds., *Language acquisition studies in generative grammar.* Amsterdam: John Benjamins.

Thornton, R., and K. Wexler. 1999. *Principle B, VP ellipsis, and knowledge of binding.* Cambridge, Mass.: MIT Press.

Tomblin, J. B. 1989. Familial concentration of developmental language impairment. *Journal of Speech and Hearing Research* 54, 287–295.

Tomblin, J. B., and P. R. Buckwalter. 1994. Studies of genetics of specific language impairment. In R. Watkins and M. Rice, eds., *Specific language impairments in children.* Baltimore, Md.: Paul H. Brookes.

Torrens, V. 1995. The acquisition of inflection in Spanish and Catalan. In C. T. Schütze, J. B. Ganger, and K. Broihier, eds., *Papers on language processing and acquisition.* MIT Working Papers in Linguistics 26. Cambridge, Mass.: MIT, MITWPL.

Tsimpli, I. M., and S. Stavrakaki. 1999. The effect of a morphosyntactic deficit in the determiner system: The case of a Greek SLI child. *Lingua* 108, 31–85.

Tsushima, T. O., M. Takizawa, S. Sasaki, K. Siraki, M. Nishi, P. Kohno, P. Menyuk, and C. Best. 1994. Discrimination of English /r-l/ and /w-y/ by Japanese infants at 6–12 months: Language specific developmental changes in perception abilities. Paper presented at the International Conference of Spoken Language and Processing 4, Yokohama, Japan.

Tyack, D., and D. Ingram. 1977. Children's production and comprehension of questions. *Journal of Child Language* 4, 211–228.

Vainikka, A. 1994. Case in the development of English syntax. *Language Acquisition* 3, 257–325.

Vainikka, A., and T. Roeper. 1995. Abstract operators in early acquisition. *The Linguistic Review* 12, 275–310.

Valian, V. 1990. Syntactic subjects in the early speech of American and Italian children. *Cognition* 40, 21–81.

Valian, V., J. Hoffner, and S. Aubry. 1996. Young children's imitation of sentence subjects: Evidence of processing limitations. *Developmental Psychology* 32, 153–164.

van der Lely, H. K. J. 1997. Language and cognitive development in a grammatical SLI boy: Modularity and innateness. *Journal of Neurolinguistics* 10, 75–107.

van der Lely, H. K. J., and L. Stollwerck. 1997. Binding theory and grammatical specific language impairment in children. *Cognition* 62, 245–290.

van der Lely, H. K. J., and M. Ullman. 1996. The computation and representation of past-tense morphology in specifically language impaired and normally developing children. In A. Stringfellow, D. Cahana-Amitay, E. Hughes, and A. Zukowski, eds., *BUCLD 20: Proceedings of the 20th annual Boston University Conference on Language Development*. Somerville, Mass.: Cascadilla Press.

van Ooyen, B., J. Bertoncini, A. Sansavini, and J. Mehler. 1997. Do weak syllables count for newborns? *Journal of the Acoustical Society of America* 102, 3735–3741.

Verrips, M., and J. Weissenborn. 1992. Routes to verb placement in early German and French: The independence of finiteness and agreement. In J. Meisel, ed., *The acquisition of verb placement*. Dordrecht: Kluwer.

Vihman, M. M. 1993. Early phonological development. In J. Bernthal and N. Bankson, eds., *Articulation and phonological disorders*. Englewood Cliffs, N.J.: Prentice-Hall.

Vihman, M. M., and R. Miller. 1988. Words and babble at the threshold of language acquisition. In M. D. Smith and J. L. Locke, eds., *The emergent lexicon*. New York: Academic Press.

Volterra, V., O. Capirci, G. Pezzini, L. Sabbadini, and S. Vicari. 1996. Linguistic abilities in Italian children with Williams syndrome. *Cortex* 328, 663–677.

Wagner, K. R. 1985. How much do children say in a day? *Journal of Child Language* 12, 475–487.

Waibel, A. 1986. Suprasegmentals in very large vocabulary word recognition speech perceptions. In E. C. Schwab and H. C. Nusbaum, eds., *Pattern recognition by humans and machines*. New York: Academic Press.

Wang, Q., D. Lillo-Martin, C. T. Best, and A. Levitt. 1992. Null subject versus null object: Some evidence from the acquisition of Chinese and English. *Language Acquisition* 2, 221–254.

Wasow, T. 1977. Transformations and the lexicon. In P. Culicover, T. Wasow, and A. Akmajian, eds., *Formal syntax*. New York: Academic Press.

Waxman, S. R. 1994. The development of an appreciation of specific linkages between linguistic and conceptual organization. *Lingua* 92, 229–257. [Reprinted in L. R. Gleitman and B. Landau, eds., *The acquisition of the lexicon*. Cambridge, Mass.: MIT Press, 1994.]

Waxman, S. R. 1998. Linking object categorization and naming: Early expectations and the shaping role of language. In D. L. Medin, ed., *The psychology of learning and motivation 38*. San Diego, Calif.: Academic Press.

Waxman, S. R., and R. Gelman. 1986. Preschooler's use of superordinate relations in classification. *Cognitive Development* 1, 139–156.

Waxman, S. R., and T. Kosowski. 1990. Nouns mark category relations: Toddlers' and preschoolers' word-learning biases. *Child Development* 61, 1461–1473.

Waxman, S. R., A. Senghas, and S. Benveniste. 1997. A cross-linguistic examination of noun-category bias: Its existence and specificity in French- and Spanish-speaking preschool-aged children. *Cognitive Psychology* 32, 183–218.

Webelhuth, G. 1995. *Government and Binding Theory and the Minimalist Program*. Oxford: Blackwell.

Wechsler, D. 1992. *Wechsler Intelligence Scale for Children*. 3rd ed. London: Psychological Corporation.

Weinberg, Amy. 1990. Markedness versus maturation: The case of subject-auxiliary inversion. *Language Acquisition* 1, 165–194.

Weissenborn, J. 1990. Functional categories and verb movement: The acquisition of German syntax reconsidered. In M. Rothweiler, ed., *Spracherwerb und Grammatik: Linguistische Untersuchungen zum Erwerb von Syntax und Morphologie. Linguistische Berichte*.

Weissenborn, J. 1992. Null subjects in early grammars: Implications for parameter-setting theories. In J. Weissenborn, H. Goodluck, and T. Roeper, eds., *Theoretical issues in language acquisition*. Hillsdale, N.J.: Lawrence Erlbaum.

Werker, J. F. 1995. Exploring developmental changes in cross-language speech perception. In L. R. Gleitman and M. Liberman, eds., *An invitation to cognitive science*. Vol. 1, *Language*. 2nd ed. Cambridge, Mass.: MIT Press.

Werker, J. F., J. H. Gilbert, K. Humphrey, and R. C. Tees. 1981. Developmental aspects of cross-language speech perception. *Child Development* 52, 249–355.

Werker, J. F., and C. E. Lalonde. 1988. Cross-language speech perception: Initial capabilities and developmental change. *Developmental Psychology* 24, 672–683.

Werker, J. F., and J. E. Pegg. 1992. Infant perception and phonological acquisition. In C. A. Ferguson, L. Menn, and C. Stoel-Gammon, eds., *Phonological development: Models, research, implications.* New York: Timonium.

Werker, J. F., and L. Polka. 1993. The ontogeny and developmental significance of language specific phonetic perception. In B. de Boysson-Bardies, S. de Schoenen, P. W. Jusczyk, P. MacNeilage, and J. Morton, eds., *Developmental neurocognition: Speech and face processing in the first year of life.* Dordrecht: Kluwer.

Werker, J. F., and R. C. Tees. 1984. Cross-language speech perception: Evidence for perceptual reorganization during the first year of life. *Infant Behavior and Development* 7, 49–63.

Werker, J. F., and R. C. Tees. 1999. Influences on infant speech processing: Toward a new synthesis. *Annual Review of Psychology* 50, 509–535.

Westerståhl, D. 1985. Logical constants in quantifier languages. *Linguistics and Philosophy* 8, 387–413.

Wexler, K. 1992. Some issues in the growth of control. In R. K. Larson, S. Iatridou, U. Lahiri, and J. Higginbotham, eds., *Control and grammar.* Dordrecht: Kluwer.

Wexler, K. 1994. Optional infinitives, head movement and economy of derivation. In N. Hornstein and D. Lightfoot, eds., *Verb movement.* Cambridge: Cambridge University Press.

Wexler, K. 1999. Very early parameter setting and the unique checking constraint: A new explanation of the optional infinitive stage. In A. Sorace, C. Heycock, and R. Shillock, eds., *Language acquisition: Knowledge representation and processing.* Amsterdam: North-Holland.

Wexler, K., C. T. Schütze, and M. Rice. 1998. Subject case in children with SLI and unaffected controls: Evidence for the Agr/Tns model. *Language Acquisition* 7, 317–344.

Whitman, J. 1994. In defense of the strong continuity account of the acquisition of verb-second. In B. Lust, M. Suñer, and J. Whitman, eds., *Syntactic theory and first language acquisition.* Vol. 1, *Heads, projections, and learnability.* Hillsdale, N.J.: Lawrence Erlbaum.

Wijnen, F. 1988. Spontaneous word fragmentations in children: Evidence for the syllable as a unit in speech production. *Journal of Phonetics* 16, 187–202.

Wijnen, F. 1992. Incidental words and sound errors in young speakers. *Journal of Memory and Language* 31, 734–755.

Williams, E. 1980. Predication. *Linguistic Inquiry* 11, 208–238.

Williams, J., S. Barrett, B. Boyes, and J. Lowe. 1961. Supravalvular aortic stenosis. *Circulation* 24, 1311–1318.

Woodward, J. Z., and R. N. Aslin. 1990. Segmentation cues in maternal speech to infants. Paper presented at the International Conference on Infant Studies, Montreal.

Zanuttini, R. 1997. *Negation and clausal structure*. Oxford: Oxford University Press.

Zribi-Hertz, A. 1984. Orphan prepositions in French and the concept of null pronouns. *Recherches Linguistiques* 12, 46–91.

Zwart, J.-W. 1997. The Germanic SOV languages and the Universal Base Hypothesis. In L. Haegeman, ed., *The new comparative syntax*. New York: Longman.

Index